ST...

POWER

CRIME

STATE

POWER

CRIME

Edited by

ROY COLEMAN   **JOE SIM**   **STEVE TOMBS**   **DAVID WHYTE**

Los Angeles | London | New Delhi
Singapore | Washington DC

First published 2009

SAGE Publications Ltd
1 Oliver's Yard
55 City Road
London EC1Y 1SP

SAGE Publications Inc.
2455 Teller Road
Thousand Oaks, California 91320

SAGE Publications India Pvt Ltd
B1/I 1 Mohan Cooperative Industrial Area
Mathura Road, New Delhi 110 044
India

SAGE Publications Asia-Pacific Pte Ltd
33 Pekin Street #02-01
Far East Square
Singapore 048763

British Library Cataloguing in Publication data

A catalogue record for this book is available from the British Library

ISBN 978-1-4129-4804-3
ISBN 978-1-4129-4805-0

Library of Congress Control Number: 2008943286

Typeset by C&M Digitals (P) Ltd, Chennai, India
Printed and bound in Great Britain by CPI Antony Rowe, Chippenham, Wiltshire
Printed on paper from sustainable resources

Mixed Sources
Product group from well-managed forests and other controlled sources
www.fsc.org Cert no. SGS-COC-2953
FSC © 1996 Forest Stewardship Council

CONTENTS

CONTRIBUTORS

Anette Ballinger is Lecturer in Criminology at Keele University, UK. Her research interests include gender and capital punishment in the twentieth century. She is the author of the award-winning book *Dead Woman Walking: Executed Women in England and Wales 1900–1955* (Ashgate, 2000) (Hart Socio-Legal Prize, 2001), and has written several book-chapters and journal articles on the subject of gender and punishment in modern history including: 'The guilt of the innocent and the innocence of the guilty: the cases of Marie Fahmy and Ruth Ellis', in A. Myers and S. Wight (eds) (1996), *No Angels*, Pandora; 'Researching and redefining state crime: feminism and the capital punishment of women', in S. Tombs and D. Whyte (eds) (2003), *Unmasking the Crimes of the Powerful: Scrutinising States and Corporations*, Peter Lang; and 'The "worse" of two evils? Double murder trials and gender in the 20th century', in A. Barton, K. Corteen, D. Scott and D. Whyte (eds) (2006), *Expanding the Criminological Imagination: Critical Readings in Criminology*, Willan. She is currently working on a book entitled *Capitalising on Punishment: State Power, Gender and Women Who Kill*, to be published by Ashgate.

Lois S. Bibbings is a Senior Lecturer in the School of Law and an Honorary Research Fellow in the Centre for Ethics and Medicine at the University of Bristol. Her research interests revolve around feminisms, masculinities and sexualities. She has published largely in the broad areas of legal history, crime and bodily issues. Current projects focus upon: relational ethics and models of autonomy, end-of-life care, nineteenth-century masculinities, gendered criminality, along with the refusal of violence and conscientious objection (1916–present). Her multidisciplinary book *Telling Tales About Men: Conceptions of Conscientious Objectors to Military Service During the First World War* considers these men's experiences, their beliefs, perceptions and actions, whilst at the same time exploring the 'nature' of history and the forms which writing about the past can take (Manchester University Press, Autumn 2009).

Jon Burnett has published widely on state racism and community cohesion and obtained his PhD from the University of Leeds in 2008. His work has appeared in several edited books, and in a wide range of academic and wide circulation journals, including *Race and Class*, *Journal of Crime Media and Culture* and *Red Pepper*. He is Information and Communications Officer at Positive Action for Refugees and Asylum Seekers in Leeds. His chapter in this book is written in a personal capacity.

Roy Coleman is Lecturer in Criminology and Sociology at the School of Sociology and Social Policy, University of Liverpool. His main research and teaching interests are in the related areas of crime control, surveillance and social divisions, urban regeneration and state formation. Published work appears in journals, including the *British Journal of Sociology*, *Critical Criminology* and *Crime, Media, Culture*. His book *Reclaiming the Streets: Surveillance, Social Control and the City* (Willan, 2004), won the Hart Socio-Legal Book Prize in 2005.

Peter Gill is Honorary Fellow at the University of Liverpool, UK. In addition to journal articles on policing and intelligence issues, he is the author of *Policing Politics* (Cass, 1994) and *Rounding Up the Usual Suspects?* (Ashgate, 2000) that provide comparative analyses of North America and the UK regarding, respectively, security and police intelligence processes. He is a co-editor of *Democracy, Law and Security* (Ashgate, 2003) and *Transnational Organised Crime* (Routledge, 2003) that both deal primarily with European developments. More recently, he has co-authored *Intelligence in an Insecure World* (Polity, 2006) and is co-editor of the *PSI Handbook of Global Security and Intelligence: National Approaches*, 2 volumes (Praeger, 2008) and *Intelligence Theory: Key Questions and Debates* (Routledge, 2009).

Penny Green is Professor of Law and Criminology at Kings College, University of London. She has published widely on state crime and state violence. Her current research interests include theorizing torture and other forms of state violence, particularly in relation to reforming state practices in Turkey and Iraq, illegal logging, environmental harms and looted antiquities. She is the author of a number of books including *State Crime: Governments, Violence and Corruption*, with Tony Ward (Pluto Press, 2004).

Stuart Hall was born in Jamaica and educated in the UK. He has been active in left politics and in the social, peace and anti-racist movements. He was one of the founding figures of cultural studies and became Director of the Birmingham Centre for Cultural Studies in 1972 and a member of the *Policing the Crisis* team. He was Professor of Sociology at the Open University, retiring as Emeritus Professor in 1997. Since then, he has been active in cultural diversity work in the visual arts.

Lynn Hancock is Lecturer in Sociology at the University of Liverpool. She chairs the British Society of Criminology's North West Regional Group. Her main research areas are in urban criminology, with particular reference to urban change, 'crime' and criminalization, community responses to neighbourhood change and the 'place' of 'crime and disorder', policing and the role of local governance structures in these processes, the politics of community safety, social exclusion, spatial exclusion, urban regeneration, crime and social control, and public responses to criminal justice. She published *Community, Crime and Disorder: Safety and Regeneration in Urban Neighbourhoods* (Palgrave) in 2001 and has authored a number of book chapters, articles and reports on the relationships, interactions, discontinuities and dilemmas between theory, policy and practice in each of these areas.

Paddy Hillyard is Emeritus Professor of Sociology at Queen's University Belfast. His main research interests include inequality, poverty, social exclusion and political violence. He is a founder member and Director of Statewatch and a member of the Executive of the Committee on the Administration of Justice (CAJ) in Northern Ireland. His books include: *The Coercive State: The Decline of Democracy in Britain* (Fontana, 1988), with Janie Percy-Smith, *Suspect Community: People's Experience of the Prevention of Terrorism Acts in Britain* (Pluto Press, 1993), *Bare Necessities: Poverty and Social Exclusion in Northern Ireland* (Democratic Dialogue, 2003) with G. Kelly, E. McLaughlin, D. Patsios and M. Tomlinson, *Beyond Criminology: Taking Harm Seriously* (Pluto Press, 2004) edited with Christina Pantazis, Steve Tombs and Dave Gordon, and *Poverty and Conflict in Ireland: An International Perspective* (IPA, 2005) with Bill Rolston and Mike Tomlinson.

Janet Jamieson is a Senior Lecturer in Criminology in the School of Social Science at Liverpool John Moores University. Her teaching and research focuses primarily upon youth justice; children, young people and crime; and gender and the criminal justice system. With Karen Evans she has co-edited *Gender and Crime: A Reader* (Open University Press, 2008) and with Karen Broadhurst and Chris Grover *Safeguarding Children: Critical Perspectives* (Wiley-Blackwell, forthcoming).

Chris Jones and **Tony Novak** have lived and worked together since 1969. They now live on the Greak island of Samos. They have written together and separately on British social policy with a focus on social security and social work and the manner in which the state destroys and distorts the lives of the poor. Their current research includes the refugees being washed on to the shores of Samos and the experiences of Palestinian young people on the occupied West Bank.

Paul Mason is Senior Lecturer at the School of Journalism, Media and Cultural Studies, Cardiff University. He has written extensively in the field of crime and media. He has edited *Criminal Visions: Media Representations of Crime and Justice* (Willan, 2003) and *Captured by the Media: Prison Discourse in Media Culture* (Willan, 2006), and authored with Frank Leishman *Policing and the Media: Facts, Fictions and Factions* (Willan, 2003). He runs the Prison Media Monitoring Unit (PMMU), which scrutinizes British media coverage of prison and prisoners, and the Cardiff Nexus Innocence Project, which works on appeals for prisoners maintaining innocence.

Christina Pantazis is Senior Lecturer in the School for Policy Studies at the University of Bristol. Along with a number of colleagues, she has been developing work around the concept of social harm. Her particular interest is on understanding harm from a gendered perspective. Publications include *Beyond Criminology? Taking Harm Seriously* (Pluto Press, 2004), with Paddy Hillyard, Steve Tombs and David Gordon, and *Criminal Obsessions: Why Harm Matters More Than Crime* (2nd edn, Centre for Crime and Justice Studies, 2008), with Danny Dorling, David Gordon, Paddy Hillyard, Simon Pemberton and Steve Tombs, and *Poverty and Social Exclusion: The Millennium Survey* (The Policy Press, 2006), with David Gordon and Ruth Levitas. Her current research (with Simon Pemberton) focuses on the war on terror and the criminalization of Muslim communities.

Simon Pemberton is Lecturer in Social Policy at the University of Bristol. After completing his PhD, 'The production of harm in the UK: a social harm analysis', he was awarded an ESRC Post-Doctoral Fellowship to develop his doctoral work on social harm. Subsequently, he has published on the topics of state and corporate harm, poverty and human rights and, more recently, on the 'war on terror'.

Joe Sim is Professor of Criminology at Liverpool John Moores University. He has written a number of books on prisons and punishment. His most recent book is *Punishment and Prisons,* and was published by Sage in 2009.

Steve Tombs is a Professor of Sociology at Liverpool John Moores University and Chair of the Centre for Corporate Accountability. His most recent book is *Safety Crimes* (Willan, 2007), co-authored with David Whyte. He has co-edited *Beyond Criminology? Taking Harm Seriously* (Pluto Press, 2004) with Dave Gordon, Paddy Hillyard and Christina Pantazis, and *Criminal Obsessions* (Crime and Society Foundation, 2008), as well as *Unmasking the Crimes of the Powerful: Scrutinising States and Corporations* (Peter Lang, 2003), with David Whyte. He is co-author of *Corporate Crime* (Longman, 1999), with Gary Slapper, and *Toxic Capitalism* (Ashgate, 1998; Canadian Scholars' Press, 1999), with Frank Pearce. He also co-authored *People in Organisations* (Blackwell, 1996) and co-edited *Risk, Management and Society* (Kluwer-Nijhoff, 2000).

Sandra Walklate is currently Eleanor Rathbone Chair of Sociology at the University of Liverpool, having held posts previously at Manchester Metropolitan University, Keele University, the University of Salford and Liverpool John Moores. She has written extensively on policing, gender and crime, and criminal victimization with her most recent work focusing on the impact of the fear of terrorism on people's everyday lives. Her most recent publications include an edited collection *Beyond the Risk Society: Critical Reflections on Risk and Human Security* (McGraw-Hill/Open University Press, 2006), with G. Mythen, and a single-authored book *Imagining the Victim of Crime* (McGraw-Hill/Open University Press, 2007). She is editor of the *Handbook of Victims and Victimology* (Willan, 2007) and series editor for *Readings in Criminology and Criminal Justice* with the Open University Press. She held a Visiting Professorship at the Institute of Criminology at the University of Stockholm in 2006 and is currently Head of the School of Sociology and Social Policy at the University of Liverpool.

Reece Walters is a Professor in Criminology at the Open University. He has published widely on the ways in which criminological knowledge is produced, governed and disseminated, including his books *Deviant Knowledge: Criminology, Politics and Policy* (Willan, 2003), and *Critical Thinking about the Uses of Research* (Centre for Crime and Justice Studies, 2008), with Tim Hope. He also publishes in *Green Criminology*, including work on air pollution, radioactive waste and food crime.

Tony Ward is Reader in Law at the University of Hull where, in addition to various legal subjects, he teaches on the MA/LLM in Criminology and Human Rights. He is co-author of *Privatisation and the Penal System* (Open University Press, 1989), with Mick Ryan, and *State Crime: Governments, Violence and Corruption* (Pluto Press, 2004), with Penny Green. His latest book, with Gerry Johnstone, is *Law and Crime* (Sage, forthcoming), a critical introduction to criminal law for criminologists. When not moonlighting as a criminologist, his main interest is in issues concerning expert evidence and the relationship of psychiatry to criminal law.

David Whyte is Reader in Sociology at the University of Liverpool where he teaches and researches issues of corporate power and regulation and crimes of the powerful. He publishes widely on those subjects in both academic and wider circulation journals, including *Social Justice, Urban Studies, Journal of Law and Society, Critical Criminology, British Journal of Criminology, Crime Law and Social Change* and *Criminal Justice Matters*, and is a regular contributor to *Red Pepper*. His books include *Unmasking the Crimes of the Powerful* (ed. with Steve Tombs, Peter Lang, 2003), *Expanding the Criminological Imagination* (ed. with Alana Barton, Karen Corteen and David Scott, Willan, 2007), *Safety Crimes* (with Steve Tombs, Willan, 2007) and *Crimes of the Powerful* (Open University Press, 2009). David Whyte is a Board member of the Centre for Corporate Accountability and an advisory board member of Corporate Watch.

Joe Yates is Principal Lecturer and Criminology Subject Leader at Liverpool John Moores University. He sits on the Executive Committee of the National Association for Youth Justice and is director of the annual social work with juvenile offenders symposium at the Inter University Centre in Croatia. His teaching and research focuses on state responses to young people in trouble and marginalised young people's experiences of criminal justice. He has published a number of journal articles and book chapters relating to youth crime and youth justice. He is co-editor of *Applied Criminology* (Sage, 2008), with Brian Williams and Brian Stout.

PREFACE

State, Power, Crime is a challenging, wide-ranging and thought-provoking collection of essays. They set crime and the criminal justice system in the context of politics and the state, wider social relations and structures of power and inequality. In so doing, they prove once again – if evidence were needed – that the critical criminological project is alive and well and capable of raising serious theoretical issues and producing profound insights, not simply into crime and the response to it, but into what Foucault called writing 'the history of the present'.

The volume is also, in part, a celebration of the publication, 30 years ago, of *Policing the Crisis: Mugging, the State and Law and Order* by a collective of writers and researchers (none of them, as it happened, professional criminologists!) associated with the Centre for Contemporary Cultural Studies at the University of Birmingham. The analysis offered in *Policing* was influenced by the body of new critical work in crime and deviance that emerged in the 1960s. It also drew extensively on the formative work in cultural studies that was developing at the Centre. The authors of *State, Power, Crime* are scrupulously generous – almost, at times, too generous? – in acknowledging where and how they have found the questions opened up by *Policing the Crisis* productive for their own thinking and research. As one of the original *Policing* group, I would like to express our gratitude for this act of recognition and solidarity across the years, which the new volume represents.

Policing the Crisis took six years to research and write and in the beginning we knew very little about the criminological field in which we were intervening and had no already-finished theoretical approach to apply. But we were propelled in new directions by events in the so-called 'real world' and trying to effect a paradigm-shift – or what David Scott calls opening a new 'problem space', from that of a conventional criminological approach – to explain them. By 'problem space' Scott means 'the ensemble of questions and answers around which a horizon of identifiable stakes ... hangs'. A paradigm shift is thus the result of treating a historical moment or conjuncture as *also* an epistemological space, and changing what seem to be 'the questions worth asking and the answers worth having' about any problem. Our method was to redefine the object of inquiry. This meant re-constituting a particular crime and the societal response to it – long prison sentences handed down for a so-called 'mugging', committed by three young men of mixed race background against an elderly man on a piece of waste ground in Birmingham in 1972 – as a social phenomenon, a 'social fact', rather than an isolated criminological event.

Why had British society – the police, the law, the media, political leaders, spokespersons, public opinion – reacted to that event in such an extreme way at this precise historical juncture? Why did such a wide-ranging 'moral panic' develop around the 'mugging' label? How did rising urban crime become the signifier of a crisis of the whole social order? What social contradictions were driving this so-called 'crisis'? How were the themes of race, crime, youth and the working class condensed in it and why had they come to serve as its ideological conductors? How did this response function as a mechanism for constructing an authoritarian consensus in the state, an increasing reliance on the law to govern and 'police' society, provoking the build-up towards a law and order' society? What role did the state play in its construction? What fears and anxieties was this shift mobilizing?

Policing was the outcome of a process of collaborative research, analysis and theorizing, a 'work in progress', an unfinished project; and, despite the inordinate length of time it took to produce, this process was far from complete when it ended. It urgently required to be further expanded and developed. That was 30 years ago, and its questions and formulations may appear somewhat naive from the perspective of the present. But that is because of the extensive work which has gone into consolidating and sophisticating the paradigm in the intervening years. Though *State, Power, Crime* was produced in very different circumstances from *Policing the Crisis*, it is clear that its authors have shared many concerns and approaches over the years. They have also been engaged in discussion and debate, a sustained conversation, which gives their work a rare unity of perspective across their different areas of expertise.

The expansion and development that *Policing* anticipated takes many forms in the new volume. *State, Power, Crime* pursues many similar topics and themes. It carries the narrative forwards. It develops and expands the argument. It offers new conceptualizations as well as critically engaging with, challenging and putting into question aspects of the earlier work.

The first line of development concerns extending the story – the narrative history – embedded in *Policing* forwards into the following decades. Every essay in the new volume builds its own historical account, deploying this to identify key events which signify critical turning points, new developments and trends, even the opening of a different conjuncture, over the succeeding 30 years. Narratives of this kind are never innocent. They establish a certain way of understanding the relationship between past, present and future; more especially, of understanding how the significant relations between the elements of a social formation 'hang together' and how that articulation is re-configured across time. The 'story' offered in these essays is no simple chronological march, one event after another. It is a *conjunctural* history. It provides an interpretive reading of how these connections can be made and, more importantly, when significant shifts occur. It is not best understood as an account of the unstoppable forward-march of some trans-historical coercive drive lodged in the state-form itself – an approach quite foreign to the demand for historical specificity and the attention to conjunctural shifts which a Gramscian perspective requires. Such developments are never the result of a simple contradiction unrolling evenly across time throughout the whole social formation, but rather, as Louis Althusser once put it, 'an accumulation of circumstances and currents' which, though different in origins, sources and the contradictions which drive them, at certain moments 'fuse into a ruptural unity'.

Policing the Crisis was framed by the 'crisis' of the post-war settlement, the break up of the Keynesian welfare state and the period of social democratic reforms, and signalled the coming apart at the seams of the accommodations which, for a period, stabilized the political landscape and the balance of social forces in post-war British society. The book charts the way the break-up of this 'settlement' produced a progressively deepening social crisis. It explores how that crisis not only shaped the developments of crime and the criminal justice system in the period, but influenced the changing character of legal regulation and the wider control culture and their role in 'policing' – reacting to and attempting to manage and contain – the crisis. Its period of active research was therefore defined by that crisis and dealt in depth with the events of the 1960s–1970s, ending in the mid-1970s. That was before the rise of what came to be know as 'Thatcherism' and the new conjuncture shaped by neo-liberalism, anti-statism and globalization: though the latter was indeed anticipated and cannot have come as a surprise to anyone who had read *Policing* carefully, since it is one of the few genuinely predictive studies in the social sciences (which are not all that strong on accurate prediction). For example, the essay 'The great moving right show', which I published in 1978, correctly anticipated the outcome of the 1979 election, and in terms of general analysis, both this and the later work on Thatcherism were made possible by, and unashamedly stood on the shoulders of, *Policing the Crisis*.

Many of the same social constituencies are followed through in the new volume; but always as a way of marking critical developments, changes of historical contexts and shifts on the modalities of control. And some identify new subjects. For example, Ballinger and Bibbings open new terrain with their discussion of the 'gendering' of crime, sexuality and the social conditions of rule. They are focused on the rise to visibility of the category of sexual offences and the wave of new legislation around rape, domestic violence, abuse within and outside marriage and harassment. Ballinger poses profound questions about the complex gendering of hegemony and how this shifts the analysis. Bibbings privileges sexuality and the state's continuing reinforcement of an heterosexual norm. These authors add a whole new dimension and new constituencies, which were – inexplicably from the perspective of today – missing from *Policing*.

Burnett tracks the race theme that was central to *Policing* – but now in the context of the rise of, and the assault on, multiculturalism; how 'community cohesion' became in the 1990s the leading edge of that attack; why the debate about cultural identity and a vision of 'belongingness' built around citizenship, provided the focus for a new moral panic around 'immigration'. He also poses questions about the effect of the shift into neo-liberalism. He seems convinced that changes in institutional forms of the state do not fundamentally undermine its coercive character. Similarly, Coleman follows through the policing of the working classes, and youth – but now in the context of 'the urban crisis' and the strategies of 'urban regeneration' that have accompanied the 'entrepreneurialization' of the state.

Jamieson and Yates offer an insightful and carefully considered 'survey' of developments in 'the highly politicized arena of youth crime and youth justice' since the 1970s. They identify the soft-and-tough 'bifurcation' approach of the Thatcher era and the deepening of a punitive regime, especially with respect to childhood and anti-social behaviour, marked by the notorious 1998 Crime and Disorder Act and New Labour's deployment of the 'community' discourse to ground and popularize its moralizing logic.

Jones and Novak also look at shifts in regulating the poor, the underclass, unemployed youth and other stigmatized minorities through the welfare state and social policies in the so-called neo-liberal state. They, too, discuss the new modes of regulation, which include such strategies as community policing, parenting orders, curfews, tagging, Asbos and the deployment under New Labour of the all-encompassing category of 'anti-social behaviour'. They add that a return to the emphasis on 'the undeserving poor' seems to take us back to the Poor Law. Is this, then, a further example of, or different from, the 'authoritarian drift' discussed in *Policing*?

On the theme that used to be defined as 'crimes of the powerful', Tombs and Whyte's chapter is part of a major adjustment of emphasis. They identify the unprecedented rise of corporate power and wealth in the period of privatization, globalization and deregulation; and the way the corporations have acquired a social role and moral authority through such devices as 'corporate responsibility' and 'community development'. Are the global multinational corporations beyond state regulation? Are they both inside and outside the state? Is this an example of the state's 'relative autonomy' in the era of anti-statism? Both Green and Ward and Gill also locate new legal and societal responses in the context of contemporary global issues. These include what they call 'crimes of obedience': how individuals are 'legitimately' [*sic*] constrained to commit illegalities by states – of war, state-legitimated violence, security threats and terrorism. The new strategies here involve a massive expansion of intelligence and surveillance, the use of torture, control and exclusion orders, incarceration without charge or trial and other counter-terrorism measures that are given a sort of 'legal legitimacy' in the context of globalization and 'the war on terror'. These seem to be new forms of the exercise of state power through the enforcement of complicit action without legal sanction, for which the term 'Guantanamo' has come to serve as a general metaphor. Many are ambiguously positioned 'both within and beyond' the law; the state harnessing new forms of political bio-power which subject bodies who are held for long periods in legal limbo in the inbetween state of 'bare life' about which Giorgio Agamben has recently so eloquently written.

Then there are chapters that bring new theorizations or a new literature to bear on old questions. Mason offers a critique of the theorization of the media and the role of primary and secondary definers offered by *Policing*. He draws on discourse analysis and the political economy of communications, especially the latter, which returns to a more orthodox neo-Marxist political-economy approach to the sphere of ideology and the media; making use, in particular, of Schlesinger's critical examination of the original approach. Mason does not state where he thinks the balance of the argument finally lies. Walklate introduces the new discourse of the victim and considers how it is related to the New Labour struggle to win consent, with its insistence on adding 'responsibilities' to 'rights', and the general promotion of ideas about the individuation of responsibility (or what they call 'responsibilization'). Pantazis and Pemberton attempt to apply the language of 'needs' and 'harm' to the era of privatization.

Hancock raises another version of the neo-liberalism question that recurs here in many chapters, about the operation of the so-called 'exceptional state' (to which Hillyard also gives extensive treatment – see below) and how far we have advanced towards it. Can neo-liberalism and anti-statism go hand in hand with the more pervasive penetration of society by the state; and is this an example of Foucault's 'governance at a distance'? In another version of the same problem, Pantazis and Pemberton ask whether in general we are witnessing in the more recent era of the so-called 'reform agenda' a deepening of the criminalization of social problems or more humane forms of the capitalist state – or both at the same time? Walters, too, wants to know what the consequences of neo-liberalism have been for criminological thinking in general and Home Office research in particular.

There seem to be many common threads and preoccupations here from which certain key questions arise. Does the relation between state, crime and power remain roughly the same in the moment of the disintegration of the Keynesian, reformist welfare state and the emergence of the anti-statist, neo-liberal, deregulated state under Thatcherism and New Labour? Is the advance towards the 'exceptional' state with which *Policing* concludes maintained across these two different conjunctures? How do we theorize the articulation between the state, crime and power in the era of free markets, anti-statist neo-liberalism, de-regulation, the 'reform' agenda and globalization? Broadly speaking, do the trends and tendencies identified in the first conjuncture persist, without significant difference, into the second? And more conceptually how much difference *do* conjunctural shifts make and how much does historical specificity matter? These are clearly issues which lie at the heart of the way the general theoretical framework of the second book reflects on the problematic of the first.

This is pre-eminently the terrain of the two over-arching review chapters in *State, Power, Crime*: 'The "Exceptional" State' by Paddy Hillyard and the panoramic Introduction to the volume by Coleman, Sim, Tombs and Whyte. Hillyard has, of course, done vital work in charting the critical role played by the Northern Ireland crisis across the whole period in 'pioneering' the movement towards an 'exceptional' state. He accurately picks up on an uncertainty in *Policing* about committing itself as to when precisely the 'drift' towards a law and order society became an 'exceptional state' and whether the latter has arrived and is now the 'normal' state of affairs.

This is a masterfully organized chapter too detailed to summarize here. Hillyard uses the three-part schema in *Policing* – drifting towards the resort to the law to govern society; the expansion of informal social controls; the movement towards the violence threshold and the deployment of new technologies of surveillance (like CCTV, data collection and intercepts in response to terrorism and Northern Ireland) – to organize his paper and to integrate a wealth of subsequent research. This is filled out in considerable detail. The main thrust of the argument is that the trends in this direction have intensified over the past three decades and that the advance to an exceptional state has been sustained.

Coleman et al. address the key conceptual issues in a thoughtfully formulated, sophisticated and wide-ranging chapter. *Policing the Crisis* was shaped by the disintegration of the welfare state; the period since has been framed by the rise of the neo-liberal state. Are an interventionist state and the anti-statist, 'deregulation' state, two sides of the same coin or are they in some more complicated way articulated together? Is rolling back the state related to rolling out new institutional forms and arrangements, new technologies of governance and new forms of policy 'delivery' – the centrepiece of state policies and actions under New Labour in recent decades? Has globalization really undermined the role of the nation state and its capacity to intervene and regulate? Do these add up to a genuine pluralization of state power and a new form of the state, or are many of them simply favourable ways of representing the state's coercive drive – what the authors call 'liberal speak' (there was a lot of it about in what elsewhere I called New Labour's 'double-shuffle').

The authors insist that the state is a contradictory site. An emphasis on the negative and coercive aspects of state power, and the use of oppositions like public/private and coercion/consent, when staged as mutually exclusive binaries, is not, they say, helpful. However, the overall tendency of the review points towards the view that new state institutions and initiatives are always underpinned by the state's coercive capacities and that state violence remains integral to its operations.

The essays in this volume do offer irrefutable evidence of an exponential expansion, a widening of the scope and a deepening of, or penetration into, society of the state. There has been an extraordinary proliferation of the modes and sites in which these many different forms of state interventionism have been exercised. Whether this represents a continuation of the tendencies towards an 'exceptional state' evident since the 1970s or a shift of conjuncture (what Gramsci called 'a relation of forces in continuous motion and shift of equilibrium') remains an open question.

Of course, the question of the *neo-liberal* state cannot be judged from the coercive end of the spectrum alone, critical though that evidence is. If you track the argument from the perspective of the state alone, which is by definition a coercive formation, there may be a danger of exaggerating the coercive aspects at the expense of others. What Gramsci called the dual perspective – 'the dialectic between force and consent, authority and hegemony, violence and civilization' – is always in play, even when the balance tilts or lurches 'exceptionally' towards one or other end of the scale. The construction of consent is neither a powerless nor a benign process. Rather, the force/consent dialectic marks the distinction between two kinds of power – between a reliance on coercive dimensions, and a form of 'hegemonic power' which, of course, always has its coercive aspects. The latter has real effects, and the state is massively involved in it: for example, in restructuring institutions around the market forces principle, giving capital access to every aspect of public and social life, saturating society from end to end with a 'free market' common sense which is visible today in every department of society, and educating society to meet the needs of that 'new type of civilization and citizen' [sic] required by capitalist globalization.

Moreover, any question of the neo-liberal state must include the liberalization of the economy and economic life, which has been the centre of the shift towards neo-liberalism. Paradoxically, what is called 'light regulation' has been one of the preferred modes of regulation in the economic area, in letting market forces have an unfettered freedom to operate: just 'light touch' enough to keep markets open, free and in good working order; to oblige them to be competitive for the sake of the free market system as a whole; opening up the free movement and operation of capital, domestically and globally, its freedom to exploit labour differentials and resources everywhere, to invest anywhere, to bank off-shore, to keep operations off-account, and to increase the value of its assets through the unlimited expansion of risk and debt. The state here maintains weak regulatory systems, seductive low taxation regimes, 'rolling back' any impediments to the corporate rich to make money, increase share value and profitability; and incidentally facilitating the rise of the richest global super-class the world has even seen.

We have in fact seen two versions of this kind of neo-liberalism. Under Thatcherism, the emphasis was on economic liberalization and privatization of public assets and the dismantling of the mixed economy: with the more coercive side deployed to undermine and break the collective defences and constraints on market forces (for example, the criminalization of opposition in the miner's strike). Its leading edge was 'privatization'. In broad principle, New Labour (Blair and Brown) have been converted to and loyally followed through this economic liberalization approach. But it focused its attention on *the management of society* – a more regulatory social regime altogether. This has included the 'entrepreneurialization' of public life, the public sector, public services, government and social institutions and expanding the regulation of civil society and of social and individual behaviour. It has replaced 'privatization' with the broader process of 'marketization' – fatally blurring the distinction between public and private, and allowing private interests to warren and hollow out public institutions from the inside; erecting markets as the only measure of efficiency and value and destroying the very idea of 'the public'. Marketization involves the obligation on all social institutions to comply with the obligation to re-model themselves on the private market, adopt market disciplines and ways of calculating value.

Of course, adding an economic dimension does not resolve the question of the neoliberal state either. These issues are too complicated to be answered fully here. What is important is that *State, Power, Crime* poses this question of the nature of the neoliberal state sharply and clearly. It adds a wealth of evidence which must be taken into account in answering it and provides a range of conceptual formulations which point towards a resolution. In this way, though it differs from *Policing the Crisis* in mode, form of analysis and conjuncture, it shares the aspiration not to be trapped in the empiricist shallows but to test the deeper waters where the questions are worth asking. I salute its courage.

Stuart Hall

INTRODUCTION: STATE, POWER, CRIME

Roy Coleman, Joe Sim, Steve Tombs and David Whyte

Bolstered by the new wave of theoretical innovation and methodological scepticism that had tentatively begun in 1968 with the formation of the radical National Deviancy Conference (NDC), a number of seminal texts were published during the 1970s which developed the critical themes and perspectives initially identified by those participating in the NDC.[1] These texts contested not only the mystifying, algorithmic quantification of positivist criminology, and the reductive emphasis on the individualization of criminal behaviour that flowed from this methodological position, but also implicitly confronted the conjoined, cosy and intertwined relationship which many in the discipline had developed with micro and macro structures of power and domination, including the state and its institutions (Walters, this volume). This relationship was based on the rhetoric of benevolent, progressive reform, which generated a criminology of 'compliance and complicity'[2] while simultaneously excluding significant areas of social and political life that had a direct bearing on the nature of, and response to, criminal and deviant behaviour. Profoundly important political and cultural processes, including the question of the state, did not feature on the radar of conventional criminological endeavour, nor the nebulous, administrative pluralism which underpinned it. However, for critical criminologists, state power, and the interests the state served in a grossly unequal social world, became increasingly important as critical criminology moved from the amorphous conceptualization of social control underpinning labelling theory's often idealized glamorization of transgressive male criminality to a more materialist, Marxist-based interpretation of power, and, by extension, the processes of criminalization and control emanating from the state and its institutions.

By the mid to late 1970s, the work of Pearce (1976), collections by Taylor et al. (1973, 1975) and, in the latter, notably the contributions by Quinney (1975) and Schwendinger and Schwendinger (1975), all drawing upon some forms of Marxism, combined to place the state as an analytical entity on the agenda of critical criminology. Again this work was a direct and oppositional challenge to the dominant criminological discourse of the time. As Frank Pearce noted:

> Within sociology, and particularly within criminology, the serious study of the state and its agents and of the activities of the ruling class is virtually non-existent. ... [N]evertheless most of what has been written has been administratively oriented or

meritocratic in its inspiration. On the other hand, endless surveys and reports have been compiled on crime, racial disturbances, working class militancy, drug 'abuse' etc. (Pearce, 1976: 158)

However, it was not until the publication of *Policing the Crisis* (*PtC*) (Hall et al., 1978) – in 1978, the same year as Poulantzas' *State, Power, Socialism*, itself a key moment in the fervent of social science literature on 'the state' – that the complexity of the state's material and ideological interventions in maintaining, and indeed enhancing, a capitalist social order increasingly dominated by the political economy of neo-liberalism, was laid bare for critical criminological analysis.

This chapter is concerned with exploring these themes, and in doing so provides a context for the contributions that follow. It focuses on three main areas. First, it is concerned with *Policing the Crisis* itself, and the conceptualization of state power that underpinned the book's analysis. Thus, it analyses the influence of the book in relation to the debates around state power within critical criminology as they have developed since its publication in 1978; this influence is, of course, further identified in its scope, variety, and trajectories by the contributors to this collection. Second, it is also concerned with exploring the conceptualization of state power as a matter of contemporary criminological concern, and in particular its invisibility within a range of criminological work – work that is itself based on both mystifying what the state does (and does not do) and caricaturing the work of those who wish to retain a critical focus on its role in reproducing the social divisions and defending the globalized capitalist social order of the early twenty-first century, however contingent and contradictory that process might be (Gill, this volume). Finally, we consider the question of the state with respect to its place as a contradictory site where the individual actions and collective activities of state servants are open to contestation from a range of individuals and groups, both within and without the power networks of its material and ideological institutions.

Policing the Crisis and the State

Policing the Crisis was published during the dying days of James Callaghan's Labour government and before the electoral birth, in May 1979, of Margaret Thatcher's first Conservative government. Politically, the book both reflected, and reflected upon, the sense of apocalyptic panic gripping the nation in general, and fractional blocs of the ruling class in particular. This panic, Hall et al. argued, was linked by a cultural and political umbilical cord to the organic crisis of a capitalist Britain experiencing a pervasive, intensifying sense of loss and defeat, of imperialist retreat and demoralization, and of economic, political and moral decline. More generally, *Policing the Crisis* signalled what was to become a social, political and economic torrent of international proportions in the rolling out of a neo-liberal experiment across much of the globe – an experiment which took its most vicious and virulent forms in centres of Anglophone criminology, namely the UK, North America, Australia and New Zealand.

Central to the book's analysis was the moral panic around mugging and the role of black youth in this most 'un-English' of crimes. Never intended as a book about 'why or how muggers, as individuals, mug' (Hall et al., 1978: 327), Hall et al.'s neo-Marxist analysis of this crime was located within the emergence of a state form that was coercive, authoritarian and brutal. The nascent social and political clampdown generated by this authoritarian state form was hegemonically cemented in the consciousness of the wider population through mediated 'truths' about mugging generated by a competitive mass media (see Mason, this volume). At the same time, according to Hall et al., the post-war social democratic state was shedding its skin of welfare–oriented, consensual social inclusion (however idealized that might have been) in favour of a militarized, coercive social authoritarianism as a response to the moral and political threats, posed by the social detritus generated by capitalist social arrangements that were in crisis.

At the time of writing *Policing the Crisis*, Stuart Hall made explicit his reading of Poulantzas' *State, Power, Socialism* (1978b) and his agreement with the central arguments of that book, notably those around the emergence of what Poulantzas was evocatively and presciently to call 'authoritarian statism' (see Hillyard, this volume). This, Poulantzas famously defined as:

> ... intensified state control over every sphere of socio-economic life *combined with* radical decline of the institutions of political democracy and with draconian and multiform curtailment of so-called 'formal' liberties, whose reality is being discovered now that they are going overboard. (Poulantzas, 1978b: 203–4, emphasis in the original)

In practice, authoritarian statism meant relentlessly mobilizing around the criminalization and control of those groups – the welfare dependent, the economically deprived, the politically depraved (those whom Thatcher was subsequently to label the 'enemy within') and the socially and psychologically dislocated – whose corrosive presence was increasingly regarded as problematic for the maintenance of a deeply divided social order and the untrammelled working of the free market.

Hall recognized 'many similarities between [Poulantzas'] characterization and those I had been struggling to formulate in *Policing the Crisis*, "Drifting into a Law-and-Order Society", and so on' (Hall, 1988: 151–2). However, he has also maintained that there were two weaknesses or omissions in Poulantzas' initial conceptual framework built around authoritarian statism. First, Poulantzas failed to analyse how popular consent could be 'constructed by a historical bloc seeking hegemony'. In mobilizing deeply embedded psychic emotions of insecurity and discontent for its own political ends, this bloc could 'neutralize the opposing forces, disaggregate the opposition and really incorporate some strategic elements of popular opinion into its own hegemonic project' (ibid.: 152). Allied to this was a second weakness, which concerned the new right's pursuit of an 'anti-statist strategy', defined as:

> ... not one which refuses to operate through the state; it is one which conceives a more limited state role, and which advances through the attempt, ideologically, to *represent itself* as anti-statist, for the purposes of populist mobilisation ... (ibid., emphasis in the original)

This dialectic – connecting a strong, interventionist, law and order state on one hand to a rolled-back, non-interventionist state form on the other – influenced the analysis of state power and crime developed by some of the emerging generation of critical criminologists. *Policing the Crisis* was one of a number of possible impetuses for 'critical criminology', a heterogeneous collection of 'radical agendas' seeking to 'challenge the status quo, modernist modes of social control, the claims of science and other disciplinary knowledges, the dominance of patriarchy and the underlying moral order of Anglophone culture' (Carrington and Hogg, 2002: 3). More specifically, the model of analysis Hall et al. developed for understanding the dynamics of state power has influenced a range of work published over the last three decades, within which it is possible to identify two distinct strands.

First, different authors have focused on the ongoing intensification in the authoritarian interventions of a numerically expansionist, surveillance-oriented, highly militarized and nakedly aggressive state form. This coercion is apparent not only in the policing and punishment of narrowly defined, legally circum-scribed criminal behaviour, but also with respect to the control of public order and the criminalization of popular and political dissent (Scraton, 1987; Gamble, 1988; Hillyard and Percy-Smith, 1988; Barton et al., 2007a; Hillyard, this volume). In turn, this authoritarianism, and the often violent and retributive discourses on which it is based, has been legitimated and sustained by a mass media which has remained central to the creation of moral panics around crime and incivilities, particularly among the young (see Jamieson and Yates, this volume). Moreover, these same media, in the last three decades, have become increasingly more con-cerned, indeed obsessed, with the licentious trivia associated with the cult of modern personalities, rather than with identifying the structural and motivational complexities surrounding a range of contemporary social issues, including crime (Bauman, 2002; Mathiesen, 1997; Mason, this volume; Hillyard, this volume). And while the state may have undergone some important reconfigurations, particu-larly with the emergence of more privatized forms of social control, as well as 'changing from provider to purchaser of public services' during the Thatcher/Major and Blair/Brown eras, nonetheless,

> it continues to maintain a coercive core and central role in the shaping and defining of social problems and the social and legal response to such problems. ... The deliv-ery of some aspects of state power may have changed but its orchestration remains relatively unchanged. (Barton et al., 2007b: 208; see also Coleman, this volume)

A second, albeit indirect, legacy of *Policing the Crisis*, via its references to the at times (apparently) contradictory relationship between state, law and capital, has been the space the book potentially opened up for developing the idea of an 'anti-statist strategy', subsequently developed via Hall (1988), and its usefulness, or otherwise, for analysing crimes of the powerful in general and corporate crime in particular (see Tombs and Whyte, this volume). Thus, in the Thatcher/Major era, the activities of the powerless were the focus for 'the retributive interventionism of the strong state … [while] for other, more powerful groups, the eighteen years of Conservative rule meant that their activities remained relatively invisible, comparatively unregulated and effectively decriminalized' (Sim, 2000: 324). This process continued under the Blair/Brown governments. The regulation (never the *policing*) of the powerful in the last three decades has, *in general*, followed an 'anti-statist' strategy with respect to the rolling back of those state agencies responsible for the regulation of their activities – even if this anti-statism has been highly selective, and in some contexts more important in its representation than reality (see Tombs and Whyte, this volume). For the Thatcherite bloc in the Conservative Party, this strategy was loudly proclaimed through the populist and political discourse of 'freeing the market' and, by extension, risk-generating, buccaneering entrepreneurship, from the stifling strangulation generated by bureaucratic red tape in a society over-burdened by state intervention (Gamble, 1988). For Blair, then Brown, the sustained (if partly rhetorical) attack on 'red tape' has been legitimated as a necessary response to the new 'realities' of globalization. Therefore, in the thirty years since *Policing the Crisis* first appeared, the state's capacity, and indeed motivation, for intervening into and responding to the activities, criminal and otherwise, of the powerful – individuals, organizations, institutions and states themselves – which can have an enormously detrimental impact on the lives of individuals, communities and the wider society, has been and remains markedly different from the interventions of its increasing number of servants into the lives of those without power, and the inevitable process of criminalization that flows from these interventions.

None of this is to deny that the non-regulation of the powerful, for example around health and safety at work, is a process that long predates the advent of neo-liberalism,

> and can be traced to the moment at which the criminal courts saw the punishment of the wealthy or the ruling class as somehow beyond their remit. The process of law reform and the process of law implementation remains guided by a logic of social ordering – of mediating over conflict in a way that will not disturb the status quo. (Tombs and Whyte, 2007: 123)

However, the important point to note here relates to *how* the state form that has developed in the last three decades has further reinforced and intensified this process of differential law and its enforcement so that, with respect to the activities of the powerful:

> Under neo-liberal conditions, in other words, punitive enforcement becomes less feasible, and co-operative or compliance-oriented approaches become much more likely. And it is here we can see – again – a coherence with policy, since the current and recent British governments are, for all their deregulatory rhetoric, probably less interested in the removal of law *per se* (which, as Thatcher found, in the 1980s, invited political confrontation), but much more interested in changing the terms of that enforcement, towards greater compliance-type techniques which imply less actual impact upon business. (ibid.: 164–5)

Thus, while a reconfigured law and order agenda has been central to the generation of successive moral panics around the behaviour of the powerless, the failure to mitigate the harms generated by relatively powerful social actors such as corporations can be characterized as an exercise in the creation of *un*-panics (Davis, C., 2000) with respect to the lack of state concern over their depredations, certainly when compared with the desperate concern constantly articulated about the behaviour of the powerless in the mass media, state documents and ministerial and other statements made by politicians. Further, the (actual or claimed) rolling back of the state should be understood alongside its rolling out in creative and novel institutional forms. For criminology, this means that increased regulation and social control should be conceptualized in its dialectical relationship to the increase in the freedom to act with the simultaneous and creative *re*-regulation of specific individuals and targeted groups (Tombs and Whyte, this volume). These are not separate spheres of criminology, criminal justice or state activity, but inextricably linked elements of a dynamic process with respect to the risks these groups may pose to the social order, however socially constructed the idea of risk might be.

Criminology and State Power: Myopia and Invisibility

Given these academic legacies, we now turn to the question of state power and its relationship to criminology in general and consider the discipline's response to the intensification and consolidation of state power that Hall and his colleagues identified in the late 1970s. As we noted above, *Policing the Crisis*, and Stuart Hall's subsequent analysis of Thatcherism, provided some key theoretical, methodological and empirical pointers towards understanding and analysing the contours, direction and impact of the law and order state as it developed from the late 1970s under successive Conservative and Labour (New or otherwise) governments. This work was responding to the clearly demarcated authoritarianism that lay at the heart of the criminal justice and state welfare policies as they developed during this time (see Hillyard, this volume; Jones and Novak, this volume). However, neither the neo-Marxist model of state power outlined by Hall et al. (nor variants of it) has been taken up or developed by criminologists, critical or otherwise. There are four reasons for, and elements of, this academic marginalization that we want to highlight here.

Critical Fragmentation

The first issue concerns the fragmentation of the critical paradigm which began as early as 1975 but which was intensified and consolidated in the 1980s. Even as many of those associated with the NDC and the emerging critical paradigm during the 1970s and 1980s provided searing critiques of crime, criminology and state power – for example, in terms of the rule of law, the capital/labour relation, gender, race and racialization – the solidification of a law and order discourse to which *Policing the Crisis* pointed, and to which criminology was quickly to submit (Hillyard, Sim et al., 2004;

Walters, this volume), led many key critical scholars of this period rapidly to aban-don the terrain of crime and criminology. While the nuances of these developments cannot be discussed here (but see Hillyard, Sim et al., 2004; Hillyard, Pantazis et al., 2004; Tombs and Whyte, 2003a/b), suffice to say that the period from the very early 1980s saw a reinforcement of criminology's historical commitment to work on the basis of definitions of what constitutes crime produced by the state. Of course, that criminology has been largely non-reflexive on this issue and has, on the whole, accepted the notion of crime, is no mere quirk or due to a shortage of criminological endeavour but is more a consequence of the rules of formation of the discipline itself; as Carol Smart was to observe some years later, 'the thing that criminology cannot do is to deconstruct crime' (Smart, 1990: 77).

Others who had been working with neo-Marxist concepts reacted to 'The Great Moving Right Show' (Hall, 1988: 39), by themselves establishing, and then admon-ishing, what they saw as the straw men of the idealist left and urging criminologists (as well as centre-left politicians) to take crime seriously. In 'left realist' criminology, the state was characterized as one autonomous element in a much-cited, but theo-retically empty 'square of crime'. There is no little irony in the fact that left realism's failure to take the state seriously occurred just at the moment that its nature and effects were being most significantly analysed by neo-Marxist criminology (Sim et al., 1987). Taking crime seriously was then easily incorporated into the great ideological beacon of New Labour's modernizing march towards government: 'tough on crime, tough on the causes of crime'. The Blair and Brown governments then commenced to mobilize around a desperately populist, highly punitive (for the powerless) law and order and social welfare strategy which was no less toxic in its implications than policies pursued under the previous Thatcher/Major regimes (Sim, 2009).

The New Pluralism

Second, and related, the state has been made even less visible in the past thirty years. The state has been gradually airbrushed out of critical analysis largely because most criminology has continued to take official discourses on 'crime' and 'law and order' – and the solution to those problems – at face value (see Walters, this volume). Thus, new ways to describe institutional concentrations of power and resources which elide states and state power – 'partnerships', 'joined-up government', 'modernization', 'rebalancing', 'flexibility', 'community cohesion' and so forth – have been accepted and internalized relatively uncritically by academic criminology. In particular, there has been a failure to subject such terms to critical scrutiny or to question the extent to which they correspond to a form of 'new liberal speak' (Bourdieu and Wacquant, 2001).

Arguably, the 'success' of this new liberal speak of 'partnerships', 'joined-up government' and so on has been to mystify and obscure the processes of power (in ideological and material terms) that shape social orders and reflect persistent (and deepening) patterns of inequality (Burnett, this volume; Coleman, this volume). In this respect the channels of primary definition ensconced in state discourses have attempted to place limitations on the sociological imagination to which many academics have aligned themselves. Within these discourses, 'the state' (if the term is deployed at all) is depicted as a series of governmental and quasi-governmental institutions among multiple sites of power. Recent studies, for example, have argued that: state power has become pluralized into variegated orders (Shearing and Stenning, 2003); states have less recourse to coercion and repressive measures (Barry et al., 1996); states lack coherence in terms of ideological referents (Miller and Rose, 1990), and indeed ideology has disappeared altogether in some work; states and powerful corporations are themselves just as likely to be subject to surveillance and regulation as the 'powerless' (Haggerty and Ericson, 2006); and states have been superseded by a range of risk managers (Feeley and Simon, 1992).

Others *have* retained the concept of the state as an analytical and empirical object of inquiry, for example in relation to regulation, policing and security (Crawford, 2006; Loader and Walker, 2006). And this work raises a number of important questions, not least of which relate to how the state in its 'diverse forms' is becoming 'more frenetic, volatile, contradictory, and politicised' in its 'regulation of behaviour' (Crawford, 2006: 471). Yet while not without insight, there remains a general tendency across this heterogeneous work to reduce state power to the organizational form that delivers policy. Crime control partnerships between public authorities and civil society groups are thus characterized as the conduits of new forms of power under the auspices of 'responsibilization' or 'governance'. This focus leads to a theoretical and political position in which these institutional arrangements are conceptualized as merely reflecting new technologies of government – the 'how' of government and governance. Indeed, it is this focus that underpins claims regarding new epoch-defining shifts in social structure (such as 'networked governance', 'neo-feudalism' or the 'death of the social', Crawford, 2003; Rose, 1996), within which the state is constructed as a static set of institutions which are bit players in new networked arrangements.

The new forms of delivering criminal justice policy, local community safety agendas and so on are seen as a challenge to the state and state power precisely because they are seen as *external* to the state. A key conceptual mistake that is being made here is a narrow understanding of what the state is. As Gramsci noted, what is normally represented as the 'state' – the 'safeguarding of public order and of respect for the laws' (or 'state as policeman') – negates the centrality of 'private forces' in the historical development of states. Thus, he argued, the 'state as policeman' approach is a 'limiting hypothesis' (1971: 261). He counterposed the 'state as policeman' with the 'ethical' or 'interventionist' state. The visible and repressive role of the state is only a part of its core function: 'the law is the repressive and negative aspect of the entire positive, civilizing activity undertaken by the state' (Gramsci, 1971: 247). Where its substantive concern is the criminal justice system, criminology tends to adopt a limiting hypothesis of the 'negative' aspects of state power, restricted to the visible mechanisms of law and public order maintenance; those mechanisms that Poulantzas called the 'public kernel' of army, police, prisons and courts (1978b: 36). No wonder, then, when new forms of 'positive' policy delivery emerge (partnerships, coalitions with the private sector, and so on), they appear before some criminologists as a revelation. No wonder that they appear to alter seismically the foundations of the state itself. For because they are not contained within the negative aspect of state power, they appear to pluralist criminology as novel forms of power, rather than new forms of positive, civilizing activity that the state has always engaged in (on this point, see also Hall et al., 1978: 211).

There should be nothing surprising in this. We should expect criminologists who are concerned with state power to study the 'negative' aspect of state power – the key institutions of policing, criminalization and incarceration, the production of political discourse around law and order in government, and so on. But in order to develop a more useful theoretical understanding of state power, a unidimensional approach that remains bounded by the *institutional ensemble* of the state should be problematized and subjected to critical scrutiny.

New pluralist commentators, then, tend to interpret the shifts in the forms taken by the delivery of policy as constituting a new form of 'state' rather than understanding them as merely new modes of delivery – thus reinforcing fragmentation of the state form itself and aspects of the social realm it seeks to govern. As Jessop (1990: 269–70) reminds us:

> The state as such has no power – it is merely an institutional ensemble; it has only a set of institutional capacities and liabilities which mediate that power; the power of the state is the power of the forces acting in and through the state.

Yet, as Jessop goes on to point out, the precise institutional arrangements and boundaries that characterize the state – such boundaries 'are usually in doubt' (Jessop, 1990: 342) – and the social forces organized through these arrangements, should therefore not be left unproblematized as a background blur without structural underpinnings. The state is not a 'thing' but a *process* that, in its shifting boundaries and ensembles, provides the arena for the organization of social forces, continually recodifying as well as drawing upon 'public' and 'private' interests. Moreover, the 'dispersed state' form of analysis distracts attention away from points of convergence across this form – and recalls Miliband's (1969) concern to map the correspondence of interests across and through the state. At the same time, it is important to point to contradictions and tensions, and explore ideological coincidences that bind interests and provide states with a measure of coherence and unity (however fragile).

An examination of the state's role in 'leadership, in direction, education and tutelage' (Hall et al., 1978: 202) questions the naïve and reductive understanding of a strict binary divide between the 'public' and 'private' realms, whereby the former is constituted by state apparatuses and the latter by institutions of civil society. In reality, both arenas are constituted and reconstituted in struggles around the state form. It is precisely here where an alliance of forces congeals and displays relative unity and, in borrowing Gramsci's terms, 'poses itself as an organism in continuous movement, capable of absorbing the entire society, assimilating it to its own cultural and economic level' (1971: 260).

Rather than focusing on the relative size of the 'public' or 'private' sectors, the key issue here is how these categories come to have political meaning and powerful institutional effects in structuring the economy and facilitating strategies of capital accumulation. Questions that can be asked include: how the contingent balance of forces between public and private acts as to, for example, redefine notions of 'sovereignty' over a given space (see Coleman, this volume) and how state projects intersect with inequalities concerning social class, 'race', gender (see Ballinger, this volume), sexuality (see Bibbings, this volume) or age (see Jamieson and Yates, this volume). Thinking of the state form as a process and a site of strategy (in defining and promoting, for example, illusory communities as a means of shaping hegemonic compromise with subordinate populations), we can undermine both the tendencies to analyse the state as a neutral arbiter or to render the state absent, and instead analyse 'the relation between state structures and the strategies which different [and asymmetrically constituted] forces adopt towards it' (Jessop, 1990: 260).

The relationship between public and private in capitalist societies is therefore organized around a complex balance of forces, rather than being organized around separate and antagonistic elements of a society that stand in external relationship to each other. It is this symbiosis – and the way that it acts to secure the domination of a minority ruling class – that concepts of 'state' should seek to capture above all. Indeed, it was his understanding of the complex ways in which 'diverse tendencies' of the state secure hegemonic domination for the ruling class that led Gramsci to the formulation that state = political society + civil society, and which was crucial to the analysis developed by Hall et al. in *Policing the Crisis*.

Globalization as 'Reality'

A third issue, and a further manifestation of an over-simplified understanding of the state which is dominant across criminology, is perhaps best captured in terms of an acceptance of 'the "ideology of globalization"' (Poulantzas, 1975: 49). If globalization is a relatively recent phenomenon, it is one that has still not been subjected to any serious critical analysis within criminology. Thus, just as nation-state power has been ceded horizontally (to the private sector) and downwards (to the local state), as the new pluralists would have it, so too has it shifted upwards, to the new dominant actors of the global economy, be these supranational institutions or transnational corporations (Braithwaite, 2000). Those assumptions have led to a range of calls to abandon our concern with the nation state as a site of power. For Sheptycki, this means we should 'no longer study the nation state system, but rather look at the transnational-state-system' (2000: 7); for Findlay, this means we should work towards a global system of crime control based around some kind of 'global ethic' (1999: 220).

Thus much contemporary criminology invokes globalization as a structuring context for, or as a factor in, a whole series of contemporary substantive issues – whether this is the nascent forms of, increasing need for, and clear problems in genuinely achieving transnational policing, the 'rise' of new or exacerbated crime threats, such as terrorism, the trafficking of drugs, people or arms, cyber-crime and money-laundering, not least through transnational organized crime, the prevalence of new risks, insecurities and mentalities – and, of course, a seemingly undeniable, yet unquestioned, loss of state authority, usually in association with a series of claims regarding 'governance' (Braithwaite, 2000). The discourse of globalization, too, attains the status of new liberal speak precisely because it forces state power and state authority into the background of the political landscape. This has particular implications for arguments to control corporate crimes and harms produced by capitalist accumulation. Notions of 'globalization' are invoked by governments as they seek to attract or retain private capital through various forms of de- and re-regulation or impose massive cutbacks in the social wage, and more generally reproduce the 'political construction of helplessness' (Weiss, 1997: 15). Thus, state interventions to protect consumers and workers are constructed as counter-productive in the sense that they repel prospective investors, or force existing businesses to relocate elsewhere (Tombs and Whyte, 1998). From its very outset, the first Blair administration was marked by his famous pledge to 'accept globalization and work with it' (cited in Holden, 1999: 531). This very same phrase might also be used to describe academic criminology. In other words, by accepting 'globalization' at face value, criminology also assumes that there has been a diminution in the capacity of states to act in the face of global market forces.

What is missing in criminology is any critical interrogation of the contested nature of globalization itself or any consideration of what different understandings of globalization might mean for different nation states (see Pantazis and Pemberton, this volume), nor, crucially, any attempt to understand globalization as political economy. Yet, beyond criminology, if only perhaps relatively recently as a critical intellectual reaction to globalization 'orthodoxy' (Hay, 1999), there *has* been a recognition that nation states have not only been the 'principal agents of globalization', but remain 'the guarantors of the political and material conditions necessary for global capital accumulation' (Barrow, 2005: 125; see also Lee and Yeoh, 2004: 2296). Thus the state is neither peculiarly constrained (Somerville; 2004; Weiss, 2005), nor is the logic of deregulation a necessity (Mosley, 2005) in the international political economy. Indeed, as Panitch reminds us, this much had been noted by Poulantzas, in 1975 in his book *Classes in Contemporary Capitalism*:

> Far from losing importance, the host state actually becomes responsible for taking charge of the complex relations of international capital to the domestic bourgeoisie, in the context of class struggles and political and ideological forms which remain distinctively national. (Panitch, 2000: 8–9)

It is precisely these relations between state and structural power that have been severed in most recent criminological theorizing – and thus there has also been a jettisoning of the affinity between state projects and the differentials in power, access to recourses and claims to social justice found in the wider social formation at any given time. Thus, we should focus attention on what the state *is*, what it *does*, but *also* the ways in which images of the state orient subjects 'to the state and the kind of order it is engaged in producing', and how such imagery figures in a 'legitimization of domination' often through 'the generation of the figure of the enemy' (Neocleous, 2003: 5; see also chapters by Hillyard, Burnett and Gill, this volume).

State Violence

A fourth key issue for our consideration here relates to the fact that the neo-Marxist conceptualization of power always foregrounds state violence, and the threat of violence – and this is antithetical to contemporary criminology's sanitized, individualized understanding of what violence is, and how it operates. In the context of our comments above, regarding contemporary criminology's limiting hypothesis of the state in 'negative' law and order terms, it similarly constitutes the apparatuses of state power, particularly with respect to violence, in very narrow terms (if at all). Thus, although the focus tends to be on overtly violent processes and institutions, the violence that concerns criminology is *individual* violence (Tombs, 2007). Yet, violence is integral to states and state power – not least, of course, and with no little irony, to law, even in its most apparently benign forms. To grasp this latter point one can simply return to some well-known histories of the development of the criminal law, which have emphasized the crucial role that the law plays in reproducing social class in ways that mask the violence of the modern state.

The work of Thompson, Hay, Linebaugh and others has asserted how the law did not merely act as an instrument of class domination but that by limiting arbitrary power and occasionally punishing members of the ruling class, the law appeared to act in the interests of all (Hay et al., 1975; Thompson, 1975). Thus, the law was able to impose by force the new property rights of the rising merchant class. The new property rights and the methodological individualism that was developed in the criminal law acted as crucial ideological and material supports to the process of capitalist industrialization (Norrie, 1993; Carson, 1979, 1980). Some of this work was highly influential for the radical and critical criminology that was contemporaneous with *Policing the Crisis*. In particular, the National Deviancy Conference/ Conference of Socialist Economists text, *Capitalism and the Rule of Law*, published in 1979, located its analysis in the requirement of the law to mediate relations between capital and labour. Thus, we find articles on the role of the law in the reproduction and disciplining of workers (Gregory, 1979; Kinsey, 1979; Mellosi, 1979) and the working class more generally (Cohen, 1979; Fine, 1979) which contextualize our understanding of the development and application of juridical processes and the form that the rule of law assumes. The labour–capital relation in this work is explicitly constructed as a relationship that is based upon force/violence. The role of the law explored in this context therefore has a very specific aim – to guarantee by violent means a particular social order that is conducive to capital accumulation. The point that this work re-inforced, and one that is generally missed in contemporary criminology, is that the state plays a key role in reproducing coercive forms of power that *appear* to be consensual.

Although individuals, as workers, consumers, citizens and so on, are formally free to make choices, in reality those choices are highly circumscribed; they operate within highly restricted conditions; and these conditions are ultimately underpinned by state violence. Thus, workers are 'free' to buy and sell their labour, but they are not free to enter premises that have been abandoned by their employer and use the facilities to set up their own business. A local fruit grower is 'free' to enter a supermarket and spend money, but is not free to set up a stall and start selling fruit outside the supermarket. Breaking those rules would soon elicit a response of force, either from the police or from the owners of the premises who might feel legitimately empowered (by established state rules and norms) to use force to eject the offender from the premises.

Similarly, new state initiatives, no matter how they are represented, are always underpinned by the coercive capacities of states. Following Gramsci, Poulantzas and Hall et al., it could be argued that although new administrative forms (partnerships, quangos and so on) often have no formally repressive powers at their disposal, it makes little sense to analyse them in isolation from, or as existing independently of, the 'repressive' apparatuses of the state. The work of the new community safety partnerships established by the Crime and Disorder Act 1998, for example, despite their exigencies to go beyond the traditional concerns of the criminal justice system and consider issues of 'community safety' rather than 'crime', is typically implemented as part of a panoply of coercive measures in communities aimed at ensuring the cooperation of the targets of anti-social behaviour orders and curfews, alongside the 'softer' forms of community engagement. To take an example that is in the headlines as we write, the Safer Islington Partnership instituted a campaign to reduce crime and anti-social behaviour in the Blackstock Road area after it identified particular problems with anti-social behaviour and stolen property. The publicity accompanying the launch of the campaign in July 2007 noted:

> [T]he partnership will continually consult with the local community, particularly the traders. The area is populated by a large Algerian community and therefore police are enlisting the help of translators and Independent Advisory Groups to ensure local traders are kept fully up to date of the partnership activity taking place. Bi-monthly meetings supported by Fin Future [a private translation company] are also taking place to allow two-way consultation.[3]

In March 2008, Operation Mista, a police swoop operation targeted 19 premises on Blackstock Road. Operation Mista was conducted on an unprecedented scale, involving more than 1,000 officers, many of them in full riot gear. The Metropolitan Police noted that Operation Mista was 'an attempt to make a clean sweep of criminality in the area' (*BBC News*, 27 March 2008b).

Thus, there is no mutual exclusivity between the apparently 'consensual' and the coercive powers of the state (see Burnett, this volume). Although no matter how 'soft' or consensual 'partnership' or 'privatized' means of policy delivery look on the surface, it is crucial to analyse the emergence of these forms of power in relation to the forms of coercive power as well as the threat and the actual use of violence that underpin them. This is not to say that 'soft' forms of power are never consensually constructed. Rather, the point is that we cannot derive conclusions about changes in the substance of state power from the appearance of administrative arrangements. What the state *is* and what it *does* remain important sociological questions and point to the need to grasp the *reorganization* – as opposed to the relative disappearance – of it and its institutions.

And always at the centre of state interventions is violence – or, at a minimum, the threat of violence. Therefore, state violence is always implied or connected to the so-called 'soft' forms of power.

To distinguish between force and consent, violent and non-violent means of securing power, then, is to set up a false dualism. Indeed, this was made explicit in *Policing the Crisis*:

> because this domination has been secured by consent – on the basis of a wide consensus, as the saying goes – that domination not only seems to be universal ... and legitimate (not won by coercive force), but its basis in exploitation actually *disappears from view*. Consensus is not the opposite – it is the complementary face of domination ... (Hall et al., 1978: 216 emphasis in the original)

In short, the one principle that the modern state is organized around is its ability to resort to violence. The laws that establish state sovereignty create this as an entity with unrivalled power. Not only are the boundaries of the legitimacy of violence established by law (Green and Ward, this volume), but the power and authority of the state – indeed law itself – is necessarily and intimately bound to violence: 'Lawmaking is powermaking and to that extent, an immediate manifestation of violence' (Benjamin, 1921/1978: 295).

Conclusion: Contesting State Power

At its most fundamental, *Policing the Crisis* sought to place a neo-Marxist, non-reductive analysis of the state and state power on to the criminological agenda. Our analysis here points to the political and theoretical necessity for this task to be revisited, albeit one that will proceed in a changed, but not transformed, context of brutalizing capitalist excesses in the early twenty-first century. In that sense, the state – what it is, where it is and what it does – should be constantly re-problematized for 'the power of the state is the power of the forces acting in and through the state' (Jessop, 1990: 269–70). However, the state is also a site (or series of sites) where claims for social justice and 'progressive' politics are forged, fought over, resisted and sometimes implemented. Conceptualizing state power in this way means thinking about the processes of resistance and spheres of contestation that exist within social relations and how such contestation is articulated and rendered as socially and politically possible (or impossible) in relation to state power. Understanding the state therefore remains crucial not only for thinking about the operation of power and the materialization and representations of social order, but also about challenges to these processes from within and without its institutional but contradictory edifice:

> It is exactly through the state (at whatever scale) that the position and role of the citizen and his/her relationship with society is defined, institutionalized and, on occasion, contested and challenged ... . If we are concerned with formulating

emancipatory policies and strategies, the state and other forms of governance remain key areas for challenging processes of exclusion and disempowerment. (Sywngedouw, 1996: 1502)

Thus, thinking about what progressive social change might look like – as well as the possibilities for its emergence – necessitates an understanding of the state's institutional and discursive power (see Coleman, this volume). Serious consideration should therefore be given to how the state both represents and mystifies itself with respect to its relationship to the maintenance and reproduction of the current inequitable social order, as well as to the mechanisms through which critical voices within and outside the state terrain remain in a process of contestation where state forces and state actors readily appear as categories to be 'talked back to, challenged, or transformed' (Smith, 2005: 894). And, to reiterate a point made above, this task should include not simply a focus upon the state's practices and statements with respect to the marginalized and powerless – those who most manifestly appear to be the objects of state activity, not least through the category of 'crime' – but also with respect to the state's relationships with the powerful, including the relationships between and within different branches of its institutional apparatus and the different blocs and fractions who develop policies and put them into practice.

Those who have adopted a neo-Marxist analysis of the state have therefore not only consistently emphasized the contradictory nature of its institutional power base, but also its place as a site of struggle, which has been, and can be, mobilized by powerless groups to subvert policy proposals and challenge social injustice. In the 1980s, at precisely the historical moment when a rampaging Thatcherism was at its most egregiously triumphant, a range of grass-roots organizations contested the intensification in the coercive capabilities of the neo-liberal state with respect to policing, prisons, the state in Northern Ireland as well as, in the case of women and black and minority ethnic peoples, the rolling back of its institutions with respect to their right to be protected from male and racist violence (Sim et al., 1987: 7). Undoubtedly, gains were made on the basis of these interventions from these wider social movements – even if these were never secure, never adequate and always somewhat fragile.

Contesting state power and exploiting the contingencies and contradictions inherent in its operations continued into the 1990s, and beyond into the twenty-first century. It has expanded into other areas that were either less visible or not on the political and criminological agenda three decades ago, for example the campaigns which have developed around the issue of asylum seekers and their desperate treatment as less eligible subjects both within and without national and international criminal justice systems. These counter-hegemonic interventions, and the strategies which have underpinned them, have been important not only in securing changes in the laws governing a range of social issues, but they have also been important in challenging the ideological basis of the state's claims to 'truth' – for example, around deaths in custody, deaths at work and the role and place of victims in a highly politicized law and order climate (see Walklate, this volume) – as well as impacting on more reformist-oriented criminal justice organizations by pulling them onto an ideological terrain where they have supported the implementation of more radical, less compromising social policy interventions (Sim, 1994).

If this is no easy task, it nonetheless remains central to many of those working as academics within a neo-Marxist, critical criminology tradition; and it is one which challenges and transcends the ongoing caricatures of this tradition, and those who support it, as idealistic utopians out of touch with the 'real' feelings and anxieties of pejoratively and patronizingly defined 'ordinary' people and their aspirations for individual security and collective safety. In many ways, it could be argued that what this critical position represents, indeed demands, is the need for *more*, not less, utopianism and idealism in the theory and practice of social science if we are to transgress the current baleful and corrosive intellectual and political situation described by Russell Jacoby as 'an age of permanent emergencies' in which 'more than ever we have become narrow utilitarians dedicated to fixing, *not reinventing the here and now*' (Jacoby, cited in Sim, 2009, emphasis added).

Criticisms of 'idealist' critical criminology have traditionally been based upon a highly misleading juxtaposition of pragmatism vs. idealism. This has often led to an assumption that to remain ideologically outside the state somehow makes critical intervention less relevant or likely to succeed. This is perhaps best illustrated by Lea and Young's (1993: 258–60) artificial opposition of police monitoring vs. police democratization, in which the work of police monitoring groups was described as 'reactive' and simply responding to police action, rather than working for more longer-term reform of (community-based) police accountability. This argument was built on the assumption that 'idealist' police monitoring groups had never articulated policies and pursued strategies for making the police democratically accountable. However, almost all of the key contributions made by monitoring groups over the years have made concrete suggestions for improving accountability, some of which have been successful (see, for example, Part 3 of Dunhill, 1989; Institute of Race Relations, 1991; and latterly, Goldson and Coles, 2005).

The perspective set out in the left realist position endures in the work of the new pluralists, with each body of literature based upon a series of unconvincing assumptions, and reflecting a 'curious passion for the mannerism of the non-committed' (Wright Mills, 1970: 90). Among these assumptions are, first, that being idealistic can never be pragmatic or useful in winning concessions or influencing policy. Second, and following this, left realism/new pluralism is based upon the assumption that a reformist discourse and agenda can actually deliver fundamental social change, an assumption rarely borne out by evidence. Third, that it is not possible to remain outside the ideological terrain of the state and at the same time to engage on the terrain of the policy world or with the current political system. Yet, in fact, there are a number of counter-hegemonic groups that stand firmly and unapologetically in opposition to the state's criminal justice agenda but still remain engaged with government in consultations, lobbying and policy work. Those groups (including INQUEST, Families Against Corporate Killers, No Borders, Women Against Rape, and so on) provide us with often incontrovertible evidence that idealism does not necessarily constrain the effectiveness or political impact of counter-hegemonic struggle. Therefore, the question remains: how best we might develop a pragmatic idealism that revolves around making connections between, and interventions across, state, economy, politics, history and 'culture', and which stands in direct opposition to 'principled pluralism' with its 'tendencies towards fragmentary problems and scattered causation' (Wright Mills, 1970: 104).

Neo-Marxist criminologists, and the interventionist work in which they engage, thus remain strongly influenced by both *Policing the Crisis* and by Gramsci's earlier interventions concerning the need to develop an alliance-building 'war of position' (Simon, 1982: 74) with the clear intention of turning 'common sense' into 'good sense' with respect to crime, criminal justice, social policy, and so on. Such work requires engaging in, again utilizing Gramsci's words, 'patient and obstinate perseverance' (cited in Boggs, 1976: 22) if a radical transformation is to occur in these areas and in the wider structures of power and privilege that both underpin and legitimate them. This kind of criminological work is inherently oppositional and, by its nature, involves making moral choices.

Thomas Mathiesen, in his book *Silently Silenced* (2004), captured the essence of this position in a chapter which, although devoted to sociology, which he described as a 'silenced profession', has a direct resonance and relevance for criminology in general and critical criminology in particular. At the end of the chapter, he discussed the direction that critical sociological research should follow. For Mathiesen:

> ... it is of vital importance to raise a new research as seen from below, taking as our point of departure the interests of those out of power rather than those in power, those who are repressed rather than those who repress, those who are governed rather than those who govern, those who lack channels of communication to act and influence over decision-making bodies and institutions rather than of those who have such channels and, in fact, are these bodies and institutions. What I have said here has been said before. It is part of yesterday's ideology. But today it sorely needs to be repeated and revitalised. Such a programme raises many difficult questions, *inter alia* questions concerning the relations and possible conflicts between interests seen from below, which in turn raise questions of choice between values. (Mathiesen, 2004: 78)

Of course, taking as a starting point the world 'of those out of power' and 'those in power' means also focusing explicitly, albeit not exclusively, upon the key institutional site of social power, namely the state. In subjecting state power and practice to scrutiny, this collection seeks to analyse its significance in ways that acknowledge and extend the insights of *Policing the Crisis*. In doing so, this introduction has taken as a starting point some of the ideas set out by Hall et al., as well as various insights generated across a series of texts that appeared during the radical turn in criminology and the social sciences through the 1970s. At the same time, while this volume recognizes discontinuities in state formation, practices and power in the UK since the era in which *Policing the Crisis* appeared, it also acknowledges significant continuities. Moreover, while various chapters highlight some of the lacunae in *Policing the Crisis*, they also stand as testimony to its enduring and prescient theoretical and political insights – and, perhaps most importantly, to the often glaring failure of criminology to recognize or develop these insights further.

Furthermore, as Hall and his colleagues noted, *Policing the Crisis* was a book in part concerned to develop 'an intervention in the battleground of ideas' (Hall et al., 1978: x) with respect to the state's activities, direction and representation. This collection, in its own way, is designed to contribute to that 'battle of ideas'. The chapters therefore foreground issues of inequality, injustice and brutalization, and how they may be conceptualized as the routine effects of capitalist states impacting differentially upon the poor and the powerless (see Jones and Novak, this volume), the 'unheterosexual' (Bibbings, this volume), women (see Ballinger, this volume), young people (see Jamieson and Yates, this volume), and minority ethnic groups (see Burnett, this volume). Centrally, they reinsert state violence – including a recognition of those state relationships where violence is removed by the state from its own arsenal of legitimate responses (Tombs and Whyte, Hillyard, Gill, Green and Ward, this volume) – into our ways of analysing and describing aspects of the social world. More generally, they recognize that to address and understand inequality is to raise questions of 'why' (for what purpose and in whose interests, however unintentionally), and not just 'how', forms of power operate.

Thus, it is important to look beyond the organizational forms that constitute the 'state' to the way that power is configured in and through states. Perhaps ironically, given the critique of neo-Marxism in some of the work of the new pluralists, an analysis that stops at the 'institutional ensemble', to use Jessop's phrase, is likely to produce a highly reductive account of state power. We would argue that a view of state power, limited to an analysis of the technical and institutional form that we find in the new pluralism, results in a situation whereby the state as a 'target of political revolt is made to disappear' (Smith, 2005: 894) and the intersection between state and economy is obscured. We say this not to argue for a return to an economic determinist view of the state, but to point to the need for a perspective which counterbalances the narrow statism that, by definition, infects all criminology. The same is also true if we take state discourses at face value and thereby eschew their 'illusory' character in respect of how they are involved in 'the differential articulation and aggregation of interests, opinions and values' (Jessop, 1990: 342). Such discursive formations should also properly be analysed in relation to the materialization of state activity (by which we mean its shifting institutional boundaries, social composition, recourse to violence, and so on) which requires careful analysis in any exploration in respect of the power to both shape material spaces and subjectivities in relation to 'the problem of crime' and the identification of disorder. The centrality of the state then resides in the mobilization of the social forces acting through it and how these forces attempt to reshape the materiality of the state, while providing and provide tutelage in the wider society (through mobilizing ideas and ways of seeing social problems).

Ultimately, while state forces retain this power to ideologically construct and materially confine its enemies, along with a power to punish unrivalled by any other social entity, social scientists would do well to maintain vigilance on and over the enemies of social justice, social equality and democratic accountability. These enemies are far more likely to emerge within, and out of, the moving target that is state power with all of its contradictions, and to which this collection seeks to draw attention.

Notes

1 These texts included: Young's *The Drug Takers* (1971); Box's *Deviance, Reality and Society* (1971); Cohen's *Folk Devils and Moral Panics* (1972); Cohen and Taylor's *Psychological Survival* (1972); Taylor et al.'s *The New Criminology* (1973); Mathiesen's *The Politics of Abolition* (1974); Taylor et al.'s *Critical Criminology* (1975); Foucault's *Discipline and Punish* (1977); Hay et al.'s *Albion's Fatal Tree* (1975); Smart's *Women, Crime and Criminology* (1978); Brownmiller's *Against Our Will* (1976); Carlen's *Magistrates' Justice* (1976); Pearce's, *Crimes of the Powerful* (1976); Fitzgerald's *Prisoners in Revolt* (1977); Ryan's *The Acceptable Pressure Group* (1978); Ignatieff's *A Just Measure of Pain* (1978); Fitzgerald and Sim's *British Prisons* (1979); Fine et al.'s *Capitalism and the Rule of Law* (1979), and Dobash and Dobash's *Violence against Wives* (1979).
2 We are grateful to Anette Ballinger for making this point.
3 www://cms.met.police.uk/met/boroughs/islington/04how_are_we_doing/news/ multi_agency_operation_to_reduce_crime_in_blackstock_road_islington_21_08_07 (accessed 26/05/08).

1

GENDER, POWER AND THE STATE:
SAME AS IT EVER WAS?

Anette Ballinger

> Women have undoubtedly benefited from greater economic, civil and political
> freedom since the late 1960s, yet discrimination persists in systemically maintained
> gender inequalities such as segregation in employment and unequal pay. Thus,
> against some of the ungrounded naïve claims of social theory, many feminists would
> insist that changes within gender relations are indicative of the emergence of new
> forms of oppression as well as new types of freedom. (McNay, 2004: 171)

The colossal impact that *Policing the Crisis* had on social science scholars interested
in developing critical perspectives on the relationship between the state and civil
society, is beyond dispute. The book also offered a radical departure from traditional
positivist functionalism which had dominated the social sciences thus far. Crucially,
however, it followed in the footsteps of traditional criminology in one respect, by
focusing its analysis on events within the *public* sphere. Without wishing to detract
from the importance of the book's arguments, it is nevertheless important to note
that the year 1978 also saw the publication of other – equally influential books – as
far as the private sphere – and therefore the subject of gender, power and the state is
concerned. Carol Smart's *Women, Crime and Criminology* (originally published in
1976, but first published in paperback in 1978) offered the first comprehensive
feminist critique of traditional criminology and included an analysis of criminal
activities such as rape, a violent crime which thus far had 'failed to arouse much
interest within the discipline of criminology' (1978: 93).

The year 1978 also saw the publication of *Women, Sexuality and Social Control*, an
edited collection by Smart and Smart which played a key role in ensuring that hence-
forth, crime within the private sphere would become a permanent fixture on the criminological agenda. These books, and others published soon afterwards such as Hutter
and Williams' edited collection *Controlling Women* (1981), established analytical concepts
which were to become the cornerstones of feminist challenges to traditional criminology
for decades to come, and which helped to expand the criminological agenda by emphasizing the gender-specific social control experienced by women in both the public and

private spheres. Such authors drew a distinction between formal and informal social control, and through detailed analysis were able to demonstrate the role such patriarchal controls play in constructing 'normal' versus 'deviant' womanhood.

However, three decades after the publication of these pioneering works, there is much evidence which indicates that, first, formal inequality between the sexes remains a serious issue within the public sphere, and second, that violence against women within the private sphere is as prevalent as ever. For example, in terms of formal inequality, despite the introduction of legislation designed to ensure equal pay, a 17% gap in women's pay is still evident (*Guardian*, 6 April 2007). Similarly, the Chartered Management Institute found that women directors earn an average of £22,144 less that male directors (*Guardian*, 19 September 2005), and the Fawcett Society has estimated that at the present rate of change, it will take 140 years before women achieve equal pay (*Guardian*, 14 June 2007). Moreover, in 2007 the Equalities Review Report noted the existence of 'an array of "entrenched" inequalities' so extensive that 'in some areas "we have stopped the clock"'; in others, '"it is starting to turn backwards"' (*Guardian*, 1 March 2007).

In terms of violence against women, the most recent statistics available at the time of writing indicate that an estimated 50,000 rapes occur annually in Britain. Of those, approximately one-fifth are reported and the conviction rate for this fraction currently stands at 5.3%. This means that if all estimated cases are taken into account, 'a rapist has about a 1% chance of being convicted' (*New Statesman*, 18 June 2007). The conviction rate for rape which stood at 33% in 1977, has thus reached its lowest level ever (*Guardian*, 18 June 2007). While 13,247 cases of rape were reported in 2004, it has been estimated that on average, '1 in 6 had experienced rape and 1 in 3 had been sexually assaulted at some point in their lives [with] one in 7 women experiencing rape in marriage' (Phoenix and Oerton, 2005: 31).

National statistics concerned with domestic violence have consistently indicated that on average, two women are killed a week 'by a current or former partner' which 'constitutes 42% of all female victims of homicide' (*Guardian*, 19 April 2006; Edwards, 1989: 126; Boyle, 2005: 85). Additionally, the Council of Europe found 'that domestic violence is the biggest cause of death and disability for all women under the age of 44' (*Guardian*, 19 April 2006), and the journal *Emergency Medicine* published statistics indicating that approximately 80% of all domestic abuse victims are women and 'around one in three women who arrive at inner-city accident and emergency hospital departments have suffered domestic abuse' (*Guardian*, 20 June 2007). Furthermore, 25% of women have 'experienced at least one physical assault from a partner … and one incident of domestic violence is reported to the police every minute' (*Guardian*, 9 August 2006). Domestic violence accounts for a quarter 'of all violent crime' (Itzin, 2000: 357), and 30% of it 'starts or is exacerbated during pregnancy' (*Guardian*, 2 September 2004). According to Mooney (2000: 38), only 37% of men would reject the possibility of using violence against their partner, a finding which helps to explain the above statistics.

Such statistics provide firm evidence that the clock has indeed stopped, not only with regard to formal equality between men and women, but also as far as eliminating domestic violence is concerned, and has 'started to turn backwards' on the subject of rape conviction rates (Lees, 1996: 264; *Guardian*, 18 June 2007). In an era where women enjoy unprecedented levels of personal and economic freedom and opportunities, and where formal equality has received another boost via the Gender Equality Duty legislation, enforced in April 2007 – why have statistics concerning domestic violence-related female deaths remained virtually unaltered while cases of reported rape increased 165% during the 1990s (Itzin, 2000: 357) – and what are the reasons for the massive drop in successful convictions for reported rape during the past thirty years? At a time when accepted wisdom states 'we are living in a post-feminist, post-sexist era, in which women have never had it so good' (*New Statesman*, 18 June 2007) – why is this level of violence against women allowed to go largely unpunished? Why has there been such massive failure on the part of the state to ensure women's safety? Why is it that, where women are concerned, 'modern democratic states with all their might and sophistication are not capable of implementing ... basic human rights, proclaimed and upheld by all democratic constitutions, particularly the right to the inviolability and integrity of one's body ...'? (Mies, 1991: 26).

In this chapter I shall argue that we cannot understand this apparent contradiction between, on the one hand, formal, (supposedly) legal equality in the public sphere, and, on the other hand, informal inequality through (supposedly) illegal violence within the private sphere, without placing the state's role in maintaining the dominant heteropatriarchal social order at the forefront of analysis. The sheer volume of violent crimes committed against women annually arguably justifies this focus in its own right; however, it is further justified theoretically since, contrary to the initial optimism of the women's movement, it soon became clear that greater participation in the public sphere, for example through wage-employment, had not solved 'the basic problem of the patriarchal man–woman relationship' which, for many women, continued to be based on violence:

> Although the modern state as the general patriarch had assumed the monopoly over all direct violence, it had left some of it to the individual patriarch in his family ... women began to understand that rape, wife-beating, harassment ..., were not just expressions of deviant behaviour on the part of some men, but were part and parcel of a whole system of ... patriarchal, dominance over women. (Mies, 1991: 26, 27)

It is to a consideration of male violence and state power to which the chapter now turns.

A New 'Crisis of Legitimacy'? The State's Response to Rape

While the state could be seen to be 'doing' 'race' in relation to the issue of the black mugger of the 1970s as outlined in *Policing the Crisis* (Hall et al., 1978), it can also be seen to be 'doing' gender (Connell, 1994: 155) in relation to violence against women. Connell argues that the state is 'an active player in gender politics' and, 'at the very least a significant vehicle of sexual and gender oppression and regulation' (1994: 147). However, he also stresses that its role in that oppression 'is usually indirect' and 'embedded in procedure, in its way of functioning: 'This perception is extremely important. It allows us to acknowledge the patriarchal character of the state without falling into a conspiracy theory of making futile searches for Patriarch Headquarters' (Connell, 1994: 143, 146). Employing Connell's analysis of the state's patriarchal tendencies being exercised *indirectly*, through *procedures* and self-defined *'objective' structures*, I shall now analyse how the state upholds the dominant heteropatriarchal social order through 'doing' gender in its response to violence against women.

First, Connell explains how patriarchal structures and procedures operate with regard to rape, which historically has been constructed from the perspective of men:

> The legal system translates this interested point of view into impersonal procedural norms, defining ... what must be proven and what is acceptable or convincing evidence. The courts are not patriarchal because they are improperly biased against women, rather they are patriarchal through the way the whole structure of rape law operates. The more objective they are in procedure the more effectively patriarchal they are. The norm of 'legal objectivity' thus becomes an institutionalisation of men's interests. (1994: 145)

Connell is thus in agreement with those feminist critiques which identified the androcentric and patriarchal nature of law. Yet, at the same time such critiques have undoubtedly had a fundamental impact on the state during the past thirty years. Franzway et al. (1989: 11) note the scope for 'interaction between feminism and the state' grew during the 1970s and 1980s, resulting in practical reforms such as 'specially trained police officers and rape suites' (Phoenix and Oerton, 2005: 32–3). Nonetheless, just as the authors of *Policing the Crisis* argued that a crisis of legitimacy was generated with regard to law and order during the 1970s, so Phoenix and Oerton argue that a crisis of legitimacy arose with regard to rape and sexual assault during the late 1990s, as a result of issues relating to stranger versus familiar rape and reporting and attrition rates, which put the government under increasing pressure to also consider legal reforms. Within this context the Sexual Offences Act 2003 (SOA 2003) can be understood as the state's response to this crisis of legitimacy, which – in turn – allowed it to be seen as having taken critiques and concerns 'seriously' by 'doing' something about sexual violence.

Yet, as indicated by the statistics above, the SOA 2003 has done nothing to reduce the amount of sexual violence, or increase the rate of successful rape convictions. This is because conceptualizing the solution to this 'legitimacy deficit' in simplistic legal and technical terms – the law is faulty and in need of reform, such reforms will lead to the correct legal procedures for reducing incidents of sexual violence and increasing the rape conviction rate – removes them altogether from the *structural* context of the heteropatriarchal social order which feminists have identified as being responsible for gendered violence in the first place. The legal changes contained within the SOA 2003 have therefore done nothing to change 'the wider social relationships and material realities which condition men's sexual violence and women's sexual victimization. In short, the power of law remains unchallenged, as does the social context that makes sexual violation routine' (Phoenix and Oerton, 2005: 39).

Here it is important to return to Connell's point about the law operating *indirectly, through procedures*, rather than in an overt or conspiratorial manner, for, undeniably, official discourse within the SOA is willing – eager even – to take sexual violence *seriously*. According to Phoenix and Oerton it does this by presenting all victims as suffering a fate worse than death through 'extreme trauma brought on by their sexual violations ...' (2005: 39).

While this portrayal appears sympathetic to victims, such generalization of victimhood also silences those who do not fit this mould. In particular, those who insist that the state's treatment of them was as traumatic as the offence – and who therefore also insist on including structural issues connected to androcentric law – are silenced. Only those who are understood as having had their entire lives destroyed by their violation gain prominence in this all-encompassing, suffering model of victimhood (Phoenix and Oerton, 2005: 41). Official discourse is therefore also reinforcing traditional views of the weak, vulnerable, disempowered victim who needs *protection*, which, in turn, sets up the conditions for legitimizing harsher punishment to give victims confidence in the system and encourage reporting (2005: 44). Again, this strategy allows the state to be seen to be taking sexual assaults *seriously* and *doing* something about them, while simultaneously ignoring the complex social relations within heteropatriarchy where such violence has its roots. Thus, according to Phoenix and Oerton, it is a strategy which generates favourable conditions for the creation of 'a new sexual enterprise of moral authoritarianism' (2005: 53) within which harsher punishment is presented as the *only* solution to ensuring 'justice for victims'.

In sum, by providing legal responses to the problem of rape, the state can be understood to have 'done' gender by eliminating those feminist discourses which identified the law and criminal justice system as part of the problem rather than the solution, and thereby leaving the structures that create and support hegemonic masculinity unexplored and the heteropatriarchal social order undisturbed (Ballinger, 2007: 477). This is unsurprising since the state and its major institutions, such as the legal system, have been identified as being 'grounded in patriarchy' (Smart, 1989: 88). The solution to rape (or domestic violence) can therefore not be found within the law since both rape and law are 'exercises in power ... they are both exercised in the masculine mode, so one is not the solution to the other' (1989: 88). Put another way, 'the state is not an objective, neutral arbiter of the "facts"' (Walklate, 2007: 49), but has gender deeply embedded within it. Maintenance of its own interests therefore includes activities which encourage the production and reproduction of the gendered subject which in turn supports the existing social order (Smart, 1995: 79). Thus, to look towards the state to solve problems stemming from its own structure of heteropatriarchy is to ask for it to work against its own interests and self-maintenance. It is within this context that the state is drawn towards technical, legal solutions from within its own repertoire which identify individuals rather than structures, as the problem: 'This orientation towards events and people produces accounts of crime which mystify the social and historical roots of crime by suggesting that wicked or bothersome individuals are at fault rather than unjust and inequitable social structures' (Morrissey, 2003: 19). In short, while recognizing that the state is far from impervious to gendered violence, its strategy in dealing with it nonetheless plays an important role in ensuring that things are indeed likely to remain much the same as they ever were, since 'legal reform, without a fundamental overhaul of the interpretative background, amounts to little more than tinkering with the edges of systematic and structural injustice' (Jackson, cited in Chan, 2001: 169).

'Doing' Gender through Domestic Violence

The second example of the state 'doing' gender can be observed in its response to domestic violence. As with the issue of rape, feminist work relating to domestic violence has had a substantial impact on official discourse over the past three decades. In particular, the poor policing of this offence created legitimacy problems for the state during the 1980s, to the point where demands for action could not be ignored. While state discourses insisted that domestic violence was rooted in individual pathology, 'problem' families and poor housing, feminists placed its inadequate policing within the context of the patriarchal state and social order:

> ... the police are defenders of the existing order while men's violence plays a central role in upholding male supremacy within that order. There is no way the police or other agents of the state, the courts, or judiciary, can truly treat men's violence as a serious crime without undermining the social order it serves so well. (Hanmer, Radford and Stanko, cited in Kantola, 2005: 85)

The 1990s consequently witnessed a struggle between these two competing discourses. The state attempted to reduce its responsibility by 'marginalising political debates' (McKie, 2005: 48) and structural issues, and instead emphasized the role of the individual (Kantola, 2005: 80), while feminists continued to emphasize the social and structural context of domestic violence. Moreover, high-profile cases such as those of Sara Thornton, Emma Humphrys and Kiranjit Ahluwalia – all given life sentences for killing their abusive partners – caused 'a public-realm scandal' which created a crisis of legitimacy for the state (Connell, 1994: 156), as a direct result of protest campaigns by feminist activists and academics (Ballinger, 1996, 2000). The women were eventually released which, on the one hand, can be characterized as a victory for feminist discourses in relation to domestic violence. However, on the other hand, it can also be seen as evidence of the state's 'capacity to regulate the power relations of gender' (Connell, 1994: 156; see also Ballinger, 2005: 79). That is, the state was 'doing' gender by ignoring complex structural issues around the heteropatriarchal social order, and instead focused on individual retaliating victims of domestic abuse, by reducing their sentences: 'The effect of this routine of management is to construct the issue as one of a deviant minority of violent husbands, and to deflect criticisms of marriage as an institution that generates violence' (Connell, 1994: 156; also Morrissey, 2003). Rather than a victory for feminism, the release of these retaliating women can therefore be understood as a conservative strategy which helped preserve the institution of marriage in particular, as well as the wider gendered social order generally (Ballinger, 2007: 475). Yet, their eventual release also demonstrates that the patriarchal state can be brought to the point of a crisis of legitimacy to which it must respond, and 'whilst recognising that "feminist discourses lack the social power to realise their versions of knowledge in institutional practices"'(Weedon, cited in Ballinger, 2005: 79), their influence nonetheless became apparent in official discourse during the 1990s, for example in the 1993 Home Affairs Committee Report which recognized the universal nature of domestic violence and recommended that 'the government should take swift action in providing funding for refuges and in creating a coherent national strategy to tackle domestic violence' (Kantola, 2005: 93).

The response to these recommendations, however, once again reflected the state's ability to 'do' gender and manage power relations to preserve the dominant heteropatriarchal social order, for it continued to emphasize individual responsibility at the expense of social structures in its explanations of, and response to, domestic violence. Thus, in 1994 'it launched a public awareness campaign ... with the slogan "Domestic Violence is a Crime – Don't Stand for It"', and the following year the Home Office produced guidelines for voluntary organizations dealing with domestic violence (Kantola, 2005: 97), gestures which ensured the state was able to portray itself as responding to the legitimacy deficit and to be 'doing' something about this violence, while simultaneously ignoring the structural issue of national funding for refuges. Campaigns and guidelines, however well intentioned, do not provide refuge for victims of violence; on the contrary, the Dash Report indicated that 'campaigns to highlight domestic violence have failed' (*Guardian*, 9 August 2006). Hence, on the issue *most* likely to bring structural improvements to the lives of domestic violence victims by providing them with safe, alternative accommodation, the government's response was virtually non-existent – in Kantola's words – 'disappointingly bleak' (2005: 97). As Connell (1994: 156) notes, the state's non-intervention within this context provides tacit support for domestic violence and, ultimately, can be understood as a refusal to engage with strategies which threaten heteropatriarchal family life, at the expense of women's safety and well-being. For, compared to leaflets and guidelines, offering women a way out of a violent relationship carries a much greater potential to undermine and threaten the idealistic image of the private sphere as a 'safe haven' and instead exposes the family as 'the most violent group to which ... women and children are likely to belong' (Dobash and Dobash, 1979: 7).

In sum, the state was doing gender by defining domestic violence as an individual problem which could be eliminated through greater awareness. This strategy left structural issues within the heteropatriarchal social order unexplored by silencing feminist discourses, and consequently, just as the SOA 2003 has done little to reduce the volume of sexual violence or increase the rate of successful rape convictions, so the state-sponsored awareness campaign against domestic violence has done nothing to reduce the number of women killed by a current or former partner.

'Doing Gender': Financing the Social Order

The final example of the state 'doing' gender concerns the subject of funding for rape crisis centres and refuges. The financial cost of rape and other forms of sexual violence is impossible to quantify due to its hidden nature and lack of reporting. Yet, shelters, refuges and rape crisis centres suffer chronic under-funding and perpetual financial crises. In 1984 England and Wales had 68 rape crisis centres (RCCs) and helplines. In 2007 only 32 remained as a result of lack of funds, while the government scored 'just two out of ten' for its efforts in ending violence against women. The Northern Ireland Office scored one out of ten (*Amnesty Magazine*, Jan./Feb. 2007). Why, at a time when the status of the victim is experiencing unprecedented attention from the state, media and academic research, is funding for those who provide specialist knowledge and expertise in their dealings with rape and domestic abuse victims perpetually dwindling?

As discussed above, feminists have identified the state as heteropatriarchal and hence deeply implicated in upholding a social order within which women's subordination – and therefore also their victimization – is maintained. It is therefore unsurprising that women's organizations dealing with the aftermath of such victimization have fought hard to remain independent of the state and its masculinist values. Thus, since their inception in 1976, RCCs have worked according to the feminist ethos of, first, providing a service 'by and for women' (Gillespie, 1994: 16), which entails an emphasis on equality, empowerment and self-help, rather than the traditional client–professional relationship, and second, providing direct access, which means supporting those who have identified *themselves* as victims, and ultimately as survivors, and always believing their accounts, rather than relying on state-identified victims through police referrals. Finally, woman-centred organizations have focused on social structures and power relationships rather than individual violent men, and have involved themselves in campaigns for social change rather than presenting themselves as 'neutral'. For example, Women Against Rape 'won the legal recognition of rape within marriage in 1991 after a 15-year campaign' (*Amnesty Magazine*, Jan./Feb. 2007).

It is precisely these principles which challenge official discourse and the *modus operandi* of state-sponsored organizations and charities, and which have subsequently resulted in RCCs being identified as '"extreme" feminist organizations, anti-police, anti-men, and more concerned with "radical feminist politics" than providing effective support services for women who have been raped and sexually abused' (cited in Gillespie, 1994: 19). Further evidence that feminist service provision is at odds with the goals of the 'efficient and effective' service delivery ethos dominating state-sponsored organizations is apparent when compared to Victim Support, which has maintained a more traditional client–expert relationship and works in close partnership with state servants such as the police, and which 'receive[s] generous funding from the Home Office' (Gillespie, 1994: 18, 24). Its funding increased from £12.7 million in 1997/98 to £25 million in 2001/02 (*Independent*, 23 October 2002), the same year that 'half of Britain's remaining rape crisis groups exist[ed] on less than £20,000, raised entirely from donations ... one in five continues to function with less than £5,000' (*Sunday Observer*, 24 November 2002).

A similar history can be traced in the development of services for domestic abuse victims. Domestic violence costs employers in the UK £3 billion annually due to employees being unable to work as a result of injuries. It costs the criminal justice system £1 billion annually, and the NHS and social services more than £1.5 billion per year (*Guardian*, 2 September 2004, 20 June 2007). Altogether, it is estimated that domestic violence costs a total of £23 billion a year in England and Wales (*Guardian*, 18 June 2004). Beyond the financial cost lies the emotional cost, not least of which is the effect on the 750,000 children who witness it annually, 'around half of whom have themselves been badly hit or beaten' (*Guardian*, 20 June 2007). Furthermore, the British Crime Survey 2004 'found that domestic violence is the single most cited reason for becoming homeless' (*Guardian*, 18 June 2004).

Within this context, 'shelters formed an essential part of the wider political struggle against the structural oppression of women, emphasising "the goal of changing the socio-political conditions that fostered violence' (cited in Lupton, 1994: 57). Thus, like RCCs, shelter workers identified themselves as part of a 'wider social movement' and hence were committed to instigating social change and to operating in 'non-hierarchical, collectivist ways'. They also emphasized self-help and self-determination as well as 'working with women, rather than for them' (Lupton, 1994: 56, 57; Kantola, 2005). As such, shelters too, have formed a contrast to 'traditional "social provision" agencies' (Lupton, 1994: 55), and challenge official discourse and ultimately, the heteropatriarchal social order. As with RCCs, maintaining this level of autonomy has had financial consequences with most shelters surviving on uncertain grant funding and fundraising. In 1980 'over one-third received no grants at all and existing sources of funding ... were inherently insecure', a situation which worsened during the 1990s (Lupton, 1994: 60). For example, in 1998, under 'half of the refuge spaces recommended by the Government Select Committee on Violence in Marriage 25 years ago' were in place (Harwin and Barron, 2000: 207). Miller notes that shelters have been 'under enormous pressure to de-emphasise their feminist politics' in exchange for funding because state 'entities were uncomfortable with the movement's position that battering resulted from a patriarchal society' (2005: 6), and Maguire has suggested that government pressure on Victim Support to extend its services to victims of domestic abuse and sexual assault 'is a deliberate attempt to circumvent the work of feminist-inspired groups' (cited in Lupton, 1994: 69).

Thus, increasingly, funding has become subject to a willingness to follow the American model where the feminist principles of self-help, self-determination and emphasis on women as survivors have been replaced with a more traditional 'social provision' ethos, within which violence against women becomes de-politicized and redefined as 'family violence', and the battered wife becomes 'a domestic violence programme client' (Lupton, 1994: 59). This process of redefining violence against women to an individual, gender-neutral problem which can be responded to by experts and 'cured' through 'therapeutic assistance' and treatment (Miller, 2005: 6), also serves to render male violence invisible (Itzin, 2000: 376). In this way, the state is 'doing gender' by undermining the structural arguments put forward by feminist-inspired groups, who, in order to attract funding, are under increasing pressure to compromise their politics and 'reframe their basic aims and objectives' towards a more traditional social provision model (Lupton, 1994: 63).

In sum, the shrinking numbers of RCCs and shelters, and the dire financial straits they have been forced to operate in during the last three decades, provide a powerful example of the state's ability to 'do gender' by directing funding towards 'more politically acquiescent services such as Victims Support' (Lupton, 1994: 72), while simultaneously marginalizing feminist organizations resisting incorporation 'into existing state structures' (Foley, 1994: 47). These organizations – and ultimately all the victims seeking their services – have thus paid a heavy price for maintaining their independence and challenging the gendered social order. Indeed, apart from the financial cost outlined above, there is the human cost in terms of victims being unable to access the support and advice they need. With RCCs and helplines 'closing at a rate of two per month', there is a waiting list of seven months for counselling, and victims from outside catchment areas where no provision exists, are regularly turned away (Women's Resource Centre, October 2006).

The apparent contradiction between such statistics and the unprecedented increase in politicians claiming their support for the implementation of legislation concerned with 'victims rights' (Spalek, 2006: 17) is explained by Cochrane as 'proof of an institutionalised misogyny that cuts to the heart of British society, a national disgrace magnified by the apparent lack of public or political will to really tackle the issue' (*New Statesman*, 18 June 2007). It is also an example of the state's continued ability to manage gender relationships through a process of 'regressive modernisation' (Hall, 1988: 164) – that is, implementing new measures which appear to take the concerns of individual victims seriously, and thus pay lip service to 'doing' something about violence against women, while simultaneously ensuring that the social structure within which that violence continues to thrive, remains 'the same as it ever was'.

Hegemony, Resistance and Patriarchal Power

Franzway et al. note that much of the state's involvement with sexual politics is organized around efforts 'to construct, impose and sustain a particular patriarchal family form, and to provide an ideological defence of this form' (1989: 12). However, state institutions do not do this in a simplistic or conspiratorial way. On the contrary:

> ... the state's role in women's oppression is subtle to the point where it appears to be gender-neutral – or even protective towards women – by seemingly regulating the system to prevent further oppression, for example through law's enforcement of 'equal opportunity' or 'equal pay' legislation. (Ballinger, 2007: 474)

Furthermore, through the process of redefinition and gender-neutralization, the state is able to present itself as *more* inclusive than feminists, who by comparison appear outdated in their insistence on focusing on heteropatriarchy. Thus, apart from the gender-neutralization described above in relation to domestic violence arguments, the state has also had a measure of success in gender-neutralizing the arguments around rape by equating equality with sameness, a definition which has facilitated a construction of official discourse built on the idea that women commit the *same* crimes as men, and consequently, they should also be treated the same. This line of reasoning further supports and reinforces the state's desire to offer a technical solution: since the problem is out-dated laws, *legal adjustments* will provide a remedy:

> Our law is cast in terms of men committing certain offences and women committing others. ... This leads to anomalies and inconsistencies in the way offenders are dealt with for what is *essentially similar behaviour* ... this kind of differential treatment was not justified unless there was a specific reason, offences should be couched in gender-neutral terms. (Home Office, cited in Phoenix and Oerton, 2005: 46, emphasis in the original)

While this reasoning appears to expand the state's concern for victims of sexual violence by including men, it also forecloses the space 'in which the law can be capable of understanding and dealing with the gendered material social relations of sexual violence' (Phoenix and Oerton, 2005: 46), and, in particular, the different contexts within which men and women commit violence. Moreover, this 'contemporary search for equivalence' (Worrall, 2002: 48) is ultimately a conservative strategy, depoliticizing the nature of such violence and ensuring the preservation of the social order by ignoring the structural issue of male violence:

> If women are no longer victims of gender-specific oppressions, such as domestic violence, rape and sexual abuse, because men are also victims of these things, then there is no need for gender-specific ways of dealing with offenders. (Worrall, 2002: 49)

This point is reinforced by Connell who, as noted above, maintains that the legal system is patriarchal, not because it is 'improperly biased against women', but through structures and procedures, allowing it to define 'what must be proven and what is acceptable or convincing evidence'. In short, the very 'appearance of technical neutrality' by the state in its quest for gender equality, is already in itself embedding 'patriarchal points of view' and as such, is inherently heteropatriarchal in nature (Connell, 1994: 145). In that sense, 'formal politics may be seen as a dynamic factor in maintaining and strengthening the gender order: the state acts to reinforce masculine norms' (Tosh, 2004: 41).

Yet, as this chapter also indicates, the state does not operate as a simplistic patriarchal tool; on the contrary, it is concerned with the maintenance of legitimacy as well as the social order, and as such, can be understood as working in the interests of individual women at particular moments (Ballinger, 2007: 475). As Connell has observed, 'the fact that the state will restrain some manifestations of private-sphere patriarchy is significant' (1994: 156). However, I have also demonstrated that the contested ground between feminist challenges to state institutions and the state's response to, and redefinition of, such challenges during the past three decades has not been a battle between equals. While feminists have emphasized the need to challenge heteropatriarchal structures, the state has responded by redefining key issues concerning violence against women, and continues to do so. Thus, when the state is 'doing gender', it is encouraging gender relationships to remain 'the same as they ever were', ultimately preserving the social order. This process involves under-playing the role of masculinity in the continual reproduction of gendered violence. Furthermore, a focus on *individuals* rather than structural issues, such as power rela-tions within marriage, remain evident. This is exemplified by the funding of 'panic rooms' for domestic violence victims within their homes, which involves installing solid doors, 'mortice locks, steel hinges, bolts and a spy glass to transform a bedroom into a "sanctuary"' (*Guardian*, 22 February 2006). Rather than tackling the abuser or root causes of violence, this solution curtails the victim's personal freedom and civil liberties, while reinforcing traditional ideologies concerning women's confine-ment to the private sphere.

A second example concerns the Freedom Programme, a course for domestic abuse victims which 'aims to help women come to terms with traumatic experiences … build confidence and self-esteem, and … avoid harmful relationships in the future' by teaching them 'to recognise signs of abusive behaviour and how to break free from the cycle of abuse' (*MerseyMart*, 16 March 2006). This exemplifies that 'things are indeed the same as they ever were' – or at least since 1992, when Dobash and Dobash wrote that 'a narrow therapeutic focus means that … violence against women is … not linked to the … wider oppression and experiences of all women' (1992: 229).

Similarly, the discourses identified by feminists during the past three decades, which constructed victims rather than perpetrators as being responsible for rape, are still active in the twenty-first century. For example, in response to a 2004 rape study, the Association of Chief Police Officers argued that 'in most cases, the alleged victims had consumed alcohol voluntarily … in some cases, to dangerous levels' (*Independent*, 17 November 2006), thus presenting 'sexual crime prevention' as being of no concern to men, but 'the sole responsibility of women'. As such, official discourse is still focused on potential female victims who must teach themselves the self-surveillance of 'sensible drinking' while questions about 'what kind of man' would desire sexual intercourse with a comatose woman remain unasked and unanswered (*Guardian*, 5 August 2005).

More widely, despite the state's continued active involvement in promoting formal equality for women, for example via the aforementioned Gender Equality Duty legislation, state servants nevertheless continue to adhere to an agenda reflecting traditional constructions of femininity, particularly those linked to reproduction and motherhood. Thus, Bennett notes the prioritizing of women's right to breastfeed in public in the 2007 *Framework for Fairness* consultation paper. Within the context of the pay gap between men and women, Bennett asks:

> Is breast-feeding really the worst problem that women have to deal with today? ... [What about] what is going to happen when I go back to work? Will someone have taken my job? Will there be flexible working? ... Why do women MPs care more about breast-feeding than about equality? (*Guardian*, 14 June 2007)

The continuing social control of women through 'the reproduction cycle' identified by Smart and Smart in 1978, is also evident from advice given to pregnant women regarding the consumption of alcohol. Only 5% of babies 'born to *alcoholic* women have FAS' (Armstrong, 2003: 7, emphasis added), and the Royal College of Obstetricians and Gynaecologists maintains 'there is no conclusive evidence of adverse effects in either growth or IQ at levels of ... 15 units a week'. Yet, the government advised pregnant women to avoid alcohol altogether 'just in case' (*Guardian*, 21 March 2007). Within the context that pregnant women are much more likely to suffer domestic violence 'than to drink excessively during pregnancy' (Armstrong, 2003: 3), that there has been a '21% rise in maternal deaths over the past three years', and that 17,000 women 'have suffered harm on labour wards', Williams concludes that such advice 'is an outrage against women [and] against the relationship between the state and the individual' (*Guardian*, 21 March 2007). This insistence on foregrounding traditional discourses of femininity, at the expense of those associated with substantial equality, also demonstrates the continuing validity of Connell's thesis discussed above, that the state is 'the main organiser of the power relations of gender', but that its role in women's oppression is subtle to the point where it may even appear 'protective towards women by seemingly regulating the system to prevent further oppression' (Connell, 1994: 148; see also Ballinger, 2007: 474). Moreover, the state's eagerness to police private-sphere activities such as pregnant women's alcohol consumption, is particularly noteworthy within the context of its failure to police private-sphere violence, as outlined in this chapter.

Meanwhile, women continue to pay the price for the state's emphasis on maintaining law and order in the public sphere at the expense of protecting women's lives within the private sphere, as can be seen from the case of Banaz Mahmod, who was murdered by her family after having 'told police at least four times that threats had been made on her life' (*Guardian*, 13 June 2007). After reporting one such threat, police 'dismissed her as being manipulative and melodramatic' and 'failed to record the murder allegation and instead ... considered charging Ms Mahmod for a broken window that she smashed to escape' from her family (*Guardian*, 12 June 2007).

The above examples suggest that despite the state's willingness to legislate in favour of women's *formal* equality, this has done little to shift dominant ideologies and discourses around traditional femininity or the power relationship between gender and the public/private sphere. Such legislation has therefore been unable to deliver *substantial* equality. On the contrary, the changes within technical and legal procedures discussed above, have *reinforced* existing state priorities and official discourses flowing from such priorities, which subsequently have remained largely 'the same as they ever were' – that is, they have been constructed and reconstructed to enable the preservation of the hetcropatriarchal social order. The centrality of the state in constructing gender relationships, as well as its ability to define and redefine the gendered subject, thus becomes visible in what it prioritizes, but equally in *what it fails to prioritize*. Within this context:

> Material feminists tend to offer … cautious accounts of change asserting that, if gender relations are transforming at all, … it is in a gradual and complex fashion where the emergence of new forms of autonomy coincides with new forms of dependency and subordination. (McNay, 2004: 174)

Conclusion

In 1978 the authors of *Policing the Crisis* concluded:

> When we confront, not crime, but the economic, political and ideological conditions producing crime, as the basis of a possible political strategy, the issues become necessarily more complex. They bring together the most difficult matters of strategy, analysis and practice. (Hall et al., 1978: 396)

Gendering this analysis three decades later, it may be concluded that when we confront, not crime, but the economic, political, ideological *and* heteropatriarchal conditions which produce women's subordination, the issues become necessarily more complex, and the current generation of feminists doubtless face difficult matters of strategy, analysis and practice. Yet, there are signs that this generation is well equipped to tackle this task, not least through the numerous third-wave feminist groups based throughout the UK, who in response to the 'mainstreaming of the porn and sex industries', have become activists to the point where 'there's a mini-revolution going on' (*Guardian*, 9 February 2007). Moreover, six new feminist publications were established between March and September 2007, and when combined with the establishment of a host of organizations such as Rights for Women and FEM Conferences (*Observer Women*, September 2007), there is much evidence that a new generation of twenty-first-century feminists have no intention of allowing relations between gender, power and the state to remain 'the same as they ever were'. Instead, they can be understood as being engaged in forming a new 'historical bloc' which aims to 'propagate itself throughout society … posing all the questions around which the [gender] struggle rages …' (Gramsci, cited in Hall et al., 1978: 203). This hegemonic strategy will ensure that the state's role as educator and organizer of gender relationships will continue to be challenged until full gender equality, and by extension, the elimination of male violence, is achieved.

Key Reading

Connell, R.W. (1994) 'The state, gender and sexual politics: theory and appraisal', in H.L. Radtke and H.J. Stam (eds), *Power/Gender*. London: Sage.

Hanmer, J. and Itzin, C. (eds) (2000) *Home Truths about Domestic Violence*. London: Routledge.

Kantola, J. (2005) *Feminists Theorise the State*. Basingstoke: Palgrave.

Lupton, C. and Gillespie, T. (eds) (1994) *Working with Violence*. Basingstoke: Macmillan.

Phoenix, J. and Oerton, S. (2005) *Illicit and Illegal: Sex, Regulation and Social Control*. Cullompton: Willan.

2

THE HETEROSTATE: HEGEMONIC HETEROSEXUALITY AND STATE POWER

Lois S. Bibbings

─────────────────── **Introduction** ───────────────────

This chapter considers the operation of state power in relation to sexualities. It uses ideas about (hetero)sexuality developed elsewhere (in particular, see Bibbings, 2004), sets them in the context of Hall et al.'s *Policing the Crisis* (1978) and considers how the latter might help us understand the nature of the state and the mobilization of its power over the thirty years since the book was published. In so doing it also seeks to bring discussion of sexualities, an area which has often been omitted or sidelined, into the mainstream of academic and, in particular, criminological debate.[1] This is crucial because 'an understanding of virtually any aspect of modern western culture must be, not merely incomplete, but damaged in its central substance to the degree that it does not incorporate a critical analysis of modern homo/heterosexual definition' (Sedgwick, 1990: 1). Moreover, as consideration of the state and state power has also often been marginalized from criminological thinking, this chapter begins to address both of these absences.

The crisis that Hall et al. were talking about in the late 1970s was, amongst other things, a moral crisis which was taken to mean (and/or to have caused) a breakdown of social discipline, including a rise in crime, and was utilized to justify the policing of morality by an increasingly authoritarian state. Thus, *Policing the Crisis* identifies various institutions constructing a consensus around the idea that society was being undermined from within by the emergence of a new permissiveness. There was then a tendency to talk of a collapse of supposedly traditional and commonsense standards – the authors identified a series of anxieties about 'moral pollution' (1978: 285–8), the 'decay of family life' and the decline of 'traditional motherhood' (1978: 112–13). Such discourses about degeneration also often identified the apparently liberalizing legislation of the 1960s, including changes to the law relating to abortion, divorce and (male) homosexuality, along with other perceived cultural shifts in the 1960s and 1970s, as the origin of the problem. These sentiments were expressed from a range of sources, including the likes of moral campaigners Mary Whitehouse and Lord Hailsham, who called for society to be 'clean[ed] up' and juxtaposed concerns about permissiveness with the 'responsibility, decency and respectability', which they argued were supported by right-minded people (1978: 159). Here the media's role was particularly crucial in reporting different incarnations of these views, thereby reinforcing their seemingly clear and straightforward truth. However, this vision of moral consensus was not without its contradictions as, for example, whilst immorality was denounced within the press, the same publications were simultaneously supporting an intensely sexualized view of the world through sensationalist journalism and photographs of topless women ('Page Three' having begun in the *Sun* in the early 1970s). This sexualization in turn served to replicate a sense that there was increased immorality and perpetuated a consensus around the need for increased coercion.

Despite this discussion of moral decline and its associations with matters of sexuality, there was in *Policing the Crisis* no explicit consideration of the notions of sexuality being employed, nor was there any attempt to theorize the role of sexuality here. This, at least in part, was a product of the period in which the book was written, as sexuality scholarship was less advanced; notably Foucault's first volume of *The History of Sexuality* was published in French in 1976 and the English translation was published in Britain in 1979 (Foucault, 1979). As a consequence of this lack, it becomes necessary to re-cast Hall et al.'s work on morality in the light of subsequent scholarship.

From the perspective of the early twenty-first century the moral concerns and notion of state power depicted in *Policing the Crisis* could all be said to constitute a heterocrisis, in which the parameters of commonsensical normality are supposedly under attack. In this context, it is a monolithic notion of appropriate heterosexuality which is apparently threatened and requires shoring up by an authoritarian (hetero)state. Consequently, anything which is identified as being *non*heteronormative (including any behaviour which is perceived to be a deviation from this culturally constructed standard) tends to be denied, rejected and repressed by the state apparatus. This heterosexual hegemony concerns sex and gender as well as sexuality, and seeks to create and reinforce a moral consensus around the 'natural' binary order of men and women in all things. Here, then, women and men should behave (or be made to behave) in accordance with the roles that they were purportedly born to by being appropriately passive or active, submissive or assertive, non-sexual or (hetero)sexually driven. Indeed, this version of heterosexuality tends to prioritize certain femininities and masculinities over others and it foregrounds male dominance. Consequently, women are secondary and their status and treatment depends, amongst other things, upon whether they are suitably feminine, especially in relation to matters sexual – thus, we have the idea of the madonna/whore dichotomy, whereby those perceived to be virginal or virtuous (for example, faithful wives and good mothers) women deserve respect whereas promiscuous females and errant mothers, along with women who associate sexually with women, warrant little by way of deference. However, although heterosexuality is a male-centred ideology, it is not one that advantages all men as, in particular, men identified as bi, gay and trans[2] tend to be deemed to be lesser entities here.[3]

Whilst there are many ways of being *un* or *non*heterosexual, and heteronormativity is not just about sexual behaviour, the practice of sex is especially important in this context. However, it is not just heterosex that is prioritized; it is sex acts which are conceived as being 'natural' which are truly heterosexual. Moreover, this version of heterosexuality is often portrayed as being God-given – as The Right Rev. Graham Dow, the Bishop of Carlisle, explained: '[o]bviously the penis belongs in [or in some accounts 'to' or 'with'] the vagina; that this is something fundamental to the way God has made us' (*Newsnight*, 16 June 2003).[4] Here, then, procreative sex informs the paradigm of the 'natural' when it comes to sex, sexuality and relationships. What is more, in keeping with this establishment religion perspective, in this version of the world the ideal form of different-sex pairing is marriage.[5]

Revisiting the moral crisis depicted by *Policing the Crisis* in the light of these ideas about heterosexuality means that, for example, the attack on marriage, in the form of the liberalization of divorce and the increase in single-parent families, along with the decline of the full-time mother, can be recast as dangerous wanings of traditional and acceptable heterosexual feminine roles; women were no longer confined to being wives and mothers in the home. Also, the relaxation of abortion laws and the introduction of the contraceptive pill in the 1960s offered greater (hetero)sexual freedom for women both within and outside marriage, signifying that feminine virtue, along with wedlock itself, was being undermined. Similarly, the partial decriminalization of male homosexual sex in the late 1960s (s.1 Sexual Offences Act 1967) can be seen as an important part of this attack upon heterosexuality (whether appropriate or not).

Such sentiments justified moves to police those women and men who transgressed against English morality. For example, they helped perpetuate the continued persecution of those men identified as being homosexual. Thus, despite the apparent liberalization of the law, homophobia and the harsh treatment of bi and gay men continued. In fact, the very legislation which granted male same-sex encounters legality actually reinforced heterosexuality because the decriminalization was unequal (the age of consent was set at 21 rather than the long-established 16) and other crimes, such as gross indecency and importuning, continued to penalize male same-sex activities (see further below). Consequently, these measures in turn legitimated both police targeting of male homosexuals and instances of homophobia (for example, see Tatchell, 1991).

Indeed, attempts to police, control, discipline and punish those who acted outside the parameters of a supposedly normal heterosexuality were common in the decade in which *Policing the Crisis* was published. But it was not only within the criminal justice system that *non*heterosexuals were persecuted. One notable area in which men and women were disciplined was medicine. Here, being a gay, lesbian or bi person was categorized as an illness, which medics and, in particular, the 'psy' professions sought to cure, often through coercion. Unsurprisingly, the negative effects of such treatment/trauma have proved to be long-lived (Smith et al., 2004). In this context, as well as within the criminal justice system and wider society it was men who associated sexually with men rather than women who associated sexually with women who were most likely to be targeted as such men have tended to be perceived as posing the greatest danger to the heteronormativity, with its prioritization of the (hetero)male. As we shall see, this focus upon bi and gay men has persisted.[6]

This chapter seeks to develop these ideas. In doing so it draws examples from the media, family, religion, medicine and education. However, the majority of materials cited are legal as 'law remains one of the central coercive institutions of the capitalist state' (Hall et al., 1978: 177). Also, while it is recognized that European law and policy have increasingly played a role in defining the direction and the parameters of domestic changes, the focus here is upon the changes implemented in England and Wales and their effects rather than the question of their origins. This is, in part, a matter of limited space, but is supported by the fact that the decisions to instigate these measures, along with their precise shape and practical effects, have (to varying degrees) been a matter for the domestic state apparatus.

Taking a chronological approach and observing shifts in the configuration of heterostate power, the analysis below explores the heteroideologies which, it is argued, have underpinned both instances of state repression and reform from the late 1970s through to the twenty-first century. The fundamental argument here is that in the first decade of the twenty-first century the idea of hegemonic heterosexuality remains just as crucial to understandings of state power as it was in the 1970s when *Policing the Crisis* was written. Indeed, despite apparent indications to the contrary (including possible shifts in the notion of hegemonic heterosexuality) and attempts to resist the heterostate, very little has changed.

The 1980s and 1990s

In the 1980s the moral crisis discourses around sexuality to which *Policing the Crisis* alluded in the 1970s were reconstructed and took on a new urgency with the advent of HIV/AIDS. Misinformation and propaganda from various quarters, including politicians, the media and religious groups described AIDS as the 'gay plague' and used this as a justification for the persecution of bi and gay men in particular (see Small, 1987; Thomas, 1993).[7] However, it was not only *non*heterosexual men who were the targets of discrimination, hatred, vilification and (actual or threatened) violence. For instance, in 1987 a councillor in South Staffordshire 'called for 90% of lesbians and gays to be gassed to prevent the spread of AIDS'.[8]

Thus, in the Thatcher years the trends which *Policing the Crisis* identified continued, with male homosexuality as one particular focus. Here, as Thomas (1993) has argued, the ideology of the idealized and safe nuclear family was juxtaposed with the threat of the diseased gay man. This binary drew and built upon pre-existing supposedly commonsensical ideas about both the value of the normal family (and its associations with lawfulness and order) as well as longstanding homophobia (and connected ideas about abnormality, criminality and disorder). In this context, expressions of hatred could be extreme. Most often quoted are the words of Sir James Anderton, Chief Constable of Greater Manchester: '[e]verywhere I go I see increasing evidence of people swirling around in a human cesspit of their own making. We must ask why homosexuals freely engage in sodomy and other obnoxious practices, knowing the dangers involved' (*Guardian*, 16 May 1987).

This particular incarnation of the moral crisis scapegoated gay men for HIV/AIDS and viewed them as deserving punishment; thus, the criminalization and intense policing of *non*heterosexual men was justified. Whilst the higher age of consent offered some scope for this, there were two other offences which provided further opportunities for repression: gross indecency penalized gay and bi men for being sexual in public (s.13 Sexual Offences Act 1956) and men were also liable to be criminalized for 'persistently … (soliciting or importuning) in a public place for immoral [homosexual] purposes' (s.32 Sexual Offences Act 1956). The latter provision was most frequently used to prosecute 'cottaging' (anonymous male–male sex in public toilets).

Alongside this bent to criminalize gay men, there was also a tendency not to take homophobic hate crime seriously. For example, in the 1980s GALOP's (Gay London Police Monitoring Group) research questioned the role of the police both in targeting gay men and responding to homophobic attacks upon them (see GALOP, 2005: 1–3). Thus, hatred, prejudice and fears about the 'gay plague' meant that it was common practice for law enforcers to exercise informal coercive control over gay men by targeting them as criminals whilst also failing to serve them as victims.

In the 1990s the criminalizing tendency, along with homophobia and myths about the HIV/AIDS, persisted. Most notably, these all played their part in the infamous *Brown* case (1993), which involved the successful prosecution of a number of men for their same-sex sadomasochistic activities. Judicial comments about the activities echoed the homophobic themes of the time and, despite the fact that the men were prosecuted for non-sexual assaults, their apparently dangerous homosexuality and its supposed connection with HIV/AIDS were highlighted by the judiciary (see further Bibbings and Alldridge, 1993: 358).

In other spheres too in the 1980s and 1990s repression was evident. Most notably section 28 of the Local Government Act 1988 reinforced and legitimated hatred for any deviation from the heteronorm. It provided that a local authority was prohibited from intentionally promoting homosexuality, publishing material with the intention of promoting homosexuality or promoting the teaching in any maintained school of the acceptability of homosexuality as a 'pretended family relationship'. The message of the then Conservative government was clear and was intended to be broadcast by local authorities and through the state education system – *non*heterosexualities were to be discouraged (if possible), repressed and hated, while the heterosexual family was the *real* thing (see Thomas, 1993).

Even in artistic spheres, where it was more possible to behave in what appeared to be an overtly *non*heterosexual manner or to 'play' a flamboyantly camp character (at least if you were male) and not only avoid the punitive attention of the law but also enjoy fame and popularity, all was not as liberated as it might appear. Men such as Frankie Howerd, Kenneth Williams, Larry Grayson, John Inman, Danny La Rue, George Melly, Elton John, David Bowie, Julian Clary and Stephen Fry in the 1970s, 1980s and 1990s for the most part presented very particular public images of *non*heterosexuality which were (largely) unthreatening to dominant heterosexual discourses and, therefore, could be incorporated into the mainstream without disrupting the dominant narrative that such people were problematic, needed to be policed and have violence inflicted on them. Accordingly, the ability of such men to flourish often meant their employing some degree of caution and treading a potentially hazardous borderline between permittable abnormality and intolerable deviance.

In addition, the supposed abnormality of the male homosexual tended to be linked with other forms of deviance and this too encouraged and legitimated persecution, increasing the dangers of being openly bi or gay. Thus, the image of the gay man as paedophile and/or child killer was a recurrent theme in the context of tabloid media furores and moral panics about abuse and murder. Such intensely homophobic assertions or undercurrents were often present in stories expressing fears about the lone stranger male. Indeed, Collier examines these themes in relation to the portrayal of Thomas Hamilton, who killed 16 children and a teacher (1997: 183–4, 188–9).

This focus upon male same-sexuality is by no means to say that other *non*heterosexualities were not also sites of repression. For example, while no formal law prevented lesbian women from being the primary carers for their children, they risked forfeiting that role because of negative and stereotypical attitudes within the family law courts; they were unsuitable mothers who should be looked at carefully when it came to their having responsibilities for minors (see Boyd, 1992; Thomas, 1993: 37–8).

Trans people also lacked rights and recognition of their gender identity, not least in relation to marriage. The basis of this position, laid down in *Corbett v. Corbett* in 1970, was that a marriage could only be contracted between a 'natural' man and a 'natural' woman. This precedent persisted through the 1980s and 1990s, again reinforcing the commonsensical moral model of the normal heterosexual family united in matrimony.

Meanwhile, supposedly errant women who failed to conform to appropriate heteronormative femininity, especially in relation to matters sexual, were likely to be scapegoated and subjected to a range of exclusions and discriminations. For example, the laws that governed female prostitution directed their attention towards criminalizing and controlling such women, focusing upon those who were a visible presence on the streets. However, prostitution itself remained legal, whilst the men who paid for sex were largely ignored by the law (see Childs, 2000). Such males were, after all, merely obeying their 'natural' heterosexual urges and could not, consequently, be blamed. In the case of the women, however, things were conceived very differently as they were behaving in a manner which was unnatural and so deserved censor and punishment – although the idea that they were providing a *necessary service* coexisted with this condemnation (for example, see Sion, 1977).

In a similar vein, rape laws, along with attitudes within the criminal justice system and society, conveyed the message that women who strayed beyond the bounds of acceptable femininity were to blame for what befell them. For example, female complainants who were deemed to be inappropriately sexually active or immoral in their dress or behaviour were less likely to be believed by the police or by a jury and, consequently, tended to be deemed responsible for their situation (for example, see Temkin, 2000a, 2000b).

In addition, more general concerns about the breakdown of the traditional family and linked anxieties about increases in crime identified in *Policing the Crisis* continued through the 1980s and into the 1990s. These discourses tended to blame single mothers, criticizing, amongst other things, their immorality. In the 1980s Margaret Thatcher's call for a return to 'Victorian values' focused attention upon how best to bring such wayward women into line. Similarly, in the 1990s John Major's call to go 'back to basics' was a reiteration of earlier concerns about the decline of the family and, in particular, the failures of women (see further Cohen, 2002: xviii; McRobbie and Thornton, 1995: 566, 567, 569). Unsurprisingly, voices from the Established Church often expressed similar concerns, reasserting the primacy of marriage (for example, see House of Bishops, 1991).

The media continued to bemoan an increased permissiveness, particularly when it came to women, calling for a return to traditional morals and, therefore, still played an important role in the construction and maintenance of a consensus around notions of respectable sexuality (for example, see Cohen, 2002: xviii; McRobbie and Thornton, 1995: 566, 567, 569). However, again its role was not quite this clear-cut. Indeed, it was contradictory, for while women were so often being told to be more appropriately feminine and less sexual lest, for example, they be raped, the tabloids simultaneously delighted in objectifying the female (but not the male) body and portraying women as both lesser than the male and available for him. Most significantly, both types of content tended to reinforce heterosexuality by encouraging agreement about what was acceptable and normal whilst also privileging the male and policing the female (whether by berating her supposed promiscuity, holding her responsible for her sexual victimization or telling her how to be in order to attract men).

Consequently, it seems that the 1980s and 1990s were bleak, oppressive years when *non*heterosexualities, with their association with moral and crime crises, were often the subject of restriction, discrimination, violence and punishment. However, this is not to say that there were no attempts at resistance and, in some cases, the overt evasion or flouting of oppression. For example, in 1982 GALOP was founded 'to expose the systematic harassment of the gay and lesbian communities by the police and to educate them about their rights' (GALOP, 2005: 1). There were also campaigns against section 28, including the lesbian women who abseiled in the House of Lords and managed to infiltrate the BBC, disrupting the *Six O'Clock News* (see Carter, 1992). In addition, the Greater London Council funded groups like GALOP (GALOP, 2005: 1) and in 1985 South Wales miners joined the Pride march to express their thanks for support during the 1984–85 strike.[9]

───────────────── **The 1990s and 2000s** ─────────────────

At first glance it might appear that in the last decade of the twentieth and the first of the twenty-first century there has been a partial but nonetheless radical transformation of the treatment of a range of *non*heterosexualities. Indeed, many have understandably celebrated and taken up the opportunities offered by legal changes, particularly in the field of family and gender recognition law.[10] However, all is not as it seems as a number of paradoxes lie at the heart of these apparently liberatory reforms, meaning that the state is still able to maintain hegemonic heterosexuality, while simultaneously purporting to have moved beyond heteronormativity and homophobia. In addition, the continuance of a moral consensus around sexuality means that there is a gap between the rhetoric of rights and protection and the reality of discrimination and attack.

Perhaps most sweeping of all the recent reforms is the prohibition of discrimination on the grounds of sexuality in relation to employment, goods, facilities, services and education (Employment Equality (Sexual Orientation) Regulations 2003; Equality Act (Sexual Orientation) Regulations 2007) and on the grounds of sexual reassignment in the context of employment and vocational training (Sex Discrimination (Gender Reassignment) Regulations 1999). These extensions of anti-discrimination laws mean that unfair treatment may lessen in some spheres and where illegal discrimination occurs there is the possibility of challenge. However, while these measures appear to symbolize equality and rights, the reality can be very different, suggesting that a consensus about what is normal continues and that little is actually being done to remedy this. Indeed, studies indicate that discrimination, harassment and ill-treatment are widespread in relation to lesbian, gay, bi and trans people (Stonewall, 2007a, 2007b, 2008; Whittle et al., 2007).

In the criminal sphere, the status of gay male sexuality has also been transformed, thereby apparently lessening the scope for the legitimized targeting of those thought to be bi or gay. For example, the Criminal Justice and Public Order Act 1994 brought the age of consent for sexual intercourse between men down from 21 to 18 (s.145) and subsequently the Sexual Offences (Amendment) Act 2000 set it at 16 (s.1). In addition, the offences of gross indecency and importuning (which only applied to encounters between men) have also been removed from the statute books and sexual offences are (on the surface) now drafted in such a way as not to discriminate against *non*heterosexuals. This reflects a general trend towards equalizing the law, so that sexual crimes are largely constructed in a gender-neutral manner. Thus, for example, consensual adult anal sex is now legal regardless of the identity of the participants (Sch.7, Sexual Offences Act 2003). Despite this, the creation of a new 'cottaging' offence has allowed police to continue to target and entrap gay men (s.71 Sexual Offences Act 2003). As Johnson (2007) argues, although this is framed as a gender-neutral offence, it was enacted with the supposedly problematic nature of gay male sexual activity in mind and the evidence indicates that the police are using the offence as if it applied only to incidents of sexual activity between men. In this context, too, little seems to have changed.

Now also, there has been some recognition of hate crime in relation to sexuality. The Criminal Justice Act 2003 required tougher sentencing for offences motivated or aggravated by the victim's sexual orientation (s.146) and in 2008 it was proposed that there should be specific sexual orientation hate crimes (s.73 and sch.16 Criminal Justice and Immigration Bill 2008). However, here it is noteworthy that, although legislation has recognized sexual orientation as an aggravating factor, it has not introduced specific offences like those which exist in cases where race or religion are involved (although, at the time of writing in 2008, there were proposals to change this position). Thus, lesser importance has been accorded to homophobic than other forms of hate crime.

There is apparently also some evidence that the perspective of the enforcers has shifted as, instead of failing to deal effectively with crimes against gay and lesbian people, police forces now emphasize the need to take such offences seriously and are keen to stress their awareness of diversity issues relating to sexual orientation.[11] Indeed, forces actively seek lesbian, gay, bi and trans employees[12] and those appointed have the support of the Gay Police Association.[13] Now also, rather than just policing Pride and Mardi Gras events, some gay officers very publicly join in the celebration, often wearing their uniforms whilst they party.[14] But, despite all this, there seem still to be issues in relation to the policing of homophobic violence. For example, research suggests that victims sometimes fail to report such incidents to the police because of 'previous bad experiences'. Poor responses included a case where '[t]he policeman let us know he and another would get queers out of the area …' (GALOP, 2004: 15, 56, 64).

Such evidence may be taken to suggest that homophobia is far from eradicated both in the criminal law and amongst those who enforce it. In wider society, too, despite moves towards the recognition of hate crime, surveys demonstrate that the levels of this form of crime are high, suggesting that a consensus around the hetero-sexual norm persists. For example, a survey conducted in two London boroughs found that 69% of respondents reported having experienced homophobic violence, threats or harassment in their lifetime and 38% recorded such experiences in the previous twelve months (GALOP, 2004: 21, 10).

In relation to female prostitution both the law and policy have changed. In par-ticular, the Sexual Offences Act 2003 aims to protect vulnerable women and children and the Home Office strategy (Home Office, 2006a) focuses upon welfare and multi-agency interventions with the objective of improving women's lives by helping them to move out of sex work. Thus, on the surface, the state is no longer so interested in penalizing such women. Nonetheless, the regulation and policing of (appropriate) female sexuality, along with other aspects of female behaviour and identity, contin-ues to be a common thread here. Indeed, the moves towards protection and a wel-farist approach have only served to increase the surveillance and coercive control of street prostitutes. Moreover, those women who refuse or fail to leave their allegedly immoral ways behind them tend to be subjected to an increased use of prosecution (Phoenix and Oerton, 2005; Scoular and O'Neill, 2007). Meanwhile, the men who pay for street prostitutes are now also criminalized, although this too seems to result in penalizing women, who are often placed in additional danger by clients' height-ened caution (Brooks-Gordon and Gelsthorpe, 2003).

Rape law and policy has also been reformed, in part, in an apparent effort to change attitudes towards female complainants, given what has been identified as an unjusti-fiably high attrition rate (for example, see Sexual Offences Act 2003; Wilson and Fowles, 2005). However, past attitudes to appropriate female sexuality persist in society (Amnesty UK, 2005) and it seems that both the law and lawyers tend to reinforce such views about women (see, for example, Temkin and Ashworth, 2004: 342; HMCPSI/ HMIC, 2007). Further, Campbell's (2005) work on rape prevention literature points to another way in which appropriate female sexuality is policed by suggesting that such texts still stress the importance of being 'ladylike' in order to avoid being raped. At the same time, however, there has been an intensification of the sexualization of wider society with magazines like *FHM*, *Loaded* and *Nuts* focusing upon the female form, increasingly explicit sexual materials which tend to objectify women being broadcast both on freeview digital television programmes and on dedicated television channels. The common element in this proliferation of sexual materials is not merely the increasing focus upon sex, but more specifically a tendency within such material to perpetuate longstanding heternormative images of women and, in particular, of female availability to men. Yet, simultaneously, the contradictions identified in earlier decades remain as there is still a tendency to decry what is perceived as a moral decline and, in particular, a lowering of female standards. Thus, in classic style in 2006, the *Daily Mail* reported that '[t]he traditional family unit is in meltdown due to plunging moral values and the rise of single parents' – and this according to 'a survey of mothers' (28 June 2006).[15] Indeed, there is an almost continuous outpouring of condemnatory stories about women who binge-drink, fight, reveal or do not wear underwear, have serial one night stands and are often criticized for behaving like men.

In the realms of the family there has also been change with the repeal of section 28 (s.122 and Sch.8, Local Government Act 2003). However, its effects and the attitudes which lay behind it have continued into the twenty-first century. Most obviously, they are reflected in the homophobic bullying which seems to be endemic within the education system (Stonewall, 2007a). In the field of child law, too, despite changes, heteronormativity lives on as, whilst there is some recognition of the role of the same-sex social parent, there is still a reluctance to see the latter as a *real* parent (see *Re G*, 2006). Also, although the Civil Partnership Act 2004 has allowed for the formal legal recognition of same-sex relationships, with accompanying rights, here too heterocentric views endure as civil partnerships stop short of being named 'marriage' and the distinction is not merely one of nomenclature. Consequently, wedlock is reserved for the ideal relationship between a man and a woman (to the exclusion of all others) and civil partnership is a form of 'pretended' family relationship (see further Stychin, 2006; *Wilkinson v. Kitzinger*, 2006; Harding 2007). More fundamentally, the introduction of civil partnerships can be seen less as a liberatory measure and more as a reinforcement of heternomativity as it merely replicates (albeit poorly) the marriage model (Auchmuty, 2004; Barker, 2006).

Similarly, 'reforms' in relation to trans people can be viewed with more than a degree of cynicism as, although the legislation appears radical, again it serves to reinforce and reify 'normal' heterosexuality. For example, the Gender Recognition Act 2004, which allows a man or a woman to apply to be officially identified in their gender, adopts a mental illness model, foregrounding the supposed extreme unnaturalness of transgender through the concept of 'dysphoria'. In doing so, it also intensifies the control of the 'psy' professions over trans people; whilst formerly psychologists were gatekeepers to treatment, now they are also performing this role in relation to recognition (see further Bibbings, 2004: 230; Sharpe, 2007: 70, 72). The latter suggests a shift in the configuration of state power, with medics in this particular context potentially gaining more of a responsibility for judging and policing normality – although there is nothing that is entirely new here, given the past role of doctors in reinforcing sexual normality and seeking to cure homosexuality, noted above.

In the media and popular culture there are perhaps signs that the precarious and exceptional place occupied by the likes of Inman and Grayson in earlier times has expanded to such an extent as to suggest that perhaps something significant has happened. For example, Cowan (2005) notes that trans people are 'everywhere', 'in television advertisements, billboard advertisements, day-time and reality television shows, and soap operas'. Also, in fiction, we find that Harry Potter's mentor, Professor Dumbledore, is gay (*The Observer*, 21 October 2007) and even BBC's *Dr Who* has had his first openly bi companion and the latter, hero Captain Jack Harkness, now features in his own successful series (*Torchwood*). But, despite this apparent acceptability and, indeed, popularity of *non*heterosexuals (or, at least gay and bi men), in the arts and media during the decades considered here, underlying and pervasive suspicions about the *non*heterosexual male persist. Thus, homophobic constructions of the gay man as paedophile continue, as the case of magistrate and former Deputy Lord Lieutenant for Mid Glamorgan, Byron Butler suggests. When interviewed for a documentary about gay people in Wales, he explained that 'probably it's a suspicion of the mainstream that they perhaps will interfere with young people and so on and that's historically been the case', adding '[b]ut they do, don't they. That's the reality.'[16] Similar comments brought Peter Willows, a Tory councillor, into the limelight in 2006[17] and *graced* the letters pages of the *British Medical Journal* in 2004 (Igbokwe, 2004). Such views expressed by powerful (presumably heterosexual) men reveal the sense of a continuing underlying 'knowledge' that gay men *really* are paedophiles.

Within established religion, too, heterosexuality remains the ideal and, for some, the only way to be. For example, in 2003 the Rt Rev. Dr Peter Forster, the Bishop of Chester, suggested in a local press article that homosexuals should seek psychiatric help in order to reorient themselves and, thus, be cured.[18] Forster was a member of the All Souls Day Group, whose condemnation of sexual immorality in 2002 extended to all such activity outside marriage. Echoing the idea of a moral crisis utilized in *Policing the Crisis*, they also opposed the immorality and liberalism which they regarded as having infiltrated the Church and infected society. Moreover, the Group pointed ominously to an unravelling of social cohesion which they warned was leading to a national crisis.[19]

Conclusion: Beyond the Heterostate?

As we have seen in this examination of sexuality in the context of *Policing the Crisis*, hegemonic heterosexuality has been and remains central to an understanding and analysis of state power. Thus, in the 1970s, despite apparently liberalizing legislation, the overarching picture was of hatred for and punishment of unheterosexualities, particularly through the criminal law. During the 1980s and 1990s, the fear of AIDS/HIV, and its incorrect association with gay men, meant that such treatment continued and took new forms, although there were exceptions and challenges to this homophobia. Since 1997, under New Labour, notwithstanding the fact that reform appears to have become the dominant theme, heterosexist ideologies still underpin these measures. Indeed, the commonsensical ideas about normality and morality which *Policing the Crisis* depicted persist, lurking behind measures and attitudinal changes which seemingly belie their existence.

Thus, beneath the supposedly calm waters of decriminalization, anti-discrimination, recognition and rights lies a hegemonic heterosexuality which still embraces very similar notions of acceptability to those of the 1970s. At this level, liberalization is (largely) symbolic (see Aubert, 1966), serving to legitimate the heterostate whilst seeming to govern by consent. Meanwhile, the need for resistance is undone as the state has apparently removed (and is removing) injustices.[20] Moreover, this ostensible liberalization also serves to bring *non*heterosexual people into society's fold and by so doing allows for the state's increased monitoring, policing and regulation of their lives. For example, legal changes allow for the registering and oversight of *non*-heterosexual relationships under civil partnerships law, ensure the medicalization of trans people, control people's gender status, increase the surveillance and punishment of supposedly wayward women and continue to facilitate the unequal criminalization of gay men's sex lives. Thus, to some extent a different form of authoritarianism reigns here, with the state increasingly constituting, regulating and disciplining individuals and relationships, thereby allowing for an 'intensification of state control' in the field of sexuality (Poulantzas, 1978b: 203). Here, then, perhaps what we see is the 'accretion and layering of disciplinary modes of containment', with the old buttressing the new (Carlen and Tombs, 2006: 339). Moreover, if this analysis holds sway, then there is little to distinguish contemporary state responses to *non*heterosexuality from those adopted towards terrorism and crime (discussed elsewhere in this volume) in that they all (albeit in different ways) tend towards a continuance and amplification of disciplinary measures and authoritarianism. Here, then, the heterostate hangs on to its legitimacy not only as a result of a consensus around the need for law, order and morality, but also, ironically, because of its inclusion of *non*heterosexuals and the apparent recognition of their rights (see Hall et al., 1978: 321).

As a result, any notion that the heterostate is in decline is misplaced as conceptions of hegemonic heterosexuality continue to underpin the reforms and supposed cultural shifts. As a result, heterosexuality is still prioritized and privileged, whilst modes of behaviour and identities perceived to be *non*heterosexual continue to be marginalized, discriminated against and in various respects controlled and regulated – in both familiar and new ways. It seems, then, that the more things change, the more they are the same.

Nonetheless, a more optimistic but necessarily cautious perspective is possible when it comes to looking for the possibilities of resistance. Thus, it could be argued that reforms might be strategically conceived as counter-discourses and as denoting precisely what they superficially purport to deliver (and to a degree do deliver – as the vision of the heterostate presented here is not a totalizing one). In this context, legal changes could be taken to signify the end of appropriate or hegemonic sexuality as the supposed hetero/homo binary has already been breached within the law. For example, now trans people can be recognized in their gender[21] and consenting adults can legally engage in the same range of sex acts regardless of their sex/gender. More significantly, perhaps, in the sphere of relationships, it is connubial heterosexuality that is accorded the highest status, same-sex civil partnership which is next in this hierarchy and all other couples (same- or different-sex) lie at the bottom of the pile.

Beyond this, this interpretation of the redrawing of the lines of acceptability, along with contradictions within hegemonic heterosexuality, suggests the possibility that legal shifts, incongruities and paradoxes could be exploited 'in order to facilitate reform and change' (Sim et al., 1987: 49). However, it is crucial not to lose sight of the need for vigilance in attempting to employ such arguments, and both to recognize the possibility of a return to the model of the overtly authoritarian heterostate which dominated in the 1970s, 1980s and (to a lesser extent) 1990s and to be wary of new strategies which may be utilized in order to continue policing the heterocrisis.

Key Reading

Bibbings, L. (2004) 'Heterosexuality as harm: fitting in', in P. Hillyard, C. Pantazis, S. Tombs and D. Gorden (eds), *Beyond Criminology: Taking Harm Seriously.* London: Pluto Press.

Boyd, S.B. (1992) 'What is a normal family: C v. C (A Minor)?', *Modern Law Review*, 55(2): 269–78.

Harding, R. (2007) 'Sir Mark Potter and the protection of the traditional family: why same-sex marriage is (still) a feminist issue', *Feminist Legal Studies*, 15(2): 223–34.

Sharpe, A.N. (2007) 'Endless sex: the Gender Recognition Act 2004 and the persistence of a legal category', *Feminist Legal Studies*, 15(1): 57–84.

Stychin, C.F. (2006) 'Not (quite) a horse and carriage: the Civil Partnership Act 2004', *Feminist Legal Studies*, 14(1): 79–86.

Thomas, P.A. (1993) 'The nuclear family, ideology and AIDS in the Thatcher years', *Feminist Legal Studies*, 1(1): 23–44.

Notes

Thanks to the editors for their comments, to Genevieve Liveley, Michael Naughton, to my sex, gender and sexuality students and, in particular, Geraldine Hastings, Kathy Pinney, Derrick Walker and candidate 88297.

Law correct as at end April 2008

1 For example, while *The Oxford Handbook of Criminology* (Maguire et al., 2007) has begun to take account of the relevance of gender (albeit a minor somewhat segregated account), with its most recent incarnation focusing upon this topic in chapter Chapter 13 (Heidensohn and Gelsthorpe, 2007), sexuality fails to be specifically addressed beyond the most fleeting of mentions in relation to diversity (Hudson, 2007: 158). Indeed, it barely even touches upon the subject of sex crimes, despite focusing upon 'violent crime' in Chapter 21. However, this is by no means to say that

there has not been important work on sexuality within the broad area of criminology and related fields – indeed, some of this work is cited here.

2   Trans is an umbrella phrase referring to transgender, transsexual and transvestite people (e.g. see Whittle et al., 2007: 6). The latter are not considered in this chapter.

3   Of course, other factors, such as race, class, disability and nationality, are relevant in the context of analysing heterosexuality. However, given limited space, intersectionality is not addressed here.

4   Dow was commenting upon Canon Dr Jeffrey John's (brief) appointment as the first openly but non-practising gay Anglican Bishop (John was eventually persuaded to withdraw his acceptance of the Reading bishopric).

5   Resolution I.10, Lambeth Conference 1998, www.lambethconference.org/resolutions/1998/1998-1-10.cfm (accessed on 30/04/08).

6   This poses a stark contrast to the (past and continued) relative invisibility of lesbian (and bi) women – see Weeks (1990: 87–111) and Smith (1992).

7   In contrast, Watney offers a different approach to moral panics in the context of gay and lesbian sexuality and AIDS (1997: 38–57).

8   www.stonewall.org.uk/information_bank/history__lesbian__gay/89.asp#3 (accessed on 30/04/08).

9   www.stonewall.org.uk/information_bank/history__lesbian__gay/89.asp#3 (accessed on 30/04/08).

10 For example, by the end of 2006 18,059 civil partnerships were formed in the UK (Office for National Statistics, 2007) and by November 2006, 1,660 people had been awarded a Gender Recognition Certificate (Whittle et al., 2007: 7).

11 For example, see: www.avonandsomerset.police.uk/community_safety/hate_crime/what_the_police_can_do.aspx; www.avonandsomerset.police.uk/diversity/orientation.aspx. (both accessed on 30/04/08).

12 For example, see www.jobs.pinkpaper.com/ArticlePage.aspx?fid=68 (accessed on 30/04/08).

13 See www.gay.police.uk/contact.html (accessed on 30/04/08).

14 However, not all forces are comfortable about the wearing of uniforms. See www.news.bbc.co.uk/1/hi/uk/4640379.stm (accessed on 30/04/08).

15 See www.dailymail.co.uk/pages/live/femail/article.html?in_article_id=392846&in_page_id=1879 (accessed on 30/04/08).

16 See www.pinknews.co.uk/news/view.php?id=7326 (accessed on 30/04/08). Butler was reportedly investigated by the police for these comments, although it is not clear whether any further action has or will be taken.

17 Willows was convicted of a public order offence (*Daily Mail*, 12 December 2006), www.dailymail.co.uk/pages/live/articles/news/news.html?in_article_id=422199&in_page_id=1770 (accessed on 30/04/08).

18 *The Daily Telegraph*, 10 November 2003, www.telegraph.co.uk/news/main.jhtml?xml=/news/2003/11/10/nbish10.xml (accessed on 30/04/08). Following complaints, there was a police investigation into the comment but it is not clear whether further action was taken.

19 See www.ceec.info/library/positional/All%20Souls%20Day%20Statement.htm. The Group was part of the Church of England Evangelical Council, which continues to express a range of similar concerns about sex. See www.ceec.info/ (both accessed 30/04/08).

20 This is not to suggest that all resistance has ceased. For example, Stonewall and GALOP, along with the trans pressure group Press for Change, continue to campaign and research. See: www.stonewall.org.uk/; www.galop.org.uk/; and www.pfc.org.uk/ (all accessed 30/04/08).

21 See Sandland (2005) and Cowan (2005), who examine the potential offered by the moves beyond sex/gender binaries here.

3

RACISM AND THE STATE:
AUTHORITARIANISM AND COERCION

Jon Burnett

 **Introduction**

The publication of *Policing the Crisis* in 1978, primarily a study of the rise of 'mugging' in the popular imagination and the responses to it, was a pivotal document garnering understandings of a shift towards an authoritarian state. Thirty years later its importance goes beyond the construction of a racialized moral panic about street crimes associated with black youths – although this is not to deny the dynamism and clear relevance of this aspect of the book – and rests in the authors' analysis of the construction of an economic and social crisis. *Policing the Crisis* never set out to dissect the consolidation of black youths as folk devils in order to argue that there was, in fact, no crisis: that the moral panic merely acted to embed a set of racist policies and practices. Although, of course, as the authors argued, the consolidation of racism was exactly what happened. Rather, it asserted that through the 1970s there was indeed a crisis of authority reverberating through the British state, wherein 'there is an open, frontal attack on the whole idea of equality, a shameless advocacy of elitism, and a complete refurbishing of the idea of equality' (Hall et al., 1978: 314).

The crisis that the authors documented discussed in detail how the 'post-1970 capitalist state' was poised at an 'exceptional moment' (ibid.: 317). As they stated:

> First, it is a crisis of and for British capitalism; the crisis, specifically, of an advanced industrial capitalist nation, seeking to stabilise itself in rapidly changing global and national conditions on an extremely weak, post-imperial economic base. (ibid.)

Second, it was a crisis of the 'relations of social forces'; of organizing alliances and interests capable of 'providing hegemonic political leadership into and through "the transition"' (ibid.: 317–18). Third, it was a crisis of the state through which restructuring was necessary in order to facilitate entry into 'late capitalism'. 'The state', as the authors asserted, 'now has a decisive economic role, not indirectly but directly.

It secures the conditions for the continued expansion of capital' (ibid.: 318). Finally, it was a crisis 'in political legitimacy, in social authority, in hegemony, and in the forms of class struggle and resistance' (ibid.: 319).

The crisis of, and within, the 'post-1970 capitalist state' discussed in *Policing the Crisis* bore relevance to an understanding of the construction of a moral panic over 'mugging' in at least two ways. The crisis revealed itself through the figure of the black male, occupying a place in the popular imagination as a key signifier of decline, danger and disintegration. Yet it also emphasized how political responses to moral panic – responses that were punitively brutal – could be legitimized, supported and even encouraged. Put simply, through understanding the crisis, the authors emphasized how racism was linked directly to, and embedded within, the shifting role of the state. Along with Sivanandan's (1976/1982) 'Race, class and the state', it marked a key moment in understandings of racism that located statecraft at the centre of analysis.[1]

This chapter draws upon this theoretical base and, in doing so, attempts to plot the consolidation of contemporary British racism and its relation to the state. It argues that a 'new' racism is in the process of being constructed through the New Labour government. It also argues that this 'new' racism is historically situated and requires understanding alongside policies aimed at fostering particular visions of race relations post *Policing the Crisis*. Consequently, this chapter begins with a discussion of key developments in race relations policies from 1978 (the publication of *Policing the Crisis*) to the election of the New Labour government. In doing so, it takes as a starting point the space the black male occupied as a racialized folk devil in 1978 as not only a signifier of 'crime', but also as a concrete symbol upon which state racism developed more generally. Of course, 1978 was not the 'beginning' of the embedding of racism into state practice in Britain, and racism is entwined within Britain's ongoing colonial story (see, for example, Bowling and Phillips, 2002: 1–5 for a discussion). Thus while what follows is not an attempt to historically chart state racism in the UK, the emergence of a moral panic around black youths by 1978 will be contextualized by specific junctures in the period leading up to this year.

The historical discussion that begins this chapter will emphasize the manner in which, by the time the New Labour government was elected in 1997, the construction of a moral panic around black youths had shifted and been joined – not replaced – by other objects of attention. The role of the state, too, was developing. The New Labour party was elected on a promise of modernization, of shedding their links to the Labour party of 'old'. A fiercely neo-liberal government from day one, by 2005 the then Treasurer Gordon Brown talked of New Labour's role in an economy of 'turbo-capitalism' (cited in Jenkins, 2006: 255). By this time, also, the government had begun to implement its race relations policy of community cohesion. No longer relying on single definers of 'danger', community cohesion has articulated a moral panic over the fact that Britain is an increasingly multicultural nation. The simple reality of diversity is to be managed in order to fit a New Labour script that casts multiculturalism as damaging to national identity and national competitiveness.

This managerial policy has been described by Kundnani (2007a: 121–40) as a strategy of 'integrationism', and it is through analysis of this that New Labour's attempts to foster a specific vision of belonging and citizenship can be understood. Integrationism attempts to force through a race relations politic of assimilation (ibid.: 126), whereby those deemed most threatening to the nation – in varying ways – can be absorbed or excluded. Yet this integrationism further justifies, in political rhetoric, the coercive basis of community cohesion policies. The final section of this chapter discusses some of these policies and documents their brutality. In doing so, it emphasizes that while community cohesion, on the face of things, appears to be based upon a strategy of securing consensus, it is in reality coupled to a hard-edged set of policing and control measures that underpin New Labour's 'new racism'.

Shifting Contours of Racism: 1978–1997

Upon its publication, *Policing the Crisis* produced a detailed account of the racialization of the act of mugging and the way in which it was defined as almost exclusively a 'black' crime. The establishment of a racialized moral panic about black people and 'mugging' consolidated a criminogenic stereotype, wherein *race* rather than *racism* was the object of concern. By emphasizing problems of racism as problems of race, 'the government had', as Sivanandan (1976/1982: 114) suggested, 'pointed out that the purposes of reducing the numbers coming in was to improve matters for those already within – to improve race relations'. Debate and policy was channelled through a prism that articulated a zero-sum numbers game in which more immigration equalled less cohesion and order. A moral panic around 'mugging' buttressed this equation and enabled policy-makers and the press to instil a perception of black people – seen as *potential* criminals – as somehow 'un-British', as a manifestly *alien* presence. It was exactly this 'alienness' that Margaret Thatcher promised would be stopped in its tracks in 1978 with her pledge to 'finally see an end to immigration', as 'this country might be rather swamped by people with a different culture' (cited in Sivanandan, 1986: 43). The 'mugger', cast as the personification of black presence, was the folk devil upon which fears of, and racism against, this 'different culture' could be channelled: 'When things disintegrate, the Folk Devil not only becomes the bearer of all our social anxieties, but we turn against him the full wrath of our indignation' (Hall et al., 1978: 161).

Policing the Crisis made clear that a moral panic around 'mugging' and the consolidation of black people as 'folk devils' was symbiotic of institutional racism more generally. Capitalist restructuring consolidated 'cuts in public expenditure and in the Welfare State' (ibid.), and in turn linked to an economic recession in the 1970s, wherein unemployment, as noted above, affected black communities in particular. This was directly linked to the 'structured position of secondariness and subordination' (ibid.: 347) that black communities occupied. Subordination was built into a nation which had recently imported workers from across its (formally) crumbling empire in order to fill labour shortages, and where the work that was offered was frequently unskilled (no matter the skills of those carrying it out), poorly paid and dangerous. As Sivanandan (1976/1982: 102) argued, 'if the free market economy decided the numbers of immigrants, economic growth and the colonial legacy determined the nature of the work they were put to'.

By the time that the moral panic around 'mugging' began to take shape, then, this structural subordination was already well in place. The legacy of overt discrimination in housing – 'no coloureds, no Irish, no dogs' – had enforced the ghettoization of black communities in all but name (see Pilkington, 1988: 41–52), while continuing discrimination in employment contained black communities frequently in poorer, decaying, inner-city areas. Immigration legislation meanwhile, in 1962, 1965 and 1971, had worked to restrict the rights and citizenship of new and existing immigrants through creating 'categories' of settlement and status (Moore, 1975: 20–3; Sivanandan, 1976/1982: 108–24), and the criminalization of black people was rooted within targeted policing strategies of 'nigger hunting' (Hunte, 1965). In this context, the racism embedded in the stigmatization of black people as those most likely to be involved in a particular activity ('mugging') was tied to the subordination of black people through a racism that was tied to colonial legacies and the restructuring of a capitalist state.

Urban Disorders

In 1981 the instigation of 'Swamp 81', a police stop-and-search 'saturation operation' (Scarman, 1981: para 4.75), explicitly targeted black communities in Brixton, London, and in doing so bore upon them the force of the criminal justice system. Of the 943 reported stop and searches, the majority were black and more than two-thirds were aged under 21 in an operation that was justified through a rhetoric of targeting 'mugging' (ibid.). The response was rioting that, in its first weekend alone, involved more than, 7,000 police officers, and led to 196 arrests and mass injuries (Benyon, 1984).[2] The Brixton riots, consequently described by some commentators as 'uprisings' (Kettle and Hodges, 1982), were only one of a series of urban disorders that took place in 1981, along with, among other areas, Southall (London), Toxteth (Liverpool) and Moss Side (Manchester). They continued a pattern of protest that had gathered pace in the 1970s with disorders in 1976 in Notting Hill and Southall (see, for example, Kettle and Hodges, 1982), Southall again in 1979 (Campaign Against Racism and Fascism/Southall Rights, 1981; Foot, 1990), and Bristol in 1980 (Joshua and Wallace, 1983), and that emanated once more in 1985 in Broadwater Farm (London) (see Gifford, 1986; Lea et al., 1986).[3] All of these events were different in certain ways, yet they were all linked together through a common thread – racism.

However, the reality of institutional racism was denied by Lord Scarman in his government-instigated report, presented to Parliament, on the Brixton 'disorders' in 1981. 'It was alleged by some of those who made representations to me that Britain is an institutionally racist society', he explained. But '[i]f by that it is meant that it is a society which knowingly, as a matter of policy, discriminates against black people, I reject that allegation' (Scarman, 1981: para 2.22). The racism of 'a few officers on the streets' he would accept (ibid.: para 4.63), but the possibility that this could be built into the fabric of the police, and more generally the nation, was disregarded. Instead, a 'cultural' explanation of (assumptions of) black criminality was promoted – tied into a recognition of socio-political deprivation – but nevertheless rooted in a perception of incompatible histories, lifestyles, and values with regard to a specific understanding of 'Britishness'. As Gilroy has noted, this in turn marked only one example of a 'new' racism that:

> is primarily concerned with mechanisms of inclusion and exclusion. It specifies who may legitimately belong to the national community and simultaneously advances reasons for the segregation or banishment of those whose 'origin, sentiment or citizenship' assigns them elsewhere. (Gilroy, 1987: 45)

Consolidating a 'New Racism'?

The appeals to nation and sovereignty made by policy-makers, and incorporated within their actions, explicitly attempted to assert that 'race' could be marked out by 'difference' from perceptions of national identity. This was articulated in particular (although not exclusively) with regard to Asian communities, and one way in which a 'new' racism was consolidated was through the stepping-up of a concerted effort to assert that particular 'communities' were both incompatible with, and at odds with, the nation's identity and sense of itself. This is not to say that this was more important than the economic policies in which racism was embedded. It is, though, to say that this shift in racism worked alongside structural policies of discrimination and exclusion.

The contours of a 'new racism' casting Asian communities as inherently culturally inferior were brought to national attention through the 'Honeyford Affair' in Bradford in the 1980s (Halstead, 1988). Headteacher Ray Honeyford claimed that multicultural education gave precedence to cultures that were 'inferior to the British way of life' and that children should be taught only the English language (Ahmed, 1997: 92). But it was perhaps the 'Rushdie Affair', following the publication of *The Satanic Verses* in 1988, that consolidated this new racism into policing and policy. Deemed particularly offensive by certain Muslims across the globe, in Bradford protest against the novel was moderated, according to Bowen (1997: 112), by the Bradford Council of Mosques and culminated most publicly in the 'Bradford Burning' in 1989. Although, as La'Porte (1999: 8) explains, this incident involved only one copy of the book being burnt, much popular reaction to the event portrayed the presence of up to 2,000 Muslim citizens engaged in this occasion as the actions of 'fundamentalists' and 'extremists'.

The repercussions within Bradford mirrored in some ways those which played themselves out on a national scale. The Rushdie Affair was utilized as a marker, by the state, through which to question the compatibility of Islam and 'the West' through a debate over the requirements of citizenship in terms of loyalty and allegiance (Alexander, 2000: 6). In particular, questions were raised regarding what it meant to 'be' British and, more specifically, what it meant to 'be' Muslim and British (ibid.; see also Singh, 2002: 84). Indeed, the vocal and visible protests against

The Satanic Verses were manipulated in such a way as to present the events as symbolic of a 'backward tradition-bound culture struggling in the face of progressive Western values' (Alexander, 2000: 10). Yet salient to this period was also the continuation of a trend of increasing racist attacks, violence and vandalism.

In Bradford in 1991 for example, part of a cemetery used for Islamic burial rites was desecrated. Graves were vandalized and the area was daubed with fascist imagery (Bowen, 1997: 112–13). Tied to the Gulf War in 1991, West Yorkshire Police noted a 100% increase in overall racist attacks in this period, many of the victims of which were either Muslims or those perceived to be Muslim. And as the Runnymede Trust consequently (1997: 41) noted '[a]ll South Asians, it follows, are potential victims on British streets of Islamophobia'. However, simultaneously, this period also saw a concentrated stepping up of 'over-policing', on the one hand, and 'under-protection' on the other. Numerous research reports and submissions documented police discrimination against Asians in this period, including frequent 'random stops and searches' (Ahmed et al., 2001: 6) and harassment (Campaign Against Racism and Fascism, 1999). And these factors were a key dynamic in the organization of Asian self-defence collectives when tied to the failure of the police to protect against racist violence (Institute of Race Relations, 1987: 70; see also Ramamurthy, 2006, for a discussion of Asian youth movements predating and including this period).

However, racist violence was not confined to attacks against Muslims. It was the murder of black teenager Stephen Lawrence in 1993 that was to immediately define New Labour's race relations policies when they gained power in 1997.

New Labour, Racism and Race Relations

The New Labour government was elected with a landslide majority in 1997 and within a matter of weeks, and under pressure from the tireless campaigning of Stephen Lawrence's parents Doreen and Neville,[4] the then Home Secretary Jack Straw ordered a full inquiry into the death of their son, appointing a High Court Judge, Sir William Macpherson, to oversee the proceedings (Rowe, 2004: 7).[5] Published in 1999, the Macpherson Report 'was widely hailed at the time as a watershed in British race relations, not least for its official recognition of "institutional racism"' (Bridges, 2001: 61). In contrast to the Scarman Report in 1981, institutional racism was acknowledged and condemned, and as one activist suggested 'we taught Macpherson and Macpherson taught the world' (cited in Sivanandan, 2000). Yet, less than four years later, Jack Straw's successor David Blunkett declared that 'I think the slogan created a year or two ago about institutional racism missed the point' (cited in Burnett and Whyte, 2004: 28). Despite evidence of institutional racism within the criminal justice system and the wider state – painstakingly documented not just through the Macpherson Report but through long-term campaigning – the Home Secretary simply denied its relevance. How, then, had this point been reached?

The Emergence of Community Cohesion Policies

Community cohesion emerged primarily as a response to a series of urban disorders in Northern towns and cities in 2001, predominantly between Asians, white people and the police.[6] Like the rioting in the 1980s, 'the context of the 2001 disorders was set by localised histories of racism and deprivation, [and] contradictory and aggressive policing practices' (Burnett, 2007a: 115). Community cohesion policies drew explicitly from the establishment of a 'Community Cohesion Review Team' (CCRT) – led by a former leader of Nottingham Council, Ted Cantle – to investigate responses and views about the disorders and produce their findings (Cantle, 2001; see also Home Office, 2001). Central to the concept was a perception that 'many communities operate on the basis of a series of parallel lives' (Cantle, 2001: 2.1) that, in turn, was integral to a concrete reshaping of race relations policies.

This theory of 'parallel lives' rested on a (racialized) perception that the segregation that marked, and in many ways still marks, towns and cities across the country was underpinned by communities 'self-segregating'. In particular, Asian 'communities' were assumed to self-segregate – despite evidence to the contrary (Simpson, 2004) – to such an extent that communities leading parallel lives 'often do not seem to touch at any point, let alone overlap and promote any meaningful interchanges' (Cantle, 2001: 2.1). As such, the parallel lives thesis further consolidated a perception – already legitimized in policy rhetoric through the construction of a racialized discourse on Asians (and particularly Muslim Asians) in the 1980s and 1990s – that segregation was, in turn, underpinned by cultural incongruities.

In this context, the community cohesion 'agenda' offered from the outset a race relations policy that was depoliticized. Rather than considering the historical framework in which segregation had been fostered through, for example, discriminatory housing policies and workplace practices or the racist violence which had led to the disorders in 2001 (Kundnani, 2001), the community cohesion agenda put forward that (particular) communities culturally and geographically chose to disengage with others. And in this framework of pointedly downplaying the structural basis of embedded social problems the concept of institutional racism – a concept that had only been recognized by the state as a result of vigorous campaigning – was one of the first casualties (Kundnani, 2007b: 33–4).

Community cohesion, however, did not emerge as a policy concern in a political vacuum. Rather, its popularity and widespread appeal was directly related to an ongoing 'attack' on multiculturalism that created space which community cohesion was to fill. It was by sheer coincidence that the reports on the 2001 disorders were published only a few months after the terrorist attacks in America, on 11 September 2001. Yet the policy climate consolidated after these attacks and the recommendations made within the Cantle Report were key factors underpinning a critique of multiculturalism that began to take shape and gain political currency. This attack on multiculturalism was formulated on the basis of a zero-sum relationship – rooted in the work of previous governments concerned with restricting immigration and 'diversity' – that there was a trade-off between diversity and cohesion. The more 'diverse' a nation became, the less stability and cohesion there would be. Consolidated after the terrorist attacks in the UK on 7 July 2005, this attack reached something of a crescendo, with multiculturalism blamed for all manner of social problems, ranging from internal tensions (Blair, 2006), violence (Griffith and Leonard, 2002), social decline (West, 2005), and even as a contributing factor in terrorism (see, for example, Malik, 2006; Nazir-Ali, 2006).

In the context of an attack on multiculturalism, a framework had consequently emerged wherein 'diversity' was to be managed under a rubric of community cohesion. This 'management' was specifically related to a racism that cast Muslims as the 'enemy within' in the 'war on terror'. Yet it also tied into a shifting set of policies for managing entry into the nation. In this way, community cohesion, within the framework of an attack on multiculturalism, offered a 'new framework for race and diversity' (Cantle, 2005) that consolidated what Kundnani (2007b: 26) has called a 'rise of integrationism'.

New Labour's Integration Agenda: Coercion and Force

As Kundnani has stated, the rise in integrationism as a focal rationale of race relations policies has meant that 'a whole raft of problems to do with segregation, immigration and terrorism have been lumped together by the integrationists as resulting from an "excess" of cultural diversity' (2007b: 28–9). As such, the key recommendations of the Cantle Report gained ground, asserting that a set of core values must be defined and fostered between citizens that, in turn, would supposedly bind together the populace. The nature of these core values were from the outset based around a rewriting of 'Britishness' and what it meant to be 'British' and, in this way, a 'new' citizenship was consolidated through the community cohesion agenda (see Cantle, 2006). This discourse on a new citizenship – placing fastidious attention on Britishness and nationality – emerged in such popular fashion at exactly the same time as Muslims, in particular, were being described as antithetic to the same values that 'Britishness' was purported to represent. And through the auspices of the 'war on terror', Britishness was explicitly tied to the re-emergence of a national conversation about the role of the British empire. In this context, the first British citizenship ceremony was held in 2004, making an oath of loyalty compulsory for those acquiring the status of citizens (Home Office, 2004).[7] While a year later a key proponent of this 'conversation' on empire, the then Treasurer Gordon Brown declared that the 'days of Britain having to apologize for the British empire are over. We should celebrate' (cited in Pilger, 2006: 6).[8]

From one perspective, this attempt to realign (and, as we shall see, coerce) a sense of citizenship within nationality was tied to Britain's role in a deeply unpopular – and illegal – war on terror abroad. At the same time, however, integrationist policies both underpinned and legitimized the continuation, albeit in differing contexts and in differing ways, of the coercive policing and criminal justice practices that were a key focus of *Policing the Crisis* (Hall et al., 1978). Following the events of 11 September, and consolidated after the terrorist attacks in London in 2005, it was made explicit that Muslims were to accept discriminatory state attention as part of their civic duties under the war on terror. In 2005, Home Office Minister Hazel Blears stated clearly that Asian males should expect to be 'stopped and searched' disproportionately (see BBC, 2005) as part of an anti-terrorism strategy. The levels of this legitimized discrimination were huge. Anti-terrorism powers enabled police officers to 'stop' people without suspecting them of committing an offence and the use of such powers grew substantially each year after 2001 (Cowen, 2004).[9] In 2005, their use had grown to such an extent that nearly 36,000 people were targeted, a rate of just under 100 people a day (Russell, 2006). Moreover, research by Statewatch indicated that official records of stop and search powers grossly underestimated their use. By recording large numbers of stop and searches under criminal justice rather than anti-terrorism legislation, less than half of all stop and searches were recorded under anti-terrorism powers (Statewatch, 2003a). Thus in 2003, the organization suggested that there had been 71,100 stop and searches, rather than the 32,100 officially recorded, and of these less than 2% led to arrests (ibid.).

Yet the extension and use of stop and search powers were only one aspect of a much wider-ranging arsenal of tools made available under the banner of anti-terrorism policies. Detention without trial (defeated by the House of Lords as a Breach of human rights) (BBC, 2004), increases in the length of time suspects can be held without charge (Russell, 2007), control orders that undermine the presumption of innocence (Liberty, 2005), and campaigns of 'black propaganda' (Burnett, 2005) were only some of the measures consolidated in order to ensure that those who were suspected of terrorist activities were brought in line with an ideal of 'cohesive' citizens (see Burnett, 2007b). They were introduced within a context wherein integrationist discourses legitimized such coercive practices for, according to the head of the then Commission for Racial Equality and now head of the Equality and Human Rights Commission Trevor Phillips, British Muslims must be 'called' British 'again and again and again' but only as one side of a 'bargain'. The other side of the bargain was the obligation to 'work by the rules of the British people – and that excludes terrorism' (Baldwin and Rozenburg, 2004: 1).

Managing Multiculturalism

The 'war on terror' has underpinned a shift through which the consolidation of Muslims as contemporary folk devils has been cemented. This, in turn, has been legitimized by a set of integrationist theories that cast Muslims as at odds with a developing framework of 'Britishness'. At the same time, this integrationist politic has further been embedded within a shifting neo-liberal state in which, according again to Gordon Brown (2008a), it is necessary to 'consider the best means to forge societies that harness the economic opportunities of globalization and reflect both diversity and common identity'. Whereas a concerted and racially coded critique of multiculturalism has been most visibly focused on Muslims, it has simultaneously sought to manage multicultural reality through creating a new form of citizenship aligned within a neo-liberal state. This has been based around a conception of nationality that has: '[P]romoted the image of "the businessman" and the "entrepreneur" as *the* principal social role models, spreading the gospel of "entrepreneurial values" ("efficiency", "choice", "selectivity") through the land' (Hall, 2005: 323).

The implementation of a community cohesion agenda sought to consolidate a series of core values and mores that explicitly engendered a specific *form of* community cohesion. In one way, this involved a hegemonic project through which the concept of community cohesion became the dominant ideal of race relations. In turn, however, this hegemonic project provided the legitimacy for a series of ongoing policy developments that would enable the concept of community cohesion to be realized. The values that underpin the community cohesion agenda combined an attempt to couple specific ideas of 'market' and 'nation'.

What this consolidated was a set of policies engendering a form of what Sivanandan (2006) has termed 'enforced assimilation', wherein integrationist policies sought to channel a framework in which diversity was 'managed' – culturally and economically. In this context, terms of inclusion were set that directly underpinned particular ideas of economic growth, on the one hand, while seeking to align values, identity and mores on the other. With multiculturalism cast as a 'threat' to community cohesion, a managed migration strategy gained ground that was 'determined by the interests of the market-state' (Kundnani, 2007a: 146). This consolidated a development upon 'fortress Europe' (see, for example, Fekete and Webber, 1994, for analysis), through combining deterrence policies against the 'unwanted' (see Weber and Bowling, 2002) with increased routes of entry for those whose labour was required. Those with skills deemed only necessary for short periods of time, and thus employable on temporary contracts, were to be administered through a framework in which coercion was justified by a rhetoric of community cohesion. These workers were provided fewer rights and often with little recourse to protection in a system that demanded 'flexible' labour.

Simultaneously, a legislative battery of asylum legislation steadily built up measures against those seeking asylum in which, particularly with regard to those whose claims had been rejected, the most brutal policies could be enacted. These included a steady increase of 'dawn raids' (Burnett, 2008a), enforcing destitution on up to 500,000 people, vast reductions in legal aid (Asylum Aid and Bail for Immigration Detainees, 2005), and withdrawing medical treatment (Carlowe, 2001). According to the Home Office (2006b), this was, quite simply, a policy of 'integration or removal'. The message was clear – if a person's presence was deemed as not conducive to a given understanding of community cohesion, then their treatment, no matter how brutal, was justified. In turn, the terms of 'cohesion' were underpinned by a forging of neo-liberal ideals of economic growth, with an increasingly authoritarian state morality (see Burnett, 2008b). A shift towards coercive assimilation cohered around what at first glance appeared as the contradictory aims of hyper-inclusion and hyper-exclusion. However, it was exactly the attack on multiculturalism and an agenda of community cohesion that not only reconciled these aims, but consolidated them as part of the same policy processes.

Conclusion: New Labour's New Racism

According to Back et al. (2002: 450), 'cohesion' policies with regard to 'race' attempt to reconcile an 'aspiration for a model of neo-liberal economic growth based on a rhetoric of globalised economic forces with an attempt to protect the social integrity of the nation-state'. In this context, what community cohesion policies engender is a shift towards an assimilatory politics of race relations. Britishness tests, citizenship ceremonies and Britishness being taught on the school curriculum all seek to engender from one perspective a form of national homogenization. This, though, is only one part of a wider race relations strategy in which community cohesion is presented, crucially, as a benign set of policies and strategies which will engender civil renewal. Community cohesion is articulated as a series of partnerships between communities and the state, through which common solutions to problems can be found.

In this regard, the assimilatory (or to use the official term 'inclusive') politics of community cohesion are articulated as the softer or consensual face of neighbourhood policing strategies, anti-terrorism strategies, and even immigration policies. Understanding New Labour's race relations policies therefore involves placing these strategies alongside massively increasing scope for coercion and, in some cases, brutality. Primarily coercive actions are *legitimized* by policies which are articulated as fostering inclusion. Under the auspices of a war on terror, Muslims are presented primarily as the new enemy within. Their presence is held up as problematic, and even threatening to a vision of national identity, and, in this context, a shift in race relations policies towards an agenda of integrationism has sought to coerce a form of assimilation. As Fekete has argued, '"integration" is used as a coded means of making insinuations and venting prejudices about Muslims in ways that stigmatise and humiliate them' (2008: 4). Yet, it is these same integrationist discourses that are used to justify increasing stop and searches and oppressive policies enacted against these same communities.

While New Labour has embedded a 'new' racism, this is a racism that is firmly rooted in colonial and post-colonial policies of 'old'. *Policing the Crisis* set out the manner in which race relations strategies were enacted to respond to a crisis within a shifting capitalist economy. This took on the forms of racist stereotyping, policy initiatives and practice that are married to broader economic and social structuring. Crucially, the terms of contemporary racism have, at least in part, shifted. Yet the continued relevance and insight of *Policing the Crisis*, in this context, rests in part within its theoretical analysis of a moral panic around black youth and 'mugging' that encompassed ideas of statecraft. New Labour's assimilatory race relations agenda requires developing analyses that recognize both where it is 'new' and where it draws upon historically situated institutional racism.

As Hall et al. (1978) demonstrated, thorough understandings of the ways in which racialized perceptions of 'crisis' are presented can only be analysed alongside developments of institutional racism, which, in turn, can only be analysed alongside a thorough understanding of the state. The concerted ongoing critique of multiculturalism – suggesting that there is crisis within contemporary multiculturalism – is directly tied to a developing racism that presents a trade-off between diversity, on the one hand, and order and safety, on the other. New Labour's attempts to manage this 'crisis' through a form of 'market patriotism' (see Whyte, 2007) not only point to the emergence of a neo-liberal race relations politic, but they further embed new forms of institutional racism. The very fact that neo-liberal statecraft relies upon a new scope for institutional racism is telling. The inequalities embedded within are bolstered by authoritarian policies that criminalize entire communities. It is these issues that *Policing the Crisis* enables us to understand more coherently – in excavating how historically situated discourses of 'race' and racism both mediate and provide the modality of managing crisis.

Key Reading

Ansari, F. (2005) *British Anti-Terrorism: A Modern Day Witch-hunt*. London: Islamic Human Rights Commission.

Bowling, B. (1998) *Violent Racism: Victimisation, Policing and Social Context*. Oxford: Clarendon Press.

Fekete, L. (2008) *Integration, Islamophobia and Civil Rights in Europe*. London: Institute of Race Relations.

Keith, M. (1993) *Race, Riots and Policing: Lore and Disorder in a Multi-racist Society*. London: UCL Press.

Kundnani, A. (2007a) *The End of Tolerance: Racism in 21st Century Britain*. London: Pluto Press.

Notes

1 This is not to say that these works were necessarily the first of their kind. Rather, it is to suggest that they were both vital documents charting the contours of British racism at the time they were written.

2 The Brixton riots were preceded by the 'New Cross Fire' in 1981, where 14 black youths were killed in what was widely believed to be a racist arson attack.

3 Resistance by black communities has a history that, of course, long predates the events that are mentioned here. While documenting this is not the purpose of this chapter, it is worth reading Keith (1993); Law (1981); Rowe (1998); O'Malley (1977); and Sivanandan (1986).

4 See Lawrence and Busby (2006).

5 Stephen Lawrence had been brutally stabbed to death in 1993 by a group of white youths in London and what followed was a saga of 'incompetence, corruption, and institutional racism' (Bridges, 1999).

6 Information obtained by the Home Office, from relevant police force areas, estimated the combined initial cost of damage in Bradford, Burnley and Oldham (the three scenes of the most serious disorder) at over £9.5 million. Furthermore, these same sources estimated that, without including the police or other emergency services, approximately 1,450 people were directly involved overall in the violence in these three areas alone (Home Office, 2001: 7). Indeed, the scale of damage that occurred in these events was considerable, and they were described as the most serious disorders in the UK in the last twenty years (Bagguley and Hussain, 2003: 2; Home Office, 2001: 7).

7 The citizenship pledge reads 'I, (name), swear by almighty God/do solemnly and sincerely affirm that, on becoming a British citizen, I will be faithful and bear true allegiance to Her Majesty Queen Elizabeth II, her heirs and successors according to law. I will give my loyalty to the United Kingdom and respect its rights and freedoms. I will observe its laws faithfully and fulfil my duties and obligations as a British citizen' (see Travis, 2003: 7).

8 As Paul Gilroy incisively responded: 'When did we start apologising?' (cited in Fabian Society, 2006).

9 After the terrorist attacks on 11 September, stop and searches using anti-terrorism legislation on Muslims (and those assumed to be Muslim) increased dramatically. In 2002/03, this increase amounted to 302% from the previous year.

4

POLICING THE WORKING CLASS IN THE CITY OF RENEWAL: THE STATE AND SOCIAL SURVEILLANCE

Roy Coleman

Written thirty years ago, *Policing the Crisis* (*PtC*) explored the often disparate yet frequently ideologically unified reactionary forces that emerged at a time of crumbling class authority. The book presented a major step forward in developing a critical criminological theorization of the state while crystallizing a moment in the orchestration of state power in the UK in the early 1970s. The authors depicted the state in neo-Gramscian terms as a 'mediator' and 'educator': a historically contingent set of discourses and institutions embroiled in a struggle over the meaning and direction of social order. This arena of struggle highlighted the possibilities for, and threats to, an idealized universalization of class hegemony. *Policing the Crisis* focused on the politics of street mugging in order to investigate the crisis of capitalist social relations ubiquitously contested across social, economic, cultural and political realms and increasingly responded to through a law and order framework as the 'solution' to a range of social problems. This re-ignited fresh debate over the definition of 'public interest', which gained impetus throughout the 1980s and, particularly in the field of urban policy experimentation, continues to reverberate today. Thus the forces of social reaction, the definitional struggles over the public interest and the reworking of class authority all identify the public–urban realm as the arena for ideological and material restructuring in response to the crisis. Here both the social order and the anti-social begin to be mapped out ideologically and underpin the longer-term context for disciplinary intervention orchestrated through 'a reaction against the supposed "theft" of the city ... cloaked in the populist language of civic morality' (Smith, 1996: 211).

In the late 1970s *Policing the Crisis* identified the beginnings of a *policing of the urban crisis*: it was the realm of the urban that signified the 'ideological conductor' for the crisis, where definitional struggles over public authority provided the stage through which 'enemies within' were identified. The crisis for government, media, policing and business spokespersons thirty years ago was mapped through an urban imaginary – a disorderly realm, crime-ridden, unproductive and ungovernable. The urban provided the stage and a means of 'staging' the crisis. It provided the arena where the crisis could be visualized and simplified for those social forces concerned to reformulate a politics with 'rediscovered' enemies: militant workers, unruly black youth, 'spongers' and a cavalcade of dissenters. As others at the time argued, 'it was already clear that "decay and dereliction" across significant tracts of Britain's major cities were creating new problems of social and political control for the state' (Friend and Metcalf, 1982: 7) within which the disorderly street, through successive and overlapping moral panics, served as the broader index and symbol of national/urban decline.

This chapter will focus on the post-*Policing the Crisis* development of the state forms and disciplinary interventions as they relate to the social ordering of classed subjects in managing the crisis. A body of work that developed from *Policing the Crisis* sought to analyse the trajectory of crisis management and demonstrate *not* the disappearance of class and class interests, but 'their "re-presentation"' as they 'are being politically and ideologically redefined' (Hall, 1988: 5). If *Policing the Crisis* presents an insight into the anxieties (and reactions arising from those anxieties) of prevailing class authority most evident in the UK metropolis thirty years ago, then how are we today to trace such anxieties and reactions – particularly relating to constructions of belonging in the contemporary urban social order? Class – particularly working-class subjects – may be unfashionable to write about (Charlesworth, 2000) but is certainly not irrelevant academically or politically, even if 'spoken through other concepts' (Skeggs, 2004: 5) in the light of continuing class inequalities (Law and Mooney, 2006). In this sense, contemporary urban 'regeneration', with its roots in the broader social reaction that *Policing the Crisis* began to highlight, provides a pivotal arena in which policing the working class *in the city* continues to find expression and sustenance from a wider racialization of working-class subjects that found a renewed emphasis from the early 1980s (Haylett, 2001). From the vantage point of this chapter, how are we to trace dominant political class anxieties in their urban state form? What are their specifically urban institutional locations, authorized actors and ideological currency? How have the anxieties and reactions of ruling groups shifted and consolidated in the process of forging a 'new common sense' or a new urban subjectivity? These are important questions for thinking about how the process of policing the working class in a re-articulation of a radicalized and regenerated city has both continuous and discontinuous elements in relation to state and urban formation that could not be entirely predicted in the 1970s. As Cohen (1985: 205) has put it, authorities 'are haunted by the old idea that the city stands for something', and indeed haunted by what stands 'exterior' to it. The response to the crisis of authority evident in the 1970s gained momentum in, and a measure of success out of, a renewal of the city as 'standing for something' – as a unifying idea and material form that could once again rekindle lines of authority and rebuild leadership, if not around the idea of 'nation', then through 'civic pride' bolstered by contested sub-national constructions of localized urban patriotism (Coleman, 2004). Thirty years after the publication of *Policing the Crisis*, the political representation of urban streets and class subjects within them has assumed a place at the heart of urban renewal and the rehabilitation of urban authority. Since *Policing the Crisis*, the law and order imperative in urban management has been expanded, within and beyond the legal realm, and has been yoked to a class-based compulsion to 'govern through crime' (Coleman et al., 2005). UK cities continue to provide the arena for renewing and modernizing the social order that have in turn generated state forms and 'novel' discourses around governing legitimacy and its relationship to 'ungovernable' class subjects. Within the urban realm today, the 'crisis' remains palpable though veiled under an ascendant entrepreneurial vernacular within a re-galvanized 'market state' (Hall, 2003: 20). Indeed, it can be counted as some measure of success that these market state forms have revolutionized themselves on the winds of creative destruction and enabled a renewal of class authority albeit through a 'dispersed' state form (Clarke, 2004), unified ideologically – though not without contradictions and tensions – around questions of urban socio-spatial order (Coleman, 2004). However, the consolidation of the marketized state has certainly not been possible – and continues to be impossible – without the social distancing, pursuance and punishment of 'enemies within' the renewed urban frontier.

Responding to the Urban Crisis: Neo-liberal Modernization and the Enemies Within

From the beginning of the 1980s, and ensconced under the 'problem of the inner cities', the spaces of urban reproduction became the subject of greater state policy intervention in response to the crisis in capitalist social relations. The widespread urban disturbances of 1981 proved a turning point for a government keen to encourage City Fathers (businessmen) back into cities. This was no quick task – particularly for cities like Liverpool, where mistrust of new power brokers was a salient feature (Coleman, 2004), but the idea of the entrepreneurial city was born at this time. As Michael Heseltine stated, six years after the urban disturbances, government 'leadership awakens a response' and 'public and private sectors work best in partnership'. Harking back to Victorian idealism, it was in the city that 'British capitalists can show a well developed sense of public duty' (Heseltine, 1987: 3). But it was not only the spaces of cities that became objects of transformation, but also the state form through which transformation was to be rendered practicable. Under Thatcherism the local state form came under sustained ideological attack and was identified as a hindrance to a marketized view of social change (Cochrane, 1993). The flourishing of Urban Development Corporations, followed by marketing bodies and competitive bidding agencies, slowly reworked the fabric and direction of local state formation (Hall and Hubbard, 1996) through which aspects of welfare support became subordinated to entrepreneurial growth. In this sense, cities in the UK become the bedding ground for 'neoliberal policy experiments' – including marketing, urban development corporations and public–private partnerships (Brenner and Theodore, 2002: 368). The 'deeply dysfunctional yet extraordinarily malleable character of neoliberal statecraft' (ibid.: 345) was evident in the injection of a business ethos into urban authority that brought new tensions and fractures across a reconstituting local state. In its concern to reinvigorate a more business-like approach to urban management, the local state was confronted by a range of problems and oppositions at the centre of which, but by no means exclusively, stood the presence of the particularly black working class. Whether construed as criminal, deviant, disorderly or in some way unproductive, this broad group became problematic in racialized narratives of urban reclamation throughout the 1980s. At the intersection between state and urban, the problem of 'policing the working class city' (Cohen, P., 1981) thus continued to be re-posed by 'primary definers' (see Hall et al., 1978: 59–62) whose ranks became swelled from the early 1980s by newly responsibilized entrepreneurial voices (Coleman and Sim, 2000). It was the urban poor whose 'disadvantages' (or at least how the representation of these disadvantages as perceived by those external to them) became significant for those concerned to instigate new entrepreneurial strategies of economic growth and city re-imaging. On the back of neo-liberal attacks on public services and welfare as a cause of poverty, those living in the latter condition became increasingly perceived as a threat to urban order and subject to intensified policing (Friend and Metcalf, 1982) that sat alongside strategies to re-image cities in a manner that masked structural class conflicts for the purpose of levering investment (Coleman, 2004).[1]

The urban uprisings in the early 1980s re-ignited punitive discourses of 'class racism' (Haylett, 2001: 351) and sparked an entrepreneurial responsibilization strategy kindled by Heseltine's post-riot bus tour of Liverpool along with 26 financiers in 1981. The disorders raised a challenge to processes of urban rule, increasing economic polarization and reactive policing towards the poor and particularly black youth. However, the Heseltine-led response to this 'crisis' was able to articulate urban 'renewal' and 'reclamation' through the message that local government was ineffective and private enterprise, encouraged by a business-enabling state, would instigate a new culture in urban management. Following this, Business in the Community (BiC) was established in 1981 and by 1993 over 300 such bodies existed in Britain's towns and cities. For this body, the rationale for leading a new culture of urban enterprise was that:

> Strife and decay in the inner cities *and associated threats to property and public safety carry a high political risk – neglect will eventually impose a high cost on the whole business community.* (BiC, cited in Barnekov et al., 1989: 207, emphasis added)

A broad recognition that political stability and public order are issues that the business community can and must have a stake in coalesced around the rehabilitation of property rights in urban centres. As part of a broadly constituted process of modernization, this process of rebranding cities on a competitive entrepreneurial footing has both enabling and disabling effects on specific class interests in a manner that 'helps to render "natural" that which is not necessarily so' (Finlayson, 2003: 67). Modernization exhibits elements of continuity between Thatcherism and its New Labour variant, re-moulding the 'public realm' as an arena 'to sustain and enable the private sector and responsible/responsibilized subjects' (Clarke, 2004: 44). Although there are local contradictions and discontinuities in this process, the managerialization of the public realm underway in the last thirty years 'provides the framing assumptions which other discourses have to contest or negotiate' (ibid.: 38). Thus the conditions for 'modernization' under New Labour (self-responsibilized and self-governed subjects flexible and open to the possibilities of regenerated urban space) speak of and hail a certain urban subjectivity, nurtured in the ways of cultural (self-) improvement. At the same time, discourses of modern regeneration, socially constructed those groups and individuals who stand outside this paradigm as 'junk' – continuing a concern with the atavistic un-modern (or members of an 'underclass') that cannot or will not refrain from outmoded ways of being (Murray, 2005).

The re-presentation of class within a broader vision of 'social worth' has, in this sense, significance for rethinking poverty and unemployment in regenerating times, as reflected in New Labour's idea of 'modernization':

> Our culture is yob culture ... we are welfare dependent and our problems won't be solved by giving us higher benefits. We are perverse in our failure to succeed, *dragging our feet over social change*, wanting the old jobs back, having babies instead of careers, stuck in outdated class and gender moulds. We are the 'challenge' that stands out above all others, the greatest 'social crisis of our times'. (Peter Mandelson, cited in Skeggs, 2004: 88, emphasis added)

Under New Labour urban regeneration formed a key plank of its modernization programme, in which ideas of 'progress', 'the modern' and the causes of social exclusion were articulated. As a term, 'modernization' may appear to de-politicize the objects of its power but in fact it problematizes the working-class poor as a subject population to be policed and 'educated' in a very broad sense, drawing upon visual codes, emblems and repetitive cultural assigning. Behavioural and moral outlooks that appear to stand against 'modernization' and potentially, if not actually, hinder the trajectory of a regeneration strategy, came up against a notion of commodified urban space through which the rehabilitation of property – found in heritage sites, cultural and consumption zones, iconic architectures and increasing property prices – began to reinforce a performative regeneration rooted in a politics of vision throughout the 1990s (Coleman, 2005). Here a notion of *visually pleasing space,* propagated through central government urban design documents, has tied 'the look' of the urban fabric to successful regeneration (Department of Environment, Transport and the Regions, 2000). Increasingly, regeneration has come to operate around a spatial logic in which the visible has centre stage, encouraging not only the performance of consumption and tourism but, increasingly, the performed appreciation of 'culture' and 'art' in the city as signifiers of 'renaissance' (Coleman, 2005). As a driver for 're-awakening civic pride', New Labour's market vision for regeneration was to be 'supported by strong enforcement action' against a range of anti-social behaviours (Urban Task Force, 1999: 2). At the outset, the 'working-class poor', whose presence is coded as problematic in relation to regeneration discourse by virtue of their own cultural shortcomings, were depicted as vestiges of an earlier failed period of British urban development. Their 'exclusion' (for example, as unemployed or unemployable) continued to be married with discourses of individual deficiency while simultaneously divorced from economic and political restructuring.

Alongside entrepreneurial regeneration vernacular, an inclusive social imaginary targets working-class subjects. Notions of social inclusion resonate with models of crime control and a politics of law and order that *Policing the Crisis* documented at its inauguration into British urban politics. As it is being played out today, poorer constituents are addressed on an understanding of their life experience couched in negative and oppositional terms with reference to degenerate, 'anti-social' activities:

> Anti-social behaviour means different things to different people – drunken 'yobs' taking over town centres, people begging by cash points, abandoned cars, litter and graffiti. ... Anti-social behaviour creates an environment in which more serious crime takes hold. ... It blights peoples lives, undermines the fabric of society and holds back regeneration. (Home Office, 2003a: 6)

A definition of the modern-social is presented in contra-distinction to its supposed antithesis – the anti-social. Such policy strategies, aimed at neighbourhoods mired in deepening social and economic marginalization, privilege a defensive social politics where 'cohesion' and 'empowerment' rest primarily on the ability of neighbourhoods to unite against designated 'anti-social' elements. It is assumed that fighting anti-social behaviour, and a regenerated social fabric, are one and the same. The ability to display unity and 'act responsibly' against the anti-social is accorded recognition in official discourse. The articulation of regeneration operative here promotes a 'quality of life' unhindered by degenerate forces: the criminal, the unruly and the nuisance. A presumption exists that the 'blighting' of peoples' lives should be understood primarily as a problem of street behaviour – particularly the behaviour of the poor, usually young. Despite the illusion of a wide definitional scope of anti-social behaviour – meaning 'different things to different people' – there is, in truth, a fairly narrow media and governmental circumscription of what counts as 'anti-social' in public spaces; thus downplaying or discounting other social harms and anxieties. The quality of life at stake here is that of the propertied and 'responsible' individual or organization. Within this rhetoric, the voice of the newly responsibilized is constructed and privileged while those labelled 'anti-social', or those who fail to unite under its auspices, are relatively silenced.[2]

Thus modern regenerative discourses have shaped the parameters of the problems to be addressed in redrawing the moral frameworks for thinking about class, but they also cultivate, in a more empowering sense, the productive power of capital and consumption. The notion that 'businesses are part of communities and can be victims of anti-social behaviour' (Home Office, 2003a: 70) has underpinned private sector funding and management of urban surveillance systems concerned, for example, with giving 'consumers' the 'freedom and safety to shop' (Home Office, 1994: 9). Local Chambers of Commerce, and privately sponsored Town Centre Management consortia, have been incorporated into local strategic partnerships (Home Office, 1998), not merely as 'a source of funds' but as educators in the skills of 'project management and technical know-how' (ibid.: Sec. 2.33). As part of this development, 'the business friendly city' is an idea which has captured the meaning and political direction of contemporary urban 'regeneration' and has reinforced this through the development of Business Improvement Districts (BIDs). This mirrors developments in the USA, where there are around 2,000 BIDs.[3] Furthermore, BIDS have been depicted by their proponents as more flexible mechanisms for meeting local business needs in circumventing local democratic decision-making and gaining local political clout (Coleman, 2004).

In this context, the utility of 'broken windows', which linked declining quality in urban life to the disorder and nuisance of the poor (Wilson and Kelling, 2003), and 'routine activity' theory have come to the fore to stress the need for 'capable guardians' to watch over 'suitable targets' (Felson, 1998: 52). This has had particular resonance through its application in BIDs and police-led partnerships, which have circumscribed a notion of social harm and tied it firmly to the 'disorder' of petty street-level offences, 'nuisance' and 'unconventional' behaviours. Not only do these models justify a gaze that is fixed upon the poor – thus ignoring harms that generate disorder enacted by the powerful – but in doing this, they also contribute to the proliferation of harms. This is particularly so for the over-policed poor who pay the price for an 'illusion of order' as propagated by supporters of zero-tolerance policing (Harcourt, 2001). Signs of disorder – or in the words of Wilson and Kelling, the signs of 'an inhospitable and frightening jungle' (2003: 31–2) – are most forcefully articulated by new primary definers and include intolerance of litter, vandalism and damage to the physical environment. The drive to a 'hospitable city' sits alongside the orchestration of 'new malleable subjectivities' that attempt to 're-impose class subordination to divisions of labour in exchange and production' (Law and Mooney, 2006: 539). Although not always smooth running in practice, such processes point us to the importance of the wider notion of 'social policing' (Neocleous, 2000) central to the demarcation of class boundaries in the entrepreneurial city.

Urban Crisis and Class Subordination

Persuading people and organisations to care for the urban environment is partly a matter of re-awakening civic pride. (Urban Task Force, 1999: 2)

But some of them [homeless people] *just look wrong*. They do not look like someone who has fallen on hard times and are trying to do something for themselves but [look] like they are getting money for the next fix. (Superintendent, Merseyside Police and Government Office member, cited in Coleman, 2004: 177–8, emphasis added)

A-political representations of urban space as 'creative performance zones' have played a key part in local state strategies in cultivating a sense of 'cultural belonging' and in convincing local constituencies of the legitimacy of entrepreneurial city building.

But what is this culture of belonging and who has the power to define it? Again, an educational and disparaging discourse underpins this desire for a more 'hospitable' city. In Liverpool, for example, the former Chief Executive, Sir David Henshaw, articulated the anxieties of the new primary definers when he spoke of the ways in which 'sometimes Liverpool can be a mind bogglingly awful place, where the glass is always half empty. There are some things we do not do well – such as customer care, cleanliness, litter. We are still an ordinary city.' He also spoke of the 'immature and irresponsible' sensibility of Liverpool people in undermining the new entrepreneurial spirit (*Daily Post*, 15 September 2004). This thinly veiled attack on what he called 'the whingers' of the city, identified working-class foot-draggers whose sensibilities were problematic in the regeneration drive. Here, emblematic representations of class are drawn through sensitization towards desirable and undesirable urban behaviours that speak of middle-class fragility while attempting to lead the city forward through an elite mode of rebranding. In this context, 'charm schools' have been established for taxi drivers and others in frontline service industries in the light of greater expected tourist numbers as a result of Liverpool becoming Capital of Culture in 2008 (Coleman, 2004). Private sector expertise has been central to orchestrating a 'solution' to the urban crisis and in building a consensual framework for a reclamation strategy that targets and stigmatizes behaviours of a non-consumerist nature, including street trading, skating and begging. These processes are wedded to the Capital of Culture in Liverpool, described by its architects as 'the people's bid' (*The Observer*, 7 September 2003).

The development of cities post-*Policing the Crisis* has been practised through competitive bidding for funds, honours and prizes that bestow degrees of status on those cities in European, international and national competitions. Such competitions for funds and recognition have been organized around heritage, culture and architecture, and underpin the formation of networks of new primary definers, partnerships between which are deemed necessary for efficient, well-managed bids. In Liverpool, the capital of culture was purported to be worth £2 billion in investment in the run-up to 2008, with 14,000 new jobs created in the service industries to manage the expected growth in tourism (*City*, March 2003). However, structural contradictions are evident in this process. Key signifiers of regeneration, such as gentrification and rising property values, have lead, as Shelter pointed out, to actual increases in local homelessness (*Liverpool Echo*, 21 December 2004), which, in turn, point to a source of risk *within* the regeneration process for already vulnerable groups.

(i)   Policing representations of the city

The deployment of theatrical language portrays contemporary urban regeneration as forward-looking, spontaneous and playful (Coleman, 2004). However, such language is also demonstrative of corporate power in the city expressed through 'economic imaginaries' that are associated with particular 'state projects and hegemonic visions' that, in the struggle for urban leadership, 'underpin a relative structured coherence [in order] to support continued accumulation' (Jessop, 2004: 166). The newly responsibilized business cabal now governing urban spaces are often presented in the local media through the 'heroic' status of high-salaried 'city slickers', who articulate the means and meaning of state leadership, 'partnership' and local democracy (Coleman, 2004). Such theatricality and the bestowing of authority mystify the agents and processes that attempt to discipline 'social' spaces in the city and ensure 'public order'. In this sense, the activities of 'partnerships' redraw the moral, legal and cultural boundaries of local state affectivity with implications for urban order and should be seen as coterminous with the relatively more visible and longstanding public order policing associated with local police and national legal frameworks deemed to promote 'good order'. In Liverpool city centre, for example, now branded 'Liverpool One' by its developer, The Grosvenor Group, the marketing director has characterized the 'New Rules' associated with this space as expressing the 'confident and multifaceted nature' of the city:

> The 'New Rules' are the driving force behind Liverpool One and describe Grosvenor's philosophy in creating the development. They are: Make new rules, Involve every-one, Love the city, Think big, Create more, and Be best. The rules, however, are fluid and have the ability to change and evolve as the development progresses. (Spokesperson for Grosvenor, cited in *Daily Post*, 1 November 2005)

'The Rules' for the newly privatized city centre fabricate an ideal citizen – aspirational in consumption, and 'thinking big' with urban pride. Accordingly, and as an aspect of a new economic imaginary, this is depicted as 'no ordinary regeneration story' because Liverpool people 'possess so much passion, so much pride, and such a desire to shop' (ibid.). Such aspects of city representation have a powerful resonance with material developments in the city but also leave other aspects of urban experience relatively silent – silences which do not go uncontested (as noted below). The Grosvenor Development is Europe's biggest city-centre development, costing over £1 billion and covering a huge 42-acre site acquired from the City Council when the leasehold was handed over to the private developer for a 250-year period. To establish Liverpool as a 'premier European city' the form of corporate aggrandizement at work here is not only geared to maximize external investment but confers responsibility for the new city centre upon organized capital in providing private policing, gated access and 400 surveillance cameras. The privatization of 35 city-centre streets with no public right of way points to the consolidation of propertied rights in urban politics, along with the power to construct and ideologically represent such spaces. The goal is the removal of 'unsightly' and long-established local street traders in the city centre to be replaced in this space by 'continental style' French markets (*Liverpool Echo*, 29 November 2004). The modernizing regenerative agenda appears here to mean a fabrication of urban 'bustle' that is rooted in enclaves that speak to a middle-class desire for inoculation from the signs of decay, disorder and inequality. The drive to corporate-led enclosure opens up the possibility of stigmatizing behaviours of a non-consumerist nature:

I'm not sure why you would want kids hanging around if they are not spending money. ... There are lots of places in Liverpool to just hang around – outside of the city. (Charlie Parker, Liverpool Regeneration Director, cited in Granada Television, 2004)

United States style Quartermasters will have a role described by one council official as to 'control and exclude the riff-raff element' (Coleman, 2004: 233). A spokesperson for the developers articulated the logic for this strategy: 'we are developing a series of quarters for the area which will have security staff making sure that people maintain reasonable standards of behaviour' (ibid.). Maintaining 'reasonable standards' gains a different meaning in the 'biggest building site in Europe' (Liverpool City Council, 2007: 98), particularly for those who labour within it. In 2007 the Health and Safety Executive described Merseyside as 'the most dangerous place to work in the UK' (*Liverpool Echo*, 26 March 2007) in its rush to finish prestige projects for the Capital of Culture. Workers have asked whether it is 'reasonable' that union leaders are banned from Liverpool One over disputes concerning casualization, accidents and pay.

Regeneration can be read as an evolving, though no less strategic, response to the British urban crisis which underpins a complex rebalancing in the spatialization of social forces in and beyond the state. This process has not been without contestation and scepticism at the local level through ways that point to the continuity of 'traditional' class struggle. For example, a local newspaper poll in 2007 reported that 56% of those polled thought that 'renaissance' was a myth and called into question its corporatized city-centre focus (*Liverpool Echo*, 12 June 2007). Furthermore, 'outmoded' strategies of class resistance are evident in the cultural sector where Liverpool's new and revamped museums and galleries (flagships for the Capital of Culture in 2008) were the arena for strike action by its 250 staff over pay and conditions. As recognized frontline staff in the city's re-imaging strategy, workers in this sector described as 'insulting and unworthy' the terms and conditions imposed upon them by management (*Daily Post*, 25 July 2007). In August 2007, street cleaners decided to strike (with a 98% majority) against their employers, Enterprise Liverpool, who used city council funding to sub-contract the street cleaning workforce and undermine pay and conditions in the run-up to the Capital of Culture (*Daily Post*, 10 August 2007).

Hegemonic and spectacular strategies for urban renewal are not without contestation. However, taken together, such strategies have contributed to the marginalization of debate about the continuing inequality found in UK cities (in which Liverpool is ranked lowest – Joseph Rowntree Foundation, 2007), but also contributed to the local states' seeming inability to address it outside the ideologies of city-centre development and growth (Audit Commission, 2007).

(ii) The objects of power and urban order

Engineering 'safe places to do business' has reflected and reinforced new state discourses and institutional configurations. Together these have subsumed the visible signs of crisis within circumscribed debates about urban pride and particular constructions of street civility. Although the networks of primary definition may have changed since *Policing the Crisis*, the targets of primary definition have remained broadly the same in terms of direction (down the social hierarchy) and with regard to ideological representations of crime and disorder emanating from relatively powerless groups. The new primary definers have articulated the disorder of the poor as detrimental to urban renewal: 'the first broken window' (and therefore the pre-eminent sign of urban disorder) 'is the unchecked panhandler', as Wilson and Kelling (2003: 32) have put it.

This process has a compelling, if overlooked, relationship to class authority. This is the case when we consider the concept of responsibilization *not* as a free-floating individually chosen path (as preferred in neo-liberal vernacular) but as seated firmly in material practices and channels of access to political power. Responsibilization for the business class has been both reflected and reinforced by their positionality in respect to organized political power at the legal and cultural levels of state infrastructure, which has provided them with the means to articulate a 'credible' urban vision. However, for the poor, responsibilization confers a lower degree of trust *from* state institutions. Rather than being networked-in as members of the 'new' urban arrangements, they are cast as outsiders, sometimes 'users' and/or recipients, with less room for manoeuvre and recourse to organized infrastructures within which to envision a 'credible' and alternative political voice.

Given the imbalance in material power, it is the working-class poor therefore who have to 'live up to' and attain credible behavioural standards while the business class has attained *the power to act*, the means and ends of which lie beyond local democratic scrutiny. The 'relative autonomy' for capital (see Tombs and Whyte, this volume), then, highlights the disciplinary imbalance evident in parenting orders/classes, acceptable behaviour contracts, curfew zones and policing welfare fraud – aimed at the 'anti-social' poor and accompanied by a stigmatizing language of rights and responsibilities. Here, ideas of 'choice' and participation – both 'represented as part of an anti-inequality strategy' (Hall, 2003: 23) – have quite different class messages encoded within them.

This disciplinary setting is complicated by the fact that the working class are 'damned if they do, dammed if they don't'. In other words, if working-class poverty is individually and collectively pathologized, so too is working-class aspiration and attempts at upward social mobility. The target of policing and surveillance in the early nineteenth-century city was partly founded upon elite fears that any 'wealth, power and luxury' that filtered down to the lower orders 'would lead to contempt of authority and ultimately anarchy' (Dodsworth, 2007: 441). Mechanisms aimed at 'policing' the cultural and material advancement of working-class people is evident in rendering them a subject of ridicule in popular cultural forms in the nineteenth century (Maidment, 2000). Today a variant of social policing is found in the punitive identification of the 'chav' or 'scally', who although conforming to consumption discourses do so in ways 'deemed vulgar and hence lacking in "distinction" by superordinate classes' (Hayward and Yar, 2006: 14). The struggle of working-class subjects for a self-authored visibility is thus doubly problematic and subject to extra-legal sanction.

The wider abandonment and dumping of the poor in particular – and the government-inspired anti-social-come-grotesque media imagery that has accompanied this strategy – also points us to the continuing relevance of the concept of 'police property' whereby 'the dominant powers of society (in the economy, polity etc.) leave the problems of social control … to the police' (Lee, 1981: 53–4). This has taken place under the wider entrepreneurialization of urban space in which new primary definers, in calling for policing solutions (Coleman, 2004), have heightened the risks of state brutality towards marginal groups (see Harcourt, 2001). In Liverpool, for example, attempts to responsibilize homeless people (as charmed tourist guides) has also taken place alongside an increase in formal surveillance of this group.[4] The category of police property extends in the city to groups including the homeless, street traders, 'deviant' youth and those on no or low incomes. The rebranding of the city, and the identities within it, therefore, sits alongside the continuation of differential policing.

Indeed, the containment and harassment of the black population in Liverpool is indicated by the fact that one in three black people were stopped and searched in 2002/03 – a rise of 112% (*Liverpool Echo*, 2 July 2004). In addition, black people have lodged 40% of complaints against the police in relation to stop and search practices and are nearly ten times more likely than whites to be stopped and searched in the city (*Liverpool Echo*, 29 March 2004). The Racial Harassment Unit in the city has reported 'a culture of denial in the public sector' when acknowledging and responding to racist violence. The Unit itself faces the possibility of being disbanded through funds being withdrawn by Liverpool Council and Merseyside Police (*Daily Post*, 6 July 2006). Spatial demarcation and freedom of movement in the contemporary city is also taking place through longstanding processes of over- and under-policing, alongside the militarization of urban policing and space (Coleman et al., 2002). Shows of state force now work alongside the seemingly benign urban rebranding exercises that this chapter has focused on but which nevertheless move disciplinary power into blurred public and private networks which underpin a wider politics of the right to the city – entrepreneurially recrafted as 'pseudo-rights' through 'the detours of nostalgia and tourism' (see Lefebvre, 1996: 158).

Conclusion

From the time of *Policing the Crisis* we have seen the development of a local state form cajoled, aided and educated by its bigger central brother to develop an entrepreneurial style of urban management. The capitulation to capital in this process has brought fresh contradictions and tensions to the state itself and in civil society. In this institutional reshaping, property has re-emerged 'as a crucial category in the organising of social and political relations' (Blomley, 2006: 4), along with a propertizing of the self, which has implications for class identity and division (Skeggs, 2004). This raises new and difficult questions, first, concerning progressive rights claims, particularly with respect to the conundrum of how 'the massive wealth generated through real estate [is] …treated as a social dividend, rather than a private entitlement' (ibid.). While surveillance of the poor encodes them *as poor*, solely on the basis of their cultural traits, the lack of surveillance, scrutiny and moral judgement directed at the powerful remains as a relative non-starter. Second, pathologizing the working-class poor through emblematic labelling continues to place them 'as a symptom of anxiety' in order to deny them political recognition (Skeggs, 2004: 181). As the authors of *Policing the Crisis* acknowledged, 'unfortunately, you cannot resolve a social contradiction by abolishing the label that has been attached to it' (Hall et al., 1978: vii). Thus, the continuing structural contradictions underpinning class inequality and working-class subordination (and how these come to be misrepresented as socio-cultural diseases for which the poor themselves are held as individually responsible) should be addressed if we are to move towards an open and democratic debate about urban social possibilities.

Not only does entrepreneurial state-building place working-class culture and identity in a spatial quandary, but in doing it raises fresh questions around authoritarianism. From the time *Policing the Crisis* was written, authoritarianism has continued to manifest itself in processes of law-making, prison-building and extended police powers. Coercive and zero-tolerance measures that continue to target the poor are buttressed by entrepreneurial state-building, where a wider social policing around 'civic pride', idealized notions of urban patriotism and the illusory community underpin a myth of responsibilized urban selves sit uneasily with deepening urban inequality. Thus, the policing of working-class subjects has been, and continues to be, simultaneously defined through 'a moral ideology of deviance and a judicial ideology of crime' (Cohen, P., 1981: 127). The 'new' discourses of 'urban safety' propagated by contemporary primary definers dovetails with the recomposition of class authority in the 'playgrounds' of modern cities. In this context, *policing the state* – in its overt law and order *and* entrepreneurial, seemingly benevolent guises – remains a role that academics can fill in developing a critical theorizations of state discourse, practice and policy. This is particularly apt in light of the new state spaces of primary definition discussed here and their role in undermining the urban rehabitation of the poor, coupled with a mounting vigilance against their return – not merely as urban subjects but as creative participants in urban life.

Key Reading

Coleman, R. (2004) *Reclaiming the Streets: Surveillance, Social Control and the City.* Cullompton: Willan.

Coleman, R., Tombs, S. and Whyte, D. (2005) 'Capital, crime control and statecraft in the entrepreneurial city', *Urban Studies*, 42(Dec.): 2511–30

Hall, S. (1988) *The Hard Road to Renewal: Thatcherism and the Crisis of the Left.* London: Verso.

Skeggs, B. (2004) *Class, Self, Culture.* London: Routledge.

Smith, N. (1996) *The New Urban Frontier: Gentrification and the Revanchist City.* London: Routledge.

Notes

1   The incidence of urban poverty and the image problem it denotes for urban elites dates back to the early nineteenth century. In this sense, the incidence and images of poverty have had a signifying relationship to wider narratives of national and urban decline (Hall et al., 1978: 139–77; Skeggs, 2004; Marriott, 1999; Coleman, 2004) and is rooted in Victorian idealism which first tied ideas of national identity to urban civic pride (Hunt, 2004). Powerful discourses pertaining to working-class subjects and spaces (and the contamination of other prized spaces) form the historical threads that bind the aestheticization of the city with the unruly presence of certain behaviours within it.

2   Such processes have not gone unchallenged. In June 2005, when 20 new youth dispersal zones were announced in Liverpool, youth workers and local residents spoke out in Dingle (the poorest area south of the city centre) and pointed to the need to engage young people where 'the chance [for them] to be pro-active and participate is denied' (*Liverpool Echo*, 18 June 2005). At the time the local youth service was described as being in 'crisis', with 50% of staff leaving posts in 2005/06 and salary cuts of up to £5,000 per individual (*Liverpool Echo*, 1 May 2006).

3   Here, it is claimed, BIDs take on an ambitious role as 'the economic development tool for the 21st century' in that they can 'dramatically increase commercial activity, improve property values and provide a source of civic pride' (California Civic Center Group, 2002, cited in Jones et al., 2003: 51). There are 22 BIDs in the UK.

4   Evidence for this is based on current research undertaken by myself into homeless peoples' perceptions and experiences of the city. *Big Issue* vendors, for example, are subject to greater restriction on movement, comportment and appearance when working in the city. Rough sleepers have been subject to the use of ASBOs, acceptable behaviour contracts, dispersal orders and arbitrary police violence as a means of removing them from the streets.

5

YOUNG PEOPLE, YOUTH JUSTICE AND THE STATE

Janet Jamieson and Joe Yates

Introduction

> Often spectacular in form, the restlessness, visibility and anti-authority attitudes of youth came to stand, in the public consciousness, as a metaphor for social change, but even more, for all things wrong with social change. (Hall et al., 1978: 48)

As this opening quotation, from *Policing the Crisis* (*PtC*) testifies, historically, youth – or more accurately the 'threat of youth' – has served as a cipher for much wider hopes and fears about social order, progress and social change. Indeed, contemporary political and media preoccupations with hoodies, 'gangs', gun culture and 'anti-social' behaviour have elicited similar forms of adult, media and political condemnation and censure to that surrounding the 'moral panics' associated with the teddy boys, mods, rockers, skinheads, punks, muggers, football hooligans, new age travellers and persistent offenders of preceding decades (Hall and Jefferson, 1976; McRobbie and Thornton, 1995; Pearson, 1983). Indeed, in the thirty years since the publication of *Policing the Crisis* the value of moral panics around youth and crime as 'an index of the disintegration of social order; as a sign that the "British way of life" is coming apart at the seams' (Hall et al., 1978: vii), and as a precursor to authoritarian state interventionism appears undiminished.

In this chapter we will present a critical analysis of the trajectory of youth justice policy in the thirty years since the publication of *Policing the Crisis*. It will highlight the continuing purchase of 'moral panics' within the continuities and shifts apparent in the highly politicized arena of youth crime and youth justice. We argue that Britain's drift towards a 'law and order' society has gained momentum within this period and that recurring 'moral panics' regarding the threat of youth continue to be mobilized in support of ever more authoritarian responses to the troublesome and criminal behaviours perpetrated by children and young people and to the ongoing problem of maintaining social order more generally.

The Thatcher Years

In the immediate aftermath of the publication of *Policing the Crisis*, concerns about the punitive nature of state responses to issues of crime and disorder appeared particularly pertinent with regard to juvenile justice as the welfare rhetoric of 'treatment and rehabilitation', underpinned by the theories of individual and social positivism, were fiercely challenged and contested by the rhetoric of 'punishment and retribution', with an emphasis on the neo-conservative priorities of remoralization and authoritarianism (Muncie, 2004: 266–7). This shift was forged in the context of a succession of moral panics in the 1970s where – in addition to 'mugging' – football hooliganism, juvenile delinquency, trade unionism, immigration, international terrorism and sexual permissiveness were identified as evidence of a 'growing moral degeneration and, crisis of authority in Britain' (Muncie, 2002b: 337). Indeed, between 1970 and 1974 a state of emergency was declared in Britain three times (Scraton, 1985b: 251), and by the 'winter of discontent' of 1978/79 the media had deemed Britain 'ungovernable' (Hendrick, 2006: 12). Riding on the 'wave of law and order' which was 'washing over the western world' (De Haan, 1990: 20), Margaret Thatcher's 1979 election campaign gained political capital by attacking the 'soft' way in which 'dangerous young thugs' were treated by the criminal justice system (Muncie, 2004: 266–7). Lambasting those who sought to understand criminality within a broader structural framework for creating a 'culture of excuses' (ibid.), she promised that her government would 're-establish a code of conduct that condemns crime plainly and without exception' (Riddle, 1989: 171). In presenting crime as the result of a broader decline in morality, and stressing individual responsibility and obligation, Thatcherism actively reworked traditional popular ideologies and nostalgia in an 'authoritarian direction' through what Stuart Hall has referred to as a 'tactical exploitation of a series of "moral panics" in which these ideological oppositions are dramatized, set in motion, winning public attention' (1988: 144).

The Thatcher premiership was to mark a paradigm shift in the British political landscape, in which the post-war Butskelite consensus around corporatist state intervention fell apart (Hall, 1988) in favour of a free market project committed to neo-monetarist economics and erosion of the welfare state. Herein, the development of what Poulantzas has referred to as a form of Authoritarian Statism combined the 'intensification of state control over every sphere of economic life' with a 'radical decline of the institutions of political democracy and with the draconian and multi-form curtailment of so-called "formal" liberties' (Poulantzas, 1978b: 203–4, cited in Hall, 1988: 126). This represented an intensified process of criminalization as the full weight of the state was brought to bear on those perceived to be socially and politically problematic – the 'enemy within' (Milne, 2004). In turn, this was coupled with an authoritarian populism, which Hall has described as an 'unremitting set of operations designed to bind or construct a popular consent to these new forms of statist authoritarianism' (1988: 127). That this authoritarian shift might have particularly negative repercussions for members of black and minority ethnic group communities, and particularly black youth, who were presented as representing a 'direct threat to social order and moral stability' (Smith, 2007: 3), was forewarned in Thatcher's electioneering tendency to address questions of crime within a 'toxic discourse' of 'class', 'race' and 'nation', as a means of indicating the threat posed by young black men (Pitts, 2001: 5).

Almost immediately on gaining power, the Thatcher government's authoritarian statist tendencies were manifested in the introduction of 'short, sharp shock' regimes in two juvenile detention centres (Smith, 2007: 3). However, while the Conservatives' rejection of the welfarism associated with the partially implemented 1969 Children and Young Persons Act was clear, the drift towards an authoritarian rule of law was to prove 'complex and contradictory' (Muncie, 2004: 266). Indeed, at the very heart of what Hall refers to as the 'blind spasm of control' (Hall, cited in Scraton, 2003: 1), juvenile justice in the 1980s has paradoxically been characterized as one of the 'most remarkably progressive periods of juvenile justice policy' (Rutherford, 1995: 57). The Thatcher government's commitment to an authoritarian statist position (a strong, authoritarian, interventionist, law and order discourse) was underpinned by an anti-statism (an economic and ideological commitment to reducing the public sector borrowing requirement through rolling back the state and reducing welfare intervention) (see Coleman et al., this volume).

This 'anti-statist' commitment to cutting costs and 'small government' opened up space in which activists, scholars and radical practitioners, disillusioned with the excessive interventionism and 'demonstrable ineffectiveness' of stigmatizing and criminalizing 'welfarist' responses to child offenders, promoted and developed a juvenile justice system premised on the due process of law, which was to be guided by the principles of decarceration, diversion and decriminalization (Muncie, 2004; Thorpe et al., 1980; Worrall, 1997). Recognizing the value of 'radical non-intervention' (Schur, 1974) as an appropriate mechanism for minimizing the adverse effects of involvement with the justice system, informalism was promoted as an effective strategy to deal with low-level offenders (Yates, 2008); opportunities for diversion and alternatives to custodial sentences were utilized as a means to persuade magistrates and the police to intervene as little as was feasible and to impose the minimum sentence where possible (Worrall, 1997); and 'systems management' was utilized to promote decarceration (Thorpe et al., 1980). Such progressive policy and practice culminated in the 1991 Criminal Justice Act, which consolidated the diversionary, decriminalizing and decarcerative principles of juvenile justice policy via the establishment of the Youth Courts (Goldson, 2002: 129), and the promotion of a range of community sentences under a broader philosophy of 'punishment in the community', wherein prison was viewed as 'an expensive way of making bad people worse' (Home Office, 1990, cited in Muncie, 2004: 266).

This 'delicately balanced consensus forged around an improbable coincidence of interests' (Goldson and Yates, 2008: 105), which rather than being 'dragged along in the slip stream of the Adam Smith Institute' (Hall, 1988: 279, cited in Sim, 2000: 332) occupied this space in an innovative and creative manner, proved sufficiently robust to last for the best part of a decade and engendered some progressive outcomes for young people in trouble. For example, the numbers of young people aged 17 and under cautioned or convicted decreased from 204,600 in 1983 to 129,500 in 1993 while the number sentenced to immediate custody was reduced from 13,500 in 1983 to 3,300 in 1993 (Muncie, 2004: 267). However, such progressive practice was only allowed space to flourish as long as it did not detract from the state's authoritarian populist credentials. Therefore, in youth justice, what emerged was a policy of bifurcation, whereby the state was 'tough and soft simultaneously' (Smith, 2007: 5), reserving custody for the minority of hard-core persistent offenders while more cost-effective community sentences and diversionary strategies were targeted at the majority of less serious offenders (Mizen, 2004; Smith, 2007; Worrall, 1997). Indeed, as John Pratt observes, government and policy-makers were 'only prepared to sanction non-custodial alternatives on the basis that custody will be *retained* for particular segments of the offender population' (1989: 244), that is those offenders deemed as undeserving, depraved and dangerous. In Pratt's view, this ideological distinction represented a secondary form of bifurcation and rested on a distinction between the 'hard core' of offenders, whose behaviour is dramatized, and 'the rest', whose behaviour is 'normalized': a distinction which translated into those perceived to be undeserving or 'socially volatile' being subject to higher levels of surveillance and intervention (Pitts, 1990: 4).

While the 1980s are lauded as the decade of the 'successful revolution in juvenile justice' (Newburn, 2002: 453), this success was not equally shared by all young offenders (Muncie, 2004: 270). Juvenile offenders from black and minority ethnic groups were not only being dealt with more harshly at all stages of the justice process (Bowling and Philips, 2002; Fitzgerald, 1993), but were also subject to the disproportionate use of custody (Pitts, 1988), despite evidence that they were no more likely than the general population to be involved in crime (Smith, 2007). Reductions in the numbers of young people held in what were formerly known as 'approved schools' masked the over-representation of black and minority ethnic youth in remand and assessment centres (Pitts, 1990). It is of note that black and minority ethnic groups were also disproportionately likely to be victims of crime (Fitzgerald and Hale, 1996). Likewise for girls, the movement to the due process of law held much promise – not least because girls experienced both the advantages and disadvantages of welfarist justice policies to a greater extent than boys 'on the grounds that they were "at risk", "in moral danger" and "in need of protection"' – but in reality delivered greater criminalization (Worrall, 1999, 2004). In addition to such 'institutional injustices' (Goldson, 2002: 130), the Thatcher government's ideological commitment to anti-welfarism and decreased public spending resulted in repressive welfare, housing, education, training and employment policies. This represented a systematic assault on social justice which not only had a catastrophic impact on the children of the poor in general (Goldson, 1997), but also 'resulted in a much strengthened disciplining of pauperised and redundant youth independent of the criminal justice and/or penal system' (Carlen, 1996: 45–6). These negative outcomes clearly illustrate the impact of structural disadvantage which, as Pitts (1990: 25) argues, 'a classless and colour blind minimalism was unable to explain' and the extent to which bifurcation provided a strategy whereby those groups regarded as the volatile fraction of the surplus population could be managed.

A Punitive Renaissance

Just as the achievements of the 1980s appeared to have been consolidated in the 1991 Act, a range of moral panics and concerns relating to childhood and youth were to trigger a 'punitive renaissance' in juvenile justice policy (Pitts, 2001: 13). In the context of a 'widespread and deep economic recession manifest in levels of unemployment unprecedented since the 1930s' (Hay, 1995: 202), a series of disturbances broke out in Cardiff, Oxford and North Shields in 1991, followed the next year by those in Bristol, Salford, Burnley and Carlisle. In the aftermath of this unrest, Britain's societal folk devil was articulated through the discourse of a 'dangerous, immoral, dysfunctional' underclass masculinity in urgent need of discipline and control (Goldson, 1997: 131). Concerns regarding these 'barbarian' (Murray, 1990: 23) underclass males living in Britain's 'thrown away' places (Campbell, 1993: 48) coalesced with an ideological assault on single mothers (McRobbie, 1994) to create what were perceived to be 'twin crises in the family and in childhood' (Scraton, 2007a: 77). This was presented as the 'reality' of crime, afflicting poor communities, which the liberal left, with its focus on minimalism and diversion, had allegedly failed to address. That the construction of these new societal folk devils was to trigger a more punitive approach to issues of law and order in general, and for juvenile justice in particular, was ensured by doubts regarding the legitimacy of the criminal justice system (Hay, 1995) and the waning fortunes of the Conservative party (Goldson, 2002; Pitts, 2001). It was further exacerbated by a modernizing Labour party, under the increasing influence of Tony Blair, which 'played the crime card' in a manner 'unprecedented' in the history of the Labour party (Brownlee, 1998: 33).

The moral panics and associated 'folk devilling' and 'demonization' of young offenders continued apace throughout the early 1990s with the media and the police playing a key role in persistently highlighting the problems of joyriding, youth disorder, 'bail bandits' and 'persistent' young offenders (Goldson, 2002; Gelsthorpe and Morris, 2002; Muncie, 2004; Smith, 2007). Furthermore, in circumnavigating the reporting restrictions on the naming of young offenders and referring to them in animalistic terms, highly emotive media coverage served to dehumanize and 'bestialize' children who were involved in offending, portraying them as 'feral', outside the laws or respectable social norms and as a threat to social cohesion. This highly emotive moral panic regarding the behaviour of young people in general, and the 'feral children' of the poor in particular, was intrinsically linked to right-wing concerns around the moral otherness of an 'emerging British underclass' (Murray, 1990: 1), the 'New Rabble' who were 'making life in low-skill working-class communities ever more chaotic and violent' (Murray 1994: 116). The problem was presented as not being about poverty *per se*, but about a certain type of poor people, characterized by unemployment, illegitimacy and criminal involvement (Murray, 1990). McRobbie (1994: 111) asserts that the remarkable feature of the moral panics of the early 1990s was 'the lack of opposition from Labour and the silence of those close to Labour when it came to speaking out against the scapegoating of the new folk devils'. In reality, the New Labour crime control strategy, developed during this period, had these 'folk devils' firmly in its sights as it focused 'solely on those invisible, intra-class and youthful crimes of the street' (Muncie, 2000a: 16): a shamelessly political expedient strategy characterized by Jones (1996: 4) as 'tough on crime and nasty to children'.

It was the arrest and charging of 10 year-old Jon Venables and Robert Thompson, for the abduction and murder of 2 year-old James Bulger, in February 1993, which was to act as 'a catalyst for the consolidation of an authoritarian shift in youth justice' (Scraton, 1997: 170) and cement the 'authoritarian backlash' (Goldson, 2002: 131). Despite the atypicality of the Bulger case, this murder focused attention on the 'vexed question' of the age of criminal responsibility (Worrall, 1997: 134). The consensus was that Venables and Thomson had committed an adult offence and needed to be treated as such and be subjected to the full weight of adult sentencing (Worrall, 1997: 134). In the aftermath of the case, childhood was deemed to be in 'crisis' (Scraton, 1997), a 'crisis' perceived to be so 'powerful' and 'pervasive' that it threatened 'the very fabric of social and moral order' (Scraton: 1997: xii). Indeed, Brown (1997: 46) asserts that the series of moral panics which characterized the 1990s no longer strictly conformed to the 'generalized panic' described by Hall et al., but rather comprised a 'total panic: a series of discourses of fear reaching out to almost every aspect of the lives of young people'. Consequently, children, and in particular marginalized children, became increasingly conceptualized as 'both the cause and the product of wider social disorder and moral malaise' (Goldson, 1997: 38), setting the scene for an even more 'punitive turn' and the 'taking of liberties' (Goldson, 2005a: 255).

Within days of this 'extraordinary event' (Goldson, 2001: 133) John Major, the Prime Minister, articulated the terms of the authoritarian backlash as necessitating society 'to condemn a little more and understand a little less' (cited in MacIntyre, 2003). The 'death blow' to the non-interventionist delinquency management strategies of the 1980s was dealt in March 1993 by the then Home Secretary, Kenneth Clarke, who promised the creation of 200 places in secure training centres which could be utilized for the hard core of persistent and serious offenders as young as 12, whose repeated offending made them 'a menace to the community' (Pitts, 2001: 14). The punitive crusade against youth crime was to intensify with the appointment of Michael Howard to the position of Home Secretary in May 1993. In a bid to 'restore the government's political legitimacy' (Pitts, 2001: 15), Howard set about implementing his party political soundbite that 'prison works' via a 'legislative onslaught' on issues of justice and punishment (Smith, 2007: 26). This included retracting prior policy commitments to the use of police cautioning (Smith, 2007: 27), undermining the prospects of decarceration (Goldson, 2001; Worrall, 1997), strengthening punishment in the community (Nellis, 2001) and introducing mandatory minimum sentences for certain offences (Worrall, 1997).

Ultimately, the result of the Conservative party's rhetorical and substantive shift to punitiveness and incarceration was a rapid reversal of the progressive gains achieved in the previous decade. Diversionary strategies to decrease the numbers of young people appearing in court declined, with the use of police cautioning falling steadily after 1992, with an associated expansion in the numbers of 10–17 year-olds taken to court for indictable offences, rising from 60,000 in 1993 to 81,000 in 2000. Furthermore, not only were the courts increasingly disposed to utilize high (supervision orders) rather than low tariff (fines and discharges) community punishments (Smith, 2007: 37–9), there was also a 79% increase in the number of 15–17 year-olds given custodial sentences between 1992 and 1998, and a 122% increase in the number of young people serving custodial sentences between 1993 and 1999 (Newburn, 2002: 557).

New Labour's Youth Justice Priorities

That New Labour was likely to pursue and consolidate the punitive renaissance initiated by their Conservative predecessors became increasingly evident in the lead-up to the election in May 1997 as it sought to reinvent itself as *the* party of law and order (Jones, D., 2001). Indeed, it was in the aftermath of yet another election defeat in 1992 that New Labour was to definitively break from its traditional welfarist concern, which emphasized the link between crime and social and economic inequalities (Downes and Morgan, 1994), in order to consolidate its 'tough on crime' philosophy. A rapidly modernizing New Labour looked to the USA and Bill Clinton's reinvention of 'an apparently moribund political party' for a solution to end its seemingly perpetual role as the party in opposition (Pitts, 2001: 18). Embracing Clinton's ideas and assumptions regarding the role of the government in a globalized economy and his retributive zero-tolerance approach to crime (Pitts, 2001), New Labour forged a political ideology of the 'Third Way' (Giddens, 1998), which rejected the belief that 'big state' had the power to solve every social problem, favouring instead the idea of an 'enabling state', with a firm emphasis on the individualized duties and responsibilities of citizens (James and James, 2001: 211).

For New Labour, law and order was viewed as 'a vehicle for the acquisition of, and retention of, power', and left 'realist' criminology was to provide the critical paradigm which enabled it to exorcise the demons of its allegedly 'idealist' past as it embraced a rigorously authoritarian agenda (Pitts, 2000: 1). Emerging in the 1980s, left 'realism' criticized the liberal tendencies of criminology, to focus on 'the randomised and somewhat romanticised, crimes of the public sphere' (Stevens, 2006: 45). It highlighted that crime was not merely a consequence of labelling or oppressive forms of social control (Smith, 2007: 165) but had 'real' consequences, particularly for working-class communities. Focusing on the context of crime and the victim's experience, left 'realism' emphasized the disproportionately damaging and oppressive impact that crime could have on the most vulnerable individuals and communities (Kinsey et al., 1986; Lea and Young, 1984), and championed the victim's, as opposed to the offender's, perspective. The recognition of the impact of crime on 'real' people and 'real' lives, which left 'realists' advocated, provided New Labour with a legitimate means to champion the rights of the law-abiding majority by embracing ever more authoritarian approaches to questions of 'law and order' (Pitts, 2001). That youth crime was to prove a particular target of this 'tough on crime' approach was ensured by the 'hostile climate' of the early 1990s (Scraton, 2007a: 77), where within a 'context of "moral panic" (Cohen, 1972), "respectable fears" (Pearson, 1983) were mobilized, child offenders systematically "demonized" and a punitive authoritarian politics began to congeal around youth justice' (Goldson and Muncie, 2006: 209).

It is therefore no surprise that after their landslide electoral success in May 1997 that New Labour moved quickly to translate its youth justice priorities into legislation in the form of the 1998 Crime and Disorder Act. Enthusiastically embracing the Audit Commission's 1996 *Misspent Youth* Report (see Jones, 2001, for a critique), which declared the existant system a failure, the government initiated a 'root and branch reform' of the youth justice system (Home Office, 1997: 7). This programme was also informed by a US-inspired agenda of actuarialism, intensive modes of early interventionism and the use of penal custody (Goldson and Muncie, 2006: 210). Concerned to improve the system's performance and to rebuild safer communities under the overarching aim of preventing offending by young people (Johnstone and Bottomley, 1998), the 1998 Act created the Youth Justice Board for England and Wales to oversee the strategic monitoring of the youth justice system (Gelsthorpe and Morris, 2002; Newburn, 2002). The provision of youth justice services was to proceed on the basis of nationally implemented time limits for the administration of justice, national standards, performance targets and the pursuit of 'what works' via 'evidence-based practice' (Muncie and Hughes, 2002). At the local level, Youth Offending Teams (YOTs) were established to coordinate the provision of youth justice services and to facilitate 'joined up', multi-agency and inter-agency working (Newburn, 2002). The 1998 Act also introduced a host of new interventionist powers and sentencing disposals which targeted those perceived to be 'at risk'. Furthermore, it intensified early post-offence intervention, promoted a new correctionalism and expanded and diversified the range of custodial sanctions (Goldson, 2008; Goldson and Muncie, 2006).

The 1998 Act established the hallmarks of New Labour's youth justice policy, introducing a range of complex and contradictory modes of youth governance which combined the neo-liberal imperatives of 'responsibilization', 'managerialism', 'risk management' and 'restorative justice' with the neo-conservative tendencies of 'remoralization' and 'authoritarianism' (Muncie, 2006; see also Muncie and Hughes, 2002). From 1998, Goldson and Muncie (2006: 210) argue, New Labour consistently pursued the 'toughness' agenda and in so doing ensured that a 'diverse and expanding array of strategies has now been made available to achieve the governance of young people' (Muncie, 2006: 787). It is beyond the scope of this chapter to address the 'relentless stream of crackdowns, initiatives, targets, policy proposals, pilot schemes and legislative enactments' that appeared (Muncie, 2006: 771). However, suffice to say that the government's authoritarian pursuit of new powers with regard to the anti-social behaviour, surveillance, incarceration, drug testing, electronic monitoring, and the stopping and searching of children and young people has served to expand and intensify the state's role in regulation, control and punishment. Consequently, as Morgan and Newburn observe:

> Young offenders are today more likely to be criminalised and subject to a greater level of intervention than before the 1998 reforms. If dealt with pre-court their warning is more likely to be accompanied by an intervention. They are more likely to be prosecuted. If convicted they are less likely to receive a discharge or fine. If subject to a community sentence it is more likely to be onerous. And last but not least, ... the number of children and young people sentenced to custody is 35% higher than a few years before the 1998 Act. (2007: 1046–7)

The Authoritarian Pursuit of Anti-social Behaviour

While recognizing that youth justice is a crowded policy space, arguably it is perhaps the issue of 'anti-social' behaviour which has borne the burden of three successive New Labour governments' efforts to appease public concern and secure electoral gain. Engaging in a process of 'regressive modernisation' (Hall, 1988: 2), New Labour have ruthlessly mobilized a nostalgic discourse of community in order to 'crystalise and realise a vision of contemporary social arrangements' (Sim, 2009: 79). 'Community' has become the 'central collective abstraction' (Levitas, 2000: 191) in New Labour's reinvention of its social and criminal justice imperatives, prioritizing the 'mutuality of duty' and the 'reciprocity of respect' (Scraton, 2007a: 75). Chiming 'almost perfectly with the resurgent ethical and Christian socialist wing of the Labour Party' (McLaughlin, 2002: 55), communitarianism, and more specifically Etzioni's (1995) 'moral authoritarian version' (Hughes, 1998: 109), which calls for the renewal and revitalization of community values and community institutions, New Labour' discourse of 'community' has served to 'aid and abet' the 'moralising logic' inherent to its 'broad social policy project' (Hughes 2002b: 129). Herein, community is conceptualized as both a 'moral resource' and 'a moral claimant'. The former sustains individuals in fulfilling their obligations to each other and the community, while in those circumstances where individuals renege on their obligations, the latter prioritizes the community's right to protection. Thus, as a 'moral claimant', it can demand that the wrongdoers live up to their responsibilities or face the possibility of exclusion (Hudson, 2003: 84).

When this moralizing logic is applied to questions of youth crime, disorder and anti-social behaviour, 'the rights and responsibilities are seen flowing in just one direction: towards the community' (Hudson, 2003: 107). This discourse is at its most obvious in the widening of availability and the extension of powers to deal with disorder and 'anti-social' behaviour, as evidenced in the promotion of non-statutory 'acceptable behaviour contracts', 'demotion orders', 'dispersal orders', 'family intervention projects', 'fixed penalty notices', 'parenting orders' and 'anti-social behaviour, injunctions' (Burney, 2005; Goldson, 2008; Walsh, 2002). This intensification of author-itarian control over children's troublesome behaviours raises a host of concerns with regard to due process (Hudson, 2003) and net-widening (Squires and Stephens, 2005), as well as its criminalizing potential (Jamieson, 2006). Furthermore, in view of the government's flirtations with benefit withdrawal (Goldson and Jamieson, 2002) and the threat of eviction (Oliver, 2005), it is clear that those children and families living in the most challenging material circumstances comprise the prime targets of New Labour's anti-social behaviour agenda.

A brief reprieve from the Blair-led onslaught on 'anti-social' behaviour appeared a distinct possibility when Gordon Brown became Prime Minister in June 2007. Concerned that the unremitting Blairite focus on tackling 'anti-social' behaviour would serve to criminalize young people for behaviour that they would grow out of in due course, Brown quickly abandoned the 'Respect' language and rhetoric of his predecessor (Sparrow, 2008), while his closest ally, Ed Balls, Secretary of State for Children, Schools and Families, asserted that 'it's a failure every time a young person gets an Asbo' and that he wanted to live 'in the kind of society which puts Asbos behind us' (*Guardian*, 27 July 2007). Accordingly, the new Home Secretary, Jacqui Smith, urged the greater use of alternative 'early intervention' measures, such as parenting orders, acceptable behaviour contracts and support orders (Travis, 2008). However, the Conservatives were quick to try to reclaim the law and order mantle within Boris Johnson's successful London mayoral campaign by exploiting the electoral potential of the aggravation caused by 'hooliganism' and 'bad behaviour' on the capital's buses and tubes (Sparrow, 2008). Thus, in the wake of the Labour Party's humiliating performance in the local government elections in May 2008, the return to a more authoritarian emphasis within government rhetoric and policy was assured. Indeed, on 8 May 2008 Jacqui Smith reaffirmed the government's commit-ment to tackling the anti-social behaviour of a 'hard core' of trouble-makers and persis-tent offenders via the 'harassment' of 'daily visits, repeated warnings and relentless filming of offenders to create an environment where there is nowhere to hide' (*TimesOnline*, 8 May 2008).

State Power and Youth Justice

Immense transformations have occurred in the British social, political and criminolog-ical landscape since the publication of *Policing the Crisis*. Characterized as representing a particular intervention into a particular debate at a particular historic moment (Clarke, 2008; Jefferson, 2008), a number of reservations have been raised regarding the credibility and resonance of Hall et al.'s analysis in an increasingly diverse and frag-mented contemporary context (Garland, 2008). More specifically, critiques of *Policing the Crisis* have included its refusal to address the realities of criminal victimization, its over-dependence on 'moral panics' to account for the public's concern regarding crime, and its determination to prove the authoritarian 'State Britain' thesis correct (McLaughlin, 2008: 147). Yet it is also apparent that the intensifying crisis that Hall et al. describe has 'never quite been resolved', but rather 'looks deeper, more durable and more complex' (Clarke, 2008: 127–8). We would argue that the issues identified in *Policing the Crisis* continue to speak to contemporary criminological concerns and our overview of youth justice policy over the last thirty years has provided numerous illustrations of the prescient nature of Hall et al.'s analysis regarding the increasingly authoritarian character of the state's use of power to prevent, manage and control youth crime.

Our analysis bears testament to the continuing discursive currency of 'moral panics' with regard to questions of youth crime and youth justice and young people more generally. For example, evidence suggests that the state's increased propensity to 'criminalise, punish and lock up' the young female offender is not reflected in an increased criminality on the part of girls (Gelsthorpe and Sharpe, 2006: 49), but rather it is generated and legitimated by contemporary 'moral panics' regarding girl gangs and the violence and drug use of 'nasty little madams' (Worrall, 2004: 54). Indeed, Goldson and Muncie (2006: 225) assert that the pandering of successive governments to the concerns of a select 'anxious, risk adverse and fearful' public (Goldson and Muncie, 2006: 225), via rhetorical pronouncements such as 'prison works', 'zero tolerance', 'no more excuses' and 'tough on crime', has served to repoliticize[1] youth crime and youth justice since the 1990s (Goldson and Muncie, 2006). This repoliticization has encouraged public attitudes that demonize children and young people (UK Children's Commissioners, 2008) and perpetuated popular punitiveness (Goldson and Muncie, 2006). Moreover, as predicted in *Policing the Crisis*, it has also served to promote the 'routine use of the more oppressive features of the state' (Hall et al., 1978: 320), which by 2004 had earned Britain the dubious title of 'prison capital of Europe' (Morris, 2007), with proportionately more children and young people incarcerated in England and Wales than in any other country in western Europe (Council for Europe, 2004).

Alongside this state authoritarianism, a key feature of social and penal policy over the last thirty years has been a neo-conservative tendency towards remoralization (Muncie, 2006; Muncie and Hughes, 2002). 'Remoralization' imperatives arise from the perception that crime is indicative of the 'break-up of the moral fabric and cohesion of society' (Muncie and Hughes, 2002: 9). These imperatives are reflected in the state's propensity to utilize its disciplinary powers to define, legislate and sanction in relation to the duties and obligations it views as fundamental to the membership rights of a 'law-abiding' citizenship (McLaughlin, 2002). Thus as part of an ongoing project to accomplish the governance of the public sphere (Penna, 2005: 151), crime prevention and early intervention programmes for 'at risk' and offending youth are provided as a means to 'micro-manage' behaviour in order to 'remoralize' the recipients (Muncie, 2006: 782). At the same time, the expansion of coercive and punitive youth justice powers and interventions provide an expressive means by which to demonstrate society's intolerance and to demonstrate to the public that firm measures are in place to deal with criminal and anti-social behaviours (Jamieson, 2006, 2008;

Yates, 2009). Herein, the emphasis on individual responsibility and obligation has served to 'cut off' crime 'from its social roots' (Hall et al., 1978: ix) and to mask the fact that the state – and the 'law-abiding' majority – also have responsibilities, not least the responsibility for ensuring that social justice extends to all, particularly those children and young people whose lived experiences undermine their ability and willingness to become active, respectable, economically contributing and law-abiding citizens (Hudson, 2003; Squires and Stephens, 2005).

Hall et al.'s analysis with regard to the criminalization of black and minority ethic groups, and the racialization of crime, also continues to resonate strongly in the contemporary sphere. Reviews of empirical evidence demonstrate the continuing 'institutional injustices' experienced by black and minority ethnic groups within the contemporary youth justice discourses, policies and practices. In 2007, House of Commons Home Affairs Committee reported that black people were three times more likely to be arrested than their white counterparts, they were just over six times more likely to be stopped and searched by the police and, once charged, black offenders were less likely to receive unconditional bail and more likely to be remanded into custody. The Committee also noted that when sentenced, black and 'mixed ethnicity' young men were more likely to receive more punitive sentences than their white counterparts, while black people of all ages are five times more likely to be in prison than white people. In a similar vein, the committee has noted concern with regard to that fact that three-quarters of the young black male population will soon be on the DNA database in England and Wales (see also Phillips and Bowling, 2007). To complicate questions of race and justice still further, a transforming social and political context has brought to the fore concerns regarding immigration, political asylum, organized crime and terrorism, heightening fears with regard to the threat from the 'enemy within', an enemy that is increasingly personified as a young, male, radicalized, Muslim 'Arab other' (Poynting et al., 2004: 3). The state's response to such threats has been the championing of symbolic and controversial measures, such as extending the maximum time police can hold terror suspects to 42 days (Brown, 2008b), which serve to erode civil liberties and are likely to be selectively targeted, with particular regard to young black and minority ethnic group sections of the population.

Conclusion

Cohen (2002) asserts that the study of 'moral panics' remains an interesting and legitimate means of identifying and conceptualizing the state's tendency to take some things very seriously and others not seriously enough. Our analysis of youth justice policy over the last thirty years suggests that the anxieties and threats associated with marginalized, alien, 'anti-social' and 'criminal' youth, and increasingly 'criminal' children, continue to be refracted through the lens of recurring and re-imagined 'moral panics'. These anxieties and threats are then mobilized by the state to justify its continuing propensity to pursue authoritarian responses in relation to the troublesome and criminal behaviour of children and young people. However, an over-emphasis on the role of 'moral panics' is less illuminating in trying to understand the ideological and material circumstances which give rise to youth crime and anti-social behaviour. In many respects, the lived realities for marginalized young people residing in the economic hinterlands of twenty-first-century Britain are far removed from those experiences described in Hall et al.'s analysis. However, the extent to which their acute experiences of social inequality and disadvantage impact in limiting their life chances and shaping their experiences of crime is not. Thus, in addressing contemporary criminological concerns regarding the emergence of a British gang culture, Pitts (2008: 33) warns that 'sustained exposure to acute social and economic disadvantage spawns forms of crime that have catastrophic effects upon the vulnerable populations amongst whom and against whom they are perpetrated'.

Notwithstanding the contested and inconsistent nature of youth justice over the last thirty years, it is clear that the state's gaze and reach with regard to issues of youth crime and anti-social behaviour has intensified. This focus has combined with an increasingly punitive stance with regard to those who stand outside normative moral and social values (Chesney-Lind, 2006) to expose ever younger and wider constituencies of children – and increasingly their parents – to a rapidly diversifying array of preventative, early, correctional and punitive interventions (Goldson, 2008). Indeed, the eagerly anticipated return to welfare values associated with the Brown premiership has failed to materialize. Rather, the government's most recent foray into youth justice policy, in the form of the *Youth Crime Action Plan* (*YCAP*), published in July 2008, outlines a 'triple-track' approach of 'tough enforcement, non-negotiable support and challenge and prevention to tackle problems before they escalate' (Secretary of State for the Home Department et al., 2008: para. 26). In further extending existing youth justice provision, the implementation of the *YCAP* promises that 'interventions will be sooner, more pervasive and more intensive' (Broadhurst et al., forthcoming). Yet the expansionist drift that has marked the present government's reform of youth justice has not proved significantly successful in preventing youth crime (Solomon and Garside, 2008). Moreover, given the government's substantial investment in youth justice has involved the diversion of significant resources from areas of social spending, most notably health, education and social services, serious questions inevitably arise regarding the capacity of youth justice agencies to address the complex economic and social factors which underlie much youth offending (ibid.).

However, the history of youth justice is a 'history of active and passive resistance' where the 'translation of policy into practice depends on how it is visioned and reworked (or made to work) by those empowered to put it into practice' (Muncie, 2004: 275; see also Coleman et al., this volume). Certainly, the progressive hiatus that occurred in the 1980s within youth justice in a 'blind spasm of control' (Hall, cited in Scraton, 2003: 1) suggests that wholesale pessimism with regard to the future of youth justice may be misplaced. Indeed, a range of recent studies have suggested that the general public are not as punitive in their attitudes to offenders as the media, politicians and public officials would have us believe (Bottoms and Wilson, 2004; Maruna and King 2004; Roberts and Hough, 2005). At the same time, a range of persuasive (Davies and McMahon, 2007; Goldson and Muncie, 2006) and high-profile critiques (UK Children's Commissioners, 2008) of the demonizing, damaging and ultimately counter-productive impacts of youth justice discourse policy and practice have served to question the legitimacy and desirability of the extant author-itarian system. It is in the presence and persistence of these dissenting voices that the promise of a more holistic, inclusive and 'principled' approach to youth crime and youth justice may be found in the future (see Goldson and Muncie, 2006).

Key Reading

Goldson, B. and Muncie, J. (eds) (2006) *Youth Crime and Justice*. London: Sage.

Muncie, J. (2009) *Youth and Crime: A Critical Introduction* (3rd edn). London/Thousand Oaks/New Delhi: Sage Publications.

Muncie, J. and Hughes, G. (2002) 'Modes of Youth Governance: Political rationalities, criminalization and resistance', in J. Muncie, G. Hughes and E. McLaughlin (eds), *Youth Justice: Critical Readings*, London: Sage. pp. 1–18.

Pitts, J. (2001) *The New Politics of Youth Crime: Discipline or Solidarity?* Lyme Regis: Russell House Publishing.

Scraton, P. (ed.) (1997) *Childhood in Crisis?* London: UCL Press.

Smith, R. (2007) *Youth Justice: Ideas, Policy and Practice* (2nd edition). Cullompton: Willan.

Note

1   Questions could be raised regarding the extent to which talk of a 'repoliticization' of youth justice in the 1990s is entirely appropriate. While it is apparent that this refers to the extent to which youth justice and youth crime were utilized for electoral advan-tage and occupied a central space in the electoral strategies of both the main political parties, it could be argued that use of the term 'repoliticization' implies an apolitical approach to youth justice immediately preceding this period. However, as we have illustrated, the bifurcation discussed by Pratt (1989), and in particular the treatment of black youth by the criminal justice system, whether formally or informally, could be seen to provide an illustration of the highly politicized nature of youth justice. Repoliticization in this sense could be seen to represent an intensification in the extent to which youth crime, and youth justice responses to it, were mobilized by the main political parties during the period rather than the absence of the politics of race, class and gender inequality in the period preceding it.

6

POWER, POLITICS AND THE WELFARE STATE

Chris Jones and Tony Novak

──────────────── **Introduction** ────────────────

We have been looking at British social policies for over thirty years. It is an area that provides a rich context for exploring and understanding the role of the state. There are some good reasons why this is so. From its origins, the modern British state has been involved in social legislation and provision as ways have been sought to overcome, or at least contain, social problems and reproduce a social order beset with difficulties and contradictions. In this way the state has attempted to carry out its most elemental function – the reproduction of the existing social and economic system. But in a society riven by inequalities and their consequent miseries, and challenged by alternative visions, struggles and protest, this has not been an easy matter.

The social policies that have preoccupied us have been those which have focused primarily on the most disadvantaged and impoverished. These are, and remain, highly sensitive areas for any capitalist society. The continual reproduction of poverty and inequality poses many challenges to developed capitalist societies, not least since the lives distorted and corroded by poverty challenge fundamentally any meaningful notion of a civilized and decent society.

Foremost in the reasons for the state's development of its social policy in Britain, as in other capitalist societies, has been its concern with securing a labour market and the reproduction of a working class. For the most part, the need to work – and especially to work under conditions of exploitation in jobs that offer little meaning and reward – has been a matter of economic necessity (although this, too, for example in its poor laws, is something the state was crucial in helping bring about, see Novak, 1988). But labour discipline is about more than just the need to work to keep alive; it is also about people's capacity for and attitudes towards work. State social policy has played a crucial role here and has, for the working class, a long history of making all alternatives to waged work highly unattractive.

At the same time, the state has been confronted with the problem of what to do with those unable to work. Often the most vulnerable and the poorest, their treatment at the hands of the state has, for the most part, seen their needs sacrificed in favour of using them to set an example to others. The punishment of the poorest as a means to discipline the merely poor majority is one of the enduring features of the state's dealings with poverty.

Of course, and especially over the last half-century, the so-called 'welfare state' has come to impact on a large part of the population and not only the poorest. But we argue that it is in its dealings with the most disadvantaged that the state reveals its preoccupation with sustaining capitalism and securing a highly unequal and unjust social order. Social policy is consequently a site of class tensions and conflict. It has been, and continues to be, a place where the powerful confront and are confronted by the powerless. The four major turning points of British social policy, the 1830s and 1840s, the period from 1880 to 1914, the decades following the Second World War, and the rise of neo-liberalism since the mid-1970s, the latter marked presciently by Hall et al. (1978), are all characterized by moments of intense confrontation, the partial resolution of which has resulted in major changes in social policy.

The first period, in the wake of an unprecedented process of industrialization that tore people from the land, established factories and a working class to work in them, heralded a 'New' Poor Law (the old having served its purpose to help ease the destruction of feudal and peasant production). Its workhouses, known popularly as Bastilles, its principles of deterrence, its cruel grind dominated the experience of poverty for over a century and framed British social policy for its subsequent development.

By the 1880s an industrial working class had grown up, in towns and in cities, with trades unions and other organizations and a thirst for something better; the economy too rode the heights of the British Empire, and a different approach was called for. In the period before the First World War, the basic structures and principles of today's welfare state were laid down. These included a fastidious attention to administrative detail to ensure that wage labour was not undermined, firm control in the hands of state agencies and minimal provision of material aid under strict conditions.

The subsequent collapse of the economy in the depression of the 1930s intensified conflicts, as well as poverty, but was saved by the Second World War and its extraordinary aftermath. There would be no return to the chaos and misery of previous years, people decided, and they called for a rational and planned way of doing things. Thirty uninterrupted years of economic growth would pay for a welfare state that would expand into all areas of people's lives.

But the welfare state created problems, for rich and poor alike, although in different ways. Since 1979 the fourth wave of social policy development has spread its icy waters as neo-liberalism in the form of both Conservative and Labour governments has tried, with considerable success, to roll back the welfare state, re-establish the primacy of the market, and shift the balance of power by clawing back the minimalist concessions granted in the aftermath of the Second World War. Moreover, as we see below, it was a roll-back accompanied by an extension of disciplinary intervention into the lives of vulnerable people.

An Interventionist State?

The naïve capitalist (probably in the majority) dreams of a world without regulation, where no taxes are paid, and where the market can go about its business without the need of a state. But it has never been thus. A market is an unstable system: it rises and falls; it is unpredictable; millions may be thrown out of work, many more impoverished. A market does not guarantee – on the contrary – a population that is healthy, or even at least capable of doing its work, or that it has the necessary literacy and knowledge. The state has always played a steering and supporting role in developing the 'free market', and as capitalism has developed the state's role has increased.

But in what ways the state should intervene, and how far, is a matter of political struggle and context. Historically, the dominant view (that is, the view of the dominant group) was that state intervention on behalf of the poor was anathema (even while the dominant group might and did benefit from state intervention). It would distort the working of the market (including, of course, the important market in labour), create dependency, and demoralize its recipients.

State intervention increased enormously throughout the nineteenth century. It built workhouses throughout the country and established a national Poor Law system as its key instrument of social policy. As far as the poor were concerned, it was wholly punitive. As Sir George Nicholls, one of the three Commissioners appointed to implement the 1834 Poor Law Amendment Act, put it:

> I wish to see the Poor House looked to with dread by the labouring classes, and the reproach for being an inmate of it extend down from father to son. … For without this, where is the needful stimulus to industry? (cited in Poynter, 1969: 314)

In the 1880s, the leaders of the influential Charity Organisation Society (COS) wrote and agitated among their own class that any state provision other than the most minimal and necessarily authoritarian would literally demoralize the working class (Jones, 1983). The poorest they argued would not have any reason to seek paid work (especially poorly paid and under harsh conditions) and they would quickly become long-term dependents on the state. It is noteworthy that the COS was appalled by the explosion of charitable activity by the wealthy during the latter part of the nineteenth century as a response to manifest suffering in Britain's major cities. They condemned this 'emotionalism' as anti-capitalist in that it provided a source of succour independent of the labour market and argued that compassion had no role to play in the provision of welfare.

However, while this non-interventionist approach would continue to resurface, and with a vengeance after 1979, by the beginning of the twentieth century it was untenable. The social and political threat of a working class radicalized over the treatment of unemployment, poverty and destitution compelled state intervention. At the beginning of the twentieth century this pressure was also accompanied by an ever-growing awareness that destructive aspects of the market were also threatening the future. The Boer War conscription, for example, revealed a majority of working-class young men as being too feeble and ill for armed service. Thus questions were raised about Britain's capacity to defend Empire and its population's fitness for work in general. This conjuncture of political unrest with deep anxieties about the reproduction of a labour force capable of competing with Germany and the USA prompted a flurry of state initiatives from support to those considered the deserving unemployed through old-age pensions and unemployment insurance to the introduction of school meals and physical education in schools.

These new forms of state welfare, which sat alongside the punitive Poor Law, were designed explicitly to assist only the 'deserving' poor: largely, the more regularly employed, skilled and organized sections of the working class. Even these 'gains' were subject to stigmatizing conditions regarding eligibility and were minimalist in terms of the assistance offered. That the poorest were largely excluded gives a lie to a widely promulgated view that these reforms were a product of a new welfare humanitarianism.

At that time, the professional and middle-class Fabian Society was among the most vociferous and successful advocates of an interventionist social state. The Empire alone demanded an imperial working class at home and, according to the Fabians, only the state had the reach and the resources capable of meeting the challenges of poverty and political unrest. Furthermore, in answer to their critics (concentrated in the COS), they maintained that state social policy, applied by specialists and those appropriately educated in places such as their London School of Economics, would not only ensure the material reproduction of a workforce but could enhance social stability. Whereas the COS were insistent that the state's involvement in material welfare – school meals, pensions, unemployment benefits, and so forth – would *always* demoralize its recipients, the Fabians insisted that this could be prevented by efficient and close social administration under the control of specially trained professionals. The Fabians had great confidence that the emerging social sciences would do for social issues what the natural sciences had done for manufacturing. It was a belief that gathered momentum throughout the first half of the twentieth century and had a significant impact on ensuring that state social policies were never subject to meaningful democratic control but left to the 'experts' in state agencies.

More positive state intervention in the relief of poverty and the provision of welfare, although inevitable, was nevertheless reluctant, partial and hedged with conditions. After 1945, state intervention in people's lives grew enormously, but the expansion of welfare services remained by and large differentiated. With the limited exception of the National Health Service (and for that reason by far the most popular strand of the post-war welfare state), the conditions imposed for receipt of services and the differing forms and styles of provision served to reinforce divisions and inequalities of 'race', gender and class. For the majority of the population the welfare state brought limited benefits and some major contradictions. True, it involved, as intended, a pooling of risks: individuals were less exposed to the full impact of the deadly vagaries of the free market and for the poorest this was a significant improvement. But in general, the cost of the welfare state fell on the working class themselves and economic redistribution remained limited. At the same time, in so far as they remained in the control of the state, welfare services served the interests of the existing order, hence no redistribution of power. Thus schools provided a schooled rather than an educated population, while state schooling and its pernicious selection policies distorted the lives of many children. And if the NHS ensured a workforce less prone to previously common sicknesses such as TB, it never followed the principles of public health, such as espoused by the Peckham health initiative with its local and democratic control (Scott-Samuel, 1990). Nowhere did the welfare state fundamentally challenge the capitalist order and the improvements in life chances were more a result of post-war economic growth than social policy.

If the realities of the post-1945 welfare state were at best paradoxical for the working class, being a mix of gains and losses, politicians of all the major political parties and much of the media sought to portray the welfare state as a symbol of Britain's new-found commitment to justice and compassion. Its 'gains' were inflated out of all proportion as marking a step towards a more just and egalitarian society. It was no surprise, therefore, that economic decline in the 1970s – combined with the loss of Empire (Hall et al., 1978) – provided a key opportunity for an ascendant political right to scapegoat the welfare state as being one of the primary causes of economic, political and moral decline.

The election of Margaret Thatcher in 1979 heralded an ideological onslaught on state welfare. State intervention, it was argued, had gone too far. People had come to expect too much of the state, and were now to be put in their place. But the neo-liberal state is no less a form of intervention. Rather, it is an intervention of a different kind, with the regulatory and disciplinary powers of the state being extended at the expense of its welfare role.

The Poor are Different

Since the branding of the poor with the letter 'V' for vagrant in the middle ages, the poorest, because they are the poorest, experience the harshest side of welfare (Novak, 1988). This has been especially so for the unemployed, whose proximity to the labour market has evoked some of the most heartless forms of discipline, in return for the lowest level of benefit, to keep them 'in readiness' for work.

But the punishment of the poor is counted not only in the inadequacies of benefit levels or overt legislation, it is also part of the fabric of how social welfare is delivered. Some would argue that it is the experience of being in receipt of welfare that is most corrosive on the well-being of recipients (Wilkinson, 1996). From the workhouse to today's social security benefits, the social relations of state social policy have been dominated by disrespect. To be dependent on welfare means losing control to state agencies; it involves letting the state into one's most intimate relationships and homes, of securing every detail of one's financial affairs undertaken in ways which are demeaning and stigmatizing. And for what? The services offered are minimal and in many cases, especially in institutional care, brutalizing.

Through its legislation, and operationalized by an array of agencies and welfare professionals, the state has actively promoted a notion that the poor are 'different' from the rest of the population. Macnicol (1987: 296), writing specifically about the 'underclass' – a neo-liberal concept aimed at restating the notion that the poor are responsible for their poverty – noted that over the past hundred years there has been a striking continuity in the stereotypes applied to the most impoverished as a people 'remaining outwith the boundaries of citizenship, alienated from cultural norms and stubbornly impervious to the normal incentives of the market, social work intervention or state welfare'. The vocabularies have changed – from the undeserving poor, to the residuum, to problem families, the underclass and now the socially excluded. There has been some vacillation as to whether these deficiencies are due to biology or family socialization. But constant throughout is the view that the poorest are different, inferior and, if left to their own devices, constitute an 'anti-social' nuisance.

Such stereotypes mean that there is no need to interrogate what is entailed in living without sufficient resources, or exposed to the negative gaze of the state through its teachers, nurses, social workers and the like, or in living in neighbourhoods chronically stigmatized and deprived of quality resources. The deficits of the poor are considered to be so patent that it is taken as given that they can have nothing worth saying. Repeated reorganizations of state social agencies over the past fifty years have all signally failed to consider the perspectives or experiences of the poorest. Yet for those on the receiving end of insults and abuse, the pain is palpable, as John Pilger revealed during his discussion with Amy and Trisha, two single mothers living on welfare:

> '… Scroungers' said Amy. 'It's a hateful thing to call us, and it's not true. They don't *know* how hard we try to get jobs; they don't know that you're turned down the moment they know you've been in care. They don't know how few jobs there are and what a con a lot of them are' … Amy seems close to tears. (Pilger, 1998: 103)

Yet perhaps, like the workers in Campbell Bunk – the worst street in north London (White, 1986) – the attitudes and actions of the poor are not pathological but rather rooted in experience. Their unwillingness to take any work is not an imperviousness to the market but a reflection of their view that some waged work – on account of its poor pay and working conditions – is simply an affront to their humanity. Likewise, the reluctance of many working-class mothers to engage with New Labour's Sure Start programme (supposedly non-stigmatizing) is not related to their lack of concern over their children's welfare but quite the contrary: many mothers in the most deprived areas targeted by Sure Start do not trust the state with their children and (rightly) fear that negative stereotyping of their status and geography will jeopardize their children's place in their families (Foster, 2005).

The extreme stigmatizing of young, unemployed single mothers has meant that many feel that the state – whether through Sure Start or social work – will judge them negatively and thereby jeopardize their rights to parenthood. Equally telling has been the way in which Sure Start itself has been changed. According to Norman Glass, one of its architects, Sure Start:

Started off as a family support programme for parents in deprived areas has [now] become a programme in which the important thing is to get people to work, with a focus on child care services and employability. (*Times Educational Supplement*, 15 April 2005)

Not surprisingly, as White noted, with respect to Campbell Bunk, the residents' hostility to the state was:

more a reaction against authority, the forces of rejection, than a resistance to self-discipline. ... It was a feeling that no one had the right to order you about, at least in a way which threatened a dignity already over-sensitive from the processes of out-casting. (1986: 104)

But outcasting remains central to the state's management of the poor. It is imperative, under capitalism at least, that the problem of poverty is deemed to be a problem of the poor and not that of the wider socio-economic system. Hence the state does not do sympathy or trust, at least as far as the poorest are concerned. It is specialized in control, surveillance and the provision of poor quality services to poor populations. This is true across the spectrum of state social policy from housing through to schooling. And it is now evident that the neo-liberal state is intent on turning the authoritarian screw that much tighter. The neo-liberals, although for the wrong reasons, have long recognized the ineffectiveness of social democratic welfare initiatives. Growing numbers of social workers and probation officers, justified on the basis that they would rid society of many troubles, including juvenile offending, did no such thing. In fact, rather than keep the young in their families, the growth in welfare professionals seemed to fuel the growth of children 'coming into care'. For the neo-liberals this is all taken as evidence that the 'underclass' or the excluded are incapable of being helped. This was well put by Robert Whelan, an assistant director of the right-wing Institute of Economic Affairs: 'the notion that the deficit can be made good by a raft of public bodies is surely too mad to take seriously now' (*Community Care*, Jan./Feb. 2000, Issue 1306: 14).

That the state has encountered little sustained opposition to its authoritarian drift, whether through parenting orders, Asbos, tagging and curfew, or the eviction of 'nuisance' tenants, is in part due to the class specificity of its proposals. These measures are simply not applied to more prosperous neighbourhoods and populations. Their children will not be drawn into the criminal justice system under the age of 10; they will not be Asboed, they will not encounter the endless ways in which the prison with its razor wire and CCTVs and endless locks and gates has penetrated today's abandoned people and areas. Neither will they be swept off to prison.

Class Fractures

Social policy has over time deepened existing ruptures within the working class. Differences created by the labour market, such as between men's and women's work, skill, age or 'race', have been reinforced by differential benefits and treatment to different segments of workers and the unemployed, and especially to those with only a marginal contact with the labour market. It was not until the 1970s that the centuries-old inferior status of women within social security was eventually addressed, although discrimination remains. The welfare state's general mistreatment of black and ethnic minority populations – not least as legacy of Empire – still reinforces their subordination. Images and stereotypes, frequently relayed through the operation of welfare services themselves, help cement these divisions.

This ideological dimension justifies divisive policies largely on the grounds of moralism overlaid with social Darwinism. In other words, those who get least deserve less because they are not deemed worthy citizens. Hence, state welfare contributes to the formation and reproduction of a moral economy with success and defeat attributed to largely individual characteristics, with the less worthy naturally 'sinking' to the bottom. These processes have a brutalizing impact and have over time established a commonly held perception that enduring poverty and distress is primarily a consequence of individual and familial pathology.

Class solidarities have not simply been fractured by capitalism, but have also been a consequence of sectional class politics which have characterized the British 'labour movement'. The primacy accorded by the Labour party and many trade unions to the interests of the most skilled working people – taken up by the state too – was justified by the sort of moralizing familiar in state social policies. Their long subordination of women, minority ethnic populations and those with a marginal relationship to the labour market has mirrored elite opinion and sometimes gone further. The increasingly geographical separation of the most vulnerable in inner-city ghettoes or 'sink' estates has been too often welcomed by more affluent working households, who have no wish to share space with those they too deem to be 'wasters', villains and degenerate. It is in this context that state social policy's divide-and-rule approach operates, deepening longstanding stereotypes and class fractures.

A Different Kind of Welfare

Engaging with the state is always problematic and paradoxical for those who are at the 'wrong end' of capitalism. On the one hand, they are in need of state assistance but, on the other, they despair at their treatment by state agencies and officials. For this reason, they have often sought other forms of 'welfare' that reveal very different capacities and priorities (Jones and Novak, 2000).

During the nineteenth century workers created a wide array of their own support systems. Friendly Societies and trade unions were formed in part to provide assistance for their members in the event of unemployment and ill health. Sick clubs and burial clubs provided a popular alternative to the despised Poor Law. Self-education flourished in working-class schools, reading rooms and libraries long before any state provision (Simon, 1974). Despite the partiality of many of these initiatives they were nevertheless independent of the state and based on key welfare principles such as mutual aid and class solidarity (Ward, 2000).

The very existence of these various forms of independent working-class self-help and mutual aid was itself to be a decisive motive for the state's intervention and provision of welfare. Not surprisingly, the encroachment of the state in these areas provoked considerable debate and division. These debates were about the very capacity of the state to act unconditionally in the interests of the less powerful and to bring about meaningful reform that would enhance their well-being. George Holyoake of the co-operative movement trenchantly argued that the capitalist state could never be the 'friend' of the working class. As far as these activists were concerned, the state had shown through the Poor Law a cruel disregard for the welfare and support of the destitute. Indeed, the state had no 'ears for the poor' and its involvement in social measures would always be tainted and be administered in ways which would compromise class well-being.

Instead, Holyoake and many others argued for the development of an active working-class self-help movement, creating for themselves institutions and practices that met their needs and aspirations, whereby workers 'took their affairs into their own hands, and what is more to the point ... kept them in their own hands' (Holyoake, cited in Bonner, 1961: 41).

While state intervention was eventually to undermine and replace many of these initiatives, it is important to note that the tradition of working-class self-help has never died away. In diverse organizations, from residents groups, housing co-ops, community action, youth groups, literacy and evening/weekend schools, there continues to be abundant evidence of working-class self-organization which is not predicated on pathologizing the poor, and which seek to enhance well-being. There are echoes here of the 'centres of self-management' and the 'democratic organs at the base' which Poulantzas, among others, has seen as one key element in the struggle for a democratic socialism (Poulantzas, 1978b: 251–65).

As we ourselves witnessed during the 1984/85 miners' strike, welfare systems don't need to threaten dignity, even in the most extreme circumstances. Miners' wives and their supporters created an extraordinary welfare system which sustained the strike over many difficult months as the strikers felt the brunt of Margaret Thatcher's anti-union legislation and the withdrawal of benefits (Jones and Novak, 1985). It included the important provision of food, clothing and cash to meet pressing demands. It was a system that was rooted in the communities and that took heed of their morale as well as their material needs. When has the social security thrown a party because people were feeling low? When has state welfare been based on mutuality and trust and where it doesn't cost you your dignity or rights to privacy because you need a cash loan?

The Professional Welfare State

In its concern to limit and de-legitimize popular welfare from below, state welfare interventions embraced professionalism. Social policy was deemed to be so sensitive and liable to 'corrupting' populism that it had to be removed from the public domain to that of state certified and regulated professionals. Experience of democratically elected School Boards and later Poor Law Boards, where radical working-class representatives were able to secure significant control and begin to reshape policy, had alarmed the state as much as the earlier plethora of working-class-run schools (Lavalette, 2006). Hence from the beginning of the twentieth century, just as the right to vote was extended, the state increasingly required that its social policies be removed from democratic control and be placed in the hands of 'experts' and professionals.

The consequences of this domination were varied but it meant that the policies and practices implemented invariably represented the perspective of the professionals involved. Hence large hospitals were designed and built according to the influence of the consultants and not patients. In social services, there was even a time when social workers argued that the pathology of their clients meant that they were unable to define or understand their own problems (Mayer and Timms, 1970). Social work infantilized and abused its clients, as typified by this popular student text:

> Over and over again one senses, beneath a hostile veneer, an oral character; a client who never stops demanding. … The dependency is pervasive and the client sucks from neighbours, shopkeepers, bartenders and news vendors as well as family members and social workers. (Richan and Mendelsohn, 1973: 15)

It is hardly surprising, then, that when the welfare state came under siege from the rising tide of neo-liberalism from the mid-1970s onwards that few of the users and clients of services rallied to their cause. For many, the so-called welfare state was part of their problem and not part of their solution. It was stigmatizing, humiliating, deeply prying into their personal lives and with considerable power to cause major disruption. In so doing, it privileged only the professionals and experts who, with their degrees and diplomas and ensconced in state agencies, were deemed to be the only true scientific arbiters of a wide range of social problems and issues. It seemed, as one critic of this process noted, that unless you were appropriately certificated you had no right to comment on your housing, your roads, your children's schooling, your health needs and certainly not your poverty (Wootton, 1959).

The rule of the experts/professionals, which was such a feature of British social policy development for nearly a hundred years, also became a major battle ground in the neo-liberal transformation of the state's welfare system. It is a conflict which reveals much about the character of the contemporary neo-liberal state in Britain.

Given that the welfare professions have tended to recruit overwhelmingly from the liberal middle classes, it is no surprise that a minority have espoused a critical perspective on the limits of state welfare, have connected capitalism with poverty and inequalities, and demanded fundamental change to the prevailing system. To listen to some right-wing critics of state welfare one could be forgiven for thinking that such radicals constituted the majority of those employed in state welfare agencies. In reality, they have always been a tiny minority whose influence and impact has been limited. Much more troubling to the neo-liberal project was the more profound reluctance of state professionals to forgo some of their limited professional autonomy over their work. This is what is demanded by the shift to a more resource-limited, targeted and hence more managerially controlled state welfare system. The introduction of audits and inspections, often with subsequent league tables and real resource implications, have been key tools in the armoury of the new managerialism which shapes the conduct of welfare professionals and thereby encroaches on their limited autonomy.

Teachers, doctors, social workers, probation officers, nurses and other state professionals have seen major changes in employment contracts, status, security and professional training over the past thirty years. For many, these changes have been overwhelmingly negative (Jones, 2001). They involved, among other developments, the state taking increased control over the content of professional training, usually with the intent of removing all those elements which might lead to critical or independent thinking. Feminist and anti-racist scholarship within the social sciences has been especially scrutinized and diluted in the professional curricula of social work, teaching and nursing.

The consequences have been telling. Teachers now find that much of their work with children in schools is closely determined by the demands of a centrally imposed national curriculum, backed up by regular audits. Likewise in social work and probation, national guidelines and regular external inspections proscribe professional activity. Managerial supervision sets the tone of much of the day-to-day work, combined with intense scrutiny over budgets and resources. This in turn has been compounded by the shift towards a supply- rather than a needs-based approach to social policy. This involves central government allocating resources (supply) which it determines are adequate but which are not based on an assessment of need. Hence, state social policy agencies commonly confront the situation where their resources are not adequate, which leads to elaborate and highly controlled allocation procedures.

Many welfare professionals complain bitterly of being effectively proletarianized and bemoan the loss of their previous privileges of having at least some control over their work. But as always, the principal losers are those on the receiving end. There has been an evaporation of service provision and what remains is more tightly regulated, less generous and subject to increasing conditions. Little or nothing positive is provided by the state, which seems more intent on gathering vast amounts of information about the poor and especially their (increasingly, 'anti-social', then criminalized) children.

Increasingly, it feels as if Britain is returning to the old Poor Law days of the nineteenth century. Britain now prides itself on having a 'lean and mean' approach when it comes to the well-being of its most vulnerable citizens. There is certainly no sustained political pressure on the state to modify its approach. There is also little in the way of labour market pressure given the regular supply of young migrant workers (undocumented or otherwise) who are considered as far more pliant workers than those condemned to sink estates and worse. As for the latter, Nick Davies observed:

Looking at them from a strictly economic point of view, [they] are worthless. More than that they are an expensive burden – at least they will be if they are properly housed and clothed and fed, if they are going to be given decent schools and hospitals. So, why bother? ... They are worth nothing; they will be given the bare minimum. (Davies, 1997: 299–300)

State Violence

Lenin remarked that the very existence of a state is predicated on a form of violence and the wielding of power by one class over another. In the field of social policy, this violence has never been far away. At times it has been blatant, at others more muted through an ideology of 'caring' for the poor, or 'welfare'. But it has always been there, ready to regulate, discipline or punish those who do not or refuse to conform. For the very poorest, it has been a fairly constant feature of life dependent on the state.

Political responses to the 'crisis of hegemony' (Hall et al., 1978: viii) saw the abandonment of welfare ideologies evident between 1945 and 1975 and a shift to a more minimalist and authoritarian social policy, especially since 1979. Poverty is not only blamed on the poor, but is now seen to require the negative intervention of the state if its consequences are to be controlled. The time of excessive confidence in armies of highly trained professionals to improve the social order, and especially transform the poorest from welfare dependents into active citizens, have long passed. What few 'positive' interventions remain are increasingly targeted on the very young, and even there the state has incorporated disciplinary procedures should the 'softer' approach fail to ensure the appropriate involvement of parents and carers. At the same time – and it is not by coincidence – the gap between the rich and the poor has soared. Inequality in Britain, not only of income and wealth, but also of life expectancy, health and other indices of well-being, is now as great as it was in the nineteenth century and the British state is developing a welfare system to match.

Whether this is sustainable remains to be seen. In the past, the naked operation of market forces, the absence of social protection and the strife and misery this provoked forced a reaction which saw the expansion in state social policy. The fracturing of class solidarity, the shackling of trade unions and the individualization of social life has allowed much of that social policy to be reduced and transformed. Currently, one-third of the population live in poverty, mostly dependent on the state, and another third struggle day by day, often by taking multiple jobs, to avoid the same fate. At the same time, the rich flout their extraordinary incomes and new-found wealth, aided in part by the cuts in social spending which fund their tax concessions. It is an unstable and volatile situation.

This is not a peculiarly British phenomenon (Wacquant, 2008). The violence of neo-liberalism is felt increasingly globally, particularly in the least developed countries where a 'staggering 78.2 per cent of urbanites ... fully a third of the global urban population' now live in slums (Davis, 2006: 23). Moreover, Davis argues, 'there is no official scenario for the incorporation of this vast mass of surplus labour into the mainstream of the world, economy' (2006: 199). Britain and the USA seem to be setting a pattern for much of the world, with the state investing in an array of strategies which point to the abandonment of any sense that these 'surplus' populations can or should be incorporated. Hare's (2005) recent account of life for a group of 'excluded' children in Leeds provides graphic insight into the tragic consequences of such an approach.

While this grim scenario unfolds globally, on two points we can be sure. One is that until we eradicate any notion that the poorest are different and responsible for their plight, then the outlook will long continue to be grim. Second, we should never expect any state form under capitalism to be a vehicle for humane and respectful social welfare; as many of the poor have long recognized, the state is part of the problem and not part of the solution.

Key Reading

Hare, B. (2005) *Urban Grimshaw and the Shed Crew.* London: Hodder and Staughton.
Jones, C. and Novak, T. (1999) *Poverty, Welfare and the Disciplinary State.* London: Routledge.
Lavalette, M. and Mooney, G. (eds) (2000) *Class Struggle and Social Welfare.* London: Routledge.
Wilkinson, R. (1996) *Unhealthy Societies.* London: Routledge.

7

THE STATE AND CORPORATE CRIME

Steve Tombs and David Whyte

Introduction

> The 'present conditions', which make the poor poor (or the criminal take to crime) are precisely the same conditions which make the rich rich (or allow the law-abiding to imagine that the social causes of crime will disappear if you punish individual criminals hard enough). (Hall et al., 1978: x)

This disarmingly simple statement from *Policing the Crisis* (*PtC*) brims full of suggestion – though never developed by the text's authors and, however well received the text has been over the thirty years since its publication, the ideas in this statement have been subsequently ignored by almost all of what passes for criminology, despite the exponential growth in academic activity in that discipline during those thirty years. Criminology, despite all of the overtures and gestures towards corporate crime, remains constrained by the straitjacket of state-defined crime (Barton et al., 2007). Yet if we are to understand how crime and criminal justice keep the poor poor, we need to understand how they also keep the rich rich.

In *Policing the Crisis*, a notion of the 'autonomization' of the law and the state put on the agenda the dialectical relationship that is expressed both in the law's hegemonic role as a support to capital, and its tendency to intervene *against* capital when necessary as a means of absorbing and diffusing conflict. *Policing the Crisis* therefore located questions of 'crime' and 'criminalization' within Marxist debates on the relative autonomy of the state (see pp. 109–13). While *Policing the Crisis* marked out much of the conceptual terrain necessary for an adequate analysis of the state, corporate crime and regulation, this was not the task its authors had set themselves. Nor has this task been taken up by subsequent scholars, despite the unfolding of the crisis of hegemony within which Hall et al. located the new politics of law and order, and which was to change radically the terrain upon which issues of corporate crime and its regulation could be thought about and analysed.

One of the few efforts to think through these issues, Reiman's *The Rich Get Richer and the Poor Get Prison* (1979), emerged contemporaneously to *Policing the Crisis*.

Reiman sought to develop a Marxist 'response' to Sutherland's critique of the class-biased nature of criminal justice (1979: 129) by using the metaphor of the carnival mirror to show how the categories established by criminal law and the practices of criminal justice agencies distort out of all recognition our understandings of the most dangerous and harmful criminal and anti-social behaviours (1979: 56).

Just prior to *Policing the Crisis*, Pearce (1973, 1976) argued that representations of the 'crime problem' in the USA were fundamentally distorted. One of the key tasks of this work was to explore the nature of the US capitalist economy, not least in terms of what was presented as the coexistence of, on the one hand, an 'imaginary' and, on the other, a 'real' social order. In *Crimes of the Powerful: Marxism, Crime and Deviance* (1976), Pearce placed the phenomenon of corporate crime – its nature, scale, opportunity structure, 'regulation', and relative invisibility – within this disjuncture between 'the way things are supposed to happen and what actually occurs' (Pearce, 1976: 79–80). Both Reiman and Pearce showed how, in different ways, the state projects through the law an imaginary order in which 'crime' is invariably something that is the responsibility of the poor. In order to reveal the 'real' legal order of things, we needed to understand how the law and its institutions upheld a formally equal order, which in reality projected one law for the rich and another for the poor.

It is to a consideration of some of these issues that this chapter is devoted. We begin by reviewing briefly the neo-liberal hegemonic reconstruction regarding state–corporate relationships, and then turn to examine the adequacy of the dichotomy between the interventionist and *laissez-faire* state as a characterization of these relationships. We then turn to a more specific focus upon the dominant discourses through which regulation has been theorized, before arguing that state–corporate relationships, not least in terms of regulation, need to be considered not in terms of an external relationship, but rather via their complex interdependence. We briefly illustrate some of our key themes with reference to a case study of the UK construction industry, before discussing the implications of this analysis for rethinking the relationship between states and the production of corporate crime.

Hegemony and the Corporation

To re-read *Policing the Crisis* is, in many respects, to be reminded of a very different era – not least, in terms of the manifest role of corporations both nationally and internationally. The terms 'privatization', 'neo-liberalism' and 'globalization' were barely present in mainstream academic, let alone political and social discourse. While there had, by the 1970s, certainly long been a debate about the irresponsibility of multinational corporations, this remained overwhelmingly cast in terms of inequalities between North and South. And if the control of the corporate sector raised itself as a domestic issue, the scale of this task, given the reconfigured balance of economic activity between public and private sectors, and the inter-penetration of domestic economies by overseas capital, appeared qualitatively and quantitatively different from that facing us today.

In the UK, state provision of goods, services and employment within a mixed economy remained widespread in 1978. Who would have imagined then that water, gas, electricity, pensions, health care, medical and unemployment insurance, higher education and, of course, criminal justice, would all, to greater or lesser extents, be purchased in some form of 'private' marketplace? These are truly seismic changes in the organization of economic and social life. Corporations now affect – or, more appropriately, *infect* – every area of our lives, shaping our lives, quite literally, from cradle to grave, from womb to dust.

If corporations are key actors with enormous economic, political and social power, some claims associated with 'globalization' have asserted that *multinational* corporations are now replacing states as the most powerful forms of actors. However, if there have been real increases in the power of transnational capital, it would be a mistake either to accept much of the hyperbole associated with globalization literature, or to see this process as necessarily entailing the diminution of state power and the significance of state activity (Coleman et al., this volume). The increasing social and economic power of corporations may not be at the expense of, but may actually augment, the power of particular national and local states (Pearce and Tombs, 2001; Tombs and Whyte, 2003b). This raises the possibility that the contemporary global context – a key component of which is the growing power of multinational corporations – makes the state a crucial, perhaps more, important object of analysis than was the case thirty years ago (Coleman et al., this volume).

Moreover, material changes in both the international economy and across national economies have been accompanied by a series of ideological changes, which have combined to produce an increase in private capital's social status. Indeed, it is possible here to discern a *moral* aspect to the new status of private capital – one which has elevated private economic activity to the status of an intrinsically worthy end in itself (Frank, 2001). Thus, increasingly, business organizations have become not simply vehicles which represent a means to some other end (the provision of goods, services, employment, and so on), but as ends in themselves. Of course, this transformation has involved ascribing a moral status not so much to particular businesses, since such an effect would be difficult to secure given the evidence of a-morality, immorality or criminality on the part of individual business organizations, albeit often cast in fairly banal terms such as corporate greed, fat-cats, business scandals, and so on. Rather, and of course attesting to the contradictory nature of a Gramscian 'commonsense' (Hall et al., 1978: 150–6), the new moral elevation, as an outcome of hegemonic construction, accrues to business, or rather 'capital', as a whole. This 'moral capital of capital' (Tombs, 2001), or what Snider has called the 'social credibility of capital' (Snider, 2000: 171), further tends towards the removal of (and thus the control of) corporate crime from state agendas. As the moral legitimacy of business organizations has increased, so the room for manoeuvre to argue for their regulation has diminished (Snider, 2000). Indeed, as we have argued elsewhere, the re-positioning of capital within local states has augmented its role as a primary definer, not least in the spheres of crime and crime control, and its own status as victim, rather than a source, of crime (Coleman et al., 2005).

From 'Anti-statism' to 'Re-regulation'

As we have noted, many of the elements necessary for an analysis of the state and corporate crime were present in *Policing the Crisis*. Therein, we find the concepts of ideology, hegemony and commonsense, largely taken from Gramsci, and so crucial to an understanding of corporate crime and its regulation (Pearce and Tombs, 1990 and 1991); the idea of appearance both as illusion and as more than mere illusion, taken from Marx and Engels; similarly, a reminder of the role of the state in securing the transition from the extraction of absolute to relative surplus value as an instance of the role the state plays in securing the conditions of development for capitalism as a whole rather than individual sectors of capital; and on the need for an impartial law to be seen to be imposing its 'authority on sections of capital itself' (Hall et al., 1978: 207).

Moreover, the emergence of *Policing the Crisis* coincided with a significant realignment of the state, not least in its apparent relationship to economic life. If the emergence of neo-liberalism in the UK apparently marked a period of state retreat, it is important to recognize the promotion of anti-statism noted earlier (Coleman et al., this volume) as a hegemonic process. Thus any simplistic dichotomy between an interventionist, on the one hand, and a *laissez-faire* state, on the other, is ultimately unhelpful when analysing corporate crime. A key point for us is not that the state *is* anti-statist, but that it represents itself as such (Hall, 1988: 152). Thus we have to differentiate between state retreat as a real outcome of neo-liberalism and anti-statism as a hegemonic device (ibid.). In this context, it is clear that the period of the past thirty years or so is not accurately characterized simply as an era of *deregulation*. This point can be illustrated with reference to two observable policy developments in regulatory policy, via criminal or administrative law, or both.

First, rather than acting to control or restrict markets, there emerged in this period regulatory forms that *promoted* market activity. Thus, the 'freeing' of markets in the privatizations of energy, water, telecommunications and, most tortuously, in rail, was accompanied by a mass of regulatory institutions designed to establish and maintain what were effectively new markets (Prosser, 1997).

Second, there has been at times, a considerable regulatory effort aimed at controlling the excesses of capital accumulation. In the sphere of environmental crime, 1990 saw the establishment of a new, and ultimately ineffective, Environment Agency. In financial services, the deregulatory 'Big Bang' in 1986 was followed very quickly by the establishment, uniquely under a Criminal Justice Act, of the Serious Fraud Office, a body which demonstrated prosecutorial zeal prior to it being largely neutered by its political masters (Fooks, 1999). In the sphere of health and safety, the second Thatcher government ultimately retreated from a full-scale deregulatory assault (Tombs, 1996). Moreover, the last thirty years have seen changing fortunes in the context of health and safety regulation, albeit one best characterized by a long-term and, recently, accelerated emasculation of the Health and Safety Executive (HSE) as the key regulator in this area (Tombs and Whyte, 2008), while there have also emerged some symbols of criminalization, not least the new legislation on Corporate

Manslaughter, enacted in April 2008. Meanwhile, at European level, competition law and its enforcement has witnessed staggering levels of fines for 'anti-competitive' practices levied against some of the world's largest corporations.

In other words, what we have been witnessing in the neo-liberal period is a complex – and at times confused – period of re-regulation.

Theorizing Regulation

Those two observations highlight a fundamental contradiction in the regulation of corporate crime, one that warns us about thinking too didactically about its criminalization. It is not enough to simply state that there is one law for the rich and another for the poor, when it is clear that under certain conditions, the state makes an effort to criminalize some forms of corporate crime more than others. To recognize that the conditions under which some forms of corporate crime can be more easily criminalized than others is also to recognize that the role that the state plays in the field of regulation is often complex and contradictory. These prefatory points having been made, it is to a more sustained analysis of regulation that we now turn.

In the past thirty years, there has emerged a substantial body of work, within criminology but much more significantly across socio-legal studies, political science and management studies-related disciplines, which has focused on regulation. And this is of particular interest since regulation is the manifest empirical link between apparently distinct and separate state and corporate sectors. While in some ways diverse, academic research on regulation can be categorized into three dominant theoretical approaches (Whyte, 2004): a 'compliance' school, the neo-liberal perspective, and capture theories. In each of these bodies of literature, the state either does not appear at all or is treated as a 'black box', a reference point rarely described, analysed or theorized. None of this work places a critical analysis of 'the state' at its core, albeit that each is based upon an implicit theory of state institutions and their role.

The compliance perspective is derived from the 'fact' that compliance-oriented enforcement techniques (enforcement styles that seek to bargain with, and persuade, corporations to comply with law) dominate in most advanced economies. It is the acceptance of this fact that leads much of the research towards a normative endorsement of compliance-oriented regulation (see Pearce and Tombs, 1998: 223–46), a normative position that is usually based upon: a recognition and acceptance of the constraints upon state resources required to regulate corporations more punitively; a recognition of the power of business *vis-à-vis* regulators; and thus a concern not to provoke counter-productive tendencies through punitive enforcement.

Second, neo-liberal theorists, most closely associated with Friedman's Chicago School of Economics, argue that, in general, states have an interventionist tendency that obstructs the efficient regulation of economic activity. A key element of the neo-liberal ideology that took hold of political systems in the late 1970s and 1980s was the institutionalization of 'deregulation' as a centre-piece of economic policy, perhaps best summed up by the Conservative government's anti-red tape and burdens on business campaigns that have been enthusiastically adapted by the Blair and Brown governments (Tombs and Whyte, 2008).

Third, there are theories which characterize governments and state regulatory agencies as vulnerable to 'capture' by big business. Capture is achieved by a mixture of intense corporate lobbying, the consolidation of elite interests in public and private sectors, and a 'revolving door' of personnel between regulator and regulated. The implication of capture theory is therefore that regulation is counter-productive, since it has an inherent tendency to institutionalize corporate influence. Capture theory is often adopted by left analysis and by the critics of globalization (see Hertz, 2001; Monbiot, 2001) in order to demonstrate the increasing and overwhelming power of capital in the global market.

A common view across these three apparently very different perspectives is that regulation involves a process of an autonomous (state) agency intervening against an autonomous (capitalist) organization. For compliance theorists, regulatory activities aim to forge consensus across a plurality of competing claims on the part of potentially – but not fundamentally – antagonistic parties ('business', 'workers', other 'interests'), all of whom, ultimately, are viewed as having a mutual interest in an effective business sector. For neo-liberals, the optimal role of the state is to withdraw from economic and social life and to perform any arbitration role as a last resort when market mechanisms have manifestly failed. For capture theorists, the state is there to be seized and dominated by powerful, organized, *external* interests and their ways of understanding the world.

Despite what are, on the surface, significant differences between compliance, neo-liberal and capture theories of the state and regulation, what is common to each of these is a view of the relationship between the state and corporations or 'business' as one of *opposition* and *externality* – that is, the state stands as an institution or ensemble of institutions which is ontologically separate and distinct from civil society. The major distortion that this leads to is that regulatory agencies are viewed in one-dimensional terms, from a limited understanding of the state that Gramsci termed the 'state as policeman' (see Coleman et al., this volume). Gramsci used the term to suggest that we could only ever have a selective, unidimensional view of the state if we limited our understanding to the negative, repressive, law-centred role of the state. If the state is always the negative enforcer, then the relationship between state institutions and corporations is always going to be antagonistic – one facing the other in a battle of opposing wills, one seeking to secure compliance with the law, the other seeking to avoid this, and so on.

But this obscures the fact that there are also *limits upon*, and *no-go areas for*, regulation on the part of a *capitalist* state (Poulantzas, 1978b: 190–4). As we have seen in the discussion of the 'moral capital of capital' above, a key feature of neo-liberalism is that it *ideologically* undermines socially protective laws by promoting values of profit accumulation and maximization above social values. The state, as Hall et al. reminded us, performs the work of actively tutoring, educating and providing intellectual leadership for interpreting and understanding the world. It does this in order to 'enable capitalist accumulation and production to begin "freely" to unroll' (1978: 208). Thus, the state intervenes at an ideological level to give the *appearance* that capital accumulation is the norm and that anything else (unnecessarily cumbersome red tape, over zealous prosecution, and so on) is an obstruction to 'our' progress. It is therefore important to think about how the process of regulation works in this way – *as a means of tutelage itself* – both in terms of how particular ideas and discourses act to discipline the targets of regulation (individual and corporate participants in markets) *and* in terms of how they target regulators (Whyte, 2006). The dominant ideas of a social formation (in this case neo-liberal capitalism) thus influence and shape the 'habitus' of market actors, regulatory policy makers and regulatory agencies in a way that organizes the limits and no-go areas for regulation (Snider, forthcoming).

The relation of externality – the positioning of the state in direct opposition to capital – that we find in the three dominant perspectives in the regulation literature over-simplifies the role that the state plays in mediating and reconstituting class conflict. But more than this, the idea of externality reinforces the imaginary legal order that both Reiman and Pearce pointed to because it presents a way of thinking about states as acting in the public interest. Thus, if the relationship between the state and capital is one of externality, *and* the regulatory agency expresses the basic dynamic of the 'state as policeman', then state and capital can be portrayed in antagonistic terms. This logic allows the regulatory relationship to be represented as an heroic effort on the part of the state to control the excesses of capital. Of course, this idea is not mere ideology, since control efforts are part of this relationship, so that there often *is* struggle between state and capital; indeed, this is why we might expect at particular times to see tough regulatory responses against the interests of individual businesses. However, while we can see struggle, contradictions, contingencies, and so on, ultimately the role of the capitalist state is to reproduce unequal relations of power inherent within capitalism, a key issue to which we return, below.

Corporations 'Inside' and 'Outside' the State

In contrast to, and more useful than, the work outlined above, Mahon (1979), drawing upon the work of Poulantzas, argues that regulatory agencies should be understood as 'unequal structures of representation' that absorb and dissipate conflicts between opposing interests that are created 'in order to neutralise any threat to hegemony that cannot easily be contained by the normal functioning of the political and administrative apparatuses of the state' (1979: 160). Mahon reminds us that regulatory agencies are normally created following particularly contentious conflicts of interests and argues that this is precisely because conflicts that threaten the stability of the social order need to be absorbed and dissipated. Large-scale environmental damage, corporate killing and financial frauds, for example, all have the potential to create conflict between workers' organizations, community groups or consumer groups and corporations. And the struggles thereby generated often involve government departments similarly in conflict.

All regulatory agencies emerge as a compromise borne out of social conflict, so that the nature of the regulatory body and its formal mission reflect the balances of forces between *and within* states, capital and populations (Snider, 1991). Regulatory agencies, then, are not simply 'policemen' – that is, their relation to capital is not merely one of opposition and externality – but they play a much more general role in reproducing the social conditions necessary to sustain a capitalist social order. In other words, they do not only have a command and control function, but this command and control function is part of a much broader role in dissipating conflict, providing an outlet for social conflict and so on. The visible aspects of regulatory agencies (how they persuade corporations to comply with the law, enforcement and prosecution and so on) is therefore merely part of their general function in maintaining a stable social order.

This discussion of regulatory agencies demonstrates clearly how corporations exist with some degree of autonomy from states, but also that this autonomy can never be complete, since the state – through regulation – plays a crucial role in reproducing the social conditions necessary for them to survive and thrive. This analysis therefore warns us against adopting an over-simplified idea, inherent within neo-liberal and pluralist literature, of the roll-back/roll-out of the state (see Coleman et al., this volume). The power of capital depends not upon the rolling back of the state, or diminution of state power, but also on the successful mediation and dissipation of particularly contentious issues, or issues that threaten a stable social order. In this sense, we can see very clearly how states intervene in ways that are essential to the long-term interests of capital.

In a much more profound sense, states are essential to the survival of profit-making corporations within capitalist social orders. Indeed, it is not an exaggeration to say that corporations are given life by states: they can only invest, extract surplus value, and make profits because of the existence of a complex of rules that formally permit then structure their activities. Institutions of government and law establish the basis of their incorporation as organizations with particular juridical and administrative characteristics. Corporations are thus given form by the rules that govern labour and commodity markets, by regulatory laws that establish the social and economic oblig-ations of corporations and so on. In capitalist societies, then, we cannot view the state as standing in binary opposition to markets (or to corporations). The way that those juridical/administrative conditions position the corporation in relation to the state provide further evidence to show how capital's autonomy from the state can never be complete, but is always in a relationship of *relative autonomy*.[1] Corporations always exist simultaneously 'inside' and 'outside' state rules and institutions.

Indeed, when it comes to the production of corporate crime, Michalowski and Kramer (2006) show very clearly how corporate crime can be *initiated* and *facilitated* by states. This understanding of the relationship between states and corporations suggests the need to reject a notion of state as passive (external) bystanders to the production of corporate crime. Rather, it locates the relationship between states and corporations as complexly imbricated and at times consciously collusive. Corporate crime is thus a product of this complex relationship.

Maintaining a Criminogenic Market: The Case of UK Construction

Some of these considerations will now be clarified by focusing upon a specific sector and a specific type of 'crime' – safety crimes in construction. The construction industry is one of the UK's most dangerous sectors. We need to be clear, however, that despite the fact that most fatalities and injuries in this industry – as in every other industry – are likely to result from breaches of the law, few are ever processed as such (Tombs and Whyte, 2007). The sector has a fatal injury rate of over five times the all-industry average and accounts for 30% of all worker deaths. In absolute terms, it is the site of most worker deaths – some 70–80 have been killed each year in the sector since 1996/97 (Health and Safety Commission, 2007). And if we move beyond a specific focus upon safety, there appear to be very good reasons for thinking that the construction industry is criminogenic, that is, if we consider: the documented ill-health effects of working in an industry that has very high rates of asbestos-related disease; the tendency towards cartelization that characterizes the sector which generates price-fixing, bribery and corruption; the environmental damage associated with the industry; and the detrimental effects upon local human rights where its activities take place overseas.

The main causes of fatal injuries are relatively mundane and highly preventable. As the employers' body, the Federation of Master Builders, put it, 'there is nothing intrinsic about construction that suggests that somebody has to die ... [yet the] culture has become so engrained in that construction is dangerous, therefore someone is always going to get hurt' (cited in London Assembly Health and Public Services Committee, 2005: 9–10). While the levels of injury and death cannot be reduced to 'culture' (Carson, 1982; Beck and Woolfson, 1999), what the above does point to is that construction is not intrinsically dangerous; rather, the source of risk for workers is to be found in the organization of the sector and in work therein. The organization of work, the workplace and the sector are all socially constructed – and thus vary between time and place; construction work, therefore, can be more or less dangerously organized.[2] A similar point has been made about the very different 'safety' records of the Norwegian and UK offshore oil industries. Ryggvik (2000) suggests that Norway's better offshore safety record is partly a result of rights for union representatives to stop work when they feel safety is jeopardized, alongside strong offshore unions with a comprehensive network of trade union-appointed safety representatives – in marked contrast to the strident anti-trade unionism of the UK sector (Whyte, 2006). In other words, the level of death and injury is an effect of workplace power relations rather than any intrinsic quality that makes an industry unsafe.

The construction industry is probably the last remaining heavy industry of any size in Britain. It employs 2.25 million people, and contributes up to 10% of GDP, making it the single biggest industry in the UK and thus a key source of Treasury revenue.

And it is a growing industry with significant labour turnover which needs some 88,000 recruits a year (CITB-Construction Skills, 2007). It is integral to the UK economy. Government in general is the largest customer of construction industry services, while Defence Estates, responsible for the management of the Ministry of Defence's land and property holdings at home and overseas, is the 'single biggest customer of the UK construction industry' (www.bipsolutions.com/events/ctf_2007/speakers.html). The industry is central to the myriad of local and regional regeneration schemes across the UK. If this has always been the case, it is a situation accentuated and further formalized through, first, the Private Finance Initiatives (PFIs) and, more latterly, Public Private Partnerships, upon which the building of prisons, hospitals, schools, airports, and underground, rail and road networks, as well as flagship projects such as the London Olympics, the 'new' Wembley stadium and even the Millennium Dome are even thinkable. According to the Major Contractors Group, representing key UK players such as Carillion, Costain and Amec, construction companies engaged in the PFI expect to make 'between three and ten times as much money as they do on traditional contracts' (Corporate Watch, 2004). Industry sources have estimated that between 1995 and 2005, the construction economy grew by 30% (Lobban, 2005).

Our earlier observations regarding states establishing codes of rules, infrastructure, and so on, to bring corporations to life and to provide the conditions under which they are able to thrive, are clearly illustrated by the fortunes of the construction industry in recent years. For here is an industry whose success is largely down to state intervention in the economy, the creation of new regulatory mechanisms for public building programmes, the reform of planning regimes (Monbiot, 2001), and so on. In this sense, the building trade has been given a major boost by the re-regulation of the industry.

It is also worth noting in this respect that the growing economic importance of the industry in this period has been accompanied by a decline in Health and Safety Executive (HSE) enforcement activity. Research using HSE internal data for the years 1996–2001 found a 52% decline in the numbers of inspection contacts across the sector (Unison/Centre for Corporate Accountability, 2002). More recent evidence shows that enforcement action taken by HSE in the sector is also in decline: from 3,487 total notices in 2003/04 to 1,846 in 2005/06. In addition, there was a fall in offences prosecuted in the industry, from 617 in 2003/04 to 453 in 2005/06, as well as in convictions secured, from 418 to 338 across the same three-year period (www.hse. gov.uk/statistics/tables/tableef11.htm). Yet these levels of formal enforcement activity, and the trends therein, fly in the face of evidence of the scale of offending across the construction industry: the subject of occasional enforcement 'blitzes' by the HSE, these concentrated enforcement initiatives regularly lead to HSE ordering work to be halted on large numbers of construction sites (see Tombs and Whyte, 2007: 13–14), thereby indicating a high level of safety crime across the sector.

Now to juxtapose the growing economic importance of the industry with the decline in regulatory intervention is not to say that the role of the HSE is always, in the last instance, subordinated to the imperatives of the economy. In fact, HSE, albeit an increasingly emasculated agency (Tombs and Whyte, 2008), and one which sees formal enforcement as but one among a series of goals, would, all things being equal, prefer a safer (not to mention healthier) industry, and does commit resources to this. *But all things are not equal.* In this context, HSE, as an agency of the Department of Work and Pensions, stands in opposition to other, much more powerful, branches of government, including the Treasury, the Department for Business, Enterprise and Regulatory Reform, the Ministry of Defence, and the Foreign Office, to name but a few. Institutional inequality across those branches of the state is created by the outcome of competing political ideologies and practices. In an overwhelmingly pro-business climate, the economic success of business is always juxtaposed with the 'burden' of regulation. This is best summed up by the UK government's new Compliance Code for Regulators, which demands that *all* regulatory agencies responsible for controlling corporate crime 'should recognise that a key element of their activity will be to allow, or even encourage, economic progress and only to intervene when there is a clear case for protection' (www.bre.berr.gov.uk/regulation/documents/compliance_code/draft/compliance_ code_final.pdf). The parallel trends of growing economic importance and declining regulatory intervention, then, have to be first placed within the context of a complex and contradictory political sphere.

It is a sphere, however, to which the construction industry enjoys privileged access. The major companies – Tarmac, Carillion, Alfred McAlpine, AMEC, Balfour Beatty, Costain Group, John Laing, Kier Group, Mowlem, and Taylor Woodrow – are closely tied to the formal political process in the UK through a series of personal and institutional links, via their numerous trade associations, and through funding of political parties (Corporate Watch, 2004). All of those companies operate internationally and much of their financially risky business in overseas markets is underwritten by the government Export Credit Guarantee Department (ECGD). Such is the centrality of the industry that the key government department, the (instructively titled) Department for Business, Enterprise and Regulatory Reform, has its own Construction Sector Unit (CSU), the remit of which clearly indicates the complex yet symbiotic state–industry relationship:

> [The] Construction Sector Unit (CSU) takes the lead in central government in relations with the Construction Sector. CSU's aim is to continue to work with our industry, and other stakeholders to deliver a marked improvement in business performance in construction, in terms of productivity, profitability and competitiveness, in line with the construction business improvement agenda. This will secure an efficient market in the construction industry, with innovative & successful UK firms that meet the needs of clients and society that are competitive at home & abroad. (www.berr. gov.uk/sectors/construction/csu/page11616.html; see also Whyte, 2007/2008).

Conclusion

This brief, sector-specific analysis shows how the lines between legality and illegality are, at best, somewhat blurred in the construction sector. Thus the industry is based upon a large informal sector, with anywhere between £4.5 billion and £10 billion of construction work nationally undertaken as 'cash in hand'. Companies which do not pay their taxes are also likely to have a 'less safe working environment' for their workers; further, the informal economy creates market conditions that put 'pressure on legitimate builders to cut corners in order to compete for work' (London Assembly Health and Public Services Committee, 2005: 10). If it is indeed the case that this is a criminogenic industry (and see also Braithwaite (1984) on pharmaceuticals and Carson (1982) on the offshore oil industry, as further examples), it remains one that is established and maintained by, and is central to, the national and local states. In so far as its function is to support government-sponsored building programmes, generate export revenue and more generally contribute to economic growth, the construction industry can be said to have a symbiotic 'insider' relationship to the state. Meanwhile, HSE continues to go through the motions of regulation via inspections, blitzes, educative initiatives, and even the odd prosecution. In this sense, the construction industry can also be said to be external to the state. This dual relationship creates opportunities for, but also imposes limits upon, regulation, as the state is both dependent upon, but required to represent itself as regulator of, the sector.

If this is one of the key implications of the analysis presented in this chapter, we wish to make three further observations.

First, we should emphasize here that if corporations themselves are powerful entities, perhaps increasingly so, this power does not necessarily stand in opposition to state power. Nor, as the focus on construction indicates, is it augmented in a zero-sum fashion at the expense of states. Relationships between states and corporations – which operate at local, national and international levels – are complex, characterized theoretically in terms of mutual interdependence, not externality. Corporate crime is not simply a result of the success or lack of success of the state acting 'as policeman', but is produced as a result of the symbiotic relationship between states and markets. The prospects for controlling corporate crime therefore rest upon the extent to which we can break this symbiosis, even for brief moments. This does not deny that different forms of corporate crime are amenable to more or less effective enforcement at different times. But regulatory settlements are always an outcome of struggles between social classes and within corporate and state elites. Regulation, then, is an outcome of social relations of power.

Second, to assert that corporations are given life by states and rely upon state institutions for the very conditions of their existence is not to dissolve any distinction between the 'public' and 'private' sphere: if this division between 'public' and 'private' realms is merely juridical, this does not deny that this differentiated juridical construction has significant *material* consequences. Thus, for example, 'privatization' – the transfer of ownership or administration of an industry from a government authority to the 'market' – implies major consequences for workers, consumers and for the economy more generally. However, as both Gramsci and Poulantzas went to great lengths to show, the distinction between 'public' and 'private' spheres is a juridical one that has its formal template created and maintained by state apparatuses. This does not mean that the extent to which 'public' and 'private' sectors exist as *formally* separate is unimportant; but it does mean that a concept of the state that does not seek to break down the formal desegregation of 'public' and 'private' is likely to over-estimate the significance of shifts in institutional power between those sectors (see also Coleman et al., this volume).

Third, our analysis has attempted to indicate that in thinking about corporate crime and its regulation, what is really at issue is not 'crime'– rather, it is an issue of state, corporate and class power. More generally, to turn our attention to the contours and dynamics of class power, and its connection to criminal justice, now seems more pressing than ever, not least since we live in a period in which rapidly rising prison populations and security/military budgets go hand in hand with a widening gap between rich and poor – whether measured in global terms *between* developed and developing economies, or *within* the economies of the developed states. Thus 'the rich get richer and the poor get prison' remains an appropriate aphorism for our times. To turn our attention to class power, and the processes that Pearce, Reiman, Hall, and others have pointed to – the state in and of capitalist social orders – means not only engaging with, and interrogating, the relationship between state institutions and the poor, but also putting the relationship between the state and capital under scrutiny. In these tasks, criminology has signally failed.

Key Reading

Glasbeek, H. (2002) *Wealth by Stealth: Corporate Crime, Corporate Law and the Perversion of Democracy*. Toronto: Between the Lines.

Mahon, R. (1979) 'Regulatory agencies: captive agents or hegemonic apparatuses?', *Studies in Political Economy*, 1(1): 162–200.

Michalowski, R. and Kramer, R. (2006) *State–Corporate Crime: Wrongdoing at the Intersection of Business and Government*. New Brunswick, NJ: Rutgers University Press.

Pearce, F. (1976) *Crimes of the Powerful: Marxism, Crime and Deviance*. London: Pluto Press.

Pearce, F. and Tombs, S. (2001) 'Crime, corporations and the "new" social order', in G. Potter (ed.), *Controversies in White-collar Crime*. Cincinnati, OH: Anderson. pp. 185–222.

Whyte, D. (2004) 'Corporate crime and regulation', in J. Muncie and D. Wilson (eds), *The Student Handbook of Criminology and Criminal Justice*. London: Cavendish.

Notes

The arguments here have benefited from our long working relationship with Frank Pearce, and from the support and constructive insights of Roy Coleman and Joe Sim. The usual disclaimers apply.

1   This point can be understood as the mirror image of the Miliband/Poulantzas debate (Hay, 2006) about the degree to which we can say that the state (superstructures) possess autonomy from the economic base (structure).

2   For example, construction work for the 2000 Sydney Olympics produced no fatal injuries among construction workers, while work towards Athens 2004 led to 40 plus deaths (McCartney, 2005).

8

VIOLENCE AND THE STATE

Penny Green and Tony Ward

Introduction

This chapter is concerned with 'organized physical violence in the most material sense of the term: *violence to the body*' (Poulantzas, 1978b: 29). There may be a good case for defining violence more broadly in some criminological contexts (Salmi, 2004; Tombs, 2007), but what concerns us here is the close relationship between organized physical violence and the state. Not only do modern states claim a monopoly of legitimate violence in this sense (Weber, 1968); they also perpetrate or instigate most of the world's serious violent crime: the infliction of pain, injury or death in contravention of legal or moral norms (Green and Ward, 2004). It is this *illegitimate* violence, or state crime, that concerns us here.[1]

The claim of states to a monopoly of organized violence is codified in the form of law (Kelsen, 1967; Poulantzas, 1978b). Much attention has been given in recent political theory to 'states of exception': forms of state power that suspend or abrogate the normal rules of law. As Agamben (2005) points out, drawing both on the fascist legal philosopher Schmitt and the Marxist writer Benjamin, states of exception may be *legally defined* spaces or times where the ordinary rules do not apply (Guantánamo Bay being the paradigmatic contemporary example), or *extra-legal* acts of violence, such as military coups, by which a state agency suspends or abrogates the existing constitution and seeks to institute a new one. In addition, there are what may be considered *de facto* states of exception, when organs of the state do not expressly suspend or abrogate existing law but systematically act in contravention of it. In all three situations, state functionaries may be called upon to commit 'crimes of obedience': 'act[s] performed in response to orders from authority that [are] considered illegal or immoral by the larger community' (Kelman and Hamilton, 1989: 46), where 'the larger community' may comprise domestic and/or international audiences. In modern states, torture and murder cannot generally be carried out openly (O'Kane, 1996) – for the state to take open responsibility for death and suffering entails, almost invariably, a denial that it amounts to murder or torture (Cohen, 2001).

The difference between 'crimes of obedience' and 'ordinary' crime should not be overstated. Much gang violence and white-collar crime could be considered to fall within Kelman and Hamilton's definition. Whether the authority involved is a gang leader, a manager or a general, such crimes raise the central criminological question: how do people come to behave in ways that they know to contravene important social norms, norms which they have often themselves internalized? Moreover, by no means all state crimes are crimes of obedience. Many crimes are committed on the perpetrator's own initiative, but either consciously further the operative goals of a state agency or are tolerated by the agency in furtherance of its goals (Green and Ward, 2004).

To understand such crimes it is necessary to integrate macro-social accounts of state formation with micro-social accounts of individual motivation and emotion. As Tombs (2007: 543–4) remarks, this is a daunting task and 'theoretical development here remains at an early stage'. In an effort to make some modest contribution to such development, this chapter will examine the formation of the state monopoly of organized violence and the effects of state formation on the sensibilities and actions of state agents. We draw heavily on three theorists, who, despite their differences, are centrally concerned with the formation and effects of the state monopoly of violence: Charles Tilly, Nicos Poulantzas and Norbert Elias.

The State and Organized Violence

For Charles Tilly, state formation is driven by war and preparation for war. In his seminal work on the subject, he argues that 'the pursuit of war and military capacity, after having created national states as a sort of by-product, led to a civilianization of government and domestic politics' (1992: 206). Military elites have to attract resources to sustain their campaigns. With the development of capital accumulation the means of extracting resources moves from direct appropriation to taxation, and the consolidation of state power over substantial territories in turn facilitates capital accumulation. States are in a continual, though not linear, process of development and war-making remains central both to defining states and to fostering their capacity for violence. Since the mid-twentieth century, wars have become both more frequent and considerably more deadly, particularly for civilian populations (Kaldor, 2006), with six times as many deaths occurring per war (admittedly a crude measure) in the twentieth century as in the nineteenth (Sivard, 1996). In the 1960s civilians accounted for 63% of recorded war deaths, by the 1980s they accounted for 74% and, according the authors of the *World Military and Social Expenditures* report, that figure had grown in the 1990s (ibid.). The World Health Organization (WHO) calculates that in 2000 some 360,000 people were killed as a result of collective violence or armed conflict (2002: 8); this represents 20% of all global violent deaths.

Tilly emphasizes the diversity among European societies in their paths to state formation, distinguishing between *coercion intensive* political modes, when ruling elites extracted revenues for war by direct coercion, and *capital intensive* and *capitalized coercion* modes, where rulers made deals with and later incorporated sections of the capitalist class into their states in the promotion of war (Tilly, 1992: 30–1; see also Mann, 1986, 1993). In either case, advanced liberal democracies have been shaped by violent internal upheavals, civil war, revolution and war between states. The colonial empires of the European states were forged and sustained by full-scale military mobilizations and in many cases only relinquished after prolonged periods of violent conflict.

The details of Tilly's magisterial historical account do not concern us here. What we are concerned with is the relationship of violence to state formation, composition and, finally, practice. We will draw particularly on comparisons between the formation of relatively stable territorial states and those states that are characterized as 'predatory' states (often in the form of military regimes), which tend to be characterized by overt forms of internal violence. As Tilly documents, military regimes by the late twentieth century had become a standard form of governance in the developing world, with 60% of all East Asian states and 64% of all African states in the control of military forces.

While there is no one standard path to their formation, states, following Engels (1968), are defined by a number of common features: central bureaucracies, armies, prisons, courts, legislatures, police forces and public services. We will be concentrating our discussion on the claim by states to a monopoly of violence over a particular territory. For such a monopoly to exist it is not essential that the agencies that exercise it be legally defined as public bodies, so long as their coercive power is authorized by the state (Ryan and Ward, 1989: 69–70; Whyte, 2003).

One measure of the coercive capacity of states is military expenditure. Evidence from the Stockholm International Peace Research Institute (2006) suggests that while the world saw an overall reduction in military expenditure following the end of the Cold War, that decline has been sharply reversing since the late 1990s, driven largely by the USA and its military operations in Afghanistan and Iraq. In 2004 the USA spent $455.3 billion in military expenditures (Stålenheim et al., 2007: 275):

> World military expenditure is extremely unevenly distributed. In 2006 the 15 countries with the highest spending accounted for 83 per cent of the total. The USA is responsible for 46 per cent of the world total, distantly followed by the UK, France, Japan and China with 4–5 per cent each.

In terms of real growth rates in military expenditures, Central Africa recorded a huge 18.2% increase between 1995 and 1999 (compared with pre-Iraq war North America, which demonstrated a 1.3% decline; Stålenheim et al., 2007: 275):

> If the current growth in worldwide military spending continues, by the end of 2006 it will have passed the highest figure reached during the Cold War. After year-on-year increases since 1999, global military spending this year is estimated to reach an unprecedented $1,058.9 bn, which is roughly 15 times annual international aid expenditure. (Control Arms Campaign, 2006: 6)

According to the Control Arms Campaign, a state's involvement in armed conflict is directly related to its debt burden – around 20% of Third World debt has been identified as a direct result of arms imports (Control Arms Campaign, 2004).

Legitimacy

As we write, the Burmese military are shooting pro-democracy demonstrators in the streets of Rangoon. Here the violence of coercive government is at its most visible. Despite the fact that in much of the world public compliance is secured through consensual forms of governance, coercive governance is rarely far from the surface (Gramsci, 1971). Cover (1986: 1607) brings this out nicely when he points out that although most convicted defendants walk to the cells 'without significant disturbance to the civil appearance of the event, [it] is ... grotesque to assume that the civil façade is "voluntary" ... most prisoners walk into prison because they know they would be dragged or beaten into prison if they do not walk'.

Legitimacy is the key to defining state crimes. Violence can be illegitimate (state crime) or legitimate. How, then, do we define 'illegitimate'? In one of the most fiercely contested examples of the exercise of coercive power by the British state, the 1984–85 miners' strike, the legitimacy of the police role was starkly called into question. The police methods were overwhelmingly supported by government, the courts and the media, but from the perspective of those policed, and their many supporters, their actions were brutal, violent and illegitimate (Green, 1990). Other examples of criminological work which challenges state legitimacy from the perspective of the policed include Ní Aolain (2000), Pickering (2002) and Rolston (1991) on Northern Ireland; Scraton et al. (1995) on the Hillsborough disaster; and Cunneen (2001) and McCulloch (2001) on policing in Australia. In any case, where legitimacy is challenged, precisely where the boundaries of legitimate coercion are drawn depends largely on whose perspective is adopted. This is not to endorse some kind of postmodern relativism, but rather to insist that the criminologist's choice of perspective must be informed by normative criteria of social justice and human rights which resonate with both state discourses and those of domestic civil society (Green and Ward, 2004).

For example, the recent protest by Burmese monks against the abuses of the military regime was particularly resonant within Burmese society because of the moral authority monks hold there. By turning upside down their begging bowls, in an act of shocking defiance, they were explicitly refusing the alms traditionally offered by the military rulers and their families. The moral impact was enormous because in refusing alms the monks were denying the military the spiritual approval – and hence the legitimacy – contingent on the ritual of giving charity to the clergy (Mydans, 2007).

States and Sensibilities

Critical criminologists have, often with good reason, been dismissive of traditional criminology's excessive focus on the study of individual motives. However, in an effort to understand the structural nature of crime and criminal justice practice, critical criminology has tended to throw the baby out with the bathwater by largely ignoring war crimes, genocide or torture, which demand a detailed examination of individual motivation and action (see Haney et al., 1973; Milgram, 1974; Staub, 1989). We would argue that much is to be learned from understanding the processes by which individuals come to cast off their socialized inhibitions against violent and cruel behaviour, particularly in the contest of state-sanctioned violence.

In this section we outline a framework for integrating political and economic analyses of state violence with a more subjective approach which focuses on the sensibilities involved in the commission of such violence.

Elias and the 'Civilizing Process'

Norbert Elias's *The Civilizing Process* (2000) shares with Tilly's work a concern with long-term historical processes of state formation. Elias's major contribution, however, lies in the connection he makes between these changes in social structure and changes in the 'structure of affects' (2000: 169). As states emerge with a monopoly of organized physical force or violence, they 'pacify' the public space within their territories (2000: 70). Alongside an increasingly complex and differentiated economic system, a new 'drive-economy' develops which inhibits the public expression of aggression as well as bodily functions like spitting and excretion. The 'pleasure of physical attack ... is now reserved to those few legitimized by the central authority (for example, the police against the criminal), and to larger numbers only in exceptional times of war and revolution' (2000: 169–70). Over many generations, the restraint of public displays of bodily functions, including violence, 'is enforced less and less by direct physical force' and more by the pressures of social institutions, including the family; 'the social commands and prohibitions become increasingly a part of the self, a strictly regulated superego' (2000: 158). Elias accepts the Freudian account of repression and the unconscious as at least roughly accurate, but insists that it is the product of specific historical processes, not some universal human condition.

Although Elias's theory owes much to Weber, his account makes the concept of *legitimate* authority less central than Weber does. Legitimacy, in Elias's historical account, seems largely to be an effect of the brute fact of overwhelming physical and economic power, coupled with the increasing complexity of the state, which makes simple despotism impossible. Elias uses the term 'civilization' in two senses: it is both the process of repressing aggressive and other 'drives' and an ideological concept which serves to legitimize state authority and colonial expansion. The second, ideological, meaning of 'civilization' is a product of the civilizing process; but as 'civilized' virtues come to be seen as a mark of the inherent superiority of the races and classes that display them, their historical origins as effects of violent domination are forgotten (2000: 43). As Emsley (2007: 125) rightly reminds us, Elias's theory is not a Whig account of inexorable human progress.

There is, in fact, a striking amount of common ground between Elias's account of state formation and that of Poulantzas (1978b). Both writers correlate the rise of state-monopolized violence with the withdrawal of the direct use or threat of physical violence from economic relations. Both deny any necessary *causal* priority of economic change over changes in state formation,[2] although Poulantzas assigns the former an *analytical* priority that Elias does not. Both recognize the importance of forms of bodily training and self-control which cannot be equated with 'ideology'; here Elias (2000: 372–3, 408) anticipates Foucault, from whom Poulantzas (1978b: 29, 64–9) evidently learned (Hall, 1980a). Both argue that while forms of discipline or habitus[3]-formation in families, schools and other institutions reduce the need for *direct* physical violence in the public sphere, these processes depend upon the state monopoly of violence:

> a continuous, uniform pressure is exerted on individual life by the physical violence stored behind the scenes of everyday life, a pressure totally familiar and hardly perceived. (Elias, 2000: 372)

> *State-monopolized physical violence permanently underlies the techniques of power and mechanisms of consent; it is inscribed in the web of disciplinary and ideological devices; and even when it is not directly exercised, it shapes the materiality of the social body on which domination is brought to bear.* (Poulantzas, 1978b: 81, original italics)

As Eisner's (2001) review of research shows, the historical evidence from western Europe that has accumulated since *The Civilizing Process* was published provides strong support for its main theses (if anything, Eisner's simplification of Elias's theory leads him to understate its success). Elias, however, concerned himself only with European trends, and many African and Latin American countries now experience homicide rates comparable to medieval Europe. Homicide rates for those aged 10–29 range 'from 0.9 per 100 000 in the high-income countries of Europe and parts of Asia and the Pacific, to 17.6 per 100 000 in Africa and 36.4 per 100 000 in Latin America' (WHO, 2002: 25). The explanation of these massive differentials is a major challenge for criminology and social theory, and clearly raises a question about how far an Eliasian perspective can be applied to non-European societies.

As Elias was well aware, the great decline in serious non-state violence in Europe over the past eight centuries is in stark contrast to the staggering levels of mass murder and torture by modern governments (Rummel, 1994). There is a 'contradiction between the code of non-violence within states and the code of permitted violence in inter-state affairs ... between the code of total non-violence valid for the majority of citizens and the code of licensed violence, more or less under public control, valid for the police and other armed forces' (Elias, 1987: 81). Again, we must remember the European focus of these remarks, but we shall tentatively assume that this observation is broadly true for most societies with effective states (including, for example, Rwanda, where state formation predated colonial rule), even though their levels of interpersonal violence may be much higher.

Elias says frustratingly little, in general terms, about how this contradiction is resolved, but there seem to be two main possibilities (Ward and Young, 2007; Green and Ward, 2009). State violence may be seen as compatible with the code of civilized behaviour because it is under control: rational, disciplined, and either lawful or justified by some kind of 'higher law', such as national security. Or state violence may be *exempt* from control: soldiers, police and other functionaries (together in some cases with non-official personnel recruited to the state's cause) may be licensed to indulge violent passions in ways denied to the general population. These two ideal types correspond, more or less, to the two main types of masculinity that Huggins et al. (2002) identified in their sample of Brazilian torturers and murderers: the 'bureaucratic functionary' and the 'personalistic cop' (a third type, 'blended masculinity', combines elements of the other two).[4] Huggins found that both types had their uses: 'bureaucratic functionaries' were efficient torturers, while 'personalistic cops' could be left to murder on their own initiative.

Bureaucracy and Violence

In the existing literature on state violence, we tend to find an emphasis on *either* the bureaucratization of violence – rational planning, the division of tasks and the separation of decision from action – *or*, less frequently, its emotional, irrational or symbolic aspects. Outstanding examples of the former include the classic psychological studies of Milgram (1974) and the Stanford Prison Experiment (recently revisited by Zimbardo, 2007); Kelman and Hamilton's *Crimes of Obedience* (1989); Bauman's (1989) seminal sociological study of the Nazi genocide; and the studies of US military power and policy by Kauzlarich and Kramer (1998) and Kramer and Michalowski (2005). The latter camp includes several anthropological studies to be found in the excellent collections by Hinton (2002) and Sluka (2000); Graziano's (1992) 'psychosexual' account of the Argentinean dictatorship; Scheff's (1994) study of the emotional roots of war; and the brief but suggestive treatment of torture and state terrorism by Katz (1988). It is harder to find work which integrates the two approaches satisfactorily. Cohen (2001) makes a start but, as his subtitle indicates, is concerned with 'knowing about atrocities', rather than their actual perpetration. In the important work of Huggins et al. (2002), the ethnographic insights of the earlier chapters (written mainly by Huggins) feel less than completely integrated in the conclusion (written mainly by Zimbardo), which leans strongly towards the 'bureaucratic' school. Our own book (Green and Ward, 2004) draws on both strands of research and makes some attempt to integrate them in particular contexts, but we would be the first to admit that there is still a long way to go. It is here that Elias's linkage of state formation and sensibilities seems, for all its limitations,[5] a promising starting point.

It is essential to recognize both that state violence is always under some degree of bureaucratic control – otherwise it would not be *state* violence – and that it is always likely to be associated with strong emotions, as is any intense physical experience. In general, state agencies appear to be highly calculating, goal-directed organizations (Kauzlarich and Kramer, 1998). The stance of rational detachment, of aiming for long-term gains rather than immediate emotional satisfaction, is a central element of the 'civilized' sensibilities and is also, of course, essential to capitalism. Yet, as Elias (1987) argues, it is a particularly difficult attitude to take to violent conflict. Revenge and retribution retain a powerful emotional appeal in virtually all societies. So it is not surprising if state responses to violence sometimes seem to embody what some anthropologists characterize as a logic of ritual – providing emotional satisfaction through their symbolic appropriateness – rather than utilitarian calculation (Aretxaga, 2000; Mahmood, 2000; Ward and Young, 2007).

Bureaucratic organization and state violence are an inherently unstable combination. Bureaucratic organizations may seek to achieve their objectives within legal rules, or they may determine that a 'state of exception' exists and the rules have to be broken. (In practice, state agencies will often pursue a complex mixture of both courses.) If the agency seeks to confine its workers to legitimate means (or means that can be presented as legitimate), it is likely to generate strain between their official objectives and the means for achieving them (Passas, 1990; Kauzlarich and Kramer, 1998). If, on the other hand, it sanctions the use of clearly illegitimate means, the resulting secrecy and impunity creates motives and opportunities for crime that can easily run out of control.

The first of these possibilities is complicated by the fact that legal rules, as interpreted by state officials, are generally flexible enough to take a good deal of strain without being unequivocally broken (McBarnet, 1981). As is well known from studies of policing, legally defined powers are 'open-textured' (Hart, 1994; Dixon, 1997), providing a structure for discretion which is supplemented by police 'working rules'. In some circumstances, the 'working rules' will sanction patently illegal violence (see, for example, Uildriks and van Mastrigt, 1991; Skolnick and Fyfe, 1993), but there is a very large 'grey area', where the boundary between 'legitimate force' and violent crime has to be judged according to such criteria as public reaction and the police's own 'official' professional standards (Klockars, 1996) as well as the interpretation of legal standards by institutions such as coroners' juries (Shaw and Coles, 2007).

Violent police crime is often emotionally cathartic, providing relief from boredom and opportunities for 'action-oriented hedonism' (Holdaway, 1983), revenge and expressions of solidarity (for example, Cancino, 2001), but often it is also functional to the maintenance of police power. The police mandate in liberal democracies is to exercise the state's monopoly of legitimate force while displaying the minimum of overt violence within pacified social spaces (Bittner, 1975; Steinert, 2003). One way of achieving this is to exploit the 'paradox of face': as Muir (1977: 41) puts it, '*The nastier one's reputation, the less nasty one has to be*'. The price of this strategy is that police have to be genuinely nasty to those who defy them, especially if they do it in front of onlookers (Worden, 1996). In Choongh's (1997) study of two English police stations, young lower-working-class men who were perceived as insufficiently respectful to the police were arrested so that they could be brought to the police station, subjected to various humiliating orders, and beaten if they showed continued defiance. Though clearly illegal, this was an effective way of reminding the policed of the violence 'stored behind the scenes' of everyday policing.

The second possible relation of a state bureaucracy to legal rules – the 'state of exception' that explicitly sets the state above ordinary law – is also complicated by the difficulty of knowing where legality begins and ends, particularly within an 'exceptional form of state' (Poulantzas, 1978b), such as a military dictatorship. Schirmer's

(1998) remarkable interviews with Guatemalan generals and military lawyers show them repeatedly insisting that national security takes precedence over law, but equivocating as to whether this precedence of security (or 'state of exception') is itself a legal norm. Marchak (1999) reports that the Argentinean officers she interviewed believed intensely in the legitimacy of their fight against 'international communism' and were encouraged in this by their ultra-reactionary Catholic priests. Whether or not it is 'technically' legal, state terror distinguishes itself from state-defined crime by its civilizing mission: to pacify society through a rational application of the state's monopoly of violence. In times of crisis, a perceived threat of chaotic, disorganized violence provides a potent justification for increased state coercion (Hall et al., 1978: Chapter 9).

To justify the torture and murder of political opponents it may be necessary to equate every form of dissent with violent subversion. There is a certain rationality in such distortions of reality (see Píon-Berlin, 1989; Graziano, 1992) which serve to legitimize ruthless political strategies. But state terror tends to amplify its own paranoia, both because interrogation under torture is always likely to confirm the interrogator's suspicions, and because different units within the state compete with each other to identify 'subversives'. The classic example of paranoia run wild is the 'great terror' in Stalin's USSR (Getty and Naumov, 2000).

The combination of impunity and secrecy associated with state terror creates a criminal opportunity structure which officials can use to pursue private interests. Under the Argentinean and Brazilian military regimes, for example, police not only tortured detainees, and murdered them to cover up their torture, but became involved in a range of crime, such as smuggling, drug-dealing and extortion, creating acute tensions and sometimes violent conflict within the apparatus of repression (Andersen, 1993; Marchak, 1999; Huggins et al., 2002). A similar pattern can be seen in the USA, for example in New York in the early 1990s, where local 'crews' of police were able to impose their own extra-legal conception of order on their neighbourhoods while enriching themselves through drug-dealing (Chevigny, 1995; Chin, 1997).

The impression of cool, rational planning at the top level of some highly violent regimes is in stark contrast to the terror inflicted on new recruits. Soldiers and police being trained for torture and murder undergo a systematic process of brutalization (see, for example, Gibson, 1990; REMHI, 1999; Conroy, 2000; Huggins et al., 2002; Haritos-Fatouros, 2003). Through experiences such as violent assault and punishment, humiliation, enforced contact with blood and excrement, and impossible or contradictory orders, trainees are given a clear message that they have entered an enclave where the ordinary rules of pacified social space do not apply. Such training serves to break down the recruit's personality, de-sensitize him to pain (and so to the pain of others), induce a state of unquestioning dependence on and obedience to his superiors, and produce a sense of pride in the recruit's hard-won new identity as a tough, disciplined servant of the state (Huggins et al., 2002). Paradoxically, it seems that many perpetrators of 'bureaucratic' violence are shaped by a training that systematically violates norms of bureaucratic rationality.

It is, perhaps, an encouraging sign of the success of the civilizing process that such extreme measures are needed to produce professional torturers and killers. Milgram's and Zimbardo's experiments make it seem all too easy to induce very cruel behaviour in the average citizen, but to adopt torture or murder as part of one's way of life in a generally peaceable modern society is not such an easy matter. Even getting people to kill 'legitimately' in war, particularly at close quarters, is much harder than was once believed. A famous study by Marshall (1947) reported that only 15–20% of allied soldiers in the Second World War fired their weapons at the enemy. According to the US military psychologist Dave Grossman, the most advanced armed forces have responded to such findings by developing realistic simulations of killing that condition and desensitize recruits, producing a 'killing ability' that 'amounts to nothing less than a technological revolution on the battlefield' (1996: 158–9).

O'Donnell (2003: 758) notes the parallels between military training – or, he might have added, the training of torturers – and the 'violentization' that Athens (1992) claims is necessary to produce a 'dangerous violent criminal' in civilian life, but he also points out that such an explanation does not seem to fit the way violence was aroused in the Bosnian war or the Rwandan genocide. We seem to see here two different patterns of initiation into extreme violence. One involves breaking down any humane sensibilities in novice violence workers, producing 'hard men' whose identity is bound up with their ability to perform violent tasks unflinchingly (although in practice their work often gives rise to acute stress and 'burnout': Huggins et al., 2002). The other involves creating what de Swaan (2001) calls 'enclaves of barbarism': bounded spaces or situations in which ordinary rules do not apply, so that people can perform atrocities within the enclave but resume their ordinary habitus and sensibility when they leave. Such situations may create a sense of what Lifton (1986) calls 'doubling', where the actor sees his violent behaviour within the enclave as quite distinct from his everyday self:

> [I]t is as if I had let another individual take on my own living appearance, the habits of my heart, without a single pang in my soul. This killer was indeed me, as to the offence he committed and the blood he shed, but he is a stranger to me in his ferocity. I admit and recognize my obedience at that time, my victims, my fault, but I fail to recognize the wickedness of the one who raced through the marshes on my legs, carrying my machete. (Rwandan genocide perpetrator, interviewed by Hatzfeld, 2005: 43)

This murderer – not a regular state functionary, but a civilian ordered to kill by state officials – distinguishes clearly between his 'obedience', which is normal conduct in an authoritarian culture such as Rwanda's (Hintjens, 1999), and his 'ferocity' and 'wickedness', which strike him (remembering the experience from his later position as a prisoner who has confessed) as alien to his normal self. This is more than a simple 'crime of obedience': the perpetrator begins to participate out of fear, deference or conformity but then (like the guards in Zimbardo's simulated prison) gets 'carried away' with his new role, performing it with zeal, passion and perhaps even pleasure.

Hierarchical decision-making and interpersonal aggression operate together to produce what de Swaan (2001: 68) calls the 'bureaucratization of barbarism'. Violence may be performed with cold detachment or with pleasure and abandon; both types, as in the Nazi death camps (Sofsky, 1997), may exist side by side. What is essential, argues de Swaan, is the *compartmentalization* of violence. Victims must be dehumanized by propaganda and the zones of killing and torture set apart spatially, temporally and/or psychologically from the world of everyday life. Such compartmentalization, however, is difficult to sustain (Ward and Young, 2007). The Rwandan *genocidaires* did not return, as they seem to have anticipated, to a life of farming enriched by the property they had looted; they were driven into exile and triggered a war that engulfed the neighbouring Democratic Republic of Congo (Nzongola-Ntalaja, 2002: Chapter 7). The 'enclaves of barbarism' at Abu Ghraib and Guantánamo Bay have become bywords for cruelty and probably the best propaganda tools al-Qaeda possesses.

Civil Society

Despite the horrifying levels of state violence in many parts of the world, there have also been dramatic changes for the better in much of Latin America, Eastern Europe, Turkey and parts of Africa (notably Sierra Leone and Liberia). While recognizing that these developments are not necessarily unilinear (and noting the significant rise in global military expenditure following the post-Cold War decline: Stålenheim et al., 2007), it is also clear that the most significant force for change in terms of reforming violent states is organized civil society (Risse et al., 1999). The 'spiral model' formulated by Risse and Sikkink suggests a 'boomerang pattern' of influence and change 'when domestic groups in a repressive state bypass their state and directly search out international allies to try to bring pressure on their states from outside' (Risse and Sikkink, 1999: 18). Internal opposition movements and human rights organizations link with transnational networks, which in turn place pressure on international donor institutions and powerful states in order to influence repressive regimes. There are, however, very real problems with relying on non-governmental organizations (NGOs) to bring about fundamental change to state practice. Their historic role as 'brokers' between neo-liberal international donors/governments, domestic regimes and local organizations inevitably compromises the nature and scale of political change required to address state violence (Petras, 1997; and with particular reference to Turkey, see Green, 2002). Nonetheless we think it reasonable to assert that those NGOs and political movements explicitly campaigning for an end to gross human rights violations have had a qualified impact which accords with the basic tenets of the 'spiral model'.

Turkey in the first decade of the twenty-first century presents a useful illustration of the combined impact of domestic and transnational civil society. From being a state characterized by brutality, endemic violence and torture, Turkey has moved to a self-conscious position in which human rights now explicitly (though in practice very unevenly) form part of the government's legitimizing discourse. From the late 1990s, but especially since 2002, there has been an acknowledgement by the Turkish Justice and Development Party (AKP) government that state violence exists – that it is increasingly unacceptable – and a zero-tolerance stance on torture has been adopted.[6] European Union accession (partially frozen in 2007) has played a critical role in the direction that the reform process has taken, but it has been the active interrelationship between domestic[7] and international human rights and cultural NGOs[8] that has created fertile conditions for European consideration of Turkey. Turkey's conditional entry into the EU depends upon improvement in the arena of human rights and activity in these realms, especially when associated with externally sponsored interventions (such as the Foreign and Commonwealth Office, or the Council of Europe's Committee for the Prevention of Torture (CPT)), is a marker that the country is moving in the right direction – in the direction of good governance, improving human rights and recognition of minority rights. Between 2002 and 2006 Turkey witnessed real and important human rights progress[9] – certainly according to the CPT, the European Council and international NGOs like Human Rights Watch and Amnesty International. In 2003 substantial reforms in terms of the abolition of torture began to be apparent and it was generally agreed that torture could no longer be said to be 'widespread'. More recent reports suggest that ill-treatment in police stations continued to occur, but systemic elements of torture, such as the use of electric shocks, appear to have been eliminated (Amnesty International, 2004). In 2007 fewer incidents of torture were reported than in previous years but killings in disputed circumstances by security forces in the east of the country continued, as did excessive force in dealing with demonstrations (Amnesty International, 2007).

Conclusion

Criminology has far to go before it can develop an adequate criminological understanding of state violence, since the discipline has not only neglected the state but has a woefully myopic understanding of violence. Violence in all its many forms needs to be understood in relation to long-term historical changes, global configurations of culture and state formation, and its global and local economic context. State violence needs to be understood both as an expression of state power and as comprising individual acts of aggression with complex social and psychological relations to other forms of interpersonal violence.

We have argued that civil society is the most effective mechanism for countering state violence. Here, in addition to trade unions, political movements and human rights-based NGOs, we must also include those elements of civil society committed to challenging political and social processes in which minorities and their cultures are systematically devalued. We have seen how central the process of dehumanization has been in facilitating torture, war crimes and genocide (Green and Ward, 2004). In this context, criminology since Becker (1963) has a valuable and successful track record in humanizing those the state has defined as outsiders, deviants and outcasts, and the arena of state crime offers real possibilities for an extension of this work.

An international criminology must learn from and extend its own domestic humanizing discourse to bigger questions concerning state violence of the order discussed in this chapter. In a short chapter it has been impossible to do more than scratch the surface of these complex issues, but we hope to have provided some pointers for future research.

Key Reading

Cohen, S. (2001) *States of Denial: Knowing about Atrocities and Suffering.* Cambridge: Polity Press.

de Swaan, A. (2001) 'Dyscivilization, mass extermination and the state', *Theory, Culture & Society*, 18(2–3): 265–76.

Green, P. and Ward, T. (2004) *State Crime: Governments, Violence and Corruption.* London: Pluto Press.

Hinton, A.L. (ed.) (2002) *Genocide: An Anthropological Reader.* Oxford: Blackwell.

Huggins, M.K., Haritos-Fatouros, M. and Zimbardo, P.G. (2002) *Violence Workers: Police Torturers and Murderers Reconstruct Brazilian Atrocities.* Berkeley: University of California Press.

Tilly, C. (1992) *Coercion, Capital, and European States, AD 990–1992.* Oxford: Blackwell.

Notes

1 This chapter owes a great deal, especially as regards our discussion of Elias, to Peter Young, though he is not responsible for any violence we may have done to Elias's theories.

2 In this respect, what Poulantzas (1978b: 42–3) writes about Pierre Clastres could equally well be applied to Elias.

3 This is the term used by Elias in the original German and, following its popularization by Bourdieu, in the latest (2000) translation.

4 There is little research on women's involvement in state violence, but what little there is does not suggest that they behave very differently from men (Hunt, 1985; Westmarland, 2002; McKelvey, 2007).

5 This is not the place for a critique of Elias, but his treatment of colonialism, the position of women and nature of capitalism are all, at best, distinctly thin.

6 On 3 September 2007, in the Turkish Grand National Assembly, Prime Minister Raycip Tayip Erdogan reasserted his government's stance: '*I want to especially underline something again. It is our zero tolerance for torture within this period. … Yes, I say this assertively, zero tolerance for torture*' (www.ihd.org.tr/press/press20070906.html).

7 For example, the Human Rights Association of Turkey, the Islamic Mazlumder and the Turkish Human Rights Foundation.

8 This is what Risse and Sikkink (1999) have termed 'transnational advocacy networks' for the dissemination of international human rights and environmental related norms.

9 There have been nine reform packages in all, six overseen by the Justice and Development Party (AKP). They have included the abolition of the death penalty in peace-time, the abolition of the ban on minority languages in education, the repeal of the ban on broadcasting in languages other than Turkish and the abolition of the State Security Courts. A new Penal Code, revised for the first time in 78 years, which entered into force in June 2005, introduced measures making it easier to convict members of the state security services for human rights violations. It provides tougher penalties for torturers and criminalizes genocide, crimes against humanity and trafficking in people.

9

THE 'EXCEPTIONAL' STATE

Paddy Hillyard

―――――――――――――――――――― **Introduction** ――――――――――――――――――――

Policing the Crisis (*PtC*) was a seminal and prescient work. As well as examining the political, economic and the ideological characteristics of mugging, it charted the progress towards a law and order society, or what the authors termed, the 'exceptional state'.[1] There is some doubt whether or not they considered that the exceptional state had arrived or whether we were progressing towards it. Chapter 9 is entitled 'The Law-and-Order Society: *Towards* the "Exceptional State"' (emphasis added). Yet in the chapter itself they imply that 'the dialectical movement' by which the law and order panic becomes institutionalized in the exceptional form had occurred in the 1970s. They argue that the political dimension of the 'exceptional state', 'gradually emerged between 1968 and 1972 and which now appears, for the "duration" at least, to be permanently installed' (Hall et al., 1978: 306).

The authors suggest that the movement towards the exceptional state was made up of three phases. The first phase witnessed the state increasingly resorting to the law and they comment that 'the sheer comprehensiveness of the supporting legislative activity in this period, all of it culminating in the tightening of legal sanctions, is staggering' (Hall et al., 1978: 288). The second phase was the increasing use of law-enforcement personnel in the exercise of 'informal control'. The third phase involved the convergence of these and other issues 'ideologically' at what they term 'the violence threshold' (Hall et al., 1978: 288).

Hall, however, when he presented the Cobden Trust Human Rights Day Lecture a year after the book was published, made it clear that we had not yet reached the moment when Britain could be described as a 'law and order society' or an 'exceptional state'. He entitled his talk *Drifting into a Law and Order Society*, which he opened with the memorable words:

> We are now in the middle of a deep and decisive movement towards a more disciplinary, authoritarian kind of society. This shift has been in progress since the 1960s; but it has gathered pace though the 1970s and is heading, given the spate of disciplinary legislation now on the parliamentary agenda, towards some sort of interim climax. (Hall, 1980c: 3)

This chapter builds upon the initial insights developed by Hall and his colleagues and examines the coercive developments over the last thirty years.[2] It concludes in considering whether it is now appropriate to describe Britain as an exceptional state. Has the 'interim climax' passed and, if so, has the exceptional state now been achieved? The three phases described in *Policing the Crisis* are used as a structure for the chapter and in order to consider a range of coercive developments. A fourth phase – the development of a 'surveillance society' – is added. The technology for this development was just on the horizon when *Policing the Crisis* was published. Real-time surveillance of large sections of the population is now possible, further enhancing the disciplinary, authoritarian society described in *Policing the Crisis*.

These authoritarian developments in the 1970s were explored by others in the 1980s. *Law, Order and the Authoritarian State* (Scraton, 1987) provided a detailed analysis, from a critical criminological perspective, of a range of coercive criminal justice policies and practices introduced under Mrs Thatcher. *The Coercive State: The Decline of Democracy in Britain* (Hillyard and Percy-Smith, 1988) took a wider perspective and analysed a range of legislative changes within and beyond the welfare state and the criminal justice system. This led to increased coercion through the provision of greater powers of classification, categorization and intervention, powers which were non-accountable and subject to little democratic control. The key feature of *Policing the Crisis* and the work that built on its insights was that the state was at the centre of the analysis.

Since the publication of the *Coercive State*, yet more coercive measures and powers have been introduced, expanding the authoritarian and disciplinary nature of the modern British state. The central argument of this chapter is that 'counter-terrorism'[3] measures have been pivotal in the restructuring of the relationship between citizens and the state, first in relation to the conflict in Ireland and now in relation to the political violence stemming from within the Islamic community. The 'counter-terrorism' measures, however, have had a differential impact on each of three key features of the exceptional state.

Expansion in the Role of Law

The first phase towards the exceptional state, according to Hall et al., was the resort to law. *Policing the Crisis* provided rich descriptions of some of the key statutes in the early 1970s – the Industrial Relations Act 1971, the Immigration Act 1971, the Northern Ireland (Emergency Provisions) Act 1973. Labour, migrants and nationalists/ republicans in Northern Ireland were all subject to new forms of discipline through the law. It was also the beginning of a sustained attack on the welfare state. Discontentment with the post-war political and social order, it was argued, was successfully mobilized around a right-wing solution – a process which Hall described as 'authoritarian populism' (Hall, 1980a), which he later expanded upon with Jacques (Hall and Jacques, 1983; see also Jessop et al., 1984).

The legislative impulse, and the mobilization of coercive law, have continued under New Labour. Between 1997 and 2007 there have been over 400 Acts of Parliament, containing over 23,000 sections, and nearly 32,000 statutory instruments – one for every hour New Labour has been in power (Hillyard, 2007). Criminal law has formed around 14% of this output and it is estimated that it has led to the creation of 3,000 new criminal offences (Wilson, 2006). Although this is likely to be an exaggeration due to the re-enactment of old offences, nevertheless it provides a stark indicator of the scale of criminalization which has taken place. Criminal policy solutions have been introduced to ever more areas of public life. Key areas of social policy – housing, education, children and family policy, and employment – have become dominated by crime control objectives, a development that Cook and others have described as the 'criminalization of social policy' (Cook, 2006; Squires and Stephens, 2005; Rodger, 2008).

Alongside the increasing criminalization of social behaviour, the legislative output has been characterized by two other equally important, but less commented upon, features. First, there has been a normalization of 'counter-terror' measures and practices, both in terms of their incorporation into the ordinary criminal law and in making the 'counter-terrorism' legislation permanent rather than subject to annual re-enactment. Second, social control has increasingly been focused on space – a process which is labelled here as the 'spatialization of social control'.

'Counter-terrorism' Powers

The first and most significant feature of the legislative output over the last thirty years has been the centrality of 'counter-terrorism' legislation. The two pieces of legislation introduced in the 1970s to deal with Irish political violence,[4] and described by Hall et al. (1978), have both been amended and extended on a number of occasions. However, following Lord Lloyd of Berwick's inquiry into the legislation, the government enacted most of his recommendations in the Terrorism Act 2000. The old law was repealed and most of the main provisions re-enacted, but crucially the annual review of the legislation by Parliament was abolished, making the main provisions of the Act permanent. Moreover, whereas the old legislation covered 'Irish terrorism', the new legislation now covers Irish, international and domestic 'terrorism'. The first year of the new millennium was, therefore, the defining moment when 'counter-terrorism' legislation was normalized and no longer considered as exceptional, leading to a permanent twin-track system of justice, with one for 'terrorist' suspects and another for those involved in conventionally defined crime.

Following the attacks on the Twin Towers in New York in September 2001, the government hastily enacted further 'counter-terrorism' legislation.[5] New provisions concerning the funding of political violence, measures to ensure greater cooperation between government departments and agencies domestically and increased cooperation with police and judiciaries internationally, and further extensions to existing police powers, were introduced. The new powers allow the police to search for identifying marks and to demand the removal of facial coverings or face paint to obtain good photographs. They also allow the British Transport Police and Ministry of Defence Police to act outside their railway and ministry of defence jurisdictions if asked to do so. In effect, the clear distinction between the police and the army has become blurred.

In 2005, the government introduced more 'counter-terror' measures, including the controversial control orders.[6] These allow for special obligations to be imposed on individuals who have not been convicted of any criminal offence, but are merely 'suspected' of being involved in 'terrorism'. Orders may prohibit the possession or use of certain items, place restrictions on movement to or within certain areas and ban specified forms of communications and associations. In 2006, six men, who had been placed on control orders, appealed to the High Court. The judge ruled that the orders were illegal because they broke the Human Rights Act.[7]

Following the bombings and attempted bombings in London on 7 July and 21 July 2005, yet more 'counter-terrorism' measures were introduced.[8] Executive powers for proscription were extended to permit the Secretary of State, among other things, to ban those organizations or groups which 'glorify terrorism'. In addition, a range of new offences were introduced, including encouraging 'terrorism' and disseminating 'terrorist' publications. But most controversially of all, they included the power to detain 'terrorist' suspects for up to 28 days.[9] Originally, the government had suggested 90 days, arguably a cynical tactic to make it easier to obtain a shorter period. Thus, what started as a seven-day detention limit in 1974 was doubled and then doubled again in the course of thirty odd years. As Seamus Milne remarked, 'The arbitrariness of this ratcheting-up is obvious: in spite of the fact that we're talking about the country's most basic civil liberties, it has clearly been a matter of think of a number and double it' (Milne, 2007).

In 2008, the government published another 'counter-terrorism' piece of legisla-tion.[10] Among a range of further measures, it provided the power to extend the time a suspect may be detained from 28 to 42 days, contained proposals to allow judges to give longer sentences for 'ordinary' offences if they had a 'terrorism' connection, permitted secret trials to determine the confiscation of property and introduced a range of new offences. It also provided for inquests to be convened before specially appointed coroners in the interests of 'national security' or the 'public interest', making the secret state even more of a reality.

What this brief analysis has shown is that over the last eight years the 'counter-terrorism' laws have been rewritten providing a range of new executive, administra-tive and criminal law powers. As Conor Gearty (2008: 29) has observed, they are 'now unrecognizable from the slim, temporary emergency measures' introduced in 1974. They have provided a range of new, largely unaccountable, discretionary powers to the police and Secretaries of State alike, which will be explored in greater depth below.

Spatialization of Social Control

The second key feature of the legislative output has been the focus on space and ways to control its use. Coleman (2007: 171) has powerfully argued that the spatial measures may best be understood in terms of what he calls the 'neo-liberalization of the city', where the urban poor are constituted as a problem in the face of 'investment, individualization, competitiveness and market sovereignty'. The increasing spatialization of social control draws much from 'counter-terrorism' measures.

The exclusion order, which was introduced in 1974,[11] allowed the Secretary of State to ban an individual from living in England, Scotland or Wales and forcing them to live in either the Republic of Ireland or Northern Ireland. In 1986, 'exclusion orders', note that even the name is the same, were introduced to deal with wayward footballer supporters and permitted the courts to prohibit anyone who was convicted of a football-related offence from attending prescribed football matches.[12] Three years later, football supporters were subject to further spatial control through 'restriction orders'. These were aimed at stopping fans travelling abroad and required the individual to report to a police station on the occasion of a designated football match outside England and Wales.[13] In 2000, exclusion orders were extended to all offences, not just those carried out by those involved in football offences. Now anyone found guilty of an offence can be excluded from entering a specified space for up to two years.[14] In 2006, anti-social drinkers were targeted and were banned from pubs and clubs in a defined geographical area if they had engaged in criminal or disorderly conduct.[15]

Anti-social behaviour orders (ASBOs), which were introduced in 1998[16] (see Squires and Stephens, 2005), are a clear descendant of exclusion orders. The law has subsequently been modified and extended in three further pieces of legislation.[17] The police, local authorities, housing action trusts or registered social landlords can now apply to a court for an order. They can include a range of instructions prohibiting the anti-social behaviour through banning the person from spending time with a particular group of friends. But the most important element, which is often included in an order, is to ban the person from visiting certain areas. The procedure is civil and, as Sanders and Young (2007: 11) have argued, it is a way 'to neutralise the practical impact of the standard of proof' used for criminal proceedings. Nearly 10,000 ASBOs were issued between April 1999 and December 2005, but it is not known how many of these included bans from specific areas.[18]

Another form of spatial control is the curfew. Traditionally used by the military to impose control,[19] it migrated from the military to the civilian context in 1991 when the government introduced curfew orders for anyone convicted of a criminal offence. They require the person to remain in a specified place. It was not long, however, before curfew orders were introduced as an informal repressive measure, as will be seen below.

Some of these spatial forms of social exclusion and restrictions now involve electronic monitoring. Initially, electronic tagging was permitted only for those convicted of offences and made subject to some sort of order, such as the curfew order,[20] but it is now used for pre-trial suspects and post-release offenders as well. Between January 1999 and January 2009, 500,000 people were subject to some method of electronic monitoring and, unsurprisingly, with this through-put, the UK now has the largest electronic monitoring programme in the world.[21]

All the new forms of spatial exclusion for British citizens have developed in parallel with what Webber has described as a 'war on migration'. Visa controls have been strengthened, 'buffer zones' created around western Europe, controls exported to countries of origin and transit and carrier sanctions have been introduced, all with the aim of excluding refugees and migrants from Britain (Webber, 2004). The European Union, under the third pillar, has played a crucial role in these developments (Hayes, 2008). If asylum seekers and refugees do arrive, they are subject to criminalization, detention, dispersion and segregation from mainstream society. There are now ten Immigration Service Removal Centres and another five Immigration Short-term Holding Centres which, in September 2006, had between them a total population of over 2,000 people held under the Immigration Acts powers (Bennett et al., 2007).

New Labour's resort to law has been quantitatively and qualitatively different from that of the Conservatives. They have normalized emergency legislation and relied heavily on the control of space. A strong symbiotic relationship has developed between the ordinary and the extraordinary law, with each radically affecting the other and vice versa. Different measures have mutated back and forth but in more draconian form. At the same time, the sheer volume of 'counter-terrorism' legalization has fundamentally reshaped the powers of the police and executive. The introduction of control orders, the 28-day detention period, secret trials to determine the confiscation of property and a raft of new offences, including the glorification of 'terrorism' and the blurring of the distinction between the police and army, have all changed fundamentally the relationship between the state and the citizen in Britain.

Expansion of Informal Control

Hall et al. suggest that the second phase in the movement to the exceptional state is the greater use of informal control. Although they do not elaborate on what they mean, they do provide some indications concerning their thinking in this area. In essence, informal control is concerned with the 'arbitrary exercise of repression' (Hall et al., 1978: 288). They cite the use of internment in Northern Ireland and the torture of a selected number of internees as examples of 'informal' methods. Here, informal control is defined in terms of any discretion of state officials to exercise coercive powers, whether on the streets or in government offices and where accountability and sanctioning mechanisms are extremely limited or ineffectual, notwithstanding the powers having a clear basis in law. Using this definition, it will be argued that the exercise of informal control has continued to increase over the last thirty years.

Curfew orders provide one example. As was shown above, these migrated in 1991 from military use into the ordinary criminal law as a measure following conviction. In 1998, however, local authorities were given the power to impose curfew orders preventing children under 10 (and significantly, therefore, under the age of criminal responsibility) from designated places at specified hours.[22] Then, in 2001, the child curfew schemes, as predicted, were extended to children under 16 and enabled the police, as well as the local authorities, to impose curfews.[23]

A second example of an informal repressive power, which also draws upon the notion of a 'designated area', is the new police power introduced in 2003.[24] This gives the police

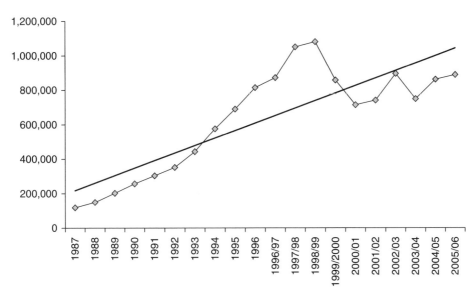

Figure 9.1 Stop and searches under section 1 of PACE, 1986–2005/06

Source: Home Office statistics.

the power to disperse groups causing or likely to cause intimidation, harassment, alarm or distress as a result of their presence in a public place. In 2005, the concept of a 'designated site' was deployed to curtail protests outside the Houses of Commons and a number of other buildings. A person now commits an offence if they enter on, as a trespasser, any 'designated site' in England and Wales or Northern Ireland.[25] The sites are an odd mixture of monarchical residences and seats of governance.[26]

A third example of the extension of informal repression is in relation to stop and search and arrest. Since the publication of *Policing the Crisis* there has been a significant expansion in police powers in both areas. In 1984 stop and search powers were extended to accommodate existing illegal police practices.[27] Ten years later they were extended to permit stop/searches to be made in anticipation of violence in any locality.[28] In 2000, further stop and search powers were given to the police to prevent acts of 'terrorism'.[29]

Arrest powers have shown a similar pattern. In 1984, the category of 'arrestable offence' was widened to allow an arrest where, for example, the name and address of the person was not obtainable.[30] 'Preventive quasi arrest powers', as Sanders and Young (2007: 115) describe them, have multiplied in recent years. For example, in 1998 the police were given the power to 'remove' school-age children from public places.[31] The most radical change was made in 2005[32] when all offences became 'arrestable offences' provided the police considered it necessary either for the investigation of a crime or the conduct of the person (Sanders and Young, 2007: 119).

Figure 9.1 shows the number of stops and searches under section 1 of the Police and Criminal Evidence Act 1984 (PACE) from 1987 to 2005/06.[33] Notwithstanding

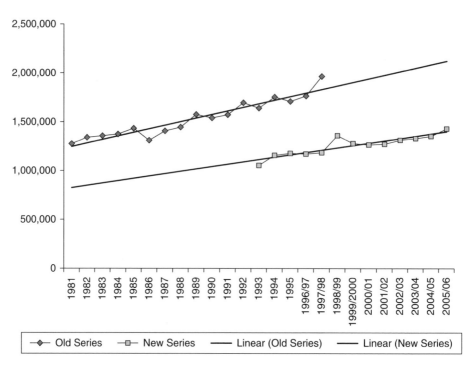

Figure 9.2   Arrests in England and Wales 1981–2005/06

Source: Home Office Statistics.

the obvious problems associated with these statistics, particularly the possibility of systematic under-recording, the figures suggest that there was a steady increase in the use of the powers over the period despite the sharp decline following the Stephen Lawrence inquiry (Macpherson, 1999). In 2005/06 nearly 900,000 people were stopped and searched in England and Wales.

Figure 9.2 shows the trends in arrests using two different data sets: one published by the Chief Inspector of Constabulary based on PACE[34] and the other by the Home Office based on legislation to monitor the treatment of ethnic minorities in the criminal justice system.[35] Both series show upward trends. Based on the new series, 1.43 million arrests occurred in England and Wales in 2005/06. It is not known how many of these involved the arrest of the same person, but it suggests that every year the police arrest much more than the total population of Birmingham, the second largest city in England and Wales, but in over 40% of arrests no further action is taken by the police.[36]

While informal control by the police has expanded, the numbers being dealt with in the courts has been steady declining. In 1981, over 44,000 people were found guilty in all courts and sentenced. But this dropped to just over 32,000 in 2006. However, those who did come before the courts were dealt with much more harshly, as can be seen in Table 9.1. The proportion sentenced by way of a fine or a discharge dropped

Table 9.1   Total number of people found guilty in all courts and sentenced, 1980 and 2006

Disposal/sentence	1980	%	2006	%
Fine	219,056	49.7	51,628	17.1
Discharges	52,298	11.9	40,300	13.3
Community sentence	80,202	18.2	102,971	34
Suspended sentence	30,881	7	20,799	6.9
Immediate sentence	53,976	12.2	73,532	24.3
Otherwise dealt with	4,551	1	13,307	4.4
Total	**440,964**	**100**	**302,537**	**100**

Source: Home Office statistics.

by half and the proportion subject to intermediate imprisonment, or some form of formal control in the community, doubled. With a quarter of all persons found guilty now being sent to prison, coupled with longer sentences, it is no surprise that the prison population has reached over 82,000. The government's solution is to expand further the capacity of jails in England and Wales by building three new 'Titan' prisons holding 2,500 inmates each. Together with other building developments, this will increase the prison capacity to 96,000 by 2014 at a cost of an extra £1.2 billion.

Surveillance

A third and equally significant characteristic of the exceptional state is the ever expanding use of surveillance as a method of control (Bunyan, 2005). Thirty years ago when Hall et al. were analysing the trends towards the exceptional state, the technology for a 'surveillance society' was only starting to be developed. Now surveillance at both the spatial and individual levels has become part of the repressive control apparatus along with the expansion in criminal law.

The attempt to stem Irish political violence played a significant role in the development of state surveillance on these islands. The army in Northern Ireland routinely collated a mass of information on individuals and their homes in republican/nationalist areas and the police, army and local businesses made extensive use of CCTV. All of these activities provided the platform for the continual development of the technologies. Following the murder of James Bulger in February 1993, the use of CCTV to survey public spaces spread rapidly in England and Wales (Coleman, 2004). Precise numbers are unknown, but there appears to be a consensus that there are about 5 million cameras in the United Kingdom – roughly one for every four households. It is further estimated that the UK has about 20% of all the cameras in the world and the average Londoner is likely to be monitored by 300 cameras as they go about their daily work (O'Neill, 2006). In contrast to the legislative output to control individuals in public spaces, there has been little or no legislation to control the surveillance of public spaces. Camerawatch has noted that 90% of CCTV installations failed to comply with the Information Commissioner's UK CCTV Code of Practice, and many installations operate illegally (Reid, 2007).

This rapid growth in the surveillance of public spaces has been accompanied by a phenomenal growth in the surveillance of individuals in a variety of different ways. First, state officials now have extensive powers to intercept telecommunications and to acquire communications data – internet usage, phone calls, mobile phone calls, faxes and emails – under Regulation of Investigatory Powers Act 2000 (RIPA) (Statewatch, 2003b). Initially, the retention of communication data was voluntary, but under a recent EU directive it is now mandatory for service providers to retain all information.

In 2004, the list of those able to acquire communications data was extended and now includes a wide range of state officials. It includes 52 police forces and 12 other law enforcement agencies, including the Royal Military Police and the British Transport Police. It also includes the Serious Organized Crime Agency, the Serious Fraud Office and HM Revenue and Customs, as well as the security and intelligence and law enforcement agencies. Outside law enforcement agencies, all 474 local authorities and over 100 public authorities are entitled to access telecommunication data. This means that some 795 organizations made up of hundreds of thousands of personnel have access to other people's telecommunication information.[37]

RIPA established an Interception of Communications Commissioner who reports to Parliament on an irregular basis, which makes statistical comparisons difficult. However, the data presented in the 2005/06 and 2006 reports (Kennedy, 2008; Swinton, 2007) suggests that nearly 7,000 people annually are having their phone calls listened to and their emails read and that around 350,000 requests are made annually for access to communication data, suggesting that communication data on 11 people in every 1,000 men, women and children in the UK are being examined annually by state officials. Further changes were introduced following the attacks on the World Trade Center when far-reaching measures were made to facilitate access by the security, intelligence and law enforcement agencies to communications data.[38]

The second form of individual surveillance has been through the development of new databases containing personal information. These take many different forms, but one of the most controversial is the national DNA database which was established in 1995[39] to identify possible suspects for offences, and links between offences. The police have been able routinely to take DNA samples of people suspected of a crime, but until 2001, if a person was acquitted or charges were dropped[40] their DNA record was destroyed. Now the records can be retained. Moreover, since 2004 the DNA samples can be taken from anyone arrested for a recordable offence. The database contains 4.2 million profiles[41] and is expanding daily. Some 37% of black men in the UK are recorded on it compared with 9% of white men (Renderson, 2006). Between 1996 and 2005 the DNA profiles of 682,585 children under 18 were added to the database,[42] and in May 2007, *The Daily Mail* reported that the police were deliberately targeting children who had committed no offence to obtain a sample of their DNA (Slack, 2007).

Another highly controversial database is the government's planned National Identity Register. The necessary legal framework was introduced in 2006[43] and provides for the issuing of identity cards. The plan is to link the cards to the new identity register, which will contain details of an individual's name, date of birth, nationality, immigration status and address. Controversially, a separate but linked database will also contain biometric data, such as fingerprints or iris patterns.

New databases are being created to control and monitor the travelling public. These can provide a detailed record of a person's movements. The automatic recognition of vehicle number plates is being used for a variety of purposes. The Oyster card system, used on the London underground, records every use of the card in and out of stations and the information is now regularly used by the police to determine the movement of individuals and groups (BBC, 2006b).

Following the 9/11 attacks, the Bush administration reached an agreement with the EU in 2003 that passenger data (PNR – Personal Name Record) involving 19 items of personal information collected by all airlines which fly to the USA, should be sent to the USA Customs and Security Agencies irrespective of whether or not the flight itself went to the USA (Statewatch, 2007). The British government, however, wants a more extensive system which covers sea, rail travel and all domestic flights. The data would be stored for 13 years and used to 'profile suspects' (Traynor, 2008).

Some of these developments, such as the automatic vehicle number recognition systems, may be used for progressive purposes, for example, the London congestion charge or to control the speed of vehicles. Many of the developments are being resisted, such as the storage of DNA or the introduction of compulsory ID cards. While there will certainly be resistance to, and contradictions and unintended consequences around, the development of these measures, the technology has created the platform for further developments and there are powerful interests within both the public and private security sectors pushing hard for its use. One of the key driving forces, as Hayes (2009) has shown, is the EU. When combined with 'arbitrary exercise of repression', the various measures form a dangerous scenario. In 2004, Richard Thomas, the Information Commissioner, warned that the country was 'sleepwalking into a surveillance society'. In 2006, he said: 'Today I fear that we are in fact waking up to a surveillance society that is already all around us' (Bennetto, 2006b).

The Threshold of Violence

The last phase in the move towards the exceptional state which Hall et al. identify is the convergence of legislative activity and the shift towards informal control around the 'threshold of violence'. This is made up of two interrelated processes. The first involves the ideological mystification of what constitutes a threat to the social order. The constant focus on crime and 'terrorist' harms and, conversely, the lack of focus on a range of much more serious harms, such as accidents at work (Tombs, 2007), road traffic 'accidents', house fires, iatrogenesis and pollution, is at the heart of this process (Hillyard et al., 2004). The second involves mobilizing 'the law' to recruit the public in support of a more authoritarian strategy. Here the media plays a key role.

Many of the developments described in this chapter were (and are) constructed as responses to the perceived threats of violence on the streets of Britain stemming from aggressive soccer supporters, drunks, congregated groups of youths, political protesters and young black men. The most important and significant responses, which have determined the shape and form of the authoritarian and disciplinary state in Britain, however, have been in relation to political violence in Ireland. It will be argued that the defining moment in the development of the exceptional state in Britain was when the authorities began to collude with informers who committed hundreds of murders – a strategy which has been described as 'proxy state violence' (Jamieson and McEvoy, 2005: 512).

From the available evidence, it appears that the strategy was introduced in the early 1980s and was based on the development of a large network of informers, by both the police and the army within the paramilitaries, which ignored their criminal and often murderous activities. Indeed, the very success of the strategy depended upon the informers committing a range of crimes, including murder, in order to be accepted as part of the paramilitary organization (CAJ, 2007). The advantage of such a strategy is that any state involvement in the actual killings can always be denied.

On the loyalist side there is evidence that one informer was involved in the killing of more than ten people (PONI, 2007). In her investigation into one of these killings, the Police Ombudsman for Northern Ireland raised grave concerns about the practices of some police officers, including their failure to arrest informants for crimes; the concealment of intelligence; sham arrests of informers; deliberately misleading interview notes; not recording the criminal activities of the informant; not informing the Director of Public Prosecutions that an informant was a suspect in a crime; withholding from police colleagues intelligence; blocking searches; misleading the courts; destroying or losing forensic exhibits; and not adopting or complying with the UK Home Office Guidelines on matters relating to informant handling, based on the Regulation of Investigatory Powers Act when it came into force in 2000.

Informers were also recruited on the republican side and were responsible for a range of serious crimes. In 2003, it emerged that one highly placed informer was alleged to be head of the IRA's Internal Security unit, or what was known as the 'Nutting Squad'. It is alleged that the British government allowed up to 40 people to be killed in order to protect the key informer's position (Harding et al., 2003). As part of the strategy, Special Branch vetted all arrests and barred criminal investigations to protect their informers. As a result, Special Branch became a 'force within a force' (Patten, 1999: 72; Stalker, 1988: 117) and accountable to no one.

Throughout the period, there have been demands for independent investigations into a number of controversial killings, particularly those in which it appeared that there was some sort of state collusion. Apart form the Stalker investigation into the killings by the Royal Ulster Constabulary (RUC) of a number of IRA members in the early 1980s (Stalker, 1988), there were no investigations into disputed killings until the first of three inquiries carried out by Sir John Stevens into collusion between the security forces and loyalist paramilitaries in 1990 (Rolston and Scraton, 2005). In May 2002 the British and Irish governments asked Canadian Judge Peter Cory to investigate the allegations in seven key cases, including the murder of two human rights lawyers, Pat Finucane and Rosemary Nelson. Collusion occurs, he argued, when the army and police 'ignore or turn a blind eye to the wrongful acts of their servants or agents or supplying information to assist them in their wrongful acts or encouraging them to commit wrongful acts' (Cory, 2004: 20–1).

Following the recommendation from Judge Cory that there was *prima facie* evidence for public inquiries to be held into three of the cases he investigated, the government cynically introduced new legislation which severely limits the scope of public inquiries and gives far greater powers to ministers to control them.[44] Under the old law, the chair controlled the inquiry. Under the new law, the powers have been placed in the hands of the government ministers. Lord Saville, the Chair of the Bloody Sunday Tribunal, which is re-investigating the events of that day following the 'whitewash' by the Widgery Tribunal in 1972 (McMahon, 1974), objected strongly to the new legislation. He said:

> I take the view that this provision makes a very serious inroad into the independence of any inquiry and is likely to damage or destroy public confidence in the inquiry and its findings, especially in cases where the conduct of the authorities may be in question.[45]

This analysis has illustrated the British state's capacity for violence against its own citizens. The law has provided little control. Indeed, it has been successfully mobilized both to cover up and deny any wrongdoing. Arguably, the use of what would be termed 'death squads' in any other part of the world represented a significant turning point in British politics. While killing by proxy had been used in different colonial struggles, the key difference was that successive governments now permitted its use in a part of the UK with little critical comment from the mass media or intellectuals. On the contrary, popular opinion was successfully mobilized to support the view that the British state was the arbiter between two warring factions. This is the moment that the exceptional state came into being in Britain.

The lack of any prosecutions for collusion in Northern Ireland has sent out a clear signal that police and army personnel and members of the intelligence services can operate beyond the law without any legal redress in the new 'war on terror'. The allegations made in 2008 that MI5 was 'outsourcing' the torture of British citizens to a Pakistani intelligence agency (Cobain, 2008) or that the five torture techniques, banned by Edward Health following their use by the British Army in Northern Ireland during the initial internment swoops, were used by the British Army in Iraq in 2003 (BBC, 2008a), are illustrative of the disdain which the authorities now hold towards the rule of law.

Conclusion

Policing the Crisis was an important work in drawing attention to the changing form of the British state and placing the changes within a broader context of the UK's continuing economic decline as a world power. The authors' description of the movement towards the development of the exceptional state were prophetic but, understandably, underplayed both the rapid growth in technology which would herald the surveillance society and the important role of the European Union. They were correct about the 'nightmare dramatizations within the repressive state apparatuses' (Hall et al., 1978: 289) and the convergence around the theme of violence in which the Northern Ireland experience was crucial in the changing politics of the time. All the main elements outlined in *Policing the Crisis* have continued apace. The resort to criminal law and 'counter-terror' legislation has intensified and there has been a further increase in informal methods of coercive control, mostly with a spatial dimension. In addition, surveillance systems now make Britain one of the most surveilled societies in the world. Furthermore, the state's capacity for violence directed at its own citizens reached new levels in Northern Ireland. And all of this has been achieved through mobilizing popular support.

Policing the Crisis did not define the criteria by which an exceptional state can be identified. Indeed, as was shown in the introduction to this chapter, there was confusion over whether the authors of *Policing the Crisis* considered that the exceptional state had arrived or whether we were drifting towards it. It has been suggested here that the key defining point in Britain becoming an exceptional state was the level of violence directed towards its own citizens in Northern Ireland and the failure to hold any of the key actors or the political elite to account. Although the continuing resort to law, the increasing use of a wide range of personnel in the exercise of informal control, intensified surveillance of the population and the widespread shift away from the ordinary criminal law to the use of 'counter-terror' law are all essential elements of an exceptional state, the key element is the capacity to sanction and then condone the widespread killings of its own citizens in an attempt to control Irish political violence. The implications for the 'war on terror' are far-reaching.

Key Reading

CAJ (2007) *War on Terror: Lessons from Ireland.* Belfast: Committee on the Administration of Justice.

Cory, P. (2004) *Cory Collusion Inquiry Report: Patrick Finucane,* HC 470. London: HMSO.

Hillyard, P. and Percy-Smith, J. (1988) *The Coercive State: The Decline of Democracy in Britain.* London: Fontana.

Scraton, P. (ed.) (1987) *Law, Order and the Authoritarian State: Readings in Critical Criminology.* Milton Keynes: Open University Press.

---------- Notes ----------

1 Agamben (2005) has since developed the concept of the 'state of exception'. While there are connections and similarities between the state of exception and the exceptional state, Agamben's analysis is genealogical and philosophical and Hall et al.'s sociological.

2 I would like to thank Dave Whyte and Joe Sim for detailed and insightful comments and valuable advice on drafts of this chapter.

3 I use this phrase to describe legislation to deal with political violence. It is placed in parenthesis to draw attention to the ambiguity and one-sidedness of the concept. It may have helped, as has been argued in relation to Northern Ireland, to maintain and sustain terrorism (CAJ, 2007).

4 Northern Ireland (Emergency Provisions) Act 1973 and the Prevention of Terrorism Act 1974 (PTA).

5 Anti-Terrorism, Crime and Security Act 2001.

6 Prevention of Terrorism Act 2005.

7 'Judge quashes anti-terror orders', *BBC News*, 28 June 2006.

8 Terrorism Act 2006.

9 Terrorism Act 2006, section 23.

10 Counter-Terrorism Bill 2008.

11 Prevention of Terrorism Act 1974.

12 The Public Order Act 1986, section 30.

13 Football Spectators Act 1989. These powers were further extended in 1999.

14 Criminal Justice and Court Services Act 2000, section 40a.

15 Violent Crime Reduction Act 2006.

16 Crime and Disorder Act 1998.

17 The Police Reform Act 2002, the Anti-Social Behaviour Act 2003, Serious Organised Crime and Police Act 2005.

18 Home Office Crime Reduction website, retrieved 2 March 2008 from: www.crimereduction. homeoffice.gov.uk/asbos/asbos2.htm.

19 In 1972 the British Army imposed an illegal curfew on the Falls area of West Belfast. No one was allowed in or out of the designated area for three days (see Campbell and Connelly, 2003).

20 Criminal Justice Act 1991.

21 Electronic Monitoring Briefing – January 2009. Personal communication from Home Office.

22 Crime and Disorder Act 1998.

23 Criminal Justice and Police Act 2001.

24 Criminal Justice Act 2003, section 30.

25 The Serious Organised Crime and Police Act 2005, section 128.

26 The sites are listed and maps are also provided. See the Serious Organised Crime and Police Act 2005 (Designated Sites under Section 128) Order 2007, Statutory Instruments 2007, No. 930.

27 Police and Criminal Evidence Act (PACE) 1984.

28 Criminal Justice and Police Act 1994, section 60. For more information on these different series, see Hillyard and Gordon (1999).

29 Terrorism Act 2000, section 44.

30 Police and Criminal Evidence Act 1984, section 25.

31 Crime and Disorder Act 1998, section 16.

32 Serious Organised Crime and Police Act 2005, section 110.

33 See Home Office and Ministry of Justice annual bulletins on Arrests for Recorded Crime (Notifiable Offences) and the Operation of Certain Police Powers under PACE.
34 Criminal Law Act 1977, section 62.
35 Criminal Justice Act 1991, section 95.
36 The precise figure is unknown (see Hillyard and Gordon, 1999).
37 The Regulation of Investigatory Powers (Communications Data) Order 2003, Statutory Instrument 2003, No. 3172.
38 Anti-Terrorism, Crime and Security Act 2001.
39 Criminal Justice and Public Order Act 1994.
40 Criminal Justice and Police Act 2001.
41 *Hansard*, 21 February 2008, Col. 821w.
42 *Hansard*, 20 December 2005, Col. 2890w.
43 Identity Cards Act 2006.
44 Inquiries Act 2005.
45 Letter to Baroness Ashton at the Department of Constitutional Affairs, 26 January 2005.

10

INTELLIGENCE, TERRORISM AND THE STATE

Peter Gill

Introduction

What appears to be a 'security panic' in the wake of the September 2001 attacks in the USA, suggests parallels between the moral panic surrounding 'mugging' that inspired and informed the analysis of the relationship between the state and law and order in *Policing the Crisis* (Hall et al., 1978) and the current concerns of the 'war on terror'. However, while there are similarities, a direct comparison between 1970s 'street robbery' and 2000s 'political violence' would be rather artificial. Therefore, drawing on the theoretical framework for understanding the relation between state, law and violence set out in *Policing the Crisis*, this chapter compares events in Northern Ireland after 1969 with current concerns over 'terrorism'.[1]

Very large quantities of ink have been spilt on the subject of terrorism since 9/11 and much of this undoubtedly reflects an excessive over reaction to that attack – by academics as well as governments (see Guelke, 2006; Kegley, 2003, includes an excellent variety of conventional and critical discussions). This chapter focuses on the specific role of intelligence which, despite being characterized as 'the second oldest profession' (Knightley, 1986), has received remarkably little attention within the mainstream disciplines of political science or criminology. Most academic discussion in the UK has been historical. Until the 1990s this concentrated on the twentieth-century world wars but an increasing flow of file releases during the 1990s has widened this to include the inter- and post-war periods, or at least, those aspects where the files have been selected for release rather than destruction (Aldrich, 2002). Since 9/11 there has been more attention from a variety of scholars, mainly in international relations, but it still receives little attention outside the specific field of 'intelligence studies'.

The current context for intelligence is not propitious. Generations of secrecy have resulted in widespread ignorance about what intelligence does, but evidence that agencies are the means by which states – democratic or otherwise – carry out secret actions that they could not do legally or would not want to admit to reinforce suspicion. The end of the Cold War and a growth in a rights culture requiring all state agencies to be on a legal footing, including a procedure by which aggrieved citizens might obtain remedies, saw increased openness and accountability in the 1990s but the shockwaves emanating from 9/11 are still being felt. This combination of failures to prevent attacks and correctly identify the absence of weapons of mass destruction (WMD) in Iraq has led to widespread mistrust of intelligence *at the very time* that government insists that its contribution to security is essential. In one sense, intelligence agencies are suffering from the same ever-increasing reliance on expert knowledge, combined with critical reflexivity, that has led to a growing distrust of government more generally (Hudson, 2003: 44; and see Loader and Walker, 2007: 197). But this afflicts intelligence even more strongly because most of what agencies do remains secret and because their 'knowledge' may be so tenuous in the first place. As we shall see below, this has a crucial significance in terms of the current workings of law within counter-terrorism.

States and Security

In *Policing the Crisis*, Hall et al. perceived three phases that characterized the relation between state, law and violence in the 1970s as it became institutionalized in an 'exceptional' form of the state: the overwhelming tendency of the state to move in the direction of the law; increased employment of law enforcement agencies in exercising 'informal' control; and, finally, their convergence at the threshold of 'violence' (1978: 288).

Those phases took place in response to a crisis that was understood, first, as a crisis of and for British capitalism as it struggled with world recession and, more specifically, to cope with changing conditions from 'a weak, post-imperial economic base'. Second, there was a resulting crisis in social relations between contending political interests and forces involving especially the incorporation of the working class into managing capitalism. Third, it was a crisis of the state as it assumed a decisive role in the economic management of capital, thus becoming drawn earlier into conflicts between economic classes that required a 'corporate' style of crisis management. Fourth, it was a crisis of political legitimacy, touching on issues of consent and coercion. As the techniques of the former waned in the face of various but not especially coherent forms of resistance after 1970 – strikes, Northern Ireland, counter-culture …, assumed to be the product of conspiracies – then the more repressive features of the state became more prominent so that coercion became the natural form by which the state sought to secure consent (Hall et al., 1978: 317–20). The crisis was experienced by 'the majority' as a succession of moral panics, which eventually converged so that 'the enemy becomes both many-faceted *and* "one"' (1978: 323). The proliferating demons – drugs, pornography, hooligans, vandals, muggers – appeared as parts of a 'general conspiracy' and the resulting law-and-order society required the state to put things right, if necessary at the expense of freedoms enjoyed in more relaxed times.

The society is battening itself down for 'the long haul' through a crisis. There is light at the end of the tunnel – but not much and it is far off. Meanwhile, the state has won the right, and indeed inherited the duty, to move swiftly, to stamp fast and hard, to listen in, discreetly survey, saturate and swamp, charge or hold without charge, act on suspicion, hustle and shoulder, to keep society on the straight and narrow. Liberalism, that last back-stop against arbitrary power, is in retreat. It is suspended. The times are exceptional. The crisis is real. We are inside the 'law-and-order' state. (1978: 323)

Terrorism, Then and Now

Though the term 'globalization' was not in common use in 1978, it would be wrong to conclude that Hall et al. were unaware of international developments: examining the factors leading to the authoritarian backlash to the late 1960s, they note: 'the constant attention to international developments suggests that it was the convergence of forces inside and outside society tending to disrupt its equilibrium which hastened on the reaction' (1978: 258). The crisis in Northern Ireland (NI) is one of the factors they have in mind and it represents an important comparison to be made with current developments since British experience of political violence there is cited by both advocates and critics of the official contention that the threat posed by al-Qaeda is qualitatively different. *Policing the Crisis* traced briefly the onset of the NI crisis as the product of the 'long and disastrous history of repression' (1978: 258) over more than 400 years, the introduction of British troops in NI in August 1969, internment in 1971 and the suspension of Stormont after Bloody Sunday in January 1972. The crisis deepened to the accompaniment of the 'steadily repeated view' that the whole situation was 'the product of that collective insanity and irrationalism called "Ireland" ... [that signified] the Ulster crisis as beyond comprehension, without reason and rationale, a mindless madness' (1978: 297).

Of course, the narrative in *Policing the Crisis* concludes around 1976, and we might note briefly some of the main developments in counter-terrorism in NI thereafter. The basic legal structures remained intact – subsequent changes to the Prevention of Terrorism Act in 1989 were directed at extending the powers to provide for financial investigation of rackets by which paramilitary groups in NI funded their activities, but also to extend the coverage of the provisions of extended detention and proscription to include 'international terrorism' (see Walker, 2002). The period of military dominance, including internment (1969–75), was identified in *Policing the Crisis* as an 'example of the overwhelming tendency of the state to move in the direction of the law', which blurred the thin line distinguishing the legal from the arbitrary exercise of 'informal' repression (Hall et al., 1978: 288), and it was acknowledged eventually as a political and security disaster. This produced the most significant policy shift in 1976 as the British state sought to regain lost legitimacy by restoring 'police primacy' as part of an attempt to 'criminalize' the issue. However, this required amendments to normal 'due process', including the Diplock courts sitting without juries. This issue of the suitability or not of 'criminal justice' to deal with serious political violence remains a current theme, as we shall see below.

There were other developments that are relevant to current concerns. For example, technological surveillance was developed in the NI 'laboratory' to an extent that rendered the population the most surveilled anywhere in Europe, and some of these have found their way back 'home'. Vehicle registration identification systems, for example, were introduced as part of the 'ring of steel' around the City of London in the 1990s and also underpinned the introduction of congestion charging in London. Also, the introduction of police primacy was less than smooth. 'Intelligence wars' between different police and military intelligence units characterized NI, especially in the early years, but some of the tactics used by these units have only slowly become clear, courtesy of several inquiries consequent on the 'peace process' (discussed briefly below). During the conflict itself it became clear that army and police units would sometimes orchestrate the circumstances in which paramilitaries would be subjected to summary justice and killed rather than arrested, even if that were a possibility. The SAS killing of a Provisional IRA (PIRA) unit about to attack the police station at Loughall in 1987 is one example (Geraghty, 1998: 124–7); some murders by Royal Ulster Constabulary (RUC) officers in the early 1980s were similar but became enmeshed in a long controversy surrounding the investigation of the killings by John Stalker of the Greater Manchester Police (e.g. Gill, 1994: 194–6).

Throughout the 1980s, however, the suspicion grew in NI that other murders, usually presented to and by the media at the time as 'senseless' or 'sectarian', were not what they seemed; rather, they were sponsored or supported by the security forces. An inquiry was conducted by John Stevens, later Commissioner of the Metropolitan Police, and over 40 individuals were prosecuted or disciplined. A second inquiry (also unpublished) took place some years later and then, in May 1999, Stevens was asked to conduct a third inquiry, with particular reference to the murder of Pat Finucane in 1989, and a brief report was published in April 2003 (Stevens, 2003). While Stevens aimed to produce evidence that could be used in prosecution; in parallel, and as a result of the 1998 Good Friday agreement, Canadian Judge Peter Cory was asked to investigate the deaths of two RUC officers, Bob Buchanan and Harry Breen, Lord Justice Gibson and his wife, Robert Hamill, a young Catholic who was kicked to death by a loyalist mob while armed RUC officers were nearby, Pat Finucane and Rosemary Nelson, Catholic lawyers involved in the defence of people charged with violent offences and Billy Wright, a dissident Loyalist murdered in the Maze prison in 1997. Cory's mandate was not to make a final determination but to assess whether there was sufficient evidence of collusion as to warrant public inquiries, which, indeed, he did.

Cory and Stevens both concluded that there was strong evidence of collusion between the army, police, security service and paramilitaries. Their reports identified typical acts: making information available to counter-gangs that assisted them in targeting opposition (often via informers or by 'leaking' documents); failing to pass credible threat information on to those who could act; and turning a blind eye to the criminal acts of informants, including conspiracy to murder. But they also detailed the attempts by the agencies concerned to mislead investigators and overseers: obstruction of enquiries by concealing documents; destroying evidence in the possession of investigators, for example arson at John Stevens' incident room; and misleading courts (Stevens, 2003: 3.3–3.4; Cory, 2003: 1.284–1.288). In other words, the violence threshold identified by Hall et al. had clearly been crossed.

Now, most of the violence arising from the NI conflict took place there, though there were various campaigns in Britain, including the Birmingham pub bombing in 1974, that precipitated the passage of the first Prevention of Terrorism (Temporary Provisions) Act and also produced one of a notable series of miscarriage cases which were not finally acknowledged through appeals until the early 1990s. The PIRA threat was perceived as essentially a domestic problem, though it did have international implications in terms of fund-raising, acquiring weapons and occasional attacks on service personnel in Germany. Yet, PIRA was a tightly run, hierarchical organization which, as we now know, was penetrated at a high level (see, for example, Gill and Phythian, 2006: 68–70). In the early 1980s it was estimated to have about 10,000 sympathizers in NI, 1,200 of whom would support 'around 600 active terrorists' (Hennessy, 2007: 17). They were concentrated in some areas of the province, though active service units abroad might be more elusive and their *modus operandi* entailed more risk since those planning attacks wanted to escape and prior warnings were regularly provided, if not always accurate. Finally, their motivation – to drive Britain out of Ireland – was rational, even if unwelcome to the state and government. Thus, even if Hall et al. noted how the NI violence was presented to the British public as 'mindless', crucially, the security authorities knew full well it was not and reacted accordingly. How else can we account for MI6 personnel maintaining 'back channels' to PIRA through the worst periods of violence?

Against this picture, the current threat is presented by the UK government as distinctive in four respects: it is an international threat, with suspected terrorists coming from a range of African and Middle Eastern countries, if not actually born in the UK; the threat comes from various individuals, groups and networks, sometimes overlapping to assist each other but independent of state support; they intend to cause mass casualties and often to kill themselves in the process; and those involved are driven by particularly violent and extreme beliefs (HMG, 2006a: paras 31–7). Further, it appears that people may make a rapid shift from 'sympathizer' to potential bomber, and the profile of those seen as potentially dangerous keeps shifting. Like generals, intelligence analysts are prone to 'fighting the last war': after 9/11 the assumption was that the 'inevitable' attack in UK would come similarly from those travelling into the country to carry it out, not from a group born in the UK. After 7/7, greater attention was given to 'homegrown' bombers, but it is doubtful that the net had spread to include those working as hospital doctors, such as those involved in the thwarted attacks in June 2007. At different times, attention has been directed to various places of radicalization – mosques, prisons or gymnasiums – but another aspect of the current situation that is new is the role of the internet as a source of information and ideas – a very different target from penetrating a branch meeting.

So what is different is the increased *uncertainty*. Now, while '[t]errorism *is* the politics of uncertainty' (Ericson, 2007: 36, emphasis in the original), the *relative* certainty with which government calculated the numbers and identities of PIRA activists has been replaced by a veritable 'numbers game' (see Hall et al., 1978: 251). For example, Hennessy reports that by late spring 2005 there were estimated to be 2,000 'serious sympathizers', of whom 200 might be prepared to carry out a terrorist attack (2007: 37), but another source suggests that by July 2005 the number of 'primary investigative targets' known to MI5 had risen from about 250 in 2001 to 800 (Bennetto, 2006a). In a lecture in November 2006, Eliza Manningham-Buller, then Director General of MI5, referred to 200 'groupings or networks' involving 1,600 actively plotting or facilitating terrorist acts in UK or abroad, acknowledging 'many we don't know of' and suggesting that there could be 100,000 'sympathizers' based on polls of those believing 7/7 bombings were justified (2007: 67). A year later, her successor, Jonathan Evans, spoke of 2,000 known to be involved in terrorist activity in the UK, again referring to the probability of as many again who were unknown (Evans, 2007).

The 'Move to Law'

But just as the greater use of law was identified by Hall et al. as the first phase of the state's attempt to deal with crisis, so law has been one of the most significant responses to 9/11. But while terrorist legislation of the 1970s referred specifically to Northern Ireland, the increased uncertainty of a quarter-century later saw much more wide-ranging law based on the precautionary principle (for example, Ericson, 2007: 21–4). There is insufficient space to discuss the various measures in detail (for that, for example, see Walker, 2002, 2007), but the reasons for the legislation are important. Prior to 9/11 the Terrorism Act 2000 had already consolidated previous legislation but also extended it beyond Irish or 'international' terrorism, to cover all forms of violence motivated by political, religious or ideological factors. The definition was broader than that in 1974, which related to violence just for political ends. Yet, despite its recent passage, the Act was deemed to be inadequate to deal with the situation after 9/11 and the Anti-Terrorism, Crime and Security Act was passed swiftly, including various measures that had lain on Whitehall desks for some time but had not been brought forward before, including the freezing of assets. Most controversially, the Act introduced indefinite detention without trial for those non-citizens deemed by the Home Secretary to be security threats if they could not be deported because they would be likely to suffer torture in their home country. The House of Lords found this provision to be contrary to the European Court of Human Rights (ECHR) in December 2004 and, as a consequence, the government introduced the Prevention of Terrorism Act 2005.

In order to continue the policy of 'prevention', the government substituted a regime of 'control orders', by which suspects – whether citizens or non-citizens – might be subjected to limitations on their freedom of movement and association, for example, by 'tagging' and curfews. The government did not believe these would require any derogation from the ECHR, but they would impose 'derogating orders' if they wanted to subject someone to house arrest. No such orders have been imposed but about 30 'non-derogating orders' have been, subject to limited oversight by the High Court, whose power to reject orders is only if ministerial reasoning is found to be 'seriously flawed'. Of those detained, some have chosen to return voluntarily to their own country and some have absconded, but judicial challenges by others have, again, led the House of Lords to criticize the measures. The main grounds for this have been the length of some of the curfews (for example, 18 hours as 'unreasonable' but 16 hours is probably okay), but the core problem is with the process by which the orders may be challenged by detainees. This involves the use of 'special advocates' who act on behalf of the detainee but in a highly restricted way. They are chosen by government and subject to security clearance so that they may read the 'closed' (that is, intelligence) material on which the Minister makes her decision. However, the special advocate may only meet with the detainee *before* she has read this material; in other words, the detainee has no idea of the case against them when speaking with the advocate. The Court of Appeal upheld this 'principle' in October 2008 and, despite continuing controversy as to the consistency of control orders with the ECHR, Parliament renewed the provisions for a further year in March 2009.

However, in the meantime, the 7/7 London bombings prompted a further law, the Terrorism Act 2006, which criminalized 'acts preparatory to terrorism', the incitement or encouragement of others to commit acts of terrorism, including the 'glorification' of terrorism, the sale, loan or other dissemination of publications encouraging or assisting terrorism, and the giving or receiving of training in terrorist techniques. It also increased police powers to detain suspects without charge from 14 to 28 days. In the wake of the 7 July bombings, it is unsurprising that Tony Blair's response – 'the rules are changing' – apparently received widespread public support (*Guardian*, 22 August 2005: 4). However, over the next six months, the government were prevented by parliamentary opposition from getting all they wanted. For example, the government's initial proposal was to increase the period of possible pre-charge detention to 90 days.[2]

So, the development of the law since 9/11 has followed a different pattern compared with the original Prevention of Terrorism Act (PTA). That Act obtained broad cross-party support at the time, maintained it through subsequent renewal debates and no need was perceived to change it in response to subsequent bombings, for example, that aimed at the Cabinet in the Grand Hotel in Brighton in 1984. Since 9/11 the legislation has been introduced in reaction to events or disabling judicial decisions, but has been informed by more of a preventive logic as it has sought to empower authorities to intervene earlier in what *might* become an attack. But the problems of obtaining what qualifies as 'evidence' in a decision by the Crown Prosecution Service to prosecute, that is, that which provides a better than even chance of obtaining a conviction and the simple unwillingness of the intelligence agencies to have their sources and methods exposed within a trial, combine to rule out prosecution in some cases. Unprepared to run the political risk of being seen not to have acted to prevent any future attack, the state has sought to develop other methods – detention, control orders – as a solution to its problem.

It is this which has revealed the growing gap between the government's uncertain assessment of the risk of further attacks and its ability to prevent them by means of the criminal justice process. The only process by which this gap can be filled is intelligence; hence the continuing controversies over periods of pre-charge detention, control orders and deportations. In all these cases, government positions are based on intelligence information and advice which normally cannot be revealed and which are greeted with widespread scepticism, if not actual disbelief, in many quarters. Here, of course, recent governments have contributed to their own discomfort by misleading Parliament and people in 2002 and 2003 regarding the 'intelligence' on the existence of weapons of mass destruction in Iraq, and subsequent police operations have reminded us at regular intervals that 'intelligence' is always an uncertain basis for action, for example, the killing of Jean Charles de Menezes in 2005, the subsequent wounding at Forest Gate and the non-existent 'ricin plot'.

'Stamp Fast and Hard'

The second phase identified by Hall et al. in 1978 was the increased use of informal executive action to supplement the move to law. Since the publication of *Policing the Crisis*, the general shift towards prevention as the preferred policy for crime and other disorder has been reinforced by the post-9/11 perception of the terrorist threat as unprecedentedly unpredictable and lethal. The political problem for the state is to avoid measures which reinforce the alienation of the community within which those who might resort to violence live. For example, UK policy since 2003, known as CONTEST, has had four main strands, including (1) *prevention,* by means of 'tackling disadvantage and supporting reform', (2) 'deterring those who facilitate and encourage terrorism', (3) 'engaging in the battle of ideas' by challenging extremists' justification for the use of violence, and (4) the *pursuit* of terrorists and their operations by gathering intelligence, disrupting terrorist activity and international cooperation (HMG, 2006b: 1–2). It can be seen that there are contradictions inherent in the first of these, as revealed by leaked Cabinet, Home and Foreign Office papers on the position of the Muslim community in the UK. These papers revealed the 'strong cause of disillusionment' among Muslims as being the perception of the 'double standard' in British and US policy, which was reflected in bias towards Israel compared with Palestine and that the 'war on terror' and the wars in Iraq and Afghanistan were seen as acts against Islam (FCO/HO, 2004: 4–5).[3] But there are further problems in the 'move beyond law' when aspects of intelligence operations can be so damaging.

Even assuming that targeting is successful, that is, avoiding false positives and false negatives, gathering information presents problems. Technical means have advanced considerably since the 1970s but, then, so have the challenges, for example, freely available encryption for communications, transmission *via* fibre optics and the easy availability (and disposability) of mobile phones and hotmail addresses. But the key method is 'human intelligence', or informers, who are not only indispensable for countering terrorism, but also provide the potential for the greatest abuses of state power because of the lengths to which agencies may go in order to protect their 'sources'. A recent report from the Police Ombudsman for Northern Ireland, Nuala O'Loan, provides a chilling insight into Special Branch practices in an area of North Belfast during the 1990s: failing to comply with rules on informant handling, creating deliberately misleading interview notes, providing misleading documents to colleagues, the Director of Public Prosecutions and courts, destroying or losing forensic exhibits and concealing intelligence indicating the involvement of informants in murder (Police Ombudsman for Northern Ireland, 2007: 11–13). In comparing the situation with that today, of course, it has to be noted that security agencies in Northern Ireland took advantage of the fact that violence was inter-communal as well as anti-state. The circumstances in Britain now are different but the history of the use and abuse of informers should provide a cautionary tale.

Nothing indicates the marginalization of the criminal justice process as much as the policy of disruption. In one sense, there is nothing new: the Metropolitan Police were established in 1829 to *prevent* and detect crime, but the increasing perception among police and security officials of the criminal justice system as an increasingly complex series of hurdles, over which they must jump in order to obtain a conviction, while New Public Management establishes an array of performance targets, makes the avoidance of the whole process increasingly attractive. Add in the government's priority to prevent attacks above prosecutions and the intelligence agencies' insistence that their sources and methods may not be made public and it becomes clear that much counter-terrorism takes place invisibly. As noted above, the international dimension of the current threat distinguishes it from Northern Ireland and, consequently, 'international cooperation' is the third 'leg' of the government's pursuit strategy. This takes many forms. Some are quite formal, such as efforts in the EU to harmonize responses to terrorism, of which the main manifestation after 9/11 was the agreement for a common arrest warrant, thus short-circuiting the need for more complex extradition procedures. Much intelligence cooperation, however, takes place informally and is mainly bilateral rather than multilateral. Again, this reflects the sensitivity of agencies to losing control over their information. However, not surprisingly, given the secrecy of these exchanges, they are just as prone to abuse as the use of informers. This has been well illustrated by the US practice of kidnapping and outsourcing torture, aka 'extraordinary rendition', which has brought intelligence since 9/11 into even further disrepute (Marty, 2007).

So, when the UK state seeks to counter terrorism we see, typically, the development of a bifurcated system: policing, law and the criminal justice process are complemented by intelligence and covert action by police, security or military. To some extent the former needs to be insulated from the latter in order to safeguard 'due process', but there are many points at which they intersect. In Northern Ireland, the latter dominated until 1976. Thereafter, the Diplock courts process was introduced and represented the former while the 'dirty war', including collusion in the murder of alleged Republicans, continued, following the long tradition of British counter-insurgency operations. Now, the situation is rather more complex. First, since 9/11 the government has faced much more systematic opposition to its making of law on terrorism than it did during the 1970s. Second, once it has legislated, the provisions have been more likely to be successfully challenged now that the ECHR has been virtually incorporated into UK law by the Human Rights Act 1998. The judiciary has become far less deferential to the government (for example, the Lords' rejection of detention without trial in 2004) than it used to be on matters of national security (see Lustgarten and Leigh, 1994). Thus it has become more difficult for governments to re-model the criminal justice system in order to facilitate prosecution of those against whom terrorist acts are alleged. Third, however limited they may be, there are now a variety of oversight procedures in place regarding the authorization of communications interception and other surveillance powers, summarized in the Regulation of Investigatory Powers Act (RIPA), and parliamentary oversight of current policies that just did not exist in the 1970s (Gill and Phythian, 2006: 161–6; Intelligence and Security Committee, 2006).

Thus, *as far as we know*, a greater proportion of counter-terrorism now than then is being conducted within the view of the law, regulation and oversight. Many 'disputed killings' in NI remained un- or under-investigated for many years and it is only with the workings of the peace process since 1998 that some serious accounting is going on. Since 9/11 police have certainly increased yet further their capacity for violence, for example, taking advice from Sri Lanka and Israel on dealing with suicide bombers. The readiness to use new techniques became evident on 22 July 2005 when Jean Charles de Menezes was shot at Stockwell underground station. However unsatisfactory it is that the only prosecution of the Metropolitan Police in connection with the shooting of an innocent man was under health and safety legislation, it is important to note that there was an immediate independent investigation of the shooting, attempts by the Metropolitan Commissioner to delay it were unsuccessful and most of the facts of the shooting are now known. This would not have happened had the circumstances arisen in 1978.

If prosecution represents one end of a spectrum of counter-terrorist policy and murder the other, then some part of the middle ground between law and executive action is covered by policies of exclusion (see, for example, Bigo, 2006). Again, there is nothing specifically new in this – states have for a long time excluded those foreigners perceived to represent some threat – and the very idea of security in political communities has been developed via notions of some 'other' or 'enemy' (see Garland, 2001: 184, 193–4). Positive vetting was developed at the start of the Cold War on the basis of excluding those with communist sympathies from employment in security or military work, and a central provision of the Prevention of Terrorism Act 1974 was the power of ministers to exclude suspected terrorists from Britain. Security intelligence methodologies have always been based on notions of *categorical* suspicion – membership of particular movements or parties – but this idea has now been taken up by more routine practices of risk control so that people become suspicious via their membership of some group (for example, Hudson, 2003: 53–67). The clearest example of this since 9/11 is the new emphasis being given to profiling as a 'social ordering practice' (Lacey, 1994: 28–34), of which most of us have experience at airports but which, for some, is more of a daily reality in, for example, police stop and search practices. The deleterious impact of these (and other) practices on whole communities were detailed in the Irish case by Paddy Hillyard (1993) and, more recently, by the Metropolitan Police Authority in the case of London: 'Anti-terrorism stop and search is doing untold damage to certain communities' confidence in the police, and its effectiveness in countering terrorism is in serious doubt' (Metropolitan Police Authority, 2007: 4 and 44–51).

This brings us full circle. Fuelled by the panic about 'mugging', police use of stop and search was a major factor in the deteriorating relationship between young black and minority ethnic men in London, Liverpool and other cities through the 1970s that culminated in serious rioting in 1981. Stop and search powers are now more extensive – the Police and Criminal Evidence Act 1984 established uniform powers throughout the country with respect to crime but the Terrorism Act 2000 enables police to identify whole areas within which they may stop and search without the need to show reasonable suspicion (s. 44). The disproportionate impact of this upon young men of Asian appearance is clear but has so far not provoked resistance on the scale of that in the 1980s.

Conclusion

Has state power been consolidated rather than undermined by recent counter-terrorism practices? It is implicit in the discussion in this chapter that there can be no general answer to this conclusion, but perhaps one that deals with particular states at particular times. Any definitive answer to this question about the UK state in 2009 would require more careful empirical analysis than has been carried out by this author, but we can identify key issues.

First, state perceptions of the terrorist risk have changed from that in the 1970s. This reflects in part a tendency to describe any political violence that is happening *now* as 'mindless' because governments are anxious to discredit it as part of their effort to control it – the government can no more acknowledge now the link between its own foreign policies and their contribution to the alienation of some young Muslims than it could the impact of their social economic and policing policies on young black men in the 1970s. Governments are concerned with short-term political control, not long-term social analysis, however damaging this may be. But a combination of 'mindlessness' and the difficulty of locating those who actually *do* plan to use political violence has led to a seeming security panic. This is manifest in successive pieces of legislation that widen the net of 'targeting' to include not just those intending to commit violence but also those disseminating information about or 'glorifying' terrorism. This follows the precautionary logic and reinforces the intelligence agencies' methodology for mapping networks of suspects and, thereby, certainly is a consolidation of state power. But, on the other hand, if it leads security authorities into general surveillance and harassment of a largely peaceful Muslim population and increases the alienation of those who would otherwise not entertain violence, it might prove to be counter-productive. Any resulting cycle of legislation, surveillance, alienation and fear risks a vicious spiral that is destructive of security.

Thus, if one were to measure current state security capacities in terms of legal powers and budgetary allocations, then it is clear that state power in the UK has been consolidated; yet it is not the whole story. There has been a second 'move to law' in the security field since the 1970s which, to some extent, counters the impact of the first. This has been accompanied by the development of a different legal regime via the incorporation of the ECHR into law and its use by a judiciary that appears to be somewhat less deferential to the executive on matters of national security than was the case in the 1970s. There have been radical changes to the governance of intelligence agencies in the last thirty years, especially since the end of the Cold War. A central aspect of this – in both 'old' and 'new' democracies of Europe and elsewhere – is that intelligence agencies and activities that were governed, if at all, by executive decisions are now subject to legal regulation and oversight. Now, we must acknowledge the possibility that this new architecture serves primarily to 'legalize' what the agencies have always done rather than actually restrict it, and, indeed, the effectiveness of such regulations and oversight are very uneven. However, the constraints on the secret and unchecked abuse of executive power in the name of security *are* now greater than in Northern Ireland in the 1970s.

State intelligence agencies now work within a context of greater external supervision and authorization of their surveillance techniques and 'interferences with property' (Security Service Act 1989: s. 3), which, given their political sensitivity, will certainly inhibit any move to Hall et al.'s third phase – violence. Had these democratic constraints not been introduced, there is every chance that the agencies' response to post-9/11 concerns would have been as excessive as it was in Northern Ireland. However, we need to be concerned at the remaining gap in 'oversight' represented by military special forces, who represent the last resort of a state determined to exercise unchecked executive power and violence against 'enemies'. The 14th Intelligence Company, which was created in Northern Ireland in the 1970s for plain clothes surveillance, has now been absorbed into the Special Reconnaissance Regiment, intended for 'close target reconnaissance' (www.eliteukforces.info/special-reconnaissance-regiment, accessed 4 March 2008). Although mainly intended for work abroad, its members were involved in the botched surveillance operation in London leading to the Stockwell shooting in July 2005. The involvement of such units in surveillance in the UK as well as renditions abroad is still highly secret. But, having learned about the impact of the Army Force Research Unit, police Special Branch and Security Service activities in Northern Ireland, we are in a better position to challenge any systematic attempt to deploy these techniques in Britain in 2008. To be sure, the challenge is great because these techniques are designed specifically to operate outwith any legal framework, but the knowledge we have now, and the fact that it is 'legitimized' by official inquiries, gives us the opportunity to reinforce and pester the improved processes for political control of intelligence techniques and their oversight that have been established since the 1970s.

As it is, we face a different problem: the gap between the 'demand' for security and the state's ability to provide it widens continuously. Even the increased selling of security by the snake oil salespersons of the private sector cannot fill this gap. Indeed, their prosperity depends on the continuous growth of the very fears they claim to assuage. If the gap becomes too wide, there is a danger of a descent into hysteria (Garland, 2001: 131–5) or 'risk-crazed governance' (Carlen, 2007), in which (and here there is a direct resonance with the 1970s) the new security laws and practices are visited disproportionately on the Muslim minority. There is an unfortunate tendency for some ministers to conflate everything from 'hoodies' to terrorists when declaiming against lawlessness and we can predict the high likelihood that new 'anti-terrorist' measures will be used against future protesters against airport expansion, new nuclear power stations or climate change, *but* there is a key difference now: the state is not facing the kind of *generalized* crisis of legitimacy that it was in the 1970s. It is debatable whether the best characterization for the state we are in is still the 'authoritarian' state or whether it might not be the 'security', 'surveillant' or even the 'panicked' state. Whatever label we attach, states in capitalist democracies play a role in providing for general security as well as particular securities and the crucial political question is whether they can be prevented from acting repressively towards minorities now that we are more keenly aware of the security *dangers* of authoritarian practices visited on a small group than we were in the 1970s.

In crisis, the possibility of democratic control is weakened and effectiveness, not norms, becomes the standard for judging policies (Habermas, cited in Hudson, 2003: 169–70). Therefore, oversight is needed to cover both the practical effectiveness and ethical dimensions of risk control (Hudson, 2003: 156–7; Gill, 2004). Of course, there is a danger that new processes are deployed as much to assist ministers in the management of national security bureaucrats as to provide 'democratic accountability' and that their reports may remain little more than voices in the wilderness. Rights are a vital counter to the discourse of utilitarianism in risk society (Hudson, 2003: 223) but can they and political opposition provide only 'formal and pyrrhic victories' (Hall et al., 1978: 289)? I suggest that the responsibility is ours to resist authoritarianism, not just because it is repressive, especially to minorities, but also because it will be unsuccessful in achieving the security that people legitimately seek.

Key Reading

Burke, J. (2004) *Al Qaeda: The True Story of Radical Islam.* London: Penguin.
Gill, P. and Phythian, M. (2006) *Intelligence in an Insecure World.* Cambridge: Polity Press.
Hewitt, S. (2008) *The British War on Terror.* London: Continuum.

Kegley Jr., C.W. (ed.) (2003) *The New Global Terrorism: Characteristics, Causes, Controls.* Upper Saddle River, NJ: Prentice-Hall.

Wilson, R.A. (ed.) (2005) *Human Rights in the 'War on Terror'.* New York: Cambridge University Press.

Notes

1 Much ink has been spilt in the quest to define this term and some would not use it at all because it is used pejoratively by states to designate enemies and dissenters whether violent or not. That is indeed the case. However, the term is used here as a shorthand to describe 'the use or threat of serious violence for political purposes by state or non-state actors'.

2 In 2007 the government re-entered this debate by proposing a maximum period of pre-charge detention of 42 days but was unable to obtain parliamentary approval.

3 A Foreign Office official, Derek Pasquill, was charged under the Official Secrets Act for leaking the documents but was acquitted.

11

CRIME PREVENTION, COMMUNITY SAFETY AND THE LOCAL STATE

Lynn Hancock

--- **Introduction** ---

Policing the Crisis mapped the shift towards the 'exceptional state' over the post-war period. Hall et al. (1978) emphasized the state's increasingly coercive attempts to secure popular consent against the backdrop of deepening economic and political crises in the 1970s. The authors explore how young black people came to represent the fulcrum of the crisis in the public imagination: the 'new crime' of 'mugging' – in which young black men were widely believed to be implicated – came to signify a step-change in the developing social malaise that was reportedly enveloping Britain by the 1970s. Hall et al. (1978), in focusing their analysis on the social reaction to 'mugging', highlighted the significance of understanding how the state mobilized the 'law-abiding', 'moral majority' against 'soft', liberal social policies and approaches that had purportedly propelled Britain into a dysfunctional condition, and to which decisive, authoritarian interventions must attend. In this way, *Policing the Crisis* captured the beginnings of what was to become commonplace in the politics of crime control – sustained appeals to 'community', 'public opinion' and 'popular sentiment' – and the reconfiguration of the relationship between citizens and the state that this represents. State endeavours to both *redraw* ideas about 'crime', exemplified in the concept of 'mugging' and what it represented, and, at the same time, to foreclose the terms of debate about 'crime' were key concerns of *Policing the Crisis*. The parallels with contemporary ideas about 'anti-social behaviour', where attempts to clearly define what is 'anti-social behaviour' have been regarded by national and local policy-makers as being particularly unhelpful, are easy to draw. And, similarly, the commitment to encompass a wider range of behaviours, activities and conditions within understandings of 'anti-social behaviour', especially those that lie beyond the criminal law, has not been designed to open up a debate about the range of social harms that may cause 'alarm, distress and/or intimidation' (Home Office, 2003a: section 30).

Therefore, from the time that *Policing the Crisis* was written to now, the problem of the state and its power in leading and orchestrating debates about 'crime' remain a central problematic within the work of critical scholars.

Hall et al.'s (1978) analysis was located at the national state level, which raises questions about how the increasingly authoritarian attempts at this level to resolve the crisis of hegemony were responded to at the level of the local polity as the relationship between central and local government was reconfigured in the decades which followed. While a detailed mapping of local state responses lie beyond the scope of this chapter, it remains important nevertheless to understand the changing nature of central–local relations – the power of the central state over the local state – to reveal some of the key factors which shaped the direction of community safety and crime prevention policies, and acknowledge the significance of local autonomy in these developments. Local governments' attempts to *resist* the centre's efforts to curb their functions following the election of the Thatcher government in 1979 (Atkinson and Wilks-Heeg, 2000) and, conversely, their endeavours to *extend* them against central resistance (following the publication of the Morgan Report's recommendation that community safety become a statutory duty for local authorities in 1991, for example) illustrate the importance of these relations.

At this juncture, however, it is important to remember that relative autonomy (at local or national level) need not necessarily imply a neo-pluralist standpoint on the state. Some of the more sophisticated Marxist accounts not only recognize but assert the importance of some autonomy if the legitimization function of the state is to be exercised. Furthermore, informed by Gramsci's insights, Hall et al. (1978: 206) go further when they argue that 'the state could only provide the "theatre" for the organisation of hegemony, by working *through consent*. … Only by winning consent can the state exact both obligation and obedience' (emphasis in the original). However, as these authors note, 'won *for what*?' 'Won *by whom*?' (1978: 215, emphasis in the original). In turn, we are alerted to the question of how consent is secured at the local level and, drawing upon Hall et al. (1978), I employ the notion of tutelage to inform a discussion of these questions later in this chapter.

When *Policing the Crisis* was published in 1978, 'crime prevention' and 'community safety' had yet to arrive on the political agenda (Tilley, 2002). However, the term 'community safety' was being employed and promoted by 'police monitoring groups' which were forming at that time in Greater London and in other metropolitan authorities, but particularly after the election of New Left labour councils in 1981 (McLaughlin, 1994; Hughes, 2002a). Informed by left political analyses and with a focus on community action, monitoring groups campaigned against police brutality and highlighted the failure of the state to respond to racist attacks and domestic violence. Groups gave advice, engaged in support work and pushed for the democratic control of the police (McLaughlin, 1994). Later, the concept of 'community safety' was employed in the Morgan Report (1991) to transgress narrow, conventional definitions of 'crime'. By using the term in preference to 'crime prevention', it was hoped that 'greater participation from all sections of the community' would be achieved (Home Office, 1991, cited in Squires, 2006: 240; Hughes, 2002a). For some, then, the concept of 'community safety' offered opportunities for a 'replacement discourse' in which a range of social harms could be recognized, in contrast to the much narrower focus on 'crime prevention' (van Swaaningen, 2002; Gilling, 2007). Conservative governments in the 1980s and 1990s clearly rejected the 'community safety' orientation. Moreover, despite some conceptual 'slippage' among commentators in the late 1990s (Hughes, 2002b), 'New Labour preferred the [arguably narrower still] nomenclature of crime and disorder reduction' (Gilling, 2007: 2) when they came to power in 1997.

Writers regarded the Conservative governments' push towards crime prevention – the growth of multi-agency partnerships (MAPs) alongside situational approaches in the 1980s and 1990s – and the institutionalization of crime and disorder reduction policies and partnerships under New Labour, in their different ways, as attempts to secure state legitimacy (see Gilling, 2007). And, as this new 'institutional architecture' (Hughes, 2007: 192) emerged, academic analyses revealed state power as being both absent and present (and reconfigured) in studies of community safety and crime prevention. If, and how, the state has been rendered visible has depended upon the kind of interdisciplinarity underpinning analyses, shifts in thinking in related disciplines, the political priorities of writers and the kinds of institutional contexts in which such thinking takes place (Cohen, S., 1981; Hillyard, Sim et al., 2004). 'Administrative criminologists', whose focus has been on the techniques of crime prevention, the evaluation of programmes, and who have promoted the priorities of the new 'crime science', not only have failed to encompass a discussion of the state, but would question the value of so doing:

> If the discipline is not to become sidelined and irrelevant criminologists must make changes that go far beyond a re-focusing of research topics. The changes must address criminology's mission, its theories and its methodologies with the collective result of making the discipline more directly relevant to crime control … . (Clarke, 2004: 55)

Economics, biology, demography, geography, town planning, engineering, public heath and so on provide the preferred disciplinary insights in this kind of criminology (Clarke, 2004). And, as Hughes et al. (2002: 330) argued, despite this apparent 'inclusiveness', the 'underlying structural causes of crime and related harms in communities' are rendered marginal.

In as much as technicist, risk-focused 'anti-social criminologies' (Hughes et al., 2002: 336) have become 'hegemonic' in a context where they were revealed, increasingly, to fit neatly with the neo-liberal project of western governments (Hughes, 2002b; Stenson and Edwards, 2003; Gilling, 2007), there has also been a growing body of research that has tried to foreground social-democratic priorities in crime prevention (Hughes, 2002b, 2007). Moreover, informed by developments in social and political theory and related disciplines, a body of writing has emerged where sociologists and critical criminologists have placed an understanding of macro socio-economic transformations and the (changing) role of the state at the heart of their analyses of crime prevention and community safety and, in particular, the new 'institutional architecture' that has now become apparent. This body of writing forms a key focus of this chapter, although it is beyond its scope to review this work in its entirety. However, the chapter does question, counter to the current government's assertions, the extent to which power has been 'dispersed downwards' to 'communities' in the current arrangements for crime prevention and community safety and, following Hall et al. (1978), raises critical issues about the state's role as an 'educator' in this setting.

Community Safety and the Rejection of the Local State: the 1980s and 1990s

In the 1980s, the Thatcher governments promoted the view that responsibility for crime prevention lay with individuals and households as part of the prevailing neo-liberal ethos and the desire to 'activate' citizens to take on responsibility for their own safety (Gilling, 2007). In this period situational crime prevention was envisaged as the main method of enhancing individual security and, indeed, it sat neatly in an ideological framework in which the notion of 'opportunity' was prioritized in government thinking (Gilling, 2007). Furthermore, the Conservatives exploited Labour's seemingly 'soft' approach to 'law and order' (Gilling, 2007) – illustrated, for example, with reference to the Greater London Council's funding of police monitoring groups after the 1981 election. Indeed, calls for the police to be rendered accountable democratically were constructed as an 'anti-police' stance (Gilling, 2007). The government rejected the view that large-scale urban unrest in the early and mid-1980s had anything to do with neo-liberal social or economic policies; neither, it was argued, were they the consequence of authoritarian, paramilitary policing practices. However, it is not difficult to see how the assertion that, on the one hand, the state was a guarantor of security was contradictory when, on the other, the view that citizens should provide for their own safety was advanced simultaneously (Gilling, 2007). Thus, alongside growing 'punitive populism' (Bottoms, 1995, cited in Gilling, 2007) and the discrediting of alternative accounts, there were also attempts to re-secure police legitimacy through measures such as 'community policing' (Gilling, 2007), police–community consultative committees (Uglow, 1988; Jones and Newburn, 1997) and experiments with multi-agency partnerships (MAPs) (Gilling, 2007).

From the onset, critical work took issue with the simple view that MAPs were a 'benevolent' development that facilitated 'better' policy on the basis of 'better' information (from the range of parties at the table) and were able to respond to problems more holistically, flexibly and efficiently (see Sampson et al., 1988). Consensus-based, pluralistic analyses were rejected in favour of approaches which revealed the power relations, conflicts and compromises within local crime prevention 'partnerships' (Crawford, 1997, 1998a; Hughes, 1998). These analyses raised important questions about the extent to which partnerships responded to 'communities' concerns, and also revealed the tensions and compromises between central and local government (Hancock, 2001).

The Safer Cities Programme, first launched in 1988 (and its fore runner – the 'Five Towns' initiative), is notable in that it revealed the Thatcher government's explicit rejection of a designated role for local government in community safety (Tilley, 1993; Crawford, 1998a; Hughes, 1998), a stance that would continue for most of the following decade. Sustained ideological opposition to local government meant that the Morgan Report's main recommendation to make community safety a statutory local authority function was ignored when it was published in 1991 (Crawford, 1998a; Hughes, 1998). Local activity, funded through City Challenge and, later, the Single Regeneration Budget (SRB), gathered pace in this period, however (Gilling and Barton, 1997; Hancock, 2001). These efforts created some scope for relatively progressive community safety activities and community-based action in some local authority areas. NACRO, for example, had developed significant work in distressed communities from the late 1970s (Crawford, 1998a). This said, as local activity funded through these frameworks expanded in the 1990s, commentators became increasingly concerned about the 'criminalisation of social policy' as welfare agencies became involved in community safety under the urban policy programmes which funded them: social exclusion and disadvantage became less important as issues in themselves; rather, they were objects of intervention because of their implications for crime and disorder (Crawford, 1997; Gilling and Barton, 1997; Hancock, 2001).

Critical commentators drew attention to the local 'democratic deficit' so apparent in the Safer Cities structure, a point emphasized in the Morgan Report in 1991 (Crawford, 1998a; Follett, 2006). Central government's antipathy towards local government, however, precluded any consideration that local authorities should take on the function of community safety as part of their service provision, which may have provided for a greater sense of legitimacy for programmes and policies as a function of the local democratic process (Crawford, 1998a). The Conservative governments' priorities were to exercise direct central control over Safer Cities' arrangements and activities, and in their attempts to 'leapfrog' local structures (Crawford, 1998a: 55) sought to secure legitimacy for central government in general and the criminal justice system in particular (Gilling and Barton, 1997).

Tilley (1993) discussed some of the key constraints upon the Safer Cities programme, which were strongly related to central government's New Right ideology, but he noted the diversity of initiatives nevertheless. Among the factors said to account for such variation was the absence of specific guidance on the kinds of interventions to be implemented under the programme. (Other explanations included the wide-ranging occupations from which the personnel coordinating local programmes were drawn, and a Home Office that was inexperienced as far as service delivery was concerned; see Tilley, 1993; Hughes, 1998; Crawford, 1998a, for further discussion.) Indeed, the perceived success of earlier NACRO initiatives, with their emphasis on social crime prevention, tenant empowerment and so on, were likely to have influenced a more progressive approach in some localities, especially in areas where NACRO successfully tendered for the management of these initiatives.[1] This said, critical reviewers questioned the extent to which autonomy at the local level could be allowed to develop given the competitive funding regimes that underpinned Safer Cities, City

Challenge and Single Regeneration Budget funded interventions (see Crawford, 1997, 1998a; Gilling and Barton, 1997; Hughes, 1998). Those seeking funding under these programmes were required to form partnerships with the private sector (seek private finance). It was a competitive rather than a needs-based process, and initiatives were time-limited (Gilling and Barton, 1997). In this context, powerful organizations, such as the police, were able to claim expertise and play a pivotal gate-keeping role. Furthermore, the very structure of these arrangements – characterized by short-termism and led by performance indicators – shaped crime prevention policy (Crawford, 1997). As Crawford put it, this process:

> ... can serve to extend a particular vision of crime control ... [which tends] largely to be pragmatic and managerial. The forms of intervention tend to be short-term and situational. Those interventions which are more amenable to simple evaluation so beloved of funding bodies, the commercial sector and the media are consequently accorded priority. As such, they tend to focus on target hardening, 'designing out' crime, and other 'technological fixes' at the expense of interventions which question the social causes of crime. (Crawford, 1997: 232)

The shift away from the more broadly conceived 'community safety' to a much narrower conception of 'crime and disorder' under New Labour from 1997, the growing significance of auditing crime and disorder under the Crime and Disorder Act 1998, and the promotion of particular types of interventions under the banner of 'what works', each served to further constrain local programmes. It is to a consideration of these issues which the chapter now turns.

Crime and Disorder Reduction and the Local State under New Labour

Despite attempts to ameliorate the 'democratic deficit' as local authorities (with the police) were given statutory duties to prevent crime and reduce disorder under the Crime and Disorder Act of 1998 (Follett, 2006), central control was effectively enhanced after 1998. The legislation required that specific agencies (probation, police authority health and fire authorities) cooperate with crime and disorder reduction partnerships (CDRPs) and identified other agencies, which the 'responsible authorities' (local authorities and the police) should invite to the partnership table (Gilling, 2007).[2] In this way, government efforts to compel agencies to cooperate challenged the 'voluntaristic' ideals that tend to be associated with 'partnership' (Gilling, 2007). Similarly, claims that government was promoting 'local solutions to local problems' were undermined by centrally-driven interventions (to address street crime and anti-social behaviour, for example) which were promoted irrespective of local conditions and preferred approaches (Gilling, 2007: 79). Home Office guidance, designated 'best practice', and new funding streams made available through the Crime Reduction

Programme launched in 1999 were designed to shape the way that crime prevention and, increasingly, 'anti-social behaviour' interventions were oriented (Gilling, 2007). Moreover, the nature and influence of 'policy networks', although differently constituted from the embryonic networks which were important for shaping degrees of diversity earlier in Safer Cities programmes (Tilley, 1993; Hughes, 1998), took on a particular and potent shape with the rise of 'crime science' and evaluation research in this period. Indeed, evaluation research became deeply enmeshed and intertwined with policy programmes under Tony Blair's governments: in this context, 'political considerations penetrate[d] methodological concerns in the new dispensation of "evidence-based policy making"' (Hope, 2004: 295).

In addition to these various methods of inducing and shaping local government's compliance with central objectives, the Crime and Disorder Act 1998 established formal procedures to strengthen central government's control over local crime and disorder reduction partnerships. Under this legislation, the Home Secretary was able to call for reports on any aspect of lead agencies' duties and retained the power to intervene directly in partnerships, for example (Hancock, 2001). The extent to which the central state was able to impact on local governance arrangements and interventions has, however, remained a matter of contention. Many writers agree that power has been increasingly vested in the central state. Nevertheless, utilizing the power-dependence model of local governance,[3] some writers argue the importance of recognizing that considerable scope remains for exercising autonomy at the local level (see Hughes, 1998, 2007; Edwards and Hughes, 2005). Edwards and Hughes (2005: 352), for example, argued that because the central state is in a relation of power-dependence to secure its objectives '[t]he necessity of bargaining with others generates political competition and the possibility of advancing certain governing strategies while resisting others'. These authors reject the idea that outcomes are the result of 'pluralist interest group politics', however, since the capacity and resources to govern are unevenly distributed. They emphasized the importance of examining the 'geo-historical contexts that constitute the struggle for authoritative action' (Edwards and Hughes, 2005: 352). However, the material nature of power in some 'geo-historical contexts' deserves more attention in shaping the nature and direction of local–state interventions, as I explore later in the chapter. The next section considers some of the ways in which the changing role of the state has been conceptualized in accounts of the development of crime prevention arrangements.

Conceptualizing the Changing Role of the State

A number of writers have drawn upon neo-Marxist analyses of the changing role of the state, especially regulation theory, and Foucauldian-informed analyses, in attempts to make sense of new forms of governance 'at a distance'. Analyses have also blended and developed different approaches (see Stenson and Edwards, 2001, for example) but there remains disagreement between authors over the extent to which the changing 'institutional architecture' of crime prevention represents the emergence of 'state rule at a distance' (Shearing, 1996, cited in Crawford, 1998a: 253).

Crawford (1998a), for example, has taken issue with Osborne and Gaebler's (1992) 'steering and rowing' analogy, which is so often quoted in 'government at a distance' debates. Crawford asked: 'who is steering and who is rowing?' For him, the different mechanisms in place for rendering the various agencies in MAPs accountable (upwards) suggested a variety of 'steerers' and a 'fleet of boats' (1998a: 255). The view that there has been a simple strengthening of the state's role, as suggested by the 'steering' analogy, for example, is rejected in this account. But neither had there been a decentralization of power, despite concerted efforts to 'responsibilize communities', to privatize, marketize and promote MAPs, which, together, promoted the widely held view that there has been a 'hollowing out' of the state. For Crawford, 'these positions provide an insight into current changes, and yet both are partial. We are witnessing weaknesses, as well as strengths, emerging as relations across the public and private divide are being reconfigured' (1998a: 259). The picture, for Crawford, was more ambiguous and complex, and, moreover, these changes challenged the 'basis of legitimacy, authority and responsibility', resulting in new conflict, friction and strains. In these kinds of setting, he argued, the capacity for greater punitiveness is strengthened as 'politicians in search of their own legitimation have fallen back on punitive rhetoric and the strong repressive state apparatus'; for Crawford (1998a: 259), punitive populism 'is an expression of the state confronting its very own weaknesses and discontents', a core argument in *Policing the Crisis* in analysing the shift towards the 'exceptional state'. However, in Crawford's account, he is primarily concerned to flag up the importance of emotionality and constructions of morality for understanding criminal justice policies and, in particular, to critique some versions of the 'dispersal of power' thesis (Rose and Miller, 1992, cited in Crawford, 1998a: 257) which conveyed the idea that 'governmental technologies' are 'overly rational, unified and instrumental'.[4]

Although his analysis is located at the level of the central (British) state, and consequently there is little detailed analysis of the ways the processes he discusses play themselves out at local or regional level, Crawford's more recent (2006) work represents an important contribution to the literature in this area. Here he takes issue with the ways the 'regulatory state' or 'post regulatory state' has been theorized as well as other modes of analysis (Foucauldian governmentality approaches, for example) which have implied a diminished role for the state. Moreover, Crawford is more emphatic that the state is not 'redundant'; rather, state ambitions have been 'greatly extended' (2006: 471), although this is not to say they are realized in any simple sense, or indeed that they are coherent and uncontested. One key strength of this work is his focus on the deeply pervasive nature of state intervention: 'few aspects of social life have been left out of this zealous gaze' (2006: 456) as a multitude of new measures have been rapidly developed to coerce, cajole and persuade individuals to submit to the state's 'social ordering strategies' (Lacey, 1994: 28) against a backdrop where 'conduct' and 'behaviour' are increasingly politicized.

The Local State and Urban Growth Coalitions[5]

There are spatial and temporal settings in which particular kinds of perceived behaviours are increasingly regarded as being a threat to urban fortunes (Hancock, 2007). The politicization of 'conduct' is deeply intertwined with the goal of creating a particular kind of business-friendly urban order and the development of 'pro-growth ideologies' (Logan and Molotch, 1987; Coleman, 2004). This signals the importance of examining the local state and how 'social ordering' in the neo-liberal city is aligned to the ambitions of the growth coalition (Coleman, 2004). Coleman et al.'s (2002) and Coleman and Sim's (2005) analyses, centred on Liverpool, are particularly useful in this regard. These authors discuss how crime control is deeply enmeshed with 'entrepreneurialized forms of rule that stress marketing, "quality of life" indicators and other promotional discourses that cities have adopted in the competition to attract and retain investment' (Coleman and Sim, 2005: 105), and which in turn shape the nature and texture of crime control policies and practices as well as their justifications (Coleman, 2004). Such rationalizations centre on claims to protect 'the public interest', although very specific notions of (public) safety are mobilized in this setting. Crime control strategies focus on marginal groups and 'spaces of spectacle where contaminants may spill' (Coleman and Sim, 2005: 106), while other harms, such as those perpetrated against women in the private sphere and against relatively powerless groups (the homeless, for example), are ignored or downplayed.

Coleman et al. (2002: 93–4) note how the ideological message conveyed to communities beyond the city centre is one where 'everyone benefits', not least from the 'trickle-down' effect of the wealth to be generated from the city centre's economic revitalization. In this context, they draw attention to the way funding is directed towards very particular kinds of projects (CCTV, for example) yet appear to be lacking for social interventions, frequently preferred by community groups (see also Hancock, 2001). This work therefore re-emphasizes the importance of issues that fail to make it on to local government agendas and the significance of 'non-decision-making'[6] when analysing power at the local level. Furthermore, the idea that power is being 'dispersed' to communities made by the 'hollowed-out state' thesis is clearly challenged in this context. This is examined further in the following section.

Community Empowerment?

Policing the Crisis emphasized the importance of appeals to 'public opinion', the 'orchestration' of public understandings and the significance of responding to 'public sentiment' for making sense of the shift towards the 'exceptional state' in the 1970s. In the intervening period, academic interest in public opinion on criminal justice has developed considerably to reveal a more complex understanding of public opinion (see Hancock, 2004). At least in part, such interest developed because of the increasingly frequent claims that state strategies accord with and are responsive to public preferences, which has become commonplace in the practice of government, and the (related) exponential growth of opinion surveys and other tools to gather the views and perceptions of the lay public since the publication of *Policing the Crisis*. Furthermore, we have also witnessed greater efforts to directly 'involve' citizens in local policy-making and service delivery from the 1980s (Hancock, 2004).

Some of the early public involvement strategies, such as the police–community consultative committees referred to earlier, were widely regarded as tokenistic, cynical attempts to secure, or re-secure, the legitimacy of the police following urban unrest in a number of British cities during 1981, for example (Uglow, 1988; Hancock, 2004). Few contemporary writers regard recent government efforts in this kind of way, however (Ryan, 1999, 2003). Rather, the influence of Etzioni-style communitarianism (1993, 1997; Hancock and Matthews, 2001) and 'third way' partnerships (see Crawford, 2001) in New Labour's political philosophy have inspired a programme of initiatives to re-invigorate public participation since 1997. The biannual 'Citizenship Survey' is meant, in part at least, to assess the impact of the growing number of initiatives at the local and national level (Home Office, 2003b).

How, then, are we to make sense of the apparent contradiction that the (local or national) state is promoting responsiveness to community concerns against evidence to the contrary, without regarding such efforts simply as a 'scam'? My argument in this final section is that government efforts to extend public participation are tension-ridden and contradictory when mapped against the much more powerful influences on policy-making, some of which we have encountered above, and the variety of conditions which remain *disempowering* as far as 'community participation' is concerned.

I have argued elsewhere there are three main reasons for gathering information from the public and securing their involvement in a range of settings (Hancock, 2004): to secure (or re-secure) the legitimacy of, and consent for, agencies or their policies by providing an ostensible accountability mechanism; to make 'better' decisions, thereby improving efficiency and saving money (this becomes increasingly important as institutions are subject to tighter financial regimes); and to re-engage the public with a sense of 'citizenship' and civic involvement. These are not, of course, mutually exclusive. This said, it is important to recognize the discontinuities between state intentions and outcomes and, moreover, to understand the way interventions in other areas of social and urban life are deeply disempowering to obtain a fuller picture. A few examples will suffice to illustrate: in a context where key areas of policy (housing, for example) are determined by the central state and particular modes of provision (through the market) are promoted, local governments and partnerships are likely to be unable, if not unwilling, to respond to community concerns (see Hancock, 2001: Chapter 6) where they do not 'fit' with the direction of these policies (opposing housing stock transfers, for example[7]). Similarly, community groups have expressed disquiet about the kinds of initiatives promoted by contemporary attempts to regenerate cities (particularly arts and culture-led projects) that, they felt, were 'not for them'; rather, they were designed to attract tourists and visitors. Moreover, the jobs promised by regenerative initiatives have been found to be less plentiful in number and more poorly paid (part-time, service industry work) than the claims made by regeneration partnerships (Hancock, 2001: 128, 2007). However, alternatives to the dominant modes and methods of urban regeneration, against the power of 'primary definers' in the 'entrepreneurial city' (Coleman and Sim, 2005), are unlikely to be heard in policy-making forums or regarded as unreasonable and 'extreme' against the pervasive 'pro-growth ideology'. Both of these examples illustrate (in two key areas that so strongly influence life chances: housing and jobs) that residential community groups frequently conceptualize neighbourhood problems differently from those agencies sitting at 'partnership' tables, and in this context it would be a rare event indeed if community participants were empowered in the directions community groups prefer.

Rather than acknowledging such discord, however, one of the distinguishing features of government discourse around 'partnership' is that it assumes, and seeks to create, a community of interest around a particular set of urban policy and community crime reduction strategies. Communities in this context become, as Imrie and Raco (2003: 6) put it, the 'object[s] of policy' and 'policy instrument[s]'. Nowhere is this confusion more apparent than in an array of government strategies on 'anti-social behaviour', 'neighbourhood renewal' and 'social exclusion' (Hancock, 2006, 2007). It is muddled thinking which arises because the government 'operate[s] with a simplistic communitarian vision' (Matthews, 2003: 7). Important questions about the extent to which communities are able to act as empowered agents are raised in this context, particularly when seen against the backdrop of discourses that are also deeply disempowering. Communities are represented as being 'victimized' and 'problematic' on a range of indicators in the discourses surrounding these strategies. Socially excluded groups in distressed neighbourhoods are frequently portrayed as 'problems to be fixed' (Morrison, 2003: 143). Families, people's skills, bodies and so on in a variety of ways are devalued; they are contrasted with the 'included' – the 'we' in the policy documents. 'They' are 'misrecognized' (Morrison, 2003: 140).[8] And, against these images of (broken) working-class communities, the vision of 'normality' in the consumption-led regenerating city is emphatically middle-class (Lees, 2003; Mooney, 2004; Jones and Wilks-Heeg, 2004).

In this way, 'inclusion' policies which appeal to 'community empowerment', and the communitarian discourses[9] underpinning them, gloss over class divisions (see Coleman, this volume) and obscure both the manner in which power relations are defended in the contemporary city and also the 'claims to moral and cultural superiority' which support such defences (Haylett, 2001: 366). Instead, definitions of local problems, increasingly, are purportedly shared by the 'community' as a whole, and it is the 'community' which, it is claimed, will benefit from crime and disorder reduction policies and the regenerative effects that, it is assumed, will follow from their enforcement (Hancock, 2007). In the event that communities lose out in their struggles for preferred interventions, social crime prevention for example, the nature of power may be revealed, although it may or may not result in conflict.

There are many factors that influence the capacity of community groups to engage in actions around community safety (see Hancock, 2001: Chapter 6) but here, following Hall et al. (1978), I wish to attend to the way local and central states act in an 'educating role' to organize consent. 'Tutoring' takes place in a myriad of ways, including through policy programmes, forms of expertise and through the state's influence on the mass media and other 'cultural systems' (Hall et al., 1978). Thus, the ways in which working-class communities are portrayed in policy discourses, referred to above, can be read as part of an educative process. For the purposes of the present discussion it is also useful to note the ways in which the state-organized consent became much more important, yet 'more delicate, more problematic' with the extension of the franchise in Hall et al.'s analysis (1978: 206). However, the comparison lacks some 'fit' because, for example, many of the arrangements for 'community involvement' lack the legitimacy of the electoral system.

To secure public consent requires that the state 'knows' the public's opinions and demonstrates *some* willingness to respond to them. And it is through an understanding of the importance of organizing consent that we can best understand the New Labour governments' efforts to (1) furnish the public with more information about crime, the criminal justice system and how it has operated since 1997; and (2) to gather increasing amounts of information about public experiences of (some) victimizations, fears about (some) crimes and perceptions of criminal justice (through an expanded British Crime Survey, for example). Indeed, the use of additional ways of obtaining (and reflecting) public opinion on 'crime' and criminal justice matters is greater than ever in the current period, as testified in the proliferation of focus groups, 'consultation' exercises, and so on (Hancock, 2004). What I wish to draw attention to also is that the 'gathering' of specific (and selective) kinds of information, and in turn the dissemination of these data, can be seen as part of state tutoring process too. At the same time, this is not to say that efforts to 'mould' public opinion are necessarily effective, given the complexity of public opinion and the ways in which public understandings and preferences, and indeed their relation to criminal justice policies, are frequently misunderstood (see Hancock, 2004).

This said, analyses of how powerful interests shape the terms of community participation (including whose views matter) in crime prevention policies and community regeneration programmes at the local level are as important in contemporary setting as it was to recognize the interests served by appeals to the 'moral voice' of the 'law-abiding community', whose protection legitimated increasingly punitive law and order interventions in the 1970s (Hall et al., 1978). Karn's (2007) recent research suggests, for example, that professionals representing various public and private agencies in urban neighbourhood regeneration partnerships in the contemporary context search for 'moral' or 'authentic' voices in their consultation and involvement strategies. Moreover, those whose views count as valid interpretations of a community's interests are those which most closely align with agencies' goals. Oppositional positions are likely to be marginalized as 'unrepresentative' of the 'community', if they are regarded as part of 'the community' at all (Karn, 2007). Karn summarizes that:

Participatory practices constitute 'the community' as those who participate constructively, co-operatively and reasonably within the process. Consultation practices are in this sense constitutive of the very community to whom professionals claim to be responding. ... Non-participation or cynicism implies, at best, unco-operativeness, at worst, destructiveness. (2007: 199)

It is this compliant community (and its future) that needs 'protection' from 'others' who are regarded as placing community regeneration in jeopardy. Punitive and exclusionary interventions (anti-social behaviour orders and evictions) are not only rationalized in this context, but also offer opportunities to demonstrate the willingness of the police or local authority to respond to 'community' concerns and enhance their legitimacy (Karn, 2007).

In addition to this, the increasingly influential 'what works' policy entrepreneurs have also had an educative effect on people's understanding of 'solutions' to crimes, as key messages mediated through consultation arrangements, policy discourses and the broadcast media have filtered into popular talk about crime. Particular kinds of strategies or interventions, which are said to be effective, may be relatively easily measured and, consequently, may be more likely to be funded, have been vigorously promoted over the past decade. However, there remain considerable contradictions within, and risks associated with, the process of trying to secure consent in this way: diminishing levels of public confidence, with its resultant implications for the capacity of agencies to claim legitimacy for their projects and programmes, become a real possibility when (elevated) public expectations are not met. In this context, the lesson from *Policing the Crisis* is that the state is more apt to react with authoritarian, punitive criminal justice policies to re-secure consent.

Summary and Conclusion

I have discussed the importance of examining the development of crime prevention and community safety through an understanding of the local state and its relation with the central state and the ways in which this relation has changed over time. In so doing, the discussion attended to the constraints and priorities the central state increasingly imposes at the local and community level. The contention that power has been 'dispersed' to communities was explored critically by highlighting a number of ways in which this assertion can be contested. Following Hall et al. (1978), the role of the state as an 'educator' and 'organizer of consent' remains particularly useful in this context. However, there remain empirical questions about the extent to which 'consent' at the local level has been won.

Thirty years on, it remains pertinent to retain a critical focus on the complexities of orchestrating public opinion about crime. Then, as now, such 'opinion' is never 'socially innocent' and is 'constrained by the available frameworks of understanding and interpretation' (Hall et al., 1978: 136) – the complexities around which this chapter has focused attention on in the contemporary setting. Furthermore, tutored understandings about crime take place alongside material changes that the institutional architecture of the state form, which in turn intersects with and redraws the parameters of social injustice. The primary goal of city authorities and their partners in the post-industrial city is to boost inward capital investment. The idea that disadvantaged groups will benefit from the 'trickle-down' and 'trickle-out' effect of investment in the city centre provides the justification for both targeting regeneration activity in the urban centre, and punitive strategies to address both the 'incidence and perception of anti-social behaviour' (Home Office, 2003b: para 4.53, cited in Hancock, 2007: 60) in both the centre and outer-city. Regenerating distressed neighbourhoods and ameliorating social exclusion, it is claimed, rests upon eliminating signs of 'disorder' to influence inward investment and improve 'community confidence' (Hancock, 2007: 62). The 'gap' between the most disadvantaged areas and the rest of the country (Social Exclusion Unit, 2001) remains stubbornly wide, however:

> Liverpool remains the most deprived district in England despite an influx of regeneration cash and a government drive to reduce inequality. ... New investment spurred by its status as European City [sic] of Culture has failed to boost local income or employment, according to the Department for Communities and Local Government (DCLG). ... The city's deprivation score, using 2007 figures, has barely changed since the previous indices for multiple deprivation (IMD) showed it was bottom of the league in 2004. (Gaines, 2008)

Those who lack political and economic power (young people and the homeless, for example) are subjected to ever more intensive forms of policing and regulation. For example, from 1 March to 31 August 2008 (in Liverpool's year as Capital of Culture) whole neighbourhoods were included in designated zones under Section 30 of the Anti-Social Behaviour Act 2003 to facilitate the dispersal and exclusion of young people to control 'anti-social behaviour'. Earlier action to disperse young people in a designated zone, in Garston during 2005, prompted young people to voice concerns about being bullied by the police. Their concerns about safety were exacerbated as their avoidance strategies took them to unfamiliar places in response to a policy which failed to recognize how young people congregate in groups *because* of their concerns about safety (Rice et al., 2005). However, recognition in policy terms of the range of harms perpetrated against politically and economically marginalized groups remains as far away in 2008 as it was thirty years earlier when *Policing the Crisis* was published.

Key Reading

Atkinson, R. and Helms, G. (eds) (2007) *Securing an Urban Renaissance: Crime, Community and British Urban Policy*. Bristol: Policy Press.

Coleman, R. (2004) *Reclaiming the Streets: Surveillance, Social Control and the City*. Cullompton: Willan.

Gilling, D. (2007) *Crime Reduction and Community Safety*. Cullompton: Willan.

Hughes, G. (2007) *The Politics of Crime and Community*. Basingstoke: Palgrave.

Hughes, G., McLaughlin, E. and Muncie, J. (eds) (2002) *Crime Prevention and Community Safety: New Directions*. London: Sage.

Notes

1 Crime Concern and the Society of Voluntary Organizations were the other significant organizations managing Safer Cities programmes (see Crawford, 1998a).

2 These arrangements produced a number of contradictions in themselves (see Gilling, 2007).

3 The power–dependence model places emphasis on the 'constraints' emanating from both within the state (competing interests, fragmentation) and as a consequence of external pressures (Atkinson and Wilks-Heeg, 2000; Marsh and Rhodes, 1992; Rhodes, 1996, 1997). These constraints challenge state capacity to organize other agencies to secure objectives. Put simply, if the state (or fragments of the state) is to achieve its goals, it is necessary to operate through a range of 'policy networks', including local government (Atkinson and Wilks-Heeg, 2000).

4 Stenson (2002) tries to address this criticism of governmentality theory in his adaptation of this approach.

5 'Urban growth coalitions' or 'growth machines' (Logan and Molotch, 1987; Savage et al., 2003) are defined as 'groupings of influential actors who seek growth at almost any cost' (Savage et al., 2003: 171). Logan and Molotch developed their analysis based on the understanding of the peculiar nature of 'places' as commodities and the recognition that 'place entrepreneurs attempt through collective action and often in alliance with other business people, to create the conditions that will intensify future land use in an area' (1987: 103–4). Their work emphasized the role governments at local and national level play in providing a business-friendly environment, including infrastructural support, 'place marketing' and the development of pervasive pro-growth local ideologies.

6 These concerns were raised some decades earlier by 'elite theorists' in the 'community power debate' (Atkinson and Wilks-Heeg, 2000; Bell and Newby, 1971; Saunders, 1983).

7 See www.defendcouncilhousing.org.uk/dch/.

8 'To be misrecognized ... is to be denied the status of a full partner in social interaction, as a consequence of institutionalized patterns of cultural value that constitute one as comparatively unworthy of respect and esteem' (Frazer, 2000, cited in Morrison, 2003: 140).

9 See Hughes (1998) for an accessible introduction to the various strands of communitarian thought.

12

VICTIMS AND THE STATE

Sandra Walklate

The state is a great civilizing force, a necessary and virtuous component of the good society. But if it is to take on this role, the state must itself be civilized – made safe by and for democracy. (Loader and Walker, 2007: 7)

Introduction

The quote from Loader and Walker cited above captures both the positive and the negative processes that we have all experienced in relation to both the real and imagined work that the state does, and fails to do, in ensuring that the interests of society as a whole are met. In many ways, it can be read as a normative statement. One of the purposes of this chapter is to explore the extent to which the state can, and does, live up to this ideal since over the last thirty years it is evidently the case that the power of the state has certainly not withered away, as some social commentators anticipated. On the contrary, its power both to intervene in and define what constitutes wider societal interests, or what might be called the 'social good', has become both more widespread and diffuse. This is nowhere more evident than in the way that, in these processes of diffusion, victimhood has been harnessed to serve and maintain state power. A second purpose of this chapter, then, is to offer a flavour of how some of those processes have manifested themselves in relation to the victim (of crime).

From the Margins to the Centre: Understanding Current Policy Pre-occupations with the Victim of Crime

Contemporarily, we live in a social and policy context in which, as responsibilized citizens (Garland, 1996), we accept victimization prevention policy rather than crime prevention policy (Karmen, 1990) as a routine feature of our everyday lives. As Zedner (2002: 419) has observed, it can no longer be claimed that the victim is the forgotten party of the criminal justice system. Victims are now seen to be key players in the system and much contemporary political and policy energy is dedicated to ensuring that this is the case. Yet the basis on which victims are considered to have a role to play within the criminal justice process has changed considerably since the 'trail blazing' (Waller, 1988) development of the Criminal Injuries Compensation Board (CICB) established in 1964 (now known as the Criminal Injuries Compensation Authority). That development was arguably rooted in post-Second World War understandings of the welfare state, in which the principle of insurance played a prominent role. Put very simply, if, as a citizen, you paid into the system, you were entitled to receive benefits from it, including the protection of the state if you were considered to be an innocent victim of violent crime. However, while this embryonic protective relationship built upon the historically problematic distinction between the deserving and the undeserving (Jones and Novack, this volume), it underpinned the establishment of the CICB, considered to be the last brick in the wall of the welfare state (Mawby and Walklate, 1994). This understanding of the welfare state was transformed during the 1980s. The drive to transform the (nanny) welfare state that took a hold during that decade also contributed to the transformation of the role and importance given to the crime victim. So much so that by the end of the 1980s policy responses to the victim of crime were informed increasingly by the presumption that they were the consumers/customers of the criminal justice system and its policies rather than merely citizens. The late 1970s were the turning point in which this change in policy orientation emerged, with the election of the Tory party in 1979 cementing this change of direction. Their commitment to value for money, efficiency, and effectiveness from the public sector as a whole, including the criminal justice system, set the policy tone in which concerns about the victim of crime, as a measure of that party's fiscal principles, developed.

Different writers within victimology have attempted to identify how and why the years since 1979 had such an impact, resulting in the heightened presence and visibility of the crime victim. Dignan's (2005) analysis focuses on the importance of the work of Margery Fry in putting the groundwork in place for the CICB; the role of the media (especially during the 1960s in their coverage of the Moors murders), to which we might add the role of the media in creating the image of the 'black mugger' attacking the elderly white victim (Hall et al., 1978); the increasing awareness of who was vulnerable in relation to crime (especially women, children and the elderly); the impact of terrorist activity pre-9/11 on the one hand, and the rising crime rate on the other; the wider use of the criminal victimization survey; and the increasing interest of criminologists in victimization. Goodey (2005) identifies ten variables that contributed to this change in status of the victim of crime, adding to Dignan's analysis by considering factors such as changing levels of public tolerance of crime, and the increasing use of victims' rhetoric as a vote-winning strategy by politicians. However, what cannot be denied in this raised awareness is the importance of increasing publicly available knowledge of the nature, extent, and impact of criminalvictimization, and the various strategies deployed by governments to 'respond' to this knowledge.

There have been (at least) three stories that have unfolded in the light of this more widely available knowledge: that of the structurally neutral victim; that of the structurally informed victim; and that of the community as victim. Each of these stories have their own voices, plots and sub-plots that limited space dictates cannot be detailed here (but see, for example, Walklate, 2007; Spalek, 2006; Goodey, 2005), but we shall outline them as a way of suggesting their relationship with the master story – the perpetuation of the role and the power of the state.

The Structurally Neutral Victim

The first story to trace is arguably the dominant story line: that of the structurally neutral victim of crime. In images of the structurally neutral victim we are all equal and all equally affected by crime: the harm done by crime is done to all of us. This image of the crime victim downplays the importance of structural variables such as age, ethnicity, class, gender, sexuality, and as a result it follows that if crime harms us all, policy responses to it should be of benefit to us all. As Alison Young (1996) has suggested, this vision of the victim elides victimhood with citizenship, a theme to which we shall return. A good deal of policy activity has presumed this structurally neutral image of the crime victim. Elsewhere (Walklate, 2007) I have discussed these efforts under four related headings: perpetuating welfare, tinkering with adversarialism, moving towards allocution, and restorative justice. Within this hive of activity it is possible to identify not only a plethora of initiatives that has been generated from the various victims charters (the last one being the Victims Code of Practice that came into force in April 2006), to the re-orientation of the Probation Service towards working with victims of crime, to the introduction of the Victims' Advocates Scheme to speak on behalf of the families of murder and manslaughter victims pre-sentencing (also introduced in April 2006), but also the increasing influence of policies that have travelled the globe to sow their seeds in the UK, such as for example, victim impact statements and restorative justice initiatives. In addition, it is also possible to identify a presumed 'special' status being offered to victims in these processes in the face of the fact that once a party to the criminal justice process they are complainants not victims. These developments are suggestive of a process that, as some commentators have already argued, is undermining the rights of defendants, resulting in a context in which neither the needs/rights of victims or offenders are being met (see Williams, 2003). If this is the case, the question remains: whose needs/rights are being met by these activities then?

The Structurally Informed Victim

Another story that can be traced over the last thirty years is that of the structurally informed victim. In this image of the victim, it is taken as given that the harm done by crime is differential and differentiated. In other words, the variables of age, gender, class, ethnicity, and so on are emphasized and inform the policy responses that are thereby generated. Within this story we can find the narratives of violence against women, violence against those who live in ethnic minority groups and the voices of those who are victims of hate crimes. Again, since the late 1970s there has been much campaign and policy activity on behalf of these groups, resulting in some considerable response by the criminal justice system designed to embrace such a structurally informed image of the crime victim. Again, limited space does not permit a full coverage of all that might be addressed here, but just taking violence against women as an example, it is clear that violence against women is now squarely on the policy agenda (though see Ballinger, this volume). In the UK, the Cross Government Action Plan 2007–08 stands as testimony to this.

Yet, simultaneously, this story also hints at the problems of co-option (Matthews, 1994; Chesney-Lind, 2006), of policies whose central pre-occupation is a voting public (voters include women!: *qua* Radford and Stanko, 1991; Mawby and Walklate, 1994; Williams, 1999) and which have been pursued in the face of contradictory evidence (like the pro-arrest stance in cases of domestic violence), of a good deal of activity and energy that has, as yet, failed to solve the problem of attrition, and the persistence of public attitudes (including women's attitudes) that appear to be out of line with this activity. Yet the focus on the criminal justice system as an appropriate arena for action remains despite the, at best ambivalent, evidence as to what might be achieved by this system for women (or for men that matter) in relation to their experience of violence. The question is again: why has this victim-oriented activity taken this shape and form despite the ambivalent evidence in support of it?

Part of the answer to this question lies in the inherent critique of the law posed by Hudson's (2006) phrase 'white man's law', which raises many dilemmas for feminists who appeal to the law as both a symbolic referent and as a mechanism for real change. As Ray and Smith (2001: 213) state in discussing hate crime, 'Whilst "hate crime" legislation is offered as a form of rights-based protection for vulnerable groups, there is considerable uncertainty as to its appropriateness and effectiveness'. They go on to raise a range of questions that are pertinent for those interested in an analysis of the relationship between criminalvictimization, victimology and wider social processes. For example, does social integration require universal, content-neutral rights or particular rights that address the diverse and unequal nature of social membership? Does the concept of hate crime empower, or does it cultivate a view that to be a victim or potential victim becomes a defining marker of identity? Does recognition of this kind of problem extend freedom through equal treatment or further extend the powers of the state for misuse? (2001: 213–14). This last question is of central importance to the arguments of this chapter.

The Community as Victim

Consequent to the 1998 Crime and Disorder Act another story of victimization has also emerged: that story centres the community as victim. Following on from the 1998 legislative framework, the community safety industry has grown apace and has taken as its driver the notion of the community as the victim of crime. This industry, as de Lint and Virta (2004: 466) comment, has contributed to the ever increasing 'securitization of social life ... the command to think security instead of full employment, public education or the good society'. This command to think security has, in their view, resulted in the 'de-politicization of crime prevention and community safety'. Yet at the same time many local crime and disorder reduction strategy documents (required by the 1998 legislation) have foregrounded issues relating to domestic violence, hate crime, and/or other associated 'quality of life' indicators. In other words, crime prevention and community safety have become implicitly politicized. But yet the question remains: whose safety and security is being addressed here?

What can we take from these three stories? In the first instance, as Sebba (2001) has pointed out, there is no necessary correlation between the rapid growth and development of the sheer amount of information about victims of crime and its *appropriate* use within the policy-making process, despite the fact that much of the funding for the gathering of the information has come from government departments. Indeed, each of these stories articulates the different ways in which that information has been drawn upon (or not, as the case may be) in support of the policy initiatives that have been generated as a result. However, it is also important to note that contemporary pre-occupations with risk and insecurity provide the cultural resonance and context in which we all make sense of the information available to us. So perhaps, by implication, the movement of the victim from the periphery to the centre of criminal justice, demonstrated by each of these stories, also needs to be understood by reference to the ways in which governments have sought to manage the impact of risk and insecurity since the 1950s and what these management processes themselves suggest. It is possible to trace the impact of two themes here: the shift from Government (with a capital G) to governance, and the shift from policy delivery as a public good to processes of policy delivery as private responsibilities. These themes help us explore the master plot and underlying generative mechanism in this story: the role and power of the state.

From 'Government' to 'Governance'

There have been several interconnected shifts in the political, economic and democratic processes that refract this move from Government to governance. In contemporary political terms, that is, after the election of the Labour party to government in 1997, it is usual to contrast the social democratic commitment of Old Labour party policies of the 1950s and 1960s with the neo-liberal democratic policies of New Labour at the end of the 1990s and into the twenty-first century. This shift in policy position reflects the powerful success of Conservative politics and policies in the years prior to Labour's election as well as the desire to be elected on the part of the Labour party, hence the party's need to reconsider its policy position. However, this shifting political position also belies more fundamental economic processes associated with neo-liberal democracies that have not been confined solely to the UK.

One of the key contexts for *Policing the Crisis*, the global recession of the mid to late 1970s, to be revisited in the early 1990s, took its toll economically in the UK, the USA and elsewhere, and resulted in a radical reconsideration of what the state might deliver for its citizens. This economic reorientation was marked by a change of emphasis in which market forces were prioritized as the means of delivering public services, the unleashing of these forces being deemed to be both politically and economically in the public interest. In the context of the UK, these global and local processes have had an impact on the nature of democracy itself so that many commentators now no longer talk in terms of parliamentary democracy but rather the process of governance. As Goodey (2005) suggests, this shift from parliamentary democracy (or Government with a capital G) to governance is one of the factors that have contributed to the centring of the crime victim.

Put fairly simply the idea of Government alludes to a set of principles sometimes referred to as the 'Westminster model'. This model assumed a strong cabinet, parliamentary democracy, electoral accountability, and so on. However, as Rhodes (1997: 4) states:

> Since 1945 the institutions of British government have experienced at least two revolutions. The post-war Labour government built the welfare state and its institutions, but these barely survived three decades before a reforming Conservative government sought to re-define most and abolish many. Allegedly, the Westminster model no longer works.

Rhodes (1997) argues that governance is broader than government: 'governance refers to self-organizing intra-organizational networks' in which the boundaries between the public sector, the private sector, and the voluntary sector are constantly shifting and opaque. Nowhere is this newer diffusion of influence on the policy-making process more evident than in the context of responses to the victims of crime.

For example, the Criminal Injuries Compensation Board (CICB), now the Criminal Injuries Compensation Authority, referred to earlier, was implemented without reference to the victim of crime *per se*. The formation of the CICB did have a champion (Elizabeth Fry), but as a policy it was formulated within the principles and framework of the welfare state of the 1950s – that is, it was informed by a principle of what it was reasonable to expect the state to put in place for its citizens. The same cannot be observed in the first decade of the twenty-first century. Not only has Victim Support become one of the most successful voluntary organizations over the last twenty-five years, now having a central place in informing the policy process in relation to crime victims, but there is also a massive Home Office database in the form of the British Crime Survey, which maps the impact of crime and the views of crime victims on a large number of matters, as illustrated by the stories sketched above. Moreover, there has been a proliferation of organizations purporting to speak for the victim of crime, if not as powerful in their influence as Victim Support, nevertheless vociferous in their claims. In addition, high-profile crimes, like the abduction and murder of Sarah Payne in 2000, have led to particular individuals, like Sarah Payne's parents, claiming the ear of government ministers. It is important to remember that none of the aforementioned groups is an elected representative and none is necessarily accountable to anyone other than its own interests or the interests of its organizations. These developments illustrate the process of governance and its potential influence on the policy decision-making.

So the existence and proliferation of victims groups demonstrates both the continuing 'powerful motif' of the victim (Bottoms, 1983) and the continued 'politicization of the victim' (Miers, 1978). However, in the intervening years since the inception of the CICB, the policy-making process has not only become more differentiated and diffuse, as suggested above, it has simultaneously become less partisan and more political. The crime victim is claimed by both political parties as being central to their concerns (less partisan), but whose voice is listened to? How, why, when and what about (hence the three stories sketched above) is neither easy nor straightforward (more political). Moreover, there is a second theme to be considered here that is connected to the changing political and economic terrain mapped above: the changing role of public services.

From Public Good to Private Responsibilities?

Since 1979 articulations of the 'public interest', and how these reflect an image of the public good, have taken a number of forms. Clark et al. (2000) suggest a number of representations of this. The first is the view of the public as taxpayers, with their interests being equated with economy, efficiency and effectiveness, and who, it is presumed, have an antagonistic relationship with non-taxpayers. The second is a view of the public as consumers, as active choice makers (the structurally neutral) within the public services (*qua* Mawby and Walklate, 1994, cited above). Hence the various charters of the late 1980s and early 1990s, and contemporarily with the Victims Code of Practice. The last view of the public identified by Clark et al. is one of a community of diverse interests (the structurally informed), but importantly a community which nevertheless is now 'responsibilized' (Clark, 2005) in a whole range of relationships it has with the state.

There are specific difficulties with all of these visions of the public interest. Yet despite the differences between them, arguably, they are all surface manifestations of a more fundamental and deeper changing relationship between the citizen and the state. What they share is a common view of the citizen who has rights to call upon the state, but rights that are contingent upon their willingness and ability as citizens to fulfil their obligations to the state – to behave responsibly. This is a significant shift from the relationship of the 1950s, in which the citizen had rights and the state had obligations. In this shifting relationship between the citizen and the state, managed as it is in contemporary policy terms through a modernization agenda, what counts as the public interest or a public good is at best blurred.

Waldron (1993: 358) has argued that a public good is: 'something which is said to be valuable for human society without its value being adequately characterizable in terms of its worth to any or all of the members of the society considered one by one'. In this view, the value of public goods is not reducible to their aggregate value for each member of society but what they are worth to everyone together. In other words, they are irreducibly *social*. Public goods represent something more than their economic worth.

However, what it is that public goods represent contemporarily seems to be both uncertain and unclear. What *is* clear and certain, in the context of contemporary criminal justice policy, is that sight has been lost of the potential *social* value of the criminal justice system. This is clearly demonstrated in the moves to centre the victim of crime in the criminal justice system in the absence of any widespread debate as to whether or not such moves are in the social (public) interest. In the absence of such a debate, of course, it is relatively easy for politicians and policy-makers to make claims for *Justice for All* (the title of a government White Paper published in 2002, in which the victim of crime was placed at the centre of the criminal justice policy agenda).

To summarize, this analysis of the transformative processes associated with the victim of crime clearly points to the way in which successive governments, in their desire to manage the problem of crime in changing economic circumstances in the light of an increasing awareness of the nature and extent of criminalvictimization, have looked to the victim of crime as a 'solution' to the questions that have been posed for them. Hence it is possible to trace different stories around who this victim of crime is and how they might best be responded to (managed). However, such 'solutions' need also to be situated in the wider cultural context of a society pre-occupied with risk and safety that has manifested itself as a 'culture of control' (Garland, 2001), in which reference to the victim has been central. This centring connects with what Jessop (2002) has described as the shift from a determined state to a hegemonic state. It is at this juncture that the master plot that underpins the victim story deepens.

Crime, Victims and the Culture of Control

Garland (2001) lays out the problem of how to account for the social and historical processes that have given rise to the current way of responding to crime. He offers us a 'history of the present' as a way of trying to make sense of what has contributed to the current increasing prison population, the processes of social exclusion that can be observed between ethnic groups and social classes, the multiplicity of agencies that are now involved in delivering criminal justice policy (public, private, voluntary), and the coexistence of increasingly punitive policy stances to be found, especially in the UK and the USA on the one hand, and the favourable response given to 'softer' restorative justice initiatives on the other. In the background of this analysis he considers the influence of the 'enterprise culture' so valued in the 1980s, the changes in the labour market, increasing spatial mobility, changing family structures, and the rise of individualism. In the foreground, his conceptual apparatus includes responsibilization, new managerialism and what he calls the criminal justice system's adaptation to failure, which, taken together, comprise his vision of the 'culture of control'. Put simply, if we can't solve it, we'll control it. The cumulative effect of these processes is that crime is normalized and, as a result, being a victim of crime is normalized, whether you are male, female, from an ethnic minority, young or old; the potential of being a victim is there for all of us to embrace (*qua* Green, 2006).

Much of Garland's analysis is concerned to map the similarities in the developments that have taken place in the UK and the USA as this culture of control has emerged. While this analysis has been subjected to solid critique that need not concern us at this juncture (but see, for example, Braithwaite, 2003; Feeley, 2003; Young, 2003; and Walklate, 2005), an awareness of its presence facilitates an understanding of how and why the victim of crime features so much more now in political and policy terms than they did in the 1950s and 1960s. Being a victim is now the norm. But this analysis requires more than just being aware of the nature and extent of criminalvictimization and the symbolic use of the crime victim in policy responses suggested by the three stories outlined above. It requires an understanding of how these processes come together to meet political needs on the one hand, and the underlying needs of the state on the other. So the cultural processes of normalization of which Garland speaks reflect underlying structural processes. This returns us to the role of the state suggested by Jessop's (2002) work.

Crime, Victims and the State

Some time ago, Jefferson, Sim and Walklate (1992: 15) said that: 'what is needed is an understanding of the role of the state which does more than reassert its ideological purpose and project, but neither assigns the 1980s [read here the 1990s onwards] to an economic nor a political determinism'. Quoting Jessop (1991) then, we argued that criminology not only needed to bring the state back in, but needed to put the state in its place. Revisiting some of these questions contemporarily, including revisiting Jessop (2002), it is possible to consider that while 'institutions matter' (2002: 34) (and in this context this can be used to refer to the institutions of the criminal justice system), they matter in a context in which:

> the state can be defined as a relatively unified ensemble of socially embedded, socially regularized, and strategically selective institutions and organizations, social forces and activities organized around (or at least involved in) making collective binding decisions for an imagined political community. (Jessop, 2002: 40)

and:

> hegemonic projects that seek to reconcile the particular and the universal by linking the nature and purposes of the state into a broader – but always selective – political, intellectual, and moral vision of the public interest, the good society, the commonweal, or some analogous principle of societalization. (2002: 42)

Through this kind of lens we can get a sense of the deeper structural processes that may be in play which have resulted in the surface manifestation of the 'culture of control' (Garland, 2001) in which the crime victim features so prominently, not only as a rhetorical and real policy device, but also as a claim to citizenship: the normalization of victimhood. This is the deeper victim story.

Jessop's (2002) analysis of the state, while clearly retaining its Marxist orientation, is a subtle analysis that does not demand determinism, coordination, evenness of distribution of processes, or uniformity in understanding the nature of the state and its activities, but does remind us of the importance of the possible relationship between 'deep' structure and 'surface' structure. There are two important clues that connect Jessop's analysis of the current form of the capitalist state to contemporary criminal justice policy and the victim of crime: the imagined political community, and the moral vision of the good society. So a more complete understanding of the processes relating to criminal justice victim policy in England and Wales over the last twenty-five years or so would also include an analysis of the shift from what might be called the 'determined state' to the 'hegemonic state', in which 'victimhood' has become a key strategy for the continued maintenance of the (capitalist) hegemonic state. This is a strategy that facilitates an appeal to an 'imagined political community' (we are now all victims) that simultaneously offers a vehicle for envisaging a 'good society' (justice for all).

It is difficult to deny the increasing importance of victimhood, not just as a cultural process (Furedi, 1997/2002) but also as a claim to status. In this sense, victimhood is the status whereby the state, through increasingly subtle and not so subtle global and local processes, is reasserting its power over citizenship. In this sense victimhood, in all its different expressions, is harnessed as a source of oppression in the interests of the increasingly diverse and hegemonic (capitalist) state. How this permeates a policy agenda is neither simple nor straightforward, but it is against the backcloth of these kinds of socio-political developments that we can begin to construct a more complete narrative of the historical emergence and increasing concern with the victim of crime in particular and the question of victimization in general.

Conclusion: The State as a Protection Racket

It can be argued that Garland's (2001) elegant analysis of the 'culture of control' has rather underplayed the importance of the role of the state in the manifestation of this culture. Yet there is something to be explored here. Tilly (1985) once described the role of the state as a protection racket whose legitimacy is sustained by its ability to *coerce* order as well as having access to the means of *maintaining* order. Much of the state's activity in this regard has been historically directed to those dangerous classes in dangerous places, but as Chevigny (2003: 91) has observed: 'even more basic to that work seems to have been a promise of safety, to the poor as much as to everyone else'. Loader and Walker (2001: 28) have called for a reconstitution of the connections between policing and the state since, as they assert (rightly in my view), 'the sense of belonging to and having a stake in a political community assists both directly and reciprocally in the production of the public goods of ontological security and stable cultural identity with which the public police are also concerned'. However the importance of the role of the state in providing such a public good of protection goes above and beyond the connections between the public police and the state. It also lies within understanding the criminal justice system and its practices as being in all our interests as a public good, in Waldron's (1993) sense of this concept. So perhaps we need to consider Tilly's (1985) observation on the role of the state as a protection racket a little more seriously than his rather waspish analysis suggests.

The argument here has been that notions of 'victimhood', as embedded within criminal justice policy, have become a key strategy for the continued maintenance of the (capitalist) hegemonic state. These practices appeal to an 'imagined political community' (the victim as citizen) yet simultaneously offers a vehicle for envisaging a 'good society' – a society in which we are all safe. In this way, these practices accommodate both the structurally neutral and the structurally informed images of victimization, along with the 'quality of life' approach adopted by many crime and disorder strategy documents. However, it is clear that we are not all safe. Neither are we all (equal) victims (see, for example, Dixon et al., 2006). But, simultaneously, it is the case that we are all the subjects and objects of contemporary criminal justice policy, policy that rests on the assumption that 'all of us' are potentially victims in one form or another. These contradictory forces have the resultant effect that the real needs of both individuals and communities, who may have a *just* call on resources and policies to make their lives better, and which as a consequence would be in the interests of society as a whole (a collective interpretation of 'all of us'), are subsumed or lost. Thus the state's generalized project to render us all as victim-citizens serves its interests of self-maintenance, contemporarily as a hegemonic rather than a determined project, very well. This is the state's protection racket!

Moreover, the more that democratic processes are eroded, not only by the processes of governance, the presence of globalized interests within local contexts, alongside the role of sponsors for particular policies, but also by the increasing gaps between the electorate, publicly available knowledge, and public policies, the less civilized the state has become (*qua* Loader and Walker, 2007, quoted at the beginning of this chapter). The transformation of the victim of crime from the periphery to the centre of criminal justice policy and the associated decentring of debates concerned with the criminal justice system as a social good are just one illustration of the wider and deeper maintenance of the interests of the state in the contemporary socio-economic and political condition. It remains to be seen whether or not the state can be civilized by or for democracy.

Key Reading

Garland, D. (2001) *The Culture of Control: Crime and Social Order in Contemporary Society.* Oxford: Oxford University Press.
Goodey, J. (2005) *Victims and Victimology.* London: Longmans.
Jessop, B. (2002) *The Future of the Capitalist State.* Cambridge: Polity Press.
Loader, I. and Walker, N. (2007) *Civilising Security.* Cambridge: Cambridge University Press.
Rhodes, R.W. (1997) *Understanding Governance: Policy Networks, Governance, Reflexivity and Accountability.* Buckingham: Open University Press.
Walklate, S. (2007) *Imagining the Victim of Crime.* Maidenhead: Open University Press.

13

CRIME, MEDIA AND THE STATE

Paul Mason

--- **Introduction** ---

In October 2007, Keith Jarrett, President of the National Black Police Association, addressed its annual conference in Bristol. His comments proved contentious.[1] Jarrett, whose speech was previewed in *The Observer*, called for the increased use of stop and search laws on black youths:

> From the return that I am getting from a lot of black people, they want to stop these killings, these knife crimes, and if it means their sons and daughters are going to be inconvenienced by being stopped by the police, so be it. (*The Observer*, 21 October 2007)

The proposed measures were criticized by Milena Buyum, coordinator of the National Assembly Against Racism, and Liberty director Shami Chakrabarti. Nonetheless, they were widely supported by the press. The *Daily Mail* headline read MORE STOP AND SEARCH CAN BEAT KNIFE CRIME, SAYS TOP BLACK OFFICER (22 October), while *The Express* and *The Sun* threw their weight behind the proposal: 'his brave stance deserves support' (*The Sun*, 22 October). *The Star* agreed in its leader: 'It's not racism, it's just plain common sense!' (22 October). Although *The Independent* and *The Mirror* reported opposition to the proposals, there was little acknowledgement of the over-representation of black and minority ethnic communities sentenced in, and punished by, the courts and prisons of England and Wales (Prison Reform Trust, 2007). Nor of the high victimization rates in these communities (Research Development and Statistics Directorate, 2004; Nicholas et al., 2007). Indeed, *The Telegraph* suggested that although black people were much more likely to be stopped and searched than white people in England and Wales, 'the fact that the majority of stops are carried out in inner-city areas – where black people often make up a large slice of the population – the disproportion in stops of blacks over whites is reduced' (22 October).

Thirty years earlier, Stuart Hall and his colleagues highlighted the intensification of police control measures, subsequent public fear, and moral panic around the black mugger (Hall et al., 1978). Crucially, they noted the central role of the media in reproducing the discourses of the powerful in their sociological approach to news production. Things, it seems, have changed very little. The black mugger has been supplemented/supplanted in the eyes of the journalist and the public by black and Asian gun-toting gangs, Muslim suicide bombers and foreign rapists and murderers released from prison to roam the streets. The contentions in *Policing the Crisis* concerning the structural relationship between the state and the media remain persuasive, however. Its core rationale concerning the hegemonic power of the media is still pertinent.

In this chapter I wish to explore the important role the state continues to play in media constructions of crime. What influence does it have on news content? How might the state shape the ways in which crime is constructed and for what purpose? And why are considerations of state and corporate power important in considering media discourses of crime? In particular, I review the contribution that *Policing the Crisis* has made to addressing these questions.

Studies seeking to problematize media and state discourses of crime emerged in the 1970s (Young, 1971; Cohen, 1972; Cohen and Young, 1973; Chibnall, 1977; Hall et al., 1978). Products of the new criminology (Taylor et al., 1973), these works explored the dominant ideologies and structures in news production (for useful reviews, see Kidd-Hewitt and Osborne, 1995; Reiner, 2007). They noted how the state's failure to deal with social and economic inequality was glossed over by media coverage of crime, and replaced by a series of moral panics about violent youth (Cohen, 1972), drug use (Young, 1971) and black muggers (Hall et al., 1978). Thus, what and who the state labelled as 'crime' and 'criminals', and how such deviancy should be punished were reinforced by media reportage. A media constructed, moral public consensus polarized the law-abiding majority and the criminal other. Despite changes in the media ecology and subsequent academic writing in the area, the broad contentions of the position remain.

This is not a popular position in contemporary work on media discourses of crime. Reiner (2007) notes that the hegemonic model of crime news production has been repeatedly challenged by more recent empirical work. Based on what Schlesinger (1990) has called an 'externalist' approach, research has shifted attention away from analyses of media content *per se*, towards an exploration of news production (Ericson et al., 1987, 1989; Schlesinger and Tumber, 1994; Doyle and Ericson, 1996; Innes, 1999, 2002; Mawby, 2002). In doing so, these studies raise criticisms of the hegemonic model of crime news. However, as Reiner also states:

> Empirical analyses of news production in action do emphasize its contingency and fluidity, but they do not fundamentally challenge the hegemonic model. While news may be a competitive arena of conflicting viewpoints, it is culturally and structurally loaded. The news media ... reproduce order in the process of representing it. (Reiner, 2007: 326)

Questions of state and elite power in the cultural constructions of criminality and social control begin with the writings of Marx and Gramsci.

Media Power, State and Hegemony

Marx and Gramsci, central to the critical criminology of the 1970s, have been hugely influential on studies of media power also. It is something of a paradox that so much cultural and media theory has been influenced by Marx, when he offered little which was specific, precise or definite about the media. As Manning observes, this has 'allowed scholars to work on a bewildering variety of interpretations, revisions and adaptations during the course of the 117 years since his death' (Manning, 2001: 35). However, fundamental to the Marxist conception of the mass media is the contention that the ruling class's control over material production also facilitates control over the means of 'mental production'. In other words, the industrialization of news, which was evolving in the 1850s when Marx and Engels were writing, required capital investment. The use of expensive printing presses and the consequent increase in staff costs, for example, meant that the production of news was increasingly dependent upon capital investment. Thus, like the distribution of wealth, access to the production of news was unequal. Marxist media scholars have consequently argued that the ruling classes were well positioned to regulate information: the means of mental production.

Such power meant that those in authority could secure legitimacy through giving their ideas 'the form of universality' (Marx and Engels, 1976: 45). They could promote particular self-serving ideologies, while subverting and restricting others, thus enabling a 'weakening of opposition to the established order' (Miliband, 1977: 50). For instrumental Marxist writers like Miliband, it is the self-censorship of journalists which allowed the continual control of media output:

> No journalist I have met writes what he knows will be cut. What would be the point? If he has a story which he knows will cause controversy back at the newsdesk he will water it down to make it acceptable. (cited in McCann, 1981: 260)

This position recognizes the importance of empirical media research. Miliband and others argued that it was the exploration of the inequalities of media power through the sociology of news that was essential. Accordingly, ethnographic studies of newsrooms, interviews with journalists and observation of journalistic practice were fundamental in exploring how information flows were regulated and how self-censorship operated. In contrast, the structural Marxism of Poulantzas (1978a) argued that it was the underlying structure of media power that required investigation: corporate ownership, the power of advertising, and so on. Herman and Chomsky's propaganda model, discussed further below, is such an exploration.

Marxist approaches to the media have been widely criticized for their economic reductionism. Marx's essentialist perspective uses capital to explain all other social and political practices (Manning, 2001). Antonio Grasmci, in his *Prison Notebooks* (1971) offered a more nuanced account of how Italian fascism attained social dominance (Hoare and Nowell-Smith, 2005). His hegemonic approach suggested that the ruling classes won consent through social and cultural institutions. The press, he argued, was one such instrument through which ideological legitimation of the existing social order and institutions was produced. These 'ruling ideas' or ideology offered the social cement which held together the dominant social order, and elicited a public acceptance of the status quo. However, Gramsci argued that the media remained a site of struggle, where resistance or critique could surface, and thus, as Fiske (1991: 291) argues, 'consent must be constantly won and re-won'. For Gramsci, then, the media was one arena, along with religious institutions, education and political system, where ideological battles took place over ideas, concepts and language. This hegemonic model was central to the new criminological concerns of the ideological role of the media, and to a more recent approach to media power: critical discourse analysis (CDA).

Also influenced by Marx and Gramsci, CDA maintains that texts, including those of the media, are a site of social struggle (Fairclough, 1992). It is predicated upon the notion that language is not merely transparent or representational, but is constitutive. It constructs versions of social reality that then 'enter the discursive economy to be circulated, exchanged, stifled, marginalized or perhaps come to dominate over other possible accounts' (Wetherell, 2003: 16). Critical discourse analysis is an important tool for investigating media power and state influence, as it is primarily concerned with how social inequality is reproduced through discourse (van Dijk, 1988, 1991, 1993; Fairclough, 1992, 1995; Fairclough and Chouliaraki, 1995; Wodak and Meyer, 2001; Richardson, 2007). Furthermore, it develops 'ways of analysing language which address its involvement in the workings of contemporary capitalist society' (Fairclough, 1995: 1). CDA is concerned with what we might call 'discursive ideologies', which reproduce the dominance of those with privileged access to resources. In *Policing the Crisis*, Hall et al. referred to this process as: 'definitions of the powerful become part of the taken for granted reality of the public by translating the unfamiliar into the familiar' (Hall et al., 1978: 62).

The winning of consent is often subtle. Discourses of the powerful may take the form of overt support for a particular position (longer prison sentences, greater use of police powers, for example), or outright denial of another (such as corporate crime as 'error' or 'accident' rather than negligence). However, more often they are exercises of power through inconspicuous, less visible forms. It is through persuasion, manipulation and disinformation in everyday texts that the institutions of the powerful are more likely to be legitimized. Such discourses appear routine, normal and established. But crucially they are *imperceptible* and thus potentially more likely accepted. Again, Hall et al. have noted of this practice:

> ... many of these structured forms of communication are so common, so natural, so taken for granted, so deeply embedded in the very communicative forms which are employed, that they are hardly visible at all, as ideological constructs, unless we set out to ask 'what, other than what has been said about this topic, could be said?' (Hall et al., 1978: 67)

Let us take an example from the British press. On 14 April 2006, *The Mirror* ran a story with the headline PRISON EGGS FURY. The report read:

> Prisoners at two of the country's toughest jails have been treated to luxury Easter eggs at the taxpayers' expense. Prison officers last night branded as 'offensive' the handouts worth £500 at Category A Belmarsh and £350 at Holloway women's prison in North London. Some officers are refusing to work. One said 'It is an insult to the victims'. … A source said 'It's like a holiday camp. Some prisoners said it felt like they weren't inside.'

How does this kind of reporting legitimate the dominance of the powerful and persuade the newspaper-reading public to accept this position? In *The Mirror* article this is achieved through the construction of the prison as 'a holiday camp', where prisoners feast on 'luxury' free chocolate rather than do hard time for their crimes. Meanwhile, the victims and their families continue to suffer. The *Mirror*'s story actually concerned prisoners' family 'fundays' over the Easter holiday, with Easter eggs given out to prisoners' children who were visiting. This alternative discourse of prisoners' families and the humanizing of the criminally deviant 'other' is subverted in the report. It is replaced by a dominant discourse of prison as a soft option and prisoners with too many rights. The discourse is legitimated further by quotes from prison staff. Prison officers are the only sources used in the story. One notes that the distribution of Easter eggs to prisoners' children was 'an insult to the victims'. Quotes such as these give legitimacy to the story. Here, the prison officers are what Hall et al. called 'primary definers': elite sources with privileged access to journalists, able to shape the news agenda. I shall come to this shortly.

What is normalized, taken for granted and established as routine in this story? *The Mirror* establishes two discourses here: that prisoners and their families are undeserving of any rights and that penal sanctions are not rigorous enough. This denies the British prison's primary role as an instrument of pain delivery, and as an institution of perpetual failure. The discourses of persuasion and manipulation *of what a prison is and does* is an example of a dominant discourse winning consent for state control measures. This is commonplace in British news reporting of prison (Mason, 2006, 2007).

But how do these state discourses of crime come to dominate over others? Marxist accounts suggest that it is economic interest and power that provide the opportunity for controlling media output. However, the work on critical political economy developed a more complex perspective on the relationship between economic, political and cultural processes. Thus the economic reductionism levelled at Marxist accounts of media production could be avoided.

Crime, Political Economics and the Corporate Media

Studies on the political economy of the media emerged in the 1960s in both the UK and USA. In Britain, the work of Peter Golding and Graham Murdock (Murdock and

Golding, 1973; Golding and Murdock, 1991) and Nicholas Garnham (1978) argued that there could not be consideration of cultural products without an exploration of the context in which they are produced and consumed. Equally, later work in the USA (Mosco, 1995) stressed the importance of locating the mass media in the broader structures of inequality and power. In particular, they examined how the concentration of control and influence over media content lay with a few large companies. Writing in 1973, Murdock and Golding noted that this was achieved through take-overs and mergers of rival businesses and the extension of modes of production and the internationalization of companies to facilitate a global market share. McChesney and Nichols (2002) provide a recent example of these processes. They note that AOL Time Warner own all the major Hollywood studios, the commercial US television networks, four of the five companies that sell 90% of music in the USA, publishing houses, internet service provision and many of the biggest cable television stations. Indeed, the expansion of this media space, coupled with the contraction of media ownership, presents further opportunities for what Turrow calls 'customer relationship media' (Turrow, 2007: 296) and is explained by Tinic as 'the propensity to personalize, individualize, and customize forms of electronic communications technology that were once seen to be the pre-eminent domain of large corporate or government institutions' (Tinic, 2007: 309).

Historically, such corporate expansion had been monitored and regulated by the state, which required cultural diversity underpinned by public subsidy (Golding and Murdock, 1991).[2] However, the liberalization of such policies and consequent freeing up of market forces have led to increased privatization and consequently an extension of the corporate reach into media ownership. As American journalist A.J. Liebling famously observed, 'freedom of the press is largely reserved for those who own one' (in McChesney and Nichols, 2002: 26).

The promotion of certain cultural forms over others is central to the concerns of critical political economy. Writers such as Schiller (1991) and Hamelink (1994) have contended that the global reach of the corporate media is a further expansion of economic domination and consumption by the west. This is particularly true of the USA in particular, where 'domination is precisely what cultural imperialism is all about. With that comes the definitional power ... that sets the boundaries for nationalist discourse' (Schiller, 1991: 19). This 'corporate take over of public expression' (Schiller, 1989: 135) has led to the industrial business sector controlling not only the media, but cultural production, education and public spaces too (Durham and Kellner, 2006). The net result of such corporate media power is the reduction of staff in the drive for profit and the reduction of quality in the endless chasing of audiences:

> They deliver first and foremost for their stockholders ... they serve the major corporate interest that bankroll so much of the media with fat advertising checks [sic] ... they serve a political class that returns the favour by giving media conglomerates free access to the public's airwaves while routinely removing barriers to the expansion of corporate control over communications. (McChesney and Nichols, 2002: 26)

Further, and as Tinic suggests, the synergies between the corporate and media spheres persist, influencing content:

> Today we only have to watch an episode of *Friends* to see that process at work. Where else but on television would we find a group of young, beautiful, white people who, despite being chronically under- or unemployed, lived in spacious New York City apartments and set the standard of fashion for dress and hairstyles in North America for over a decade? (Tinic, 2007: 321)

This applies equally to representations of crime and crime control. Take, for example, the influx of US crime dramas, imported cheaply by British terrestrial and cable television. Here, the dominant discourse is one of crime fighting, of heroic cop fighting on the mean streets of Los Angeles, Miami or New York. Police protagonists are flawed but ultimately heroic (Reiner, 2000; Doyle, 2003; Leishman and Mason, 2003; Mawby, 2003; Reiner et al., 2003). They are heroes in hard times (King, 1999), and avengers for a fearful public. Wider social causes of crime and uneven access to justice for the poor and disenfranchised are, of course, not dealt with in these narratives. Consequently, the deviant remain constructed as 'social junk and dynamite' (Christie, 2000: 73).

The elite control of the media is made more manifest in Herman and Chomsky's 'propaganda model'. Central to their analysis of the political economy of the US media, the model deals with the consequences of corporate control, and 'traces the routes by which money and power are able to filter out the news fit to print, marginalize dissent, and allow government and dominant private interests to get their message across to the public' (Herman and Chomsky, 1988: 2). The model is based upon five filters which, Herman and Chomsky argue, operate so naturally that journalists believe they are acting objectively and in accordance with professional news values. These filters comprise the power of the deregulated and concentrated corporate media, advertisers, powerful institutional sources, the polarization of issues into the 'fuzzy concept' of communism, used 'to serve as a political control mechanism' (Herman and Chomsky, 1988: 29), and the use of 'flak': negative, organized responses to counter stories and reports damaging to the political elite. It is through these filters that mainstream US corporate news passes.

However, the model has been subjected to criticism on a number of grounds, some more carefully considered than others (for considered accounts, see Klaehn, 2002, 2003; Sparks, 2007). It has been suggested that in proposing the existence of a structural relationship between state and journalists, Herman and Chomsky's premise 'can easily collapse into a conspiracy model' (Manning, 2001: 39). As Edward Herman has pointed out (Herman, 2000), such criticisms ignore the specific explanations of why the model was non-conspiratorial (Herman and Chomsky, 1988), and how a dominant media embedded in a market system could 'act like lemmings'. Further criticisms have argued that the model is media-centric, failing to talk to news reporters themselves (Schlesinger, 1989), and that public opposition to dominant news discourses are incompatible with the propaganda model. This latter argument contends that public dissatisfaction with President Reagan's foreign policy in Central America (LaFeber, 1988; Lang and Lang, 2004a, 2004b) and/or with the Vietnam war (Schlesinger, 1989) illustrate that the state has been unsuccessful in its attempts to convince the public of its point of view. However, in a feisty defence of the model, and arguing for its continued relevance ten years on from its original inception, Edward Herman (2000) points out that the model illustrates how the media *works* rather than *how effective* it is. He notes: 'By the logic of this criticism of the propaganda model, the fact that many Soviet citizens did not swallow the lines put forward by *Pravda* demonstrates that *Pravda* was not serving a state propaganda function' (Herman, 2000: 107). The model's continuing relevance, he suggests, is to explain how elite consensus is repackaged through the propaganda system, as democratic consent.[3]

A fundamental criticism of the propaganda model is its dependence on content rather than on journalistic practice and news production (Schlesinger, 1989; Hallin, 1994). It is far better, the critiques suggest, to investigate how particular ways of understanding the world come to dominate in news production. It is this sociology of news production that *Policing the Crisis* had gone some way to providing, back in 1978.

Sources and the Primary Definition of Crime

One of the enduring contributions of *Policing the Crisis* has been its work on the social production of news. Hall et al. were keen to draw attention to the routines of information gathering and the structures of news production which, they argued, came 'to reproduce the definitions of the powerful' (Hall et al., 1978: 61). This exploration formed part of a wider exploration of how social constructions of crime (in their case 'mugging') produced certain kinds of responses from the state. Consequently, they argued that the media, the judiciary and the police were not simply passive agencies, reacting to consensual, unambiguous notions of crime, but that such institutions were 'active in defining situations, in selecting targets, in initiating 'campaigns', in structuring these campaigns, in selectively signifying their actions to the public at large, in legitimating their actions through the accounts of situations which they produce' (Hall et al., 1978: 52). Hall et al. therefore offered an account of the relationship between the dominant ideas of the state and professional media ideologies and practices. On the face of it, and like Herman and Chomsky's propaganda model which came later, such a proposition was open to accusations of a simplistic conspiracy theory. It suggests that journalists are bullied, cajoled and pressured into producing the news which the state and elite news organizations want. However, *Policing the Crisis*, aware of such criticism, argued that such a contention would be to ignore the (relative) autonomy of journalists from such corporate control. Instead, Hall el al. suggested that it was the role of elite news sources that structured news content. Writing more than a decade later, Ericson et al. noted that:

News is a representation of authority. In the contemporary knowledge society news represents *who* are the authorized knowers and *what* are their authoritative versions of reality. ... At the same time that it informs who are the authorized knowers, it suggests, by relegation to a minor role and by omission, who is excluded from having a say in important matters. (Ericson et al., 1989: 3–4, emphasis in the original)

Back in 1978, Hall et al. were at pains to emphasize the power of news sources too. They stressed that the time constraints on journalists to meet deadlines led to an increased dependency on news sources. Coupled with this reliance were the journalistic imperatives of balance, impartiality and objectivity, requiring that reporters sought accredited representatives, such as MPs, government ministers and/or 'experts'. Such sources, they argued, acquired legitimacy through their institutional position, power or representativeness. Alternatively, they were considered by reporters to be what Deacon and Golding (1994) referred to as 'disinterested arbiters'. These 'experts' could provide comment and explanation on contemporary events without any ideological investment in the issue themselves (Greenberg, 2004).

Hall et al. drew on Becker's ideas of a 'hierarchy of credibility' (Becker, 1967). Here, Becker suggested that the media tended to reproduce the existing structure of power in society, while Hall et al. argued that two factors – journalistic reliance on sources and the professional and ideological imperatives of 'balance' –

... combine to produce a systematically structured *over-accessing* to the media of those in powerful and privileged institutional positions. ... The result of this structured preference given in the media to the opinions of the powerful is that these 'spokesmen' [*sic*] become what we call the *primary definers* of topics. (Hall et al., 1978: 58, emphasis in the original)

The media, they argued, were *secondary* definers of news. Although crucial, they reproduced the definitions of those who had privileged access to journalists, editors and so on. In what Chibnall (1977) termed the 'structured access' of news, Hall et al. argued that the media were subordinate to elite and powerful sources, such as the police officer, the government minister, the judge, and so on. It was therefore these ruling-class interests that constructed a particular image of society, images which (re)presented the ruling-class interest as the interests of all society. Here, Hall et al. made overt reference to the Marxist premise, discussed earlier, that the ruling class own and control the means of 'mental production'.

Policing the Crisis makes two other important points. Coupled with an explanation of how the press reproduce the ideologies of the powerful, it explained what it termed the *transformation* from facts and interpretation into a finished news format. Hall et al. noted two 'structural imperatives' in the news media: selectivity and the public idiom. The first concerned the ability of each newspaper to accept or reject statements from primary definers and to shape such statements to fit with its own processes, politics and 'personality'. Such selectivity, they argued, further countered the notion of an overt conspiracy between the powerful and the media. Nevertheless, there remained a relatively narrow choice, 'within certain distinct ideological limits' (Hall et al., 1978: 63). Indeed, in contemporary journalism, much has been made of the fall in numbers of journalists in the increasing drive for profit. Moreover, the shift from journalists as news gatherers to news processors has increased as the use of press releases and professionalized public relations grows (Davis, A., 2000; Franklin, 2004, 2006; Lewis et al., 2008). This is dealt with further below.

The second process Hall et al. outlined was the translation of statements from primary definers into 'the public idiom'. This was the re/presenting of elite sources' accounts in familiar language, which 'invests them with a popular force and resonance, naturalising them with the horizon of understandings of the various publics' (Hall et al., 1978: 67). For example, Shadow Home Secretary David Davis, in a statement commenting on Home Office statistics released in October 2006 said: 'These shocking statistics show the towns and communities of Britain continue to be blighted by increasing violent crime and robbery as a result of Labour's failing policies on law and order'. *The Express* headline the same day read YOB RULE ON THE STREETS OF BRITAIN: VIOLENT YOBS HAVE TAKEN CONTROL OF THE STREETS, MAKING A MOCKERY OF TONY BLAIR'S PLEDGE TO MAKE US SAFER (20 October 2006). If there were any doubt about the pertinence of *Policing the Crisis* in contemporary criminology, the continual construction of 'mugging' in the British press thirty years on would suggest otherwise. On the same day as *The Express* headline, *The Times* suggested that 'This figure is the increase in the number of "thefts from the person" estimated by the British Crime Survey (BCS) for the year ending June 2006. Thefts to the person are better known as muggings.'

The police officer, the judge and the Home Officer minister do not have it all their own way. Among the political claims and counter-claims over crime statistics, criminal justice policy or social control agendas, it is certainly the case that alternative voices are heard. In most crime news reports, one would expect to see a challenge to the contentions of the primary definer: expression from a different viewpoint. Hall et al. accepted that there were oppositional views put forward by the print media and that these appeared to offer some semblance of balance. Crucially, however, they determined that it was the primary definers that establish the 'initial definition' or primary interpretation of the topic in question. It is these primary definers that set the frame of reference, giving other voices little choice but to shape their views into the pre-existing parameters defined by elite sources. To attempt to play outside these 'rules' was to risk delegitimization, being constructed as 'extremist' or simply 'defined out of the debate' (Hall et al., 1978: 64).

By way of example, let us return to Keith Jarrett. I noted that *The Independent* and *The Mirror* reported opposition to his call for an increase in stopping and searching in the black community. A closer analysis reveals that those quoted were responding to a debate framed by a senior police officer, a primary definer. While Shami Chakrabarti, Labour MP Keith Vaz and Liberal Democrat Home Affairs spokesman Nick Clegg voiced their concerns at Jarrett's suggestion, issues such as widespread and institutional racism in the police, and the policing of disenfranchised communities were subverted. These oppositional voices are forced 'on to the terrain of the *pragmatic* – given that there is a problem about crime, what can we do about it? (Hall et al., 1978: 69). Thus counter-discourses to those of Jarrett are limited, stifled and sometimes simply silenced.

While the primary definer thesis remains persuasive, it has been challenged, disputed and contested on a number of grounds. The best known, most cited and undoubtedly most thorough of these criticisms came from Philip Schlesinger (Schlesinger, 1990; Schlesinger and Tumber, 1994). His principal concerns were based around the 'excessive media centrism' (Schlesinger, 1990: 61) and internalist methodology in the exploration of source/media relations. Borrowing from Ericson et al.'s extensive study of crime news sources in Toronto (Ericson et al., 1989), Schlesinger suggested that to draw conclusions about the news-gathering structure simply from the news reports was to ignore the critical perspective of the sources themselves. From this he noted several weaknesses in Hall et al.'s approach.

First, Schlesinger suggested that the cohesiveness and uniformity of primary definers had been over-estimated, ignoring tensions and competing discourses between them. These 'turf wars' (Manning, 2001: 16) between elite sources suggest that primary definers do not speak with one voice, a position exemplified in work on food 'scares' in the media (Miller and Reilly, 1994), news coverage of the poll tax (Deacon and Golding, 1994), foreign policy reporting (Robinson, 2001), political conflict in Northern Ireland (Miller, 1993, 1994) and New Labour's media strategy (Manning, 1998). More recently, Simon Cross, in his work on the leaking of a local paedophile story, suggests that:

> ... leaks offer a prism through which can be seen the absence of elite consensus among members – in this case the prison service, police service, probation service, as well as the political class shaping post-sentence penal policy. (Cross, 2005: 297)

Schlesinger's second contention arises from his criticism of textual analyses to establish the structural relationship of sources to news production. This was the criticism levelled against instrumental Marxist media theory and the propaganda model in particular. Schlesinger suggests that Hall et al.'s account fails to explore what occurs off the record: the ability of primary definers to brief unattributably and indirectly. In their work on the reporting of AIDS, Miller and Williams (1998) argued that the ability of some groups to influence the public debate could not be judged purely by their media profile. They pointed out that charitable organizations that receive government funding may be constrained in what they are able to communicate publicly. Terrence Higgins Trust worker, Nick Patridge, explained:

> We have to be the responsible party, that's our role. One: it protects our charitable status, secondly our combative up-front campaigning has to be in the context of charity and ... I want this organization to remain a trusted source of information. (ibid.: 128)

This is equally true of pressure groups. The Howard League, for example, are also government funded and count among their trustees ex prison governors, members of the board of visitors, parole board and judiciary. This will undoubtedly influence their public voice. Although this may suggest a shortcoming in the primary definer model, it nevertheless supports the broader contention that the media maintain a hegemonic role in reproducing existing structures of power, whether this occurs behind the headlines or below them.

It has been noted by some scholars that the primary definer model underplays the role for alternative sources to access the media. Moreover, it is suggested that there is 'a potential openness' (Schlesinger, 1990: 76) to oppositional viewpoints (Miller, 1993; Deacon, 1996; Anderson, 1997; Miller and Williams, 1998; Manning, 2001; Greenberg, 2004). It is hard to dispute such a body of empirical research. However, in crime news this appears less convincing. *Policing the Crisis* expressly states that crime reporting is, by definition, less open to alternative definitions: 'a police statement on crime is rarely "balanced" by one from a professional criminal ... criminals are neither "legitimate" nor organised' (Hall et al., 1978: 69). Work by Chibnall (1977), Ericson et al. (1989), Leishman and Mason (2003), Mason (2006, 2007), Mawby (2002) and Solomon (2006) all suggest that elite criminal justice sources, such as the police, prison officials and the Home Office, primarily define crime stories. Consequently, alternative viewpoints are considerably underreported.[4] One could add a further primary definer which has emerged in the years following the publication of *Policing the Crisis*. Reiner (2007) points out that victims have become a central focus in crime news narratives in the last thirty years, reflecting the central role they now play in the criminal justice system. Indeed, many victims groups are widely quoted in crime reporting, such as Mothers Against Guns and the Victims of Crime Trust. This latter group, despite consisting of only three permanent members has been quoted more times on prison stories than the Howard League and Prison Reform Trust combined (Mason et al., 2006c)

It is interesting to note that research on the alternative news media website *Schnews* reflected the same, albeit inverted, sourcing practices as the mainstream media (Atton and Wickenden, 2005). Thus the 'counter elite' – activists and the journalist/ witness – were still at the top of the source hierarchy of sources, rather than 'ordinary people', as one might have thought:

> The nature of its sourcing practices and the dominance of particular source types suggests a routinisation of sourcing similar to that of the mainstream, where over-accessing of particular sources for ideological reasons is as likely as over-accessing for reasons of workload and deadlines. (ibid.: 358)

Schlesinger offers several other criticisms of the primary definer model. These concern the failure of the model to offer a fully working account of the sociology of news production. He considers the model to be 'atemporal', failing to account for future shifts in the emergence of new primary definers; it does not fully explain who is defined as a 'primary definer' and the shifting levels of access elite sources may have; it fails to account for the process of contestation between sources and within institutions before they reach the press. Here, Schlesinger is more concerned with producing a more nuanced and sophisticated model for exploring news production, and concedes his argument is primarily a methodological and conceptual one. Despite such criticisms, Schlesinger and others concede that Hall et al.'s contention that the structure of journalistic practice promotes, for the most part, the interests of the powerful. Hall et al.'s argument, then, remains convincing:

> Despite these reservations, however, it seems undeniable that the *prevailing tendency* in the media is towards the reproduction, *amidst all the contradictions,* of the definitions of the powerful, of the dominant ideology. (Hall et al., 1978: 65–6)

Conclusion

The media have regularly been represented as conduits for the distribution of governmental ideology. Writers from this school of thought talk of 'the packaging of politics' (Franklin, 2004), 'the modern publicity process' (Blumler, 1999), 'designer politics' (Scammell, 1995) and 'the public relations state' (Deacon and Golding, 1994). In a media ecology in which style supersedes content, and where personalities supplant policies and photo opportunities replace news, it is unsurprising to find criminal justice agencies seeking to get in on the act. The police, prison and probation service, lawyers and judges have all professionalized their media management strategies, borrowed from the corporate sphere (Schlesinger and Tumber, 1994) and market share (Nelson, 1989; Scammell, 1995; Rosenbaum, 1997; Franklin, 2004). More importantly, as Davis notes, 'corporate and state sources have massive institutional and economic resource advantages that cannot be matched' (Davis, A., 2000: 47), including the legitimacy of institutional sources as discussed by Hall et al. (1978). Put bluntly, PR worked, so its use has increased.

In policing, for example, image making and news management has, historically, been a central concern (Mawby, 2002). The police have, for many years, been able to plan and refocus 'crime stories'. Thus, the sole onus for solutions to crime is transferred away from the police by, for example, presenting vandalism as an environmental story and substance abuse as primarily a health issue (Boyle, 1999a, 1999b; Leishman and Mason, 2003). The media, it would seem, are happy to accept this cop-sided view of events.

Similarly, the Prison Officers' Association have used press releases to pre-empt criticism. Their intervention attempts to shift media discourses away from prison conditions and treatment of prisoners towards one based on public fear, risk and danger (Mason et al., 2006a, 2006b, 2006c). Legal professionals and the court system too have engaged in forms of media management. The Department for Constitutional Affairs undertook a lengthy consultative process with media professionals and journalists in planning the televising of appeal courts. A source at the Department also suggested it had attempted to exercise some influence over the portrayal of the judiciary in the BBC series *Judge John Deed* (personal communication, October 2004).

Clearly, the use of PR is not limited to instruments of the state. Pressure groups, too, have opportunities to intervene in debates.[5] But A. Davis points out that, despite what he calls 'grounds for pluralist optimism' (2000: 51), it is government and elite sources that have disproportionate access to the media. One may argue that this is true of any challenge to existing definitions of crime, and true of subsequent social control measures. It is the carving out of alternative public spaces where real and sustainable challenges to the state can be made (Mathiesen, 2001, 2003).

As *Policing the Crisis* has made abundantly clear, one cannot talk of media constructions of crime without consideration of the state. From the dominant discourses of the powerful reproduced through elite sources, to the structured nature of news production and corporate ownership, the hand of the state is palpable. Critics will point out shortcomings in the hegemonic position I have explored. Scholars will continue to publish nuanced arguments, offer exceptions to the rule and point out omissions. Studies based on small or undisclosed interview samples will conclude that the 'reality' is more complex and contested than Hall et al., Herman and Chomsky and McChesney and Nichols suggest. They will still, however, conclude that PR, primary definers and corporate control are central to crime narratives in the media. Meanwhile, the disenfranchised will continue to be criminalized, more prisons will be built to contain them and criminal justice agencies will continue to promote their self-serving discourses to a collusive corporate media.

Key Reading

Ericson, R., Baranek, P. and Chan, J. (1989) *Negotiating Control: A Study of News Sources.* Milton Keynes: Open University Press.

Golding, P. and Murdock, G. (1991) 'Culture, communications and political economy', in J. Curran and J. Gurevitch (eds), *Mass Media and Society.* London: Edward Arnold.

Herman, E. (2000) 'The propaganda model: a retrospective', *Journalism Studies,* 1(1): 101–12.

Manning, P. (2001) *News and News Sources: A Critical Introduction.* London: Sage.

McChesney, R. and Nichols, J. (2002) *Our Media, Not Theirs: The Democratic Struggle against Corporate Media.* New York: Seven Stories Press.

Schlesinger, P. and Tumber, H. (1994) *Reporting Crime: The Media Politics of Criminal Justice.* Oxford: Clarendon Press.

Notes

1   Jarrett also suggested that 'Affirmative action in the eyes of the BPA is having the right person for the job. ... If you need black police officers then what is the point of putting someone else there who wouldn't understand? ... It takes bravery to do something that is unpopular.' The British media, and the tabloids in particular, screamed of political

correctness gone mad: 'fascist positive discrimination' cried *The Star* (25 October), PROMOTE BLACK POLICE JUST FOR BEING BLACK reported *The Express* (25 October).

2   Murdock and Golding note that British commercial channels have been regulated, in the public interest, to offer programmes which appealed to a minority interest, even if such programmes did not make a profit.

3   In an excellent account, Herring and Robinson note that the propaganda model applies equally to academia. They point out that, 'analysis of Chomsky's marginalisation by academia is worthwhile only to the extent that it contributes to academia facing up to its responsibility to acknowledge and end its active and passive participation in supporting elite interests' (Herring and Robinson, 2003: 68).

4   However, work by Schlesinger and Tumber (1994) on crime reporting, and Doyle and Ericson (1996) on prison coverage in Canadian newspapers found alternative sources were more common.

5   For a discussion of how the media support particular conservative pressure groups, such as Sarah's Law and the cutting of fuel prices, see Milne (2005).

14

THE STATE, KNOWLEDGE PRODUCTION AND CRIMINOLOGY

Reece Walters

 Introduction

We live in a contaminated moral environment. (Vaclav Havel, 1 January 1990)

Vaclav Havel, playwright, human rights activist and first President of the Czech Republic, knew from a young age what it meant to live under an oppressive and dictatorial form of government. He expressed his resistance to abusive government regimes through his literary talents, including the influential *The Power of the Powerless*, published in 1978, which resulted in him spending four years in prison. Havel argued that communist Czechoslovakia was governed by morally corrupt individuals who subverted truth in favour of a totalitarian lie that served the interests of the ruling elites. The denial of free speech and the perpetuation of intolerance contaminated public consciousness, where citizens were not only victims of state power but were its 'co-creators'. Individual silence and compliance resulted in a society of moral ill-health where 'we become used to saying something different from what we thought'. The answer to repressive state power was a mobilization of public participation and resistance that harnessed diverse endeavours to speak truth to power and uncover the lies, contradictions, hypocrisies and corruption of state power.

It is ironic that Havel should publish his account of repressive state power in the very same year that Hall et al. printed their own British version, namely *Policing the Crisis* (1978). So, on the thirtieth anniversary of *Policing the Crisis* (*PtC*), it is timely that we should reflect upon its contributions as a beacon of resistance to repressive state power; that harnessed diverse knowledges across sociology, cultural and media studies and social history to critique the social formation in Britain through the imprisonment of Paul, Jimmy and Musty for the politically and socially constructed crime of 'mugging'. As this collection attests, *Policing the Crisis* was a rich source for analysing state power, even if this has not always been adequately utilized within nor beyond criminology. For me, I wish to explore its impact on our understandings of the construction of knowledge about crime and 'crime problems'. In doing so, to ask, to what extent has the state and state power changed since 1978? And have the ways in which criminological knowledge been controlled and constructed also changed?

Policing the Crisis – Some Reflections

In order to answer the above questions, let us reflect and begin with the objects of *Policing the Crisis*, namely, the 'black urban mugger', and how this knowledge of the criminal was derived from official criminal statistics that were essentially manipulated. Such a starting point allows us to indicate how a dominant 'truth' is established by the state in the widest sense of the word; in this case, the police and the mass media with the help of politicians. As Hall et al. (1978) identify, newspapers reported that Mr Arthur Mills, an elderly widower, was stabbed to death on 15 August 1972 by three muggers. Mr Mills came to represent the 'vulnerable victim', the frail elderly or the 'easy mug' who fell prey to an emerging street violence exported from the USA to Britain (see Walklate, this volume, on the rise of the victim). Through the death of Mr Mills, we all became victims to a new 'criminal pariah', one that violated our personal space on the streets of everyday existence. The offenders, on the other hand, through the urban black youth, came to represent the 'dangerous other' in a changing British society. Subsequent Home Office research, while identifying that victims of mugging were more likely to be the young, and that the most serious forms of street robbery committed with weapons were perpetrated by white and not black people, continued to reinforce the view that African-Caribbean males were disproportionately associated with mugging (Baker et al., 1993). As a result, the media and socially constructed labels following the attack on Mr Mills became embedded in political and government discourse.

While published in 1978, *Policing the Crisis* was based on a collection of writings published from the early 1970s, a period when mainstream or positivist criminologies were challenged by a range of radical discourses, which focused on crime, deviance and social order. The advent of 'critical' criminologies (labelling theory, new deviancy theory, conflict theory, Marxism and Feminism) sparked an intellectual debate of conflict and constituted a radical shift within existing criminological discourses or attempted to do this. Criminology came to be recognized as an important part of the sociology of deviance and mainstream positivist theory was challenged for its political alliance with the state's crime control apparatus (Cohen, 1988). As we know, 'radical criminologies' rejected concepts of individual and social pathology in preference to a framework that examined crime and deviance in terms of the processes by which certain behaviours were defined, labelled and policed by the state (Scraton and Chadwick, 1991). To this extent, radical or 'critical' criminologies of the 1970s were positioned within the 'broader realm of political activism' (Muncie, 1998: 221).

These conflicts in criminology, sociology, media and cultural studies formed the intellectual trajectory for *Policing the Crisis*'s critique of the social order in Britain under an emerging authoritarian state. Through a Gramscian and Marxian analysis, *Policing the Crisis* identifies the ways in which state power, through its agencies of criminal justice, came to represent the 'final frontier of civilization, beyond which lay barbarism' (Clarke, 2008: 124). This barbarism was racial tension and class struggle, constructed and regulated by media and state power as the lawlessness corrupting British society. This authoritarian and conservative form of governance came to construct crime and criminality in ways which permitted the state to regulate the poor and powerless in society.

As a result, it was a period renowned for its control of criminological knowledge. Cohen and Taylor's (1977) work on long-term imprisonment and its effects on inmates in British prisons has been widely used as an example of how state power was mobilized to de-legitimatize critical research. In this case, Cohen and Taylor were denied permission by the Home Office to publish their work-in-progress in the journal entitled *New Society*. The Prison Department of the Home Office objected to the research focusing on specific aspects of incarceration, namely psychological trauma, as well as its 'journalistic' methodology (see Cohen and Taylor, 1977). Cohen and Taylor proceeded to publish their intended article and, as a result, were denied subsequent contact with inmates. Moreover, letters that the researchers wrote to inmates who had participated in their study were returned and the Home Office eventually refused to support the study any further. For years after publishing their work, Laurie Taylor continued to experience barriers from the Home Office. Taylor was banned by the Home Office from entering borstals and remand centres in Britain for the purposes of compiling a BBC documentary on delinquency because, as official sources revealed, 'a book he wrote several years ago about how long-term prisoners coped psychologically with their years inside … had contravened the Official Secrets Act' (Bell and Newby, 1977: 173).

As is often the case with conservative forms of governance, they did not remain localized, but travelled to other jurisdictions and during the period of *Policing the Crisis's* publication, criminologists across Europe were lamenting state interference and control of criminological knowledge. In 1980, for example, the eighth conference of the European Group for the Study of Deviance and Social Control was held in Leuven under the title, 'State Control of Information in the Field of Deviance and Social Control' (see Brusten and Ponsaers, 1981). It noted, that criminological research in Europe was seen by state officials as a means of legitimating penal law and government policy, and that researchers who criticized these positions were unlikely to receive government funding.

John Clarke, one of the original authors of *Policing the Crisis*, recently reflected upon the book's content in a thirtieth anniversary marking its publication. He concludes his piece by suggesting that its ongoing value is:

> that the sense that crisis has never quite been resolved. … Thatcherism appeared to be the natural inheritor of law and order politics, not least in the intensified suturing of the police into political rule. New Labour, however, might be seen as the true believers – with the criminalization of a greater range of social behaviour than ever before. (Clarke, 2008: 127)

This 'suturing of police into political rule' Radical criminological detours, mentioned above, from the scientific approach, became marginalized and, in some instances, disregarded by others claiming that such critical or radical endeavours represented a form of 'left idealism' (Lea and Young, 1984). While left realists challenged the proponents of neo-conservatism and right realism, they asserted that crime 'must be taken seriously' and embarked upon a socialist-based agenda that would address the 'realities' of crime at the local level. This schism within criminology's left represented a return to pragmatic ideals: a realist agenda that extricated itself from notions of crime as a socially constructed entity and focused on, in particular, questions of victimology. While left realism asserted a midway position between what it called 'left idealism' and administrative criminology, many authors argue that left realism compromised its 'radical' roots in favour of a pragmatic programme that diluted 'the new criminology's quest for radical criticism beyond correctional meaning horizons' (Pavlich, 1999: 10). In doing so, it created an intellectual platform for the modernization of New Labour, and its taking crime seriously, through 'evidence based policy', was an electoral success in 1997 and a subsequent pathway for authoritarian, law and order policies.

Policing the Ongoing Crisis and the Intensification of the Authoritarian State

New Labour's intensified authoritarian approach to social problems is evident in its punitive policies. Since 1997, the New Labour government has set about to criminalize some of the most marginalized and traumatized groups in British society, including the homeless, the welfare dependent, the young and those fleeing persecution. As a result, New Labour's infamous slogan 'tough on crime, tough on the causes of crime' has launched various state crackdowns against some of the most vulnerable and dislocated people in contemporary Britain (see Muncie and Goldson, 2005).

The introduction of some 1,018 new crimes since coming to power, the highest prison population in western, northern and southern Europe, an assault on civil liberties, 'anti-social behaviour', 'breaking drop-out culture,' and matching 'rights with responsibilities' are the 'unchanging values' of New Labour that are supposed to take 'Britain forward not back' and bring 'prosperity for all' (see Blair, 2005: 1). However, such rhetoric cannot be reconciled with the same government's recent 'war on immigration', with human rights abuses including lengthy detention, dispersal, denying benefits and removing rights of appeal. This shameful hypocrisy has become normalized within an intolerant regime of denial, cover-up and dismissal.

In such a context, the need to mobilize the critical, academic voice in the UK has recently gathered momentum. The British Sociological Association has called upon all academics in Britain to 'play a more prominent public role' and to 'push intellectual credentials' by stimulating critical debate of government policies and practices (Attwood, 2007: 1). Clearly, public debate about crime and criminal justice is required. The silence and denial of the Prime Minister's Office in recent years and Home Office officials on issues such as the 'war on terror', the treatment of dislocated peoples fleeing persecution, the over-policing of ethnic minorities, the demise of civil liberties and the erosion of the rule of law, the massive increase in fraud and corporate tax evasion, the unacceptable level of health and safety violations, and the various political 'scandals' that have become part and parcel of contemporary British life that necessitate immediate and urgent academic and government debate.

Yet this is a government that does not encourage public dialogue or entertain critical appraisal. Indeed, it actively subverts and whitewashes it. This New Labour government has demonstrated a resistance to transparency and open debate. An Attorney-General who failed to make public his entire legal opinion on the case for war; a Chancellor who actively suppressed Treasury documents about the pensions scandal; Prime Ministerial advisers arrested for suspicion of conspiracy and perverting the course of justice over cash-for-peerages and Lord Goldsmith seeking injunctions to prevent the BBC broadcasting police revelations; a Prime Minister who privately instructed the Serious Fraud Office to drop its investigations against weapons giant BAE and then conducts secret deals behind closed doors; a Cabinet accused of withholding information needed for an open debate about the renewal of Britain's nuclear fleet; government legislation that has changed the nature and parameters of 'public' inquiries; a Constitutional Affairs Minister who tacitly supported a private member's bill that attempted to prevent 'Official Information Request' disclosure of parliamentarian expenditure; Mr Blair's direct communication with former BBC directors to moderate Iraq war coverage; an immigration minister forced to resign over the sex-for-asylum scandal and no government inquiry; Number 10 silence over Mrs Blair's involvement in the deportation case of former fraudster Peter Foster; recent High Court rulings declaring illegal government decisions on immigration and the dropping of the BAE Systems investigations – the list could go on. This is not a government that openly conveys and debates the truth. It is a government that conceals, manipulates and suppresses 'truth'. This is not maladministration but a form of corruption, whereby the reliable, honest and available flow of accurate information to the public is deliberately disrupted or withheld. A public that does not have access to the truth cannot participate in debate and is thereby denied its democratic right. Such are the misguided values and practices of New Labour governance that have, unsurprisingly, influenced and become embedded in the executive of government. The results of 3 May 2007 elections across Britain and the Prime Minister's current lowest opinion poll ratings in 16 years bear testament to public discontent about New Labour's political performance.

The following section links the mistrust and repressive policies of New Labour with the operations of the Home Office Research Development and Statistics Directorate (HORDS). It explores this existing political culture of governing by half-truths and examines the ways in which the Home Office and, to a lesser extent the Scottish Executive (two key sites of criminological hegemony about crime and criminal justice), skew, manipulate and distort criminological knowledge for political gain.

Home Office

During 2006/07 the Home Office allocated 68% (£46.6 million) of its research budget for crime and criminal justice (Wheeler, 2006). During the same period, the then Home Secretary, John Reid, directed a 'pause', 'to improve the quality of Home Office research'. National headlines claimed that the pause was nothing more than an attempt to 'bury bad news', arguing that gun crime research conducted by Chris Lewis at Portsmouth University was poised to reveal the ease in which criminals could access firearms in Britain (Harper and Leapman, 2006). The Home Secretary's pause was a poisoned chalice for the Home Office. If the pause was a manoeuvre to block research damning of the government, then it was an overt act of suppression and cover-up. If it was an action taken to improve the internal functioning of the HORDS, then it was a declaration of inefficiency, or indeed, incompetence. Official statements from the Home Office identified that: 'The Home Secretary asked for a short pause in publications whilst he considered how HO publications should be dealt with in future and so as the new Home Secretary he could take a look at what is on the stocks and in the pipeline.' This identifies a clear ministerial dissatisfaction with the criminological research undertaken by the RDS. Or indeed, a Home Secretary wanting to 'vet' the stockpile of research and ensure that nothing too damning or damaging was on the horizon. Whatever the reason, the pause was not intended to promote critical scholarship of the criminal justice workings of government.

Throughout the pause (which included a cessation on the release of all taxpayer-funded research publications) quality was to be achieved by:

(i)   Strengthening the quality assurance processes for research, including the use of external peer review as well as external review of our internal processes for commissioning new work
(ii) Developing a new format for research publications that are shorter, more succinct and aimed specifically at supporting the development and delivery of Home Office policy. (Official Information Request 6262)

For those of us in academic criminology who have for years declared the biased, controlling and manipulative practices of Home Office criminological research (Tombs and Whyte, 2003a; Hope, 2006; Hillyard, Sim et al., 2004; Walters, 2003), this was nothing more than Home Secretarial endorsement for what we have known for years – that HORDS is 'not fit for purpose'. Home Office suppression of criminological research that contradicts ministerial policy and opinion is a feature of this arm of government with a long history that has intermittently received national headlines (Travis, 1994).

The Home Secretary publicly announcing the shortcomings of his own department, calling a halt to all research activities, and then radically splitting a centuries-old government institution into two to improve efficiency and restore public confidence was a declaration of existing failure. Of course there were various attempts to minimize

John Reid's announcement from within, and none more striking than that of Chloe Chitty's at the British Society of Criminology's conference in Glasgow. Chloe Chitty, a senior researcher within HORDS attempted to downplay the minister's decision to a 200-plus audience and reaffirm the 'importance' of evidence-led policy created by a constructive alliance between government and the academy. The rhetoric of 'changing times', 'new challenges' and 'global threats' was welcomed like a stinging nettle and widely rejected by many criminologists at the conference, including a small delegation who walked out during Ms Chitty's talk. The Home Office rhetoric of 'working with academics' and 'building alliances' must be seriously questioned. In June 2007, at the Open University's International Centre for Comparative Criminological Research's conference, Ms Chitty presented her views on 'the most pressing issue facing the prison is ...'. In it she stated that 'they' (the Home Office) 'were seeing' that inmates with sentences beyond six months were re-offending with less frequency than those serving shorter periods of incarceration. This led Ms Chitty to conclude that perhaps we should be looking at longer prison sentences. Professor Pete King (historian at the Open University) pointed out what any good undergraduate criminology student would have known, that there is a mountain of criminological data that identifies the fallacy in Ms Chitty's thinking. To which Ms Chitty responded 'that's very interesting, and that's why we need to be listening to academics and the work you are doing', after which she left the conference and didn't return. Not only was the ignorance profound and concerning, but this farcical rhetoric of 'partnership', 'listening', 'alliance', solving problems 'together' is laughable when we all know that the Home Office cherry-picks research findings for political ends. Hence, 'we want to listen to what you've got to say, as long at it conforms to our view, and is exactly what the Minister wants to hear'. That is not partnership, but government deceit, and it is precisely why the Home Office has been criticized and subject to severe external scrutiny (see Walters, 2008).

Much of the media attention on the Home Office shake-up focused on escaped prisoners, immigration and terrorism. Yet a sceptic may say that the Home Office's reconfiguration may have been a government ploy to avert the disquiet and anxieties posed by opposition parties and the House of Commons Select Committees. Take, for example, the Science and Technology Committee, which raised serious concerns about the research undertaken and commissioned by the HORDS. It concluded:

> Research must, so far as is achievable, be independent and must been seen to be so. We are not convinced that the current mechanisms for commissioning research deliver this objective. ... We urge the Government CSA [Chief Scientific Advisor] to investigate proactively any allegations of malpractice in commissioning, publication and use of research by departments and to ensure that opportunities to learn lessons are fully taken advantage of. We would expect the results of any such investigations to be made public. (House of Commons Science and Technology Committee, 2006: 97–8)

Finally, the parliamentary record identifies and confirms what criminologists up and down the length of Britain have been saying and experiencing for some time, that conducting research commissioned by the Home Office is a frustrating, one-sided arm-wrestle – where the Home Office ensures that it will almost always 'cherry-pick' the answer it wants. Elsewhere I have identified how Home Office criminology is politically driven; how it provides policy salient information for politically relevant crime and criminal justice issues; how its research agenda is motivated by outcomes that are of immediate benefit to existing political demands – it is the quintessential 'embedded criminology' (Walters, 2007). Critical scholarship is viewed as unwelcome, unhelpful and actively discouraged. Any credible independent research that is likely to shed a negative or critical light on the policies and practices of government will not be procured, funded, published or even debated by the Home Office. This is clearly problematic. It is widely acknowledged that the HORDS plays an important part in the funding of criminological scholarship in the UK. As Rod Morgan has accu-rately identified (2000: 70–71), the RDS is the 'largest single employer of crimino-logical researchers in the UK', where almost all of its research is 'atheoretical fact gathering', 'narrowly focused', 'short-termist', 'uncritical' and 'designed to be policy-friendly'. The Home Office has become a site of criminological hegemony in the UK within a New Labour politics of 'evidence-based research'. As such, its locus of power within the funding and dissemination of criminological scholarship has recently been met with opposition from scholars who argue for criminology to be aligned with much needed 'counter-hegemonic movements' that can actively debate and resist the tilted picture of crime created by the Home Office (see Tombs and Whyte, 2003a; Hillyard, Sim et al., 2004).

Home Office criminology has a very clear purpose: to service the 'needs' of minis-ters and members of parliament. While revealing, it is not surprising that Hillyard, Sim, Tombs and Whyte (2004: 4) identify that the HORDS has experienced a 500% increase in funding for external research in recent years, largely due to New Labour's desire for 'evidence-led policy'. Moreover, they identify from an analysis of HORDS research outputs during the period 1988–2003 that from a catalogue of 571 reports 'not one single report deals with crimes which have been committed as part of legit-imate business activities', concluding that HORDS research serves to reinforce state-defined notions of criminality while paying lip service to state and corporate crime. It is clear that the Home Office is only interested in rubber-stamping the political priorities of the government of the day. If it were concerned with understanding and explaining the most violent aspect of contemporary British society (notably the modern corporation), it would fund projects that analyse corporate negligence, commercial disasters and workplace injuries – but it doesn't. If it were concerned with issues of due process and justice, it would examine deaths of inmates in British custody (including children), the ill-treatment of mentally ill offenders, the imprisonment of women for minor offences and the unacceptable levels of miscarriages of justice – but it won't. If it were concerned with violence and human rights abuses, it would fund projects to examine the corporate/state role in Iraq, Afghanistan and Northern Ireland, or policies on asylum or the sale of weapons to war-torn African countries – but it doesn't (see Hope and Walters, 2008). If it were concerned with the health and well-being of its citizens, it would monitor and evaluate medical misadventure and the unacceptable level of preventable deaths in the NHS – but it doesn't. If it were truly concerned with citizen safety, it would examine the bias and brutality of public and private policing – but it doesn't. The Home Office remains silent on all those topics that have the potential to reflect poorly on government. As a result, it is not an institution that represents the British public – it is an organization that exists to protect the reputation of government. In doing so, the Home Office employs psychology, economics and physics graduates in preference to criminology and sociology graduates to perform quantitative and statistical analyses to pressing Westminster concerns (Walters, 2006a, 2006b).

Scottish Executive

It must be asked whether the views expressed above are unique to the Home Office or representative of other jurisdictions in the UK. The opportunity to compare the processes and practices of the Home Office with a devolved UK government emerged in 2003 while working at the University of Stirling. I had heard various accounts from scholars across different disciplines and different universities of how the Scottish Executive 'cherry-picked' research findings, suppressed reports and censored critical commentary, some of which have been reported in the press, including the Tata and Stephen's (2007) work, which concluded that the Scottish Executive's policy of fixed fees for lawyers had not delivered the promised £10 million reduction to Scotland's legal aid bill – research that the Executive suppressed for more than two years (Howie, 2007).

An opportunity to evaluate the pilot youth court funded by the Scottish Executive emerged in early 2003, of which I became a part. My subsequent encounters with the Executive's manipulation and suppression of 'independent' research, which included omitting relevant data, delaying research results and formally petitioning a university Vice Chancellor when threatened by the critical content of a government-commissioned evaluation report, have since received widespread media attention (Peakin, 2006; Howie, 2006; BBC, 2006a; Parry, 2007; MacPhee, 2007) and have been discussed elsewhere (see Walters, 2008).

In short, when academics commissioned by government fail to produce the results which reinforce existing government policy and practice, then the authorities will cherry-pick and highlight the most positive aspects of the research. Should the researcher publish alternative accounts to the favourable ones acclaimed by government, then the academic can expect various techniques of neutralization that will attempt to discredit and rebuke their work and reputation.

Resistance and Boycott

For years I have listened to civil servants (and academics) declaring the importance of an academic/government research and policy alliance. The power imbalance that exists between civil servants and the providers of knowledge (academics, consultants, members of the public) severs all possibilities of an egalitarian relationship where mutual interest and expertise can be expressed in government policy. The rhetoric of bringing the academic world closer to the workings of some sections of government policy will always encounter applause, yet, at present (at least with the HORDS), it is, in my opinion, unachievable and undesirable. As things stand, they must remain separate. To participate in HORDS and Scottish Executive (SE) criminal justice research is to endorse a biased agenda that omits topics of national and global concern in favour of regulating the poor and the powerless. If all academics boycotted HORDS and SE research and refused to provide such research with the credibility that academic credentials brings, then senior criminal justice civil servants would be forced either to change the existing agenda or to solely engage corporate researchers. If the latter was adopted, not only would Westminster and the devolved parliaments begin to question the lack of 'expertise' informing policy, but the Emperor would be without clothes.

Academics participate in government research agendas that ignore, for example, crimes committed by the most powerful and wealthy in society, while endorsing policies that aim to regulate the already over-regulated in society. Moreover, the Home Office will abort research that 'is no longer of interest to ministers or policy colleagues, either the research has been so delayed that the results are no longer of any interest or because ministers or officials have changed their priorities' (see Walters, 2003: 57). Academics may spend months or even years planning and implementing research that is funded by the Home Office, only to have the plug pulled because a minister has changed his or her mind. Academics should never operate under such conditions and until the Home Office develops a research agenda that seriously addresses crimes of the powerful and permits independent scholarship to occur without interference and to be published verbatim, then I say (as I have said elsewhere: Walters, 2003, 2007, 2008) that academics must boycott the seeking of, and participation in, HORDS and Scottish Executive criminal justice research.

A boycott on HORDS and Scottish Executive research does not mean disengagement or isolationism. I mean to promote engagement and a 'public criminology' through diverse narratives that are often regulated, curtailed or prevented by the constraints of some sections of government. What is needed is the expansion of critical knowledges of resistance. Such knowledges cannot be generated under contract HORDS where they are often silenced or neutralized. They require criminologists to stand outside the domains of commercial criminology and actively assert a position of resistance (Scraton, 2001, 2007b).

There is much to be gained through establishing networks of collective concern (with academics, professional bodies, parliamentary committees, political parties, campaign and voluntary groups) that advocate for the promotion of multiple narratives, social justice and for the dissemination of new and critical knowledges. The promotion of new critical narratives in patriarchy and power, human rights, transnational justice, as well as state and corporate crime provide important voices of resistance against an emergence of embedded criminology. What is needed is an increase and a vocal outpouring of the critical voice or what I call 'deviant knowledge' (that which is critical of contemporary forms of governance and challenges the existing social order). If criminology is to survive or is to make any sense, it must embrace diverse knowledges of resistance – in my view, criminology must be a knowledge of resistance. This calls for a politics of engagement that is often prohibited by the proscriptive and regulated culture of HORDS and Scottish Executive research, which many academics are seduced by in the name of income-generation or evidence-based decision-making. Rather than having young scholars employed *en masse* by HORDS and Scottish Executive-funded projects that are highly regulated to provide government with information that supports its political priorities, I would prefer to see established criminologists employing research fellows on grant funding or universities providing careers for young scholars to pursue research of their own interest. In doing so, they will provide important contributions to theoretical and critical knowledge.

Such knowledges represent the hallmarks of the discipline and as such we should constantly celebrate the critical voice. To take the British context, why is it that the names of Pat Carlen, Stan Cohen, Joe Sim, Stuart Hall, Barbara Hudson, Phil Scraton, Ian Taylor, Jock Young remain the most influential criminological scholars of the last forty years? The merit and value of the critical scholar stands the test of time. It is not defined by the vagaries of contemporary politics and the machinations of Whitehall; instead, it is based on a thoughtful, reflective and innovative scholarship.

Public Criminology and Voices from Below

In the spirit of Vaclev Havel, quoted in the opening to this chapter, criminological scholars have recently called for criminology to become more 'public' and to harness the power in activist movements or 'voices from below'. While there remains dissention on what this means – a voice of independent and critical autonomy (Hope, 2008) or one that works alongside government in the production of crime policy (Wiles, 2002) – it is clear that there exists a movement of mobilization to have criminologists actively engaged with diverse public voices to provide innovative responses to existing 'crime problems'. Take, for example, the words of Elliot Currie (2007: 176), one of America's foremost critical criminologists for the past three decades. He argues that a 'public criminology' is 'one that takes as part of its defining mission a more vigorous, systematic and effective intervention in the world of social policy and social action'. While criminologists have been very effective at producing answers to crime causation, programmes of rehabilitation, effectiveness or ineffectiveness of the justice system, we have been less influential in educating and capturing the imagination of the public at large. For Currie, criminology as a discipline has become 'institutionally constructed', where certain forms of knowledge and dissemination don't count. This, he argues, needs to change. The ability to write and speak to agencies, pressure groups, trade union movements, activist organization and community gatherings are all necessary in educating a more informed public – an education that must take place outside the university classroom and beyond the academic journals. In doing so, a public criminology is harnessing voices from below and not speaking and listening solely to the legislators and civil servants in the corridor of power. This does not mean that the production of technical reports for government is not a worthwhile endeavour. I believe it is. Yet, it is important that 'government' is not seen by academic criminologists as the sole domain of the HORDS. Technical reports about crime and harm produced for the NHS, the Food Standards Agency, Health and Safety Executive, Ministry of Internal Affairs and so on, are valuable assets to a more public criminology. They must not, of course, colonize all forms of criminological dissemination, but they have an important role to play in reaching the broader tentacles of government and its executive. Equally important is the engagement with other academic disciplines and with networks and partnerships with diverse audiences, including the media. As Currie (2007: 188) argues, 'truth needs advocates. It needs defenders.' Such advocacy cannot be achieved through the production, manipulation and suppression of HORDS commissioned reports – the likes of which is consuming, in my opinion, an unacceptable amount of academic criminological time and resources. Effective advocacy requires diverse and active dissemination to various publics to ensure that maximum reach.

Conclusion

Academic criminologists commissioned by the HORDS or the Scottish Executive to conduct evaluations of government policy are often in the position to unearth the relationship between politics and policy, which is why authorities often seek to control the production, distribution and consumption of emerging new knowledges about their world of policy-making and practice. When researchers reveal critical insights of these processes through their evaluative work, then those in power may seek to control the distribution and consumption of these new knowledges and question the production process itself (Presdee and Walters, 1999).

In my view, civil servants in the Home Office and the Scottish Executive do not want to 'learn' from academics – in their minds, there is little that academics can teach them. They seek credible reassurance and endorsement for political priorities and not genuine debate, challenge or disagreement; and certainly not anything spoken or written that will embarrass a minister and/or denounce the actions of government. We live in a society where sections of government manipulate or cherry-pick criminological knowledge and produce distorted pictures of the 'crime problem'. The offspring of this flawed process are polices of deceit which fail to target the most deleterious and socially injurious criminal aspects of British society. The 'Catch 22' facing government administrators is that they must produce credible 'scientific' endorsement for their own failed and misguided polices, hence the process of suppression, control and manipulation outlined above. Academic criminologists must not grant legitimacy to such a corrupt process. I suggest what is needed is an increase and a vocal outpouring of the critical voice or what I call 'deviant knowledge' (that which is critical of contemporary forms of governance and challenges the existing social order). I am strongly opposed to academics (notably to senior academics) engaging in contract research or consultancy advice with the HORDS or the Scottish Executive's agencies of criminal justice that simply grant legitimacy to the ongoing criminalization and marginalization of some of the poorest and most disadvantaged members of society.

In saying this, it is important to remember that this new authoritarian state, or what Rhodes (1997) calls 'the neo-liberal state', is not a monolith. The restructuring of the public sector has created a complex dynamic between traditionally accepted notions of 'public' and 'private', culminating in changing, ambiguous and diversifying modes of governance. As a result, it is erroneous to talk about the researcher and the 'state', as though the state represents a static and united entity (cf. Foucault, 1977). The corporatization of the public sector has produced intense competition within and across different sectors of modern government. Research, in general, and criminological research, in particular, may be highly sensitive and controversial for one area of government, and yet advantageous or desirable to another sector. Therefore, for criminology to be a public knowledge of resistance it is important that community and activist voices be harnessed and aligned with government officials within the fields of health, education, housing and employment, and not solely within government criminal justice agencies.

State produced criminological knowledge through the HORDS or the agencies of criminal justice within Scottish Executive is, to quote Vaclav Havel, 'morally contaminated'. Through biased and skewed research agenda, the British public is presented with an erroneous and partial view of crime in British society – that anti-social behaviour is a working-class youth/drug problem; that violence has become part of black culture; that increased prisons are required to rescue a fledgling criminal justice system; that parental irresponsibility and a growing lack of 'respect' are the sources of injustice, inequality and criminal behaviour, and so on. HORDS and Scottish Executive criminology continues to both perpetuate and superficially describe media stereotypes of crime and criminality that formed the basis of *Policing the Crisis*'s critique thirty years ago. As a result, a reductionist perspective is proffered, that crime can be simplified to individuals who are both responsible for its consequences and for its eradication – thus washing the government's hands of any culpability. It is not surprising that criminological narratives (mentioned above) that provoke political reaction and capture both media and public imagination are those that venture beyond bland descriptive analyses of what is already known and provide critical accounts of governmental power. To challenge state power is to enter the eye of the storm, the very epicentre of discrimination, institutional bias and social injustice. To do otherwise is to become 'co-creators' in a morally contaminated environment of intolerance, where the poor and powerless remain the objects of government scrutiny and over-regulation. Those who challenge state power will always experience various obstacles that attempt to silence or moderate their dissent. Yet, the critical voice is most needed, most respected and most influential when actively engaged in contestation with policies and practices of governmental power.

—————————————————— **Key Reading** ——————————————————

Currie, E. (2007) 'Against marginality: arguments for a public criminology', *Theoretical Criminology*, 11(2): 175–90.
Hillyard, P., Sim, J., Tombs, S. and Whyte, D. (2004) 'Leaving a "stain upon the silence": contemporary criminology and the politics of dissent', *British Journal of Criminology*, 44: 369–90.
Hope, T. and Walters, R. (2008) *Critical Thinking about the Uses of Research*. London: Centre for Crime and Justice Studies.
Scraton, P. (2007b) *Power, Conflict and Criminalisation*. London: Routledge.
Walters, R. (2003) *Deviant Knowledge: Criminology, Politics and Policy*. Cullompton: Willan.

15

NATION STATES AND THE PRODUCTION OF SOCIAL HARM: RESISTING THE HEGEMONY OF 'TINA'

Christina Pantazis and Simon Pemberton

 Introduction

Policing the Crisis (PtC) sought to capture the crises embedded in the British post-war social democratic state and the emergence of a coercive social authoritarianism. By interrogating the construction of the social and political panic around 'mugging', Hall et al. (1978) documented the state's transformation towards a punitive and populist penal strategy directed against young black men – further marginalized during, and as a result of, the economic recession of the 1970s. Central to *Policing the Crisis* was an analysis of the accompanying hegemonic forms that served to underpin coercive responses. Specifically, consent was constructed through a range of devices, pre-existing traditionalist ideologies, halcyon images of the past and the construction of young black men as the modern-day folk devils and purveyors of social harm. All of this was to be understood within the context of the perceived breakdown of moral society which followed from the permissive social democratic post-war period of the 1960s.

Thatcherism's response to the perceived decay of the moral order was to reassert the importance of moral values, and to stress the significance of individual freedoms and personal responsibility – epitomized by the rejection of social citizenship and the accompanying notion of an interventionist state. Problems such as homelessness, poverty, and criminality were now reconfigured as the responsibility of individuals rather than the social state. Thatcherism's remoulding of the state insinuated an unstinting faith in the market as a force for social 'good'. Here, the market was to be 'freed' from the meddling of state bureaucrats and the perceived power of the unions, 'low' inflation was to be maintained and wealth accumulation rewarded. These aims were to be achieved through an extensive privatization programme, the disciplining of the trade unions, taxation cuts for the wealthy, reductions in benefit levels for lone parents and children, and the removal of some benefits for selected groups, such as young people. The impact of welfare retrenchment and changes to taxation were reflected in the demonstrable increases in poverty and inequality during this period (Gordon and Pantazis, 1997; Hills, 1998). Moreover, the criminal justice system was increasingly used to deal with social problems and tensions within capitalist society, replacing the longstanding attachment to the welfare state and corporatist politics. Welfare retrenchment and creeping authoritarianism, which Hall was to identify in subsequent work (1980c, 1988), led to a range of disparate groups, from striking miners (Green, 1990) and football fans (Scraton, 1999) to young black men (Scraton, 1985a), being targeted for vilification and coercive state responses.

Following this trajectory of state-defined social harm elaborated as 'enemies within' under Thatcherism, New Labour consolidated the notion of personal responsibility through ensuring that welfare entitlements are linked to labour market activity (Levitas, 2005), as well as making offenders 'pay for their crimes'. It extended its commitment to hiving off the welfare state to private and voluntary providers (Powell, 2007), and introduced further taxation cuts for the wealthy while reducing welfare benefits for groups perceived as 'undeserving'. Although we should acknowledge that, in responding to the inherited poverty legacy (Pantazis et al., 2006), New Labour aimed to tackle child poverty, and also sought to reward 'hard-working' families through policy initiatives such as tax credits and the minimum wage. However, New Labour has also exacerbated trends towards the criminalization of social policy (see, for example, Cook, 2006; Knepper, 2007) and the exchange of welfare for punishment. At the most extreme end, prisons are serving to absorb vulnerable individuals who would have previously been supported by the welfare state and, in particular, mental health services (Pemberton, 2005, 2008).

Following these observations, how can we begin to develop and extend an understanding of social harm in capitalist social formations? Coleman et al. (this volume) note that the legacy of Hall's theoretical work on the state spawned a generation of critical criminologists who sought to highlight the socially corrosive impacts of the criminalization of 'problem groups', as well as the damaging consequences of the deregulation of corporate and state activities. These interventions have extended mainstream criminology's gaze upon the harmful actions of organizations that are analogous to conventional crimes. However, this means that harmful outcomes associated with policies of welfare retrenchment, such as unemployment, inequality and ill health, are still ignored. It is in this context that we should be reminded of Hall's (1980c) notion of anti-statism, which appears in response to his concerns over the Thatcherite demise of welfare rights. Indeed, anti-statism provides the basis of our analysis. Moreover, by identifying the harms produced or mediated through the organization of late capitalist societies, we attempt to counterpose the tendency in debates to, first, obscure the structural origins of harms and, second, to undermine the role and responsibilities of the state. In this respect we recognize that many state interventions are benevolent and can have positive impacts on people's well-being, without detracting from coercive state machinations.

The chapter is divided into two sections. The first outlines our approach to the definition and the measurement of harm using a human needs perspective. The second section identifies a series of different state formations so that levels of harm may be compared across types of state formation. The purpose of this comparative work is to assess the performance of states in mitigating harm. Our analysis seeks to challenge Thatcher's assertion that 'there is no alternative' (TINA) to global capitalism and its continued role in shaping hegemonic attitudes to harms, in particular, the implicit acceptance of the social wreckage generated by the shift towards a neo-liberal mode of organization. By comparing the UK and the USA with corporatist and social demo-cratic formations, the chapter identifies more humane forms of capitalist state – which *Policing the Crisis* signalled a shift away from in the UK thirty years ago but which nevertheless persist within the 'constraints' of contemporary globalization.

Definition and Measurement of Social Harm

To date, attempts to define the notion of social harm within criminology have largely fallen into two broad categories. The first seeks to draw on existing legal frameworks, usually human rights, to expand the notion of crime to encompass wider harms than the criminal law currently captures, including structural harms (Schwendinger and Schwendinger, 1975). However, discursive frames derived from legal discourses pose a rather obvious problem in that the tools immediately available to map these harms originate from state systems. This places clear limitations on the scope of the phenom-ena to be analysed. Thus, detaching the concept of harm from the sites of state power is crucial to generating more objective and comprehensive definitions of structural harm. A second set of definitions move away from these legal frameworks and towards sociologi-cal conceptualizations of harm. For instance, Muncie (2000a) seeks to deconstruct the notion of harm to generate a typology which encompasses both positive and negative emotions. More recently, Hillyard and Tombs (2004) categorize harm in terms of physical, financial/economic, sexual, emotional/psychological and cultural safety elements. However, neither approach sufficiently provides a theoretical basis to identify which spe-cific events should be placed into these categories. Arguably, what is required is a normative rationale that can determine which social events and acts should be considered as harmful.

The notion of harm necessitates an understanding of the human condition and the prerequisites for human well-being (Tift and Sullivan, 2001; Pemberton, 2004, 2007). To understand harm we rely on a notion of what it is to function successfully as a human being; only then can we understand the full range of harms that affect us. A range of sociological concepts have been developed in recent years that can be applied to such an investigation, including ideas about happiness (Layard, 2003) and its corollary, well-being (Gough and McGregor, 2007). However, these concepts are fraught with difficulties, including ambiguity over their precise meanings, their tendency towards subjective interpretation, and consequently the ability to formulate meaningful policy to address such issues. The concept of need – premised on an account of human essence – is better suited to an investigation of harm. As Doyal and Gough (1991: 50) argue, 'basic human needs … stipulate what persons must achieve if they are to avoid sustained and serious harms'.

Doyal and Gough's work (1984, 1991) represents perhaps the most comprehensive account of human needs (but see also Maslow, 1954; Harvey, 1973). For Doyal and Gough, physical health and autonomy are basic human needs, the minimum pre-requisites necessary for successful human action. Hence individuals must possess the 'mental ability to deliberate and to choose' and the 'physical capacity to follow through on their decision' (Doyal and Gough, 1984: 15). Physical health is more than mere survival; it requires a level of capacity that enables actors to function successfully. Autonomy requires an individual to have basic skills, sufficient mental health, and opportunities to act. However, their emphasis on sufficient mental health as a functional limitation does not take into account the disabling social, environmental, and attitudinal barriers preventing the successful autonomy of individuals. Drawing upon a social model of disability, we can rectify this limitation by focusing instead on the support systems in place for individuals.

In order for these needs to be met, a further tier of need fulfilment is required – 'intermediate needs' – which Doyal and Gough (1991: 157) define as 'properties of goods, services, activities and relationships which embrace physical health and human autonomy and all cultures.' They go on to list the following as intermediate needs: food and water, housing, work, physical environment, healthcare, childhood needs, support networks, economic security, physical security, education, birth control and childbearing. We have sought to adapt this list to make it as comprehensive as possible (Table 15.1) and simplified it where possible. For example, we have included birth control and childbearing under autonomy and healthcare rather than maintain them as separate categories because this invites further categories relevant to other social groups. We have also added information and communication, transport, political participation, and civic efficacy, which we regard as essential for autonomy, as well as 'recognition', which represents freedom from discriminatory policies, practices and attitudes (Fraser, 1997).

While we have sought to be as comprehensive as possible in our identification of needs, this is not an exhaustive or definitive account. We view this template as work in progress. Moreover, as in the case of other sociological concepts, particularly definitions of relative poverty (Piachaud, 1987), experiential knowledge(s) are of vital importance to the refinement of this 'expert' definition of need/harm. A further issue is that the non-fulfilment of different needs does not necessarily result in equal amounts of suffering and, therefore, future work may consider establishing hierarchies of harm. Neither do harms exist in isolation. As Doyal and Gough's list of needs suggest, need fulfilment is interrelated. Thus, we see the experience of harm as being interconnected, cumulative and additive in nature (Pantazis, 2004).

The following section describes the process of operationalizing our definition of need in the context of comparative analysis. Creating lists of indicators can only provide an indicative, rather than a definitive, picture of need fulfilment. They allow us to observe and comment on the satisfaction of needs (and harm) at a societal level which can facilitate a comparative analysis. A series of comparable social indicators

Table 15.1   Basic and intermediate needs required for successful human action

Need	Definition of need
Basic needs	
Physical health	Survival chances and being free from physical ill health
Autonomy	Basic skills (literacy and numeracy), sufficient mental health support, and opportunities to act
Intermediate needs	
Food and water	Availability of a healthy diet and access to clean water
Housing	Sufficiently protective housing, with basic services and adequate space per person
Living environment	A non-hazardous environment
Healthcare	Provision and access to appropriate preventative, curative and palliative care
Social participation and support	The presence of primary support groups and close and confiding relationships
Economic security	Protection against financial risk and insecurity
Physical security	Freedom from interpersonal, corporate and state violence
Transport	Access to transport facilities
Education	Access to primary, secondary and higher education and life-long learning opportunities
Information and communication	Access to reliable sources of information, communication and technology
Civic efficacy	Ability to influence decisions affecting your own life
Political participation	Ability to participate in the political process
Cultural recognition	Recognition that lifestyles (based on gender, disability, ethnicity, sexuality, religion, etc.) are equally valid – freedom from discrimination and prejudice

were selected from reports, statistical collections and databases of international organizations and supranational governmental bodies, including Laboursta (ILO), KLIM (ILO), WHOSIS (WHO), Global Burden of Disease (WHO), UIS (UNESCO), World Values Survey (WVS). Utilizing international statistics, we circumnavigate the more obvious methodological difficulties associated with comparative work, although inconsistencies remain. Furthermore, we were also unable to identify appropriate indicators for the need relating to transport and civic efficacy. Therefore, these needs do not feature in our analysis. Country coverage of other indicators (for example, domestic violence, hate crime) was patchy and, therefore, excluded.

Given the multifaceted nature of human needs, it is unlikely that a single social indicator or data source would reflect these complexities. We sought to capture this complexity through the clustering of indicators and the selection of different types of data. Service provision indicators (hospital beds, medical staff) were used to map the framework of services and benefits provided by regime type, although they fail to capture issues, such as 'access', 'take up' and 'quality' of provision. Measures of social disadvantage (relative poverty rates, unemployment) and measures of social phenomena (pollutant levels, accidents at work) were also used to quantify aspects of non-fulfilment. Attitudinal survey data were deployed to assess the fulfilment of needs related to recognition through measuring social attitudes towards marginalized groups. Furthermore, subjective measures of well-being (reported levels of freedom) were deployed to assess perceptions of need fulfilment, particularly in relation to 'less tangible' needs, such as autonomy – although we note potential disparities between objective reality and reported perceptions. Finally, some needs are more easily captured by social indicators than others. For example, the measurement of physical need fulfilment, through mortality and disease morbidity statistics, may be less problematic than capturing need fulfilment with respect to recognition. These are arguably more complex in nature, as their non-fulfilment relates to less easily observed social phenomena, such as cultural practices, interactions and meanings.

State Formations and Need Fulfilment

Since Esping-Anderson's (1990) classic work on welfare-state regimes, there has been a burgeoning interest from social scientists in categorizing countries, on the basis of a selected number of criteria, in order to compare policy outcomes (Ferrera, 1996; Huber and Stephens, 2001; Navarro and Shi, 2001; Chung and Muntaner, 2007; Eikemo et al., 2008). Within criminology, Cavadino and Dignan (2006) build upon the ideas of Esping-Anderson and others to construct a four-fold typology of welfare-state regimes in order to explore the relationship between political economy and punishment. Our preference has been to make use of this typology over other models. Their political economy approach is sensitive to the issues of welfare retrenchment and authoritarian statism that we identified in the introduction. However, unlike them, and due to space limitations, with the exception of neo-liberal states, we do not compare countries with the same state formation. On this basis, the chapter examines the following four state formations:

(1) The *neo-liberal state* is epitomized by political conservatism and economic liberalism and is characterized by a strong free market and a minimal or residual welfare state. Income differentials are extreme, with the poorest dependent on a heavily stigmatized welfare state which targets the neediest on the basis of means testing while better-off individuals supplement state welfare with private services and income protection (especially in relation to health and pensions). While formally egalitarian, there is an emphasis on 'individualized, atomized, [and] limited social rights' (Cavadino and Dignan, 2006: 15). Furthermore, the dominant penal ideology rests heavily on a law and order agenda with an emphasis on exclusionary punishment methods involving the use of prison for its incapacitation effects. The USA is regarded as the exemplar of the neo-liberal state, although the UK, Australia and New Zealand have also been pursuing neo-liberal economic and social policies since the 1980s.

(2) The *conservative corporatist state* represents the incorporation of 'national interest groups' (that is, workers' and employers' organizations). Members of these interest groups gain from relatively generous welfare payments and services which exist as social rights, although social divisions remain evident as a result of a hierarchical benefit system that is linked to the occupational structure. Reciprocity is a key aspect of the conservative corporatist state; members are provided with welfare

protection at times of market failure or misfortune, but there are obligations on the part of benefit recipients with respect to their familial and employment responsibilities. Traditional institutions such as the Church and the family also play a key role in welfare provision in such states. The dominant penal ideology is one of rehabilitation and it focuses on using a variety of penal sanctions, including moderate use of imprisonment and diversionary strategies for young offenders. The clearest example of the conservative corporatist state is Germany, although other countries include the Netherlands, Italy and France.

(3) The *oriental corporatist state*, which Cavadino and Dignan see as befitting a description of Japan, shares much in common with conservative corporatist countries but it has a distinctive social and political context and overlaps in some key areas with neo-liberal states. Cavadino and Dignan (2006: 19) describe it as a form of 'bureaucratized corporate paternalism' which is characterized as having occupational security and a hierarchical and patriarchal, but progressive, career structure, entitling workers not only to monetary rewards, but also housing and healthcare. Its dominant penal ideology is 'apology-based restoration' (2006: 15) with a focus on rehabilitation. Such states are marked by low levels of imprisonment and 'inclusionary social and penal policies that are linked with what appears to be a remarkably effective regime of informal social controls' (2006: 27).

(4) *Social democratic states* support full employment and redistributive policies, and offer a universal and generous benefit system in exchange for wage restraint by the trade unions. Every worker is entitled to benefits but they are graduated according to earnings. Therefore, temporary interruptions from the labour market do not have deleterious impacts on living standards. Generous support is also provided to non-workers, such as children and the elderly. Such states are typified by variants of penal welfarism, emphasizing state responsibility for the harmful acts of offenders, as well as the prevention of crime through a benevolent welfare system and active employment policies. Levels of imprisonment are lower than those in conservative corporatist states but higher than those found in oriental corporatist states, which has been explained in terms of its egalitarian ethos and its emphasis on collective (rather than just individual) responsibility. Sweden and Finland provide the best examples of social democratic states.

Engaging with the exercise of developing welfare regime typologies brings with it some immediate difficulties. One initial concern is that such analyses necessarily prioritize the 'nation' state, which means that the relevance and impact of divergent social policies pursued in countries with federal structures, such as the USA and Germany, are minimized. Thus, the analysis we present in the remaining part of the chapter does not take into account interregional variations of need fulfilment. A second limitation is that the designation of countries to type of state formation is not always clear-cut. The prime example of this difficulty lies with Cavadino and Dignan's categorization of the UK as an example of a neo-liberal state, on the basis of its trajectory since the 1980s. However, doing so necessarily negates its historical specificity and undervalues the legacy of the post-war settlement and the establishment of a universal and comprehensive welfare state, which in some areas could be considered still intact. With these caveats in mind, Tables 15.2–15.7 reveal levels of need satisfaction and harm according to different state formation.

Table 15.2 Physical health and autonomy by type of state formation

Need indicator	Neo-liberal		Oriental corporatist	Corporatist	Social democratic
	UK	USA	Japan	Germany	Sweden
Physical health					
Male life expectancy at birth, 2005	77	75	79	76	79
Female life expectancy at birth, 2005	81	78	86	82	83
Male Healthy Life Expectancy at birth (HALE), 2002	69	67	72	70	72
Female Healthy Life Expectancy at birth (HALE), 2002	72	71	78	74	75
Infant mortality rate (per 1,000 live births), 2005	5	7	3	4	3
Neonatal mortality rate (per 1,000 live births), 2004	3	4	1	3	2
Maternal mortality rate (per 100,000 live births), 2005	11	14	10	9	8
Autonomy					
Reported levels of freedom and control over one's life on a scale 1 (none at all) to 10 (a great deal) (mean score) α	7.22	7.98	6.0	7.43	7.41
Basic literacy					
% of population aged 15 and over unable to read or write, 2004	–	1	1	1	1
Student mean score for reading, 2003	–	495	498	491	514
Student mean score for maths, 2003	–	482	534	503	509
Student mean score for science, 2003	–	491	548	502	506
Opportunities for productive activity					
% unemployed, latest year	5	5	4	11	8
Persons unemployed for 12 months or more as a % of total unemployed, 2004	12	21	34	52	19
Annual hours worked per person, latest year	1669	1804	1784	1436	1583
Days of paid annual leave (collective agreement average or statutory minimum + public holidays), 2005	33	10	30–35	39	42
Provision of mental health services					
Total psychiatric beds per 10,000 population, latest year	6	8	28	8	6
Number of psychiatrists per 100,000 population, latest year	11	14	9	12	20
Number of psychiatric nurses per 100,000 population, latest year	104	7	59	52	32
Number of psychologists per 100,000 population, latest year	9	31	7	52	76
Number of social workers per 100,000 population, latest year	58	35	16	477	–

Sources: WHO WHOSIS database; UNICEF Country database; World Values Survey; ILO Laboursta database; ILO KLIM database; OECD (2007a) *Babies and Bosses*; WHO (2005) *Mental Health Atlas*.

Notes: α = figures for UK exclude Northern Ireland and for Germany exclude the former East Germany. **Bold** figures represent the lowest level of need fulfilment. *Italicized* figures represent the highest levels of need fulfilment.

Out of the five countries considered, life expectancy is lowest in the USA (just 75 for men and 78 for women). The populations of the USA and UK can also expect to experience a lower healthy life expectancy. Infant and neonatal mortality rates are also highest in the UK and the USA. Understanding why wealthy nations like the USA and the UK have such poor levels of performance needs to be contextualized in terms of intermediate needs relating to access to a healthy diet and healthcare resources, as well as poverty rates (Shaw et al., 1999) (discussed further below). In marked contrast, Japan (followed closely by Sweden) has the highest levels of need fulfilment with respect to health. Health needs are being fulfilled to such an extent that Japanese men can expect an extra five years of healthy life, and women seven years, in comparison to their US peers. Again, understanding such outcomes must take into account dietary patterns and lifestyle factors (Shimazu et al., 2007), and must inevitably relate to the success in meeting intermediate needs.

As well as physical health, individuals require autonomy. This captures the idea that individuals should be able to initiate successful actions based on their own deliberations. Table 15.2 shows that reported levels of freedom and control over one's life is highest in the USA (7.9) and perhaps this is unsurprising given the prominence afforded to the notion of individual liberty in US culture, history, legal and political structures. Whether or not this perception is a lived reality, however, is explored further later. Conversely, reported levels of freedom and control are lowest in Japan (6.0), which could be explained by the extent of informal social control found in Japanese social institutions such as the family and workplaces (Cavadino and Dignan, 2006). Three constituent elements define autonomy: cognitive deprivation, opportunities for economic activity and mental health (Doyal and Gough, 1991). In terms of cognitive skills, all countries display universal or near universal need fulfilment with regards to literacy. However, other basic skill indicators reveal that the USA has the lowest mean scores for reading, maths and science whereas Sweden has the highest score for reading and Japan has the top scores for maths and science.

Opportunities to be involved in productive activity encapsulates the idea that individuals should have access to paid or unpaid work, providing them with a sense of self-worth and contributing to self-development. Our focus here is on paid work due to the unavailability of relevant data concerning unpaid work. Unemployment levels are lowest in the UK due to the success of a buoyant economy and highest in Germany, where long-term unemployment is particularly acute since the integration of East Germany. Nevertheless while there are clear benefits associated with working, overly long hours can impinge upon social relationships and other activities, including caring responsibilities, voluntary work and leisure activities (Levitas, 2005), as well as cause ill-health and workplace safety risks (Spurgeon et al., 1997). Americans work the longest hours; nearly 370 hours a year more than the Germans and 220 hours more than the Swedes. The Japanese currently work just a mere 20 hours a year less than the Americans but have historically had long working hours (e.g. working hours fell from 2,021 in 1980 to 1,784 in 2006). Concern about the phenomenon of *Karoshi* – the term used to describe death or permanent disability caused by overwork which surfaced during the 1970s – eventually led the Japanese government to introduce preventative health measures (Iwasaki et al., 2006) which could explain the improved working hours. In addition to working the longest hours, Americans have the shortest annual leave entitlement (just 10 days), whereas the Swedes have the longest at 42 days. While leave entitlement may be indicative of work–life balance, we must also acknowledge that many workers may not take their full entitlement due to workload pressures (BBC, 2003) or, within the Japanese context, feelings of guilt (Harada, 1998). A final issue to be considered is the nature and quality of productive activity. Although not captured by our data, there exist a variety of ethnographic accounts which record the reality of low-paid, unskilled, casualized work within the context of neo-liberal economies (Abrahams, 2002; Ehrenreich, 2002; Toynbee, 2003). Thus, we might speculate that levels of job satisfaction, for example, may be lower in those countries where disproportionately people work in unskilled, de-unionized sectors for low pay.

Pursuing our interpretation of the relationship between mental health and autonomy, Table 15.2 also provides data on the mental health services and personnel. While Japan has the highest provision of psychiatric beds per 10,000 population, rates of different type of mental health personnel vary, with no strong discernable patterns from country to country. Sweden has the highest number of both psychiatrists and psychologists but relatively low rates of psychiatric nurses. On the other hand, the UK has the highest number of nurses but relatively low rates of psychiatrists and psychologists.

Intermediate needs provide the contexts and frameworks which lead to basic need fulfilment. It follows that divergences between state formations in basic need fulfilment will be contingent on intermediate needs. Thus, countries with relatively low levels of specific intermediate need satisfaction will accordingly fail to provide basic need provision for some groups of individuals. We hope to demonstrate the interrelationship between intermediate and basic need fulfilment when discussing the results in Tables 15.3–15.7.

Beginning with the fulfilment of food and water needs (Table 15.3), the UK, the USA and Japan have the highest percentage of infants born with a low birth weight, which in the context of the USA and UK could be explained by the experience of poverty and inequality. These two countries also have the highest rates of obesity, with nearly one-third of the US and nearly one-quarter of the UK population clinically obese. Surveys suggest those in the USA and UK are more likely to report being unable to afford a balanced diet, which may go some way in explaining these extraordinary high obesity levels, as may increases in portion sizes (Young and Nestle, 2002) and the sedentary lifestyles of people (Epstein et al., 2000). In contrast, few Germans and Swedes report not being able to afford a balanced diet and demonstrate lower levels of obesity and newborns with low birth weight. Japan has the lowest levels of obesity by far (at just 3%), which is most likely linked to a healthy diet (Shimazu et al., 2007) but also perhaps due to low levels of inequality.

Housing needs are assessed in terms of the sufficiency of shelter offered, basic services and adequate space per person. Sweden has the highest satisfaction of the fulfilment of needs related to household repairs, overcrowding and lack of warmth, which may be explained by growing state involvement since the Second World War

Table 15.3 Intermediate Needs (food and water, housing and living environment) by type of state formation

| Need indicator | Neo-liberal | | Oriental corporatist | Corporatist | Social democratic |
	UK	USA	Japan	Germany	Sweden
Food and water					
% of newborns with low birth weight, 2002	**8**	**8**	**8**	7	*4*
% of adults with BMI > 30 kg/m², 2005	23	**32**	*3*	14	11
% of households unable to have a healthy diet, most recent year	8	**11**	–	2	2
% of population with sustainable access to improved drinking sources using unimproved, 2004	100	100	100	100	100
Housing					
% of households unable to heat home, most recent year	2	**7**	*1*	3	*1*
% of households with accommodation needing repair	6	5	**17**	7	*4*
% of households with overcrowded accommodation	19	8	**21**	14	*5*
Living environment					
Emissions of sulphur oxides (kg/capita), 2005	12	**45**	6	7	*5*
Emissions of nitrogen oxides (kg/capita), 2005	27	**57**	*15*	18	23
Emissions of carbondioxide (kg/capita), 2005	40	**273**	*23*	50	67
% of households with accommodation exposed to noise/traffic nuisance	*7*	17	**32**	8	*7*

Sources: OECD (2006a) *Measures of Material Deprivation in OECD Countries*; OECD (2007b) *Factbook*; UNICEF country database.

Notes: **Bold** figures represent the lowest level of need fulfilment. *Italicized* figures represent the highest levels of need fulfilment.

in housing provision (Nessein, 2003). The transformation marks the state's planned approach to housing production, controls over the private sector and perhaps, most importantly, its commitment that 'the whole population shall have access to healthy, spacious, well planned and suitably equipped dwellings of good quality at affordable prices' (Turner, 1996: 106). However, need is greatest in Japan with respect to household repairs and overcrowding, while being able to maintain a warm home is a problem for a significant minority of the US population.

Living environment covers unacceptable levels of pollutants – what Doyal and Gough (1991) refer to as 'physical environment'. Although comparative data of unacceptable levels do not exist, data are available on the actual total levels of emissions relating to sulphur oxides, nitrogen oxides and carbon dioxide. Emissions of such dangerous pollutants, which are linked to loss of life, particularly among the elderly and the sick (COMEAP, 1998), are by far the highest in the USA. Compared to the country with the next worst rates of emissions, the USA has nearly four and two times the amount of the UK's sulphur oxides and nitrogen oxides, respectively, and four times the amounts of Sweden's carbon dioxide. The high levels of pollutants experienced within the USA could in part be explained by the process of deregulation which has taken place over the last thirty years – serving to weaken the structures which govern industrial processes (Pearce and Tombs, 1998).

Healthcare provision is included as an intermediate need (Table 15.4, p. 226) but is also related to basic physical health needs. We may expect to see a positive relationship between healthcare provision and physical health. However, a significant minority of the American population cannot access healthcare when they need to because of cost; four times as many compared to the Japanese and two and half times as likely as the populations of the UK, Germany and Sweden. This is despite the fact that the total health expenditure as a percentage of GDP is highest in the USA than in any of the countries we are considering (15% of GDP, compared to 11% in Germany, 9% in Sweden, and 8% in Japan and the UK) (OECD, 2007b). US healthcare is not universally available free at the point of need, but instead accessed by those with the financial means via healthcare insurance, leaving 46,995,000 people without access (US Census Bureau, 2007). Neither does healthcare expenditure necessarily translate into more healthcare professionals. For instance, the USA has the lowest number of hospital beds per 10,000 population. Compared to other forms of health systems, such as the UK's NHS or the social insurance scheme of Germany, market-based health systems spend a much higher proportion on administration (Lowe, 1993), possibly accounting for the USA's relative lack of beds and professionals.

There are consistent patterns with regards to social participation and support, with Japan emerging as the country exhibiting the highest levels of social isolation and lowest levels of participation in cultural and sporting organizations. Staggeringly, one-third of Japanese people rarely or never spend time with friends and a further 28% (not reported in the table) rarely or never spend time with family. In the UK, reduced contact with friends and family has been linked to paid work responsibilities (Levitas, 2005). Thus cultural values which promote the importance of work and duty towards the employer (Harada, 1998) may account for the patterns of sociability in Japan. In contrast, Sweden, which has relatively low working hours, has the smallest proportion of people lacking contact with friends but the highest proportions who are members of sporting and cultural organizations.

Economic security is assessed in terms of relative poverty, inequality and the adequacy of state safety nets (Table 15.5, p. 227). The USA exhibits the highest levels of economic insecurity on three out of the four indicators of need. The replacement rate for unemployment benefit is lowest in the USA (just one-third) and old age pension the second lowest (just over half). Unsurprisingly, therefore, indicators of relative poverty and inequality are also highest in the USA. Although the UK follows closely behind on rates of poverty and inequality, one in four of the US working population lives in

Table 15.4 Intermediate needs (healthcare and support networks) by type of state formation

Need indicator	Neo-liberal		Oriental corporatist	Corporatist	Social democratic
	UK	USA	Japan	Germany	Sweden
Healthcare					
% of households with restricted access to healthcare	3	**8**	*2*	3	3
Physicians per 1,000 population, by latest year	**2**	3	*2*	3	3
Nurses per 1,000 population, latest year	*12*	9	**8**	10	10
Dentists per 1,000 population, latest year	1.0	*1.6*	**0.7**	0.8	0.8
Hospital beds per 10,000 population, 2005	39	**33**	*129*	84	52
% contraceptive prevalence rate, latest year	*84*	73	**56**	75	–
% births attended by skilled health personnel, latest year	**99**	**99**	*100*	*100*	–
Social participation and support					
% of population who rarely or never spend time with friends	7	8	**34**	14	*5*
% of population who are members of sport or cultural groups	**12**	58	21	32	*74*

Sources: OECD (2006a) *Measures of Material Deprivation in OECD Countries*; WHO WHOSIS database; ILO KLIM database.

Notes: **Bold** figures represent the lowest level of need fulfilment. *Italicized* figures represent the highest levels of need fulfilment.

relative poverty defined in terms of earning less than two-thirds of median earnings, while the 40% lowest-earning population has just 16% of the share of household income. The US welfare system has never had the level of coverage or high benefit rates that have characterized some European countries, yet the current situation has been exacerbated by the fierce processes of retrenchment instigated during the 1980s that have curtailed 'benefits both in size and duration', 'increased means testing eligibility', in order to 'pare down expenditure on social programmes' (Miller and Markle, 2002: 105). In contrast, Sweden has generous replacement rates for unemployment benefit and pensions (73% and 66%, respectively), and reports the lowest levels of relative poverty (a mere 6%). Indeed, Sweden compares favourably against other EU countries in having the second lowest relative poverty rates, being beaten only by one other social democratic state, Finland (Schult, 2002).

The USA's high level of economic insecurity is matched by a similarly high level of physical insecurity (Table 15.5). The USA's performance is worse on every indicator

Table 15.5   Intermediate needs (economic and physical security) by type of state formation

Need indicator	Neo-liberal		Oriental corporatist	Corporatist	Social democratic
	UK	USA	Japan	Germany	Sweden
Economic security					
Average of net replacement rates over 60 months of unemployment, unemployment benefits plus additional social support, 2004	63	**31**	57	73	73
Old age pension replacement rates (net), 2004	41	52	**39**	58	66
Share of workers earning less than two-thirds median earnings, 2005	21	**24**	16	16 (2002)	6
% share of household income, lowest 40%, 1994–2004	18	**16**	25	22	23
Physical security					
Homicide, rate per 100,000 population, 2004[a]	1.59 E/W 2.31 S 2.31 NI	**6**	–	1	1
Deaths from intentional violence per 100,000 population, 2002	1*	**5**	1	1	1
% of women reporting sexual assault in the previous year, 2003–04	0.9	**1.4**	0.8	0.4	1.3
Self-inflicted deaths per 100,000 population, 2002	9	10	**25**	14	13
Road traffic deaths per 100,000 population, 2002	7	**16**	9	9	6
Rates of fatal injuries at work α, latest year	0.6	**4**	0.01	2.38	1.6
Prison population rate per 100,000 population, 2006 or latest year	143	**738**	62	97	78

Sources: Eurostat (2008) *Statistics in Focus, Crime and Criminal Justice*; OECD (2006b) *Society at a Glance*; WHO Global burden of disease database, ILO Laboursta database; van Dijk et al. (2007) *Criminal Victimization in International Perspective*.

Notes: α = Rates of fatal injuries for Japan relate to per 1,000,000 hours worked; for Germany, Sweden, the USA, and the UK they relate to per 100,000 employees or workers employed.
[a] = E/W England and Wales; S Scotland; NI Northern Ireland.
* England and Wales only.
Bold figures represent the lowest level of need fulfilment. *Italicized* figures represent the highest levels of need fulfilment.

of physical security. Despite spending more on law and order (and defence) as a proportion of GDP than any other country (barring the UK) (Solomon et al., 2007), the USA fails to offer comparable levels of physical security for its people. Supposedly the 'land of the free' (Goldson, 2005b: 78), the USA incarcerates more people than any other country in the world (Walmsley, 2002). The creation of what Miller (2001: 158) has described as 'carceral hyperinflation' has its roots in the politicization of criminal justice debates, in which social problems have increasingly attracted punitive sanctions. This process, which stems back to the 1970s, intensified under Ronald Reagan's 'war on drugs', resulting in the catastrophic criminalization of already marginalized social and racialized groups (Wacquant, 2001). With more than 2 million people now imprisoned, one in three 20–29 year-old African-American males is on probation, prison or parole (Young, 1999). Yet the 'prison works' mantra espoused by politicians appears to have failed to safeguard individual physical integrity. As well as having the highest rates of incarceration, the USA has the highest rates of death caused by intentional violence than any other country. Japan, which has the lowest rates of incarceration (just 62 per 100,000 population compared to the USA's 738) has a rate of violence which is nine times smaller than that of the USA (0.6 per 100,000 population compared to the USA's 5.4). Rates of women reporting sexual assault are also highest in the USA (followed closely by Sweden) but lowest in Japan, although these results should be treated cautiously as 'women in countries where gender equality is more advanced are more inclined to report sexual incidents' (van Dijk et al., 2007: 77). Deaths from road traffic accidents are also highest in the USA (three times as high as in Germany, which has the lowest number of deaths). On the other hand, levels of self-inflicted deaths are highest in Japan. Cultural tolerance of suicide compared to that of western society, combined with relatively high levels of unemployment during recent economic recession have been offered as explanations for these rates, particularly among men aged between 40 and 54 (Takei et al., 2000; Young, 2002; and Koo and Cox, 2008).

Language and literacy skills are crucial to establishing and improving human autonomy. Table 15.6 shows that country fulfilment of education needs varies according to educational sector. While access to primary education is considered one of the major stumbling blocks towards the achievement of progress for the majority of developing countries, it has yet to be fully realized in the USA, with net primary school enrolment rates being just 92 and net secondary school rates being even lower at 89, although its graduation rate is comparable to other countries. Alongside the lowest rates of enrolment, the USA (with the UK) has the highest pupil–teacher ratios. The highest levels of educational need fulfilment can be found in Japan and Sweden. As with education, the ability to access reliable and high-quality information is fundamental to people's capacity to make informed decisions about their lives. There are remarkably few indicators to measure the fulfilment of this need. What does exist largely relates to access rather than the quality of information. Sweden has the highest level of need fulfilment measured in terms of access to the internet, telephones and newspapers, with the USA achieving the highest rates of personal computer ownership.

Need fulfilment with respect to political participation is assessed via involvement in the electoral process and involvement in political groups, including trade unions, as well as reported confidence in parliament. Sweden reports the highest levels of participation in national elections (77%), as well as the highest involvement in political organizations and trade unions (73%). The lowest electoral participation levels were

Table 15.6 Intermediate needs (education, information and political participation) by type of state formation

Need indicator	Neo-liberal		Oriental corporatist	Corporatist	Social democratic
	UK	USA	Japan	Germany	Sweden
Education					
Net primary school enrolment rate, 2000–05	99	**92**	*100*	–	99
Primary pupil–teacher ratio, 2005	17	14	**19**	14	*10*
Net secondary school enrolment rate, 2006	95	89	*100*	–	99
Secondary pupil–teacher ratio, 2005	**15**	**15**	13	14	*10*
% of tertiary graduates to the population at the typical age of graduation, 2003	38	34	36	**21**	39
Information and communication					
Number per 100 population, internet users, 2002–04	63	63	50	**43**	*75*
Number per 100 population, with phones, 2002–04	159	123	**118**	153	*180*
Personal computers per 1,000 inhabitants, 2002	406	*659*	**382**	431	621
Daily newspapers: total average circulation per 1,000 literate inhabitants, 2004	355	–	–	**313**	*584*
Political participation					
Lowest age of electorate	*18*	*18*	**20**	*18*	*18*
% of electorate voting, 2005 or latest year	69	**55**	62	72	*77*
% of population who are members of political groups or the union	**13**	50	**13**	14	*73*
% reporting little or no confidence in parliament, 1999α	65	62	**78**	65	*49*

Sources: UNESCO UIS database; OECD (2007b) *Factbook*; World Values Survey.

Notes: α = figures for the UK exclude Northern Ireland and for Germany exclude the former East Germany. **Bold** figures represent the lowest level of need fulfilment. *Italicized* figures represent the highest levels of need fulfilment.

reported in the USA (55%). Yet the comparatively low figure excludes the 4 million Americans (disproportionately composed of African-Americans) who are excluded from voting because they are serving a felony sentence or have previously been convicted of a felony (Mauer, 2002). Japan has the lowest observed levels of need fulfilment, with just 13% reporting membership of a political organization and 78% reporting little or no confidence in parliament, although we should also acknowledge that majorities in each of the UK, USA and Germany also report low levels of trust in their national parliaments.

Sweden displays the highest levels of need fulfilment relating to the recognition of different lifestyles, cultures and identity (Table 15.7). Indeed, it has the highest levels of need satisfaction on each indicator covering the dimensions of gender, ethnicity, disability and sexuality. This may be explained by the post-war Swedish states' pursuit

Table 15.7 Intermediate needs (recognition) by type of state formation

Need indicator	Neo-liberal		Oriental corporatist	Corporatist	Social democratic
	UK	USA	Japan	Germany	Sweden
Recognition					
Gender					
Gender wage gap, 2005	0.79	0.81	**0.69**	0.76	*0.85*
% of parliamentary seats held by women, 2005 or latest year	20	15	**9**	32	*45*
% of women in employment	67	65	**57**	60	*72*
% reporting that men should be privileged work over women during periods of job scarcity, 1999α	23	10	**32**	27	*2*
Gender Development Index[a]	0.944	**0.937**	0.942	0.935	*0.955*
Gender Empowerment Measureβ	0.783	0.762	**0.557**	0.831	*0.906*
Ethnicity					
% reporting that they would not want a neighbour who was a different race, 1999α	**9**	8	–	4	3
% reporting that theywould not want a neighbour who was Muslim, 1999α	**14**	11	–	10	9
% reporting that they would not want a neighbour who was an immigrant/ foreign worker, 1999α	**16**	10	–	7	3
% reporting that they would not want a neighbour who was Jewish, 1999α	**6**	9	–	5	2
% reporting that they would not want a neighbour who was a Gypsy, 1999α	**37**	–	–	32	20
Disability					
% of disabled 20–64 year-olds in employment, late 1990s	**39**	49	–	46	53
Disability benefit expenditure as % of GDP, 1999	1.3	0.7	–	**1.0**	*2.1*
% reporting that they would not want a neighbour who was emotionally unstable α	39	**52**	–	22	17
Sexuality					
Legal age of consent for gay males	16	Variable	13–18	14/16	15
Legal age of consent for gay females	16	Variable	13–18	14/16	15
Legal age of consent for heterosexuals	16	Variable	13–18	14/16	15
% reporting that they would not want a neighbour who was homosexual α	**24**	23	–	13	6

Sources: OECD database on earnings dispersion; World Values Survey; UNDP Human Development Index database; OECD (2003) *Transforming Disability into Ability.*

Notes: α = figures for the UK exclude Northern Ireland and for Germany exclude the former East Germany.
a = The Gender-related Development Index (GDI) attempts to capture achievement in the same set of basic capabilities included in the Human Development Index.
b = The Gender Empowerment Measure (GEM) measures gender equality in key areas of economic and political participation and decision-making, i.e. women's representation in parliaments, managerial and professional work, participation in the labour force, etc. **Bold** figures represent the lowest level of need fulfilment. *Italicized* figures represent the highest levels of need fulfilment.

of a series of progressive agendas in relation to gender equality (Nyman, 1999; Hobson, 2003), migrants' social rights (Sainsbury, 2006), and disability rights (Lilja et al., 2003). In terms of non-fulfilment of need, a number of patterns can be discerned. Japan has the lowest levels of need fulfilment for gender recognition, with the highest gender wage gap (0.69), the lowest percentage of parliamentary seats held by women (9%), the lowest percentage of women in employment (57%), and the lowest Gender Empowerment Measure (0.557). Although economic and political pressure led to policy reform during the 1990s, Japanese society is dominated by a family model that designates women as full-time housewives and mothers (Osawa, 2000). In relation to ethnicity, the highest levels of unfulfilled need appear within the UK, closely followed by the USA, although data was unavailable for Japan. UK respondents reported not wishing to live next door to someone of a different ethnicity (9%), a Muslim (14%), an immigrant (16%) and a Gypsy (37%). We might expect that with the current focus on the war on terror and the targeting of Muslims after 9/11 (Pantazis and Pemberton, 2006) the figure for not wishing to have a Muslim as a neighbour to have increased. Similarly, the UK (24%) and USA (23%) reported the highest percentages of people not wanting to live next door to someone who was a homosexual, which is starkly contrasted to attitudes among the Swedish sample (6%). This pattern is repeated for disability, with the UK and USA again demonstrating the lowest levels of need fulfilment. The UK has the lowest percentage of disabled individuals in employment and the USA spends the lowest percentage of its GDP on disability benefits. Both the UK and USA report the highest percentage of people not wanting to live next door to someone who was emotionally unstable (39% and 52%, respectively), in contrast to more tolerant attitudes among the Swedish sample (6%).

Conclusion

The chapter has sought to put the state back on the agenda when considering the range of factors in the generation and responses to social harm. 'Harmful states' are not the inevitable outcome in response to capitalist crisis. From our empirical analysis, we make four observations about state formations and need fulfilment. The first is that one of the most consistent patterns in our data was the poor performance of the USA, a country boasting the greatest wealth. As an exemplar of the neo-liberal state – the embodiment of Gamble's (1988) couplet 'free economy; strong state' – the US reliance on the free market, and a tough and punitive approach to offenders, has led to a rapidly expanding penal estate. The US neo-liberal model assumes the benefits accrued through economic growth outweigh the inequalities that are inherent in this form of organization. While some may benefit from the freeing of the market, a series of collateral harms result which far outweigh those occurring in other regimes. It is a social formation which formally offers life opportunities without mechanisms for a large proportion of the population to realize them. Moreover, our analysis demonstrates a disjuncture between the formal recognition of rights and equality espoused by the USA and the lived reality as reflected in the recognition indicators.

Second, the UK since the late 1970s has followed a neo-liberal trajectory and has paid close attention to the USA for inspiration and for examples in lesson-drawing across a range of social and public policies (Dolowitz et al., 2000; Jones and Newburn 2002; Pantazis and Pemberton, 2008). This is most apparent in the massively expanding imprisonment rates in England and Wales following governments' adoption of a highly punitive penal strategy since the early 1990s. The UK is also marked by high levels of economic insecurity, reflected in the persistence and extent of relative poverty and inequality. We would argue that 'remnants' of social democratic institutions such as the NHS have served to mitigate the worst excesses of these neo-liberal shifts.

Third, our analysis reveals the contradictions of paternal forms of capitalism as epitomized by Japan. Work occupies a central role in the satisfaction of need for the Japanese population, guaranteeing access to healthcare, education, pensions and leisure (Cavadino and Dignan, 2006). With wages being determined by family responsibilities and seniority rather than productivity or the market value of employee skills, low levels of inequality and to some extent poverty are ensured. However, the delivery of welfare through corporate structures leads to two key considerations: first, loyalty to one's employer and work results in a series of harms, including long working hours, low levels of social participation and high rates of suicide; second, women's low participation in the workforce restricts their access to welfare, which may explain Japan's poor performance relating to gender recognition. Finally, although Sweden operates within a capitalist structure, our analysis demonstrates that it offers an impressive level of need fulfilment as a result of state interventions, in the form of universal and generous welfare benefits, healthcare and access to education, planned housing policy, and a commitment to full employment. With comparable levels of GDP to the UK, the Swedish example would suggest that less harmful models of capitalist state formation are possible within the context of the 'constraints' of con-temporary global capital. Although these state formations remain vulnerable to the 'pressures' of global capital and have at times diluted their commitments to equality and social citizenship (Broberg and Roll-Hansen, 1996), these pressures have not been translated into an abandonment of a more 'humane' form of capitalist state in all contexts.

The analysis presented here shows that states are highly differentiated, both in relation to the harms they produce and in terms of the spaces that remain, within which the production and effects of such harms can be resisted. Thus, recognizing the variation between state forms, even under conditions of a global struggle for neo-liberal hegemony, is significant both for the *analysis* of state forms and for develop-ing sites of *resistance* to state power. In contrast to totemic claims to 'no alternatives' that have become part of the neo-liberal orthodoxy, through attempts to globalize the 'race to the bottom' model of capitalism, alternatives not only remain possible but, as the analysis here shows, already exist in a wide variety of forms. This chapter testifies to the unevenness and constantly unfolding nature of state power, to the opportunities for exploiting the spaces that exist between the rhetoric and realities of state power and, thus, for the need for critical social science to foreground an analysis of states and state power.

————————————————— Key Reading —————————————————

Dorling, D., Gordon, D., Hillyard, P., Pantazis, C., Pemberton, S. and Tombs, S. (2008) *Criminal Obsessions: Why Harm Matters More than Crime* (2nd edn). London: Centre for Crime and Justice Studies.

Hillyard, P., Pantazis, C., Tombs, S. and Gordon, D. (eds) (2004) *Beyond Criminology: Taking Harm Seriously*. London: Pluto Press.

Muncie, J. (2000a) 'Decriminalising criminology', in G. Lewis, S. Gerwitz and J. Clarke (eds), *Rethinking Social Policy*. London: Sage.

Pemberton, S. (2007) 'Social harm future(s): exploring the potential of the social harm approach', *Crime, Law and Social Change*, 48(1–2): 27–41.

Schwendinger, H. and Schwendinger, J. (1975) 'Defenders of order or guardians of human rights?', in I. Taylor, P. Walton and J. Young (eds), *Critical Criminology*. London: Routledge.

Tift, L. and Sullivan, D. (2001) 'A needs-based, social harm definition of crime', in S. Henry and M. Lanier (eds), *What Is Crime? Controversies over the Nature of Crime and What To Do about It*. Lanham, MD: Rowman & Littlefield.

BIBLIOGRAPHY

URL addresses correct as at July 2008.

Abrahams, F. (2002) *Below the Breadline: Living on the Minimum Wage.* London: Profile Books.

Agamben, G. (2005) *State of Exception.* Chicago: Chicago University Press.

Ahmed, I. (1997) 'The quest for racial justice in Bradford', in C. Rank (ed.), *City of Peace: Bradford's Story.* Bradford: Bradford Libraries.

Ahmed, N., Bodi, F., Kazim, R. and Shadjareh, M. (2001) *The Oldham Riots: Discrimination, Deprivation and Communal Tension in the United Kingdom.* London: Islamic Human Rights Commission.

Aldrich, R.J. (2002) '"Grow your own": Cold War intelligence and history supermarkets', *Intelligence and National Security*, 17(1): 135–52.

Alexander, C. (2000) *The Asian Gang: Ethnicity, Identity, Masculinity.* Oxford: Berg.

Amnesty International (2004) *Turkey: Restrictive Laws, Arbitrary Application – The Pressure on Human Rights Defenders.* (EUR 44/002/2004). London: Amnesty International.

Amnesty International (2007) *Turkey: The Entrenched Culture of Impunity Must End.* (EUR 44/008/2007). London: Amnesty International.

Amnesty UK (ICM) (2005) *Sexual Assault Research Summary Report.* London: Amnesty UK.

Andersen, M.E. (1993) *Dossier Secreto: Argentina's Desaparecidos and the Myth of the 'Dirty War'.* Boulder, CO: Westview Press.

Anderson, A. (1997) *Media, Culture and the Environment.* London: Routledge.

Anderson, B. and Rogaly, B. (2005) *Forced Labour and Migration to the UK.* London: COMAS/TUC.

Ansari, F. (2005) *British Anti-Terrorism: A Modern Day Witch-hunt.* London: Islamic Human Rights Commission.

Aretxaga, B. (2000) 'A fictional reality: paramilitary death squads and the construction of state terror in Spain', in J.A. Sluka (ed.), *Death Squad.* Philadephia: University of Pennsylvania Press.

Armstrong, E.M. (2003) *Conceiving Risk, Bearing Responsibility.* Baltimore, MD: Johns Hopkins University Press.

Asylum Aid and Bail for Immigration Detainees (2005) *Justice Denied: Asylum and Immigration Legal Aid – A System in Crisis.* London: Asylum Aid and Bail for Immigration Detainees.

Athens, L.H. (1992) *The Creation of Dangerous Violent Criminals.* Urbana, IL: University of Illinois Press.

Atkinson, H. and Wilks-Heeg, S. (2000) *Local Government from Thatcher to Blair: The Politics of Creative Autonomy.* Cambridge: Polity Press.

Atkinson, R. and Helms, G. (eds) (2007) *Securing an Urban Renaissance: Crime, Community and British Urban Policy.* Bristol: Policy Press.

Atton, C. and Wickenden, E. (2005) 'Sourcing routines and representation in alternative journalism: a case study approach', *Journalism Studies*, 6(3): 347–59.

Attwood, R. (2007) 'Academics told to push intellectual credentials', *The Times Higher Educational Supplement*, 13 April.

Aubert, V. (1966) 'Some social functions of legislation', *Acta Sociologica*, 10(1–2): 98–120.

Auchmuty, R. (2004) 'Same-sex marriage revived: feminist critique and legal strategy', *Feminism and Psychology*, 14(1): 101–26.

Audit Commission (2007) *Annual Audit and Inspection Letter, Liverpool City Council.* London: Audit Commission.

Back, L., Keith, M., Khan, A., Shukra, K. and Solomos, J. (2002) 'New Labour's white heart: politics. Multiculturalism and the return of assimilation', *The Political Quarterly*, 73(4): 445–54.

Bagguley, P. and Hussain, Y. (2003) *Citizenship, Ethnicity and Identity: British Pakistanis after the 2001 'Riots'*. University of Leeds Working Paper. Leeds: University of Leeds.

Baker, M., Geraghty, J., Webb, B. and Key, T. (1993) *Street Robbery. Police Research Group*. Crime Prevention Unit Series Paper No. 44. London: Home Office.

Baldwin, T. and Rozenburg, G. (2004) 'Britain must scrap multiculturalism', *The Times*, 3 April.

Ballinger, A. (1996) 'The guilt of the innocent and the innocence of the guilty', in A. Myers and S. Wight (eds), *No Angels*. London: Pandora.

Ballinger, A. (2000) *Dead Woman Walking: Executed Women in England and Wales 1900–1955*. Aldershot: Ashgate.

Ballinger, A. (2005) '"Reasonable" women who kill: re-interpreting and re-defining women's responses to domestic violence in England and Wales 1900–1965', *Outlines: Critical Social Studies*, 7(2): 65–82.

Ballinger, A. (2007) 'Masculinity in the dock: legal responses to male violence and female retaliation in England and Wales 1900–1965', *Social & Legal Studies*, 16(4): 459–81.

Barker, N. (2006) 'Sex and the Civil Partnership Act: the future of (non) conjugality?', *Feminist Legal Studies*, 14(2): 241–59.

Barnekov, T., Boyle, R. and Rich, D. (1989) *Privatism and Urban Policy in Britain and the United States*. Oxford: Oxford University Press.

Barrow, C. (2005) 'The return of the state: globalization, state theory, and the new imperialism', *New Political Science*, 27(2): 113–45.

Barry, A., Osborne, T. and Rose, N. (1996) 'Introduction', in A. Barry, T. Osborne and N. Rose (eds), *Foucault and Political Reason: Liberalism, Neo-liberalism and Rationalities of Government*. London: UCL Press.

Barton, A., Corteen, K., Scott, D. and Whyte, D. (eds) (2007a) *Expanding the Criminological Imagination*. Cullompton: Willan.

Barton, A., Corteen, K., Scott, D. and Whyte, D. (2007b) 'Conclusion: expanding the criminological imagination', in Barton, A., Corteen, K., Scott, D. and Whyte, D. (eds) *Expanding the Criminological Imagination*. Cullompton: Willan.

Bauman, Z. (1989) *Modernity and the Holocaust*. Cambridge: Polity Press.

Bauman, Z. (2002) *Society under Siege*. Cambridge: Polity Press.

BBC (2000) 'The black and black divide', *BBC News Online*, 17 October, www.news.bbc.co.uk/1/low/uk/974603.stm.

BBC (2003) 'Workers not taking holidays', *BBC website*, www.news.bbc.co.uk/1/hi/uk/2946134.stm.

BBC (2004) 'Terror detainees win Lords appeal', *BBC News Online*, 16 December, www.news.bbc.co.uk/1/hi/uk/4100481.stm.

BBC (2005) 'Muslim police stops "more likely"', *BBC News Online*, 2 March, www.news.bbc.co.uk/1/hi/uk/4309961.stm.

BBC (2006a) *Newsnight Scotland*, 4 December.

BBC (2006b) 'Oyster data is "new police tool"', *BBC News*, 13 March.

BBC (2006c) 'Judge quashes anti-terror orders', *BBC News*, 28 June.

BBC (2008a) 'On Whose Orders?', *Panorama*, 25 February.

BBC (2008b) 'Raid on street in crime crackdown', *BBC News Online*, 27 March, www.news.bbc.co.uk/1/hi/england/london/7317060.stm.

Beck, M. and Woolfson, C. (1999) 'Safety culture – a concept too many?', *The Health and Safety Practitioner*, 16(1): 14–16.

Becker, H. (1963) *Outsiders*. Glencoe, IL: Free Press.

Becker, H. (1967) 'Whose side are we on?', *Social Problems*, 14(3): 239–47.

Bell, C. and Newby, H. (1971) *Community Studies: An Introduction to the Sociology of the Local Community*. London: George Allen and Unwin.

Bell, C. and Newby, H. (eds) (1977) 'Epilogue', in C. Bell and H. Newby (eds), *Doing Sociological Research*. London: Allen and Unwin.

Benjamin, W. (1921/1978) 'Critique of violence', in P. Demtz (ed.), *Reflections: Essays, Aphorisms, Autobiographical Writings* (trans. E. Jephcott). New York: Schocken Books.

Bennett, K., Heath, T. and Jeffries, R. (2007) *Asylum Statistics United Kingdom 2006*. 14/07, London: Home Office.

Bennetto, J. (2006a) 'MI5 conducts secret inquiry into 8,000 al-Qa'ida "sympathisers"', *The Independent*, 3 July.

Bennetto, J. (2006b) 'Big Brother Britain 2006: "We are waking up to a surveillance society all around us"', *The Independent*, 2 November.

Benyon, J. (1984) 'The riots, Lord Scarman and the political agenda', in J. Benyon (ed.), *Scarman and After: Essays Reflecting on Lord Scarman's Report, the Riots and their Aftermath*. Oxford: Pergamon Press.

Bhattacharya, J., DeLeire, T., Haider, S. and Currie, J. (2003) 'Heat or eat? Cold-weather shocks and nutrition in poor American families', *American Journal of Public Health*, 93(7): 1149–54.

Bibbings, L.S. (2004) 'Heterosexuality as harm: fitting in', in P. Hillyard, C. Pantazis, S. Tombs and D. Gordon (eds), *Beyond Criminology: Taking Harm Seriously*. London: Pluto Press.

Bibbings, L.S. and Alldridge, P. (1993) 'Sexual expression, body alteration, and the defence of consent', *Journal of Law and Society*, 20(3): 356–70.

Bigo, D. (2006) 'Security, exception, ban and surveillance', in D. Lyon (ed.), *Theorizing Surveillance: The Panopticon and Beyond*. Cullompton: Willan.

Bittner, E. (1975) *The Functions of Police in Modern Society*. New York: Jason Aronson.

Blair, T. (2005) *Britain Forward, Not Back: The Labour Party Manifesto 2005*. London: HMSO.

Blair, T. (2006) 'The duty to integrate: shared British values', Speech hosted by the Runnymede Trust, London, 8 December, www.number-10.gov.uk/output/Page10563.asp.

Blomley, N. (2006) 'Editorial: Homelessness and the delusions of property', *Transactions of the Institute of British Geographers*, 31(1): 3–5.

Blumler, J. (1999) 'The modern publicity process', in M. Ferguson (ed.), *Political Communication: The New Imperatives*. London: Sage.

Boggs, C. (1976) *Gramsci's Marxism*. London: Pluto Press.

Bonner, A. (1961) *British Co-operation: The History, Principles and Organisation of the British Co-operative Movement*. Manchester: Co-operative Union.

Bottoms, A.E. (1983) 'Neglected features of the contemporary penal system', in D. Garland and P. Young (eds), *The Power to Punish*. London: Heinemann.

Bottoms, A.E. (1995) 'The philosophy and politics of punishment and sentencing', in C. Clarkson and R. Morgan (eds), *The Politics of Sentencing Reform*. Oxford: Clarendon.

Bottoms, A.E. and Wilson, A. (2004) 'Attitudes to punishment in two high-crime communities', in A.E. Bottoms, S.A. Rex and G. Robinson (eds), *Alternatives to Prison: Options in an Insecure Soceity*. Cullompton: Willan.

Bourdieu, P. and Wacquant, L. (2001) 'NewLiberalSpeak: notes on the New Planetary Vulgate', *Radical Philosophy: A Journal of Socialist and Feminist Philosophy*, 105(Jan./Feb.): 2–5.

Bowen, D.G. (1997) 'Peacemaking after *The Satanic Verses* protests', in C. Rank (ed.), *City of Peace: Bradford's Story*. Bradford: Bradford Libraries.

Bowling, B. (1998) *Violent Racism: Victimisation, Policing and Social Context*. Oxford: Clarenden Press.

Bowling, B. and Phillips, C. (2002) *Racism, Crime and Justice*. Harlow: Longman.

Box, S. (1971) *Deviance, Reality and Society*. London: Holt, Rinchart and Winston.

Boyd, S.B. (1992) 'What is a normal family: *C v. C (A Minor)*?', *Modern Law Review*, 55(2): 269–78.

Boyle, K. (2005) *Media and Violence*. London: Sage.

Boyle, R. (1999a) 'Spotlight Strathclyde: police and media strategies', *Corporate Communications*, 4(2): 93–7.

Boyle, R. (1999b) 'Spotlighting the police: changing UK police–media relations in the 1990s', *International Journal of the Sociology of Law*, 27: 229–50.

Braithwaite, J. (1984) *Corporate Crime in the Pharmaceutical Industry*. London: Routledge and Kegan Paul.

Braithwaite, J. (2000) 'The new regulatory state and the transformation of criminology', in D. Garland and R. Sparks (eds), *Criminology and Social Theory*. Oxford: Clarendon Press.

Braithwaite, J. (2003) 'What's wrong with the sociology of punishment?', *Theoretical Criminology*, 7(1): 5–28.

Brenner, T. and Theodore, N. (2002) 'Cities and geographies of "actually existing noliberalism"', *Antipode*, 24(3): 349–79.

Bridges, L. (1999) 'Incompetence, corruption and institutional racism', *Journal of Law and Society*, 26(3): 298–322.

Bridges, L. (2001) 'Race, law and the state', *Race and Class*, 43(2): 61–76.

Broadhurst, K., Grover, C. and Jamieson, J. (forthcoming) *A Commentary on the Youth Justice Action Plan*.

Broberg, G. and Roll-Hansen, N. (eds) (1996) *Eugenics and the Welfare State: Sterilization Policy in Denmark, Sweden, Norway, and Finland*. East Lansing, MI: Michigan State University Press.

Brooks-Gordon, B. and Gelsthorpe, L. (2003) 'Prostitutes' clients, Ken Livingstone and a new Trojan horse', *The Howard Journal of Criminal Justice*, 42(5): 437–51.

Brown, G. (2008a) Speech on managed migration and earned citizenship, The Camden Centre, London, 20 February, www.number-10.gov.uk/output/Page14624.asp.

Brown, G. (2008b) '42 day detention: a fair solution', *TimesOnLine*, 2 June, www.timesonline. co.uk/tol/comment/columnists/guest_contributors/article4045210.ece.

Brown, S. (1997) *Understanding Youth and Crime: Listening to Youth*. Buckingham: Open University Press.

Brownlee, I. (1998) 'New Labour–new penology? Punitive rhetoric and the limits of managerialism in criminal justice policy', *Journal of Law and Society*, 25(3): 313–35.

Brounmiller, S. (1976) *Against Our Will*. Toronto: Bantam.

Brusten, M. and Ponsaers, P. (eds) (1981) 'State control of information in the field of deviance and social control', Working Papers in European Criminology (2). Leuven: European Group for the Study of Deviance and Social Control.

Bunyan, T. (2005) 'While Europe sleeps', in T. Bunyan (ed.), *Essays for Civil Liberties and Democracy in Europe*, Essay No. 11. London: Statewatch, www.ecln.org/essays.html.

Burke, J. (2004) *Al Qaeda: The True Story of Radical Islam*. London: Penguin.

Burnett, J. (2005) 'Hearts and minds in the domestic "war on terror"', *Campaign Against Racism and Fascism*, 18 October, www.carf.demon.co.uk/feat60.html.

Burnett, J. (2007a) 'Community cohesion: a new framework for race and diversity', *Race and Class*, 48(4): 115–18.

Burnett, J. (2007b) 'Britain's "civilising project": community cohesion and core values', *Policy and Politics*, 35(2): 353–7.

Burnett, J. (2008a) 'Dawn raids', *PAFRAS Briefing Paper No. 4*. Leeds: Positive Action for Refugees and Asylum Seekers.

Burnett, J. (2008b) 'Community cohesion in Bradford: neoliberal integrationism', in J. Flint and D. Robinson (eds), *Community Cohesion in Crisis? New Dimensions of Diversity and Difference*. Bristol: The Policy Press.

Burnett, J. and Whyte, D. (2004) 'New Labour's new racism', *Red Pepper*, 124: 28–9.

Burney, E. (2005) *Making People Behave: Anti-social Behaviour, Politics and Policy*. Cullompton: Willan.

CAJ (2007) *War on Terror: Lessons from Ireland*. Belfast: Committee on the Administration of Justice.

Campaign Against Racism and Fascism (1999) 'The politics of numbers: police racism and crime figures', *Campaign Against Racism and Fascism*, June/July, www.carf.org.uk.

Campaign Against Racism and Fascism/Southall Rights (1981) *Southall: The Birth of a Black Community*. London: Institute of Race Relations and Southall Rights.

Campbell, A. (2005) 'Keeping the "lady" safe: the regulation of femininity through crime prevention literature', *Critical Criminology*, 13(2): 119–40.

Campbell, B. (1993) *Goliath: Britain's Dangerous Places*. London: Methuen.

Campbell, C. and Connelly, I. (2003) 'A model for the "war against terrorism"? Military intervention in Northern Ireland and the 1970 Falls Curfew', *Journal of Law and Society*, 30(3): 341–75.

Cancino, J.M. (2001) 'Walking among giants 50 years later: an exploratory analysis of patrol officer use of violence', *Policing: An International Journal of Strategies and Management*, 24: 144–61.

Cantle, T. (2001) *Community Cohesion: A Report of the Independent Review Team*. London: Home Office.

Cantle, T. (2004) *The End of Parallel Lives? The Report of the Community Cohesion Panel*. London: Home Office.

Cantle, T. (2005) *Community Cohesion: A New Framework for Race and Diversity*. Basingstoke: Palgrave Macmillan.

Cantle, T. (2006) 'Parallel lives', *Index on Censorship*, 35(2): 85–90.

Carlen, P. (1976) *Magistrates' Justice*. London: Martin Robertson.

Carlen, P. (1996) *Jigsaw: A Political Criminology of Youth*. Buckingham: Open University Press.

Carlen, P. (2002) 'Carceral Clawback', *Punishment and Society*, 4(1): 115–21.

Carlen, P. (2007) 'Imaginary penalities and risk-crazed governance', Annual Research Lecture, British Society of Criminology, NW Regional Branch, University of Liverpool, 28 March.

Carlen, P. and Tombs, J. (2006) 'Reconfigurations of penality: the ongoing case of the women's imprisonment and reintegration industries', *Theoretical Criminology*, 10(3): 337–60.

Carlowe, J. (2001) 'The doctor won't see you now…', *The Observer Online*, 24 June, www. guardian. co.uk/society/2001/jun/24/health.life.

Carrington, K. and Hogg, R. (2002) 'Critical criminologies: an introduction', in K. Carrington and R. Hogg (eds), *Critical Criminology*. Cullompton: Willan.

Carson, W.G. (1979) 'The conventionalisation of early factory crime', *International Journal of the Sociology of Law*, 7(1): 37–60.

Carson, W.G. (1980) 'Early factory inspectors and the viable class society – a rejoinder', *International Journal of the Sociology of Law*, 8(2): 187–91.

Carson, W.G. (1982) *The Other Price of Britain's Oil*. Oxford: Martin Robertson.

Carter, V. (1992) 'Abseil makes the heart grow fonder: lesbian and gay campaigning tactics and Section 28', in K. Plummer (ed.), *Modern Homosexualities: Fragments of Lesbian and Gay Experience*. London: Routledge. pp. 217–26.

Cavadino, M. and Dignan, J. (2006) *Penal Systems: A Comparative Approach*. London: Sage.

Chan, W. (2001) *Women, Murder and Justice*. Basingstoke: Palgrave.

Charlesworth, S.J. (2000) *A Phenomenology of Working Class Experience*. Cambridge: Cambridge University Press.

Chesney-Lind, M. (2006) 'Patriarchy, crime and justice: feminist criminology in an era of backlash', *Feminist Criminology*, 1(1): 6–26.

Chevigny, P. (1995) *Edge of the Knife: Police Violence in the Americas*. New York: New Press.

Chevigny, P. (2003) 'The populism of fear: politics of crime in the Americas', *Punishment and Society*, 5(1): 77–96.

Chibnall, S. (1977) *Law and Order News: An Analysis of Crime Reporting in the British Press*. London: Tavistock Press.

Childs, M. (2000) 'Commercial sex and criminal law', in D. Nicolson and L. Bibbings (eds), *Feminist Perspectives on Criminal Law*. London: Cavendish.

Chin, G.J. (ed.) (1997) *New York City Police Corruption Investigation Commissions, 1894–1994, Vol. VI: Mollen Commission Report*. Buffalo, NY: William S. Hein.

Choongh, S. (1997) *Policing as Social Discipline*. Oxford: Clarendon Press.

Christie, N. (2000) *Crime Control as Industry: Towards Gulags, Western Style?* London: Routledge.

Chung, H. and Muntaner, C. (2007) 'Welfare state matters: a typological multilevel analysis of wealthy countries', *Health Policy*, 80(2): 328–39.

CITB-Construction Skills (2007) *Annual Report and Accounts 2006*. London: HMSO, www.citb.org.uk/pdf/annualreport/annualreport2006.pdf.

Clark, J. (2005) 'New Labour's citizens: activated, empowered, responsibilised, abandoned?', *Critical Social Policy*, 25(4): 447–63.

Clark, J., Gewirtz, S., Hughes, G. and Humphrey, J. (2000) 'Guarding the public interest? Auditing public services', in J. Clark, S. Gewirtz and E. McLaughlin (eds), *New Managerialism: New Welfare?* London: Sage.

Clarke, J. (2004) 'Dissolving the public realm? The logics and limits of neoliberalism', *Journal of Social Policy*, 33(1): 27–48.

Clarke, J. (2008) 'Still policing the crisis?', *Crime, Media and Culture*, 4(1): 123–9.

Clarke, R.V. (2004) 'Technology, criminology and crime science', *European Journal on Criminal Policy and Research*, 10: 55–63.

Cobain, I. (2008) 'MI5 accused of colluding in torture of terrorist suspects', *The Guardian*, 29 April.

Cochrane, A. (1993) *Whatever Happened to Local Government?* Buckingham: Open University Press.

Cohen, P. (1979) 'Policing the working-class city', in B. Fine et al. (eds), *Capitalism and the Rule of Law: From Deviancy Theory to Marxism*. London: Hutchinson.

Cohen, P. (1981) 'Policing the working-class city', in M. Fitzgerald, G. McLennan and J. Pawson (eds), *Crime and Society: Readings in History and Theory*. London: Routledge Kegan Paul.

Cohen, S. (1972) *Folk Devils and Moral Panics*. Harmondsworth: Penguin.

Cohen, S. (1981) 'Footprints on the sand: a further report on criminology and the sociology of deviance in Britain', in M. Fitzgerald, G. McLennan and J. Pawson (eds), *Crime and Society: Readings in History and Theory*. London: Routledge and Kegan Paul.

Cohen, S. (1985) *Visions of Social Control*. Cambridge: Polity Press.

Cohen, S. (1988) *Against Criminology*. New Brunswick, NJ: Transaction Books.

Cohen, S. (2001) *States of Denial: Knowing about Atrocities and Suffering*. Cambridge: Polity Press.

Cohen, S. (2002) *Folk Devils and Moral Panics* (3rd edn). London: Routledge (1st edn, 1972).

Cohen, S. and Taylor, L. (1972) *Psychological Survival*. Harmondsworth: Penguin.

Cohen, S. and Taylor, L. (1977) 'Talking about prison blues', in C. Bell and H. Newby (eds), *Doing Sociological Research*. London: George Allen and Unwin.

Cohen, S. and Young, J. (eds) (1973) *The Manufacture of News: Social Problems, Deviance and Mass Media*. London: Constable.

Coleman, R. (2004) *Reclaiming the Streets: Surveillance, Social Control and the City*. Cullompton: Willan.

Coleman, R. (2005) 'Surveillance in the city: primary definition and urban spatial order', *Crime, Media and Culture: An International Journal*, 1(2): 131–48.

Coleman, R. (2007) 'Confronting the hegemony of vision: state, space and urban crime prevention', in A. Barton, C. Corteen and D. Scott (eds), *Expanding the Criminological Imagination*. Cullompton: Willan.

Coleman, R. and Sim, J. (2000) '"You'll never walk alone": CCTV surveillance, order and neo-liberal rule in Liverpool city centre', *British Journal of Sociology*, 51(4): 623–39.

Coleman, R. and Sim, J. (2005) 'Contemporary statecraft and the "punitive obsession": a critique of the new penology thesis', in J. Pratt, D. Brown, M. Brown, S. Hallsworth and W. Morrison (eds), *The New Punitiveness: Trends, Theories, Perspective*. Cullompton: Willan.

Coleman, R., Sim, J. and Whyte, D. (2002) 'Power, politics and partnerships: the state of crime prevention on Merseyside', in G. Hughes and A. Edwards (eds), *Crime Control and Community: The New Politics of Public Safety*. Cullompton: Willan.

Coleman, R., Tombs, S. and Whyte, D. (2005) 'Capital, crime control and statecraft in the entrepreneurial city', *Urban Studies*, 42(Dec.): 2511–30.

Collier, R. (1997) 'After Dunblane: crime, corporeality and the (hetero)sexing of the bodies of men', *Journal of Law and Society*, 24(2): 177–98.

COMEAP (Committee on the Medical Effects of Air Pollution) (1998) *Report: The Quantification of the Effects of Air Pollution on Health in the United Kingdom*. London: Department of Health.

Connell, R.W. (1994) 'The state, gender and sexual politics: theory and appraisal', in H.L. Radtke and H.J. Stam (eds), *Power/Gender*. London: Sage.

Conroy, J. (2000) *Unspeakable Acts, Ordinary People: The Dynamics of Torture*. Los Angeles: University of California Press.

Control Arms Campaign (2004) *Guns or Growth: Assessing the Impact of Arms on Sustainable Development*. London: Amnesty International, Iansa and Oxfam.

Control Arms Campaign (2006) Arms without Borders: Why a Globalised Trade Needs Global Controls, www.controlarms.org/documents/Arms%20Without%20Borders_Final_21Sept06.pdf.

Cook, D. (2006) *Criminal and Social Justice*. London: Sage.

Corporate Watch (2004) *UK Construction Industry Overview*, www.archive.corporatewatch.org/profiles/construction/construction.htm.

Cory, P. (2004) *Cory Collusion Inquiry Report: Patrick Finucane*, HC 470. London: HMSO.

Council for Europe (2004) *Space 1: Council of Europe Annual Penal Statistics, Survey 2004*. Strasbourg: Council of Europe.

Cover, R. (1986) 'Violence and the word', *Yale Law Journal*, 95: 1601.

Cowan, S. (2005) '"Gender is no substitute for sex": a comparative human rights analysis of the legal regulation of sexual identity', *Feminist Legal Studies*, 13(1): 67–96.

Cowen, R. (2004) 'Young Muslims "made scapegoats" in stop and search', *Guardian Unlimited*, 3 July, www.guardian.co.uk/uk/2004/jul/03/terrorism.race/print.

Crawford, A. (1997) *The Local Governance of Crime: Appeals to Community and Partnerships*. Oxford: Clarendon Press.

Crawford, A. (1998a) *Crime Prevention and Community Safety: Politics, Policies and Practices*. Harlow: Longman.

Crawford, A. (1998b) 'Community safety and the quest for security: holding back the dynamics of social exclusion', *Policy Studies*, 19(3/4): 237–53.

Crawford, A. (2001) 'Joined up but fragmented: contradiction, ambiguity and ambivalence at the heart of New Labour's "Third Way"', in R. Matthews and J. Pitts (eds), *Crime, Disorder and Community Safety*. London: Routledge.

Crawford, A. (2003) 'Contractual governance of deviant behaviour', *Journal of Law and Society*, 30(4): 479–505.

Crawford, A. (2006) 'Networked governance and the post-regulatory state? Steering, rowing and anchoring the provision of policing and security', *Theoretical Criminology*, 10(4): 449–79.

Cross, S. (2005) 'Paedophiles in the community: inter-agency conflict, news leaks and the local press', *Crime, Media, Culture*, 1(3): 284–300.

Cunneen, C. (2001) *Conflict, Politics and Crime*. Crows Nest, NSW: Allen & Unwin.

Currie, E. (2007) 'Against marginality: arguments for a public criminology', *Theoretical Criminology*, 11(2): 175–90.

Davies, N. (1997) *Dark Heart: The Shocking Truth about Hidden Britain*. London: Chatto Windus.

Davies, Z. and McMahon, W. (2007) *Debating Youth Justice: From Punishment to Problem Solving?* London: Centre for Crime and Justice Studies.

Davis, A. (2000) 'Public relations, news productions and changing patterns of source access in the British national media', *Media, Culture & Society*, 22(1): 39–59.

Davis, C. (2000) 'Corporate violence, regulatory agencies and the management and deflection of censure', unpublished doctoral thesis, University of Southampton.

Davis, M. (2006) *Planet of Slums*. London: Verso.

De Haan, W. (1990) *The Politics of Redress: Crime, Punishment and Penal Abolition*. London: Sage.

De Lint, W. and Virta, S. (2004) 'Security and ambiguity: towards a radical security politics', *Theoretical Criminology*, 8(4): 465–89.

de Swaan, A. (2001) 'Dyscivilization, mass extermination and the state', *Theory, Culture & Society*, 18(2–3): 265–76.

Deacon, D. (1996) 'The voluntary sector in a changing media environment: a case study of non-official news sources', *European Journal of Communication*, 11(2): 173–99.

Deacon, D. and Golding, P. (1994) *Taxation and Representation: The Media, Political Communication and the Poll Tax*. London: John Libbey.

Dench, G., Gavron, K. and Young, M. (2006) *The New East End: Kinship, Race and Conflict*. London: Profile Books.

Department of the Environment, Transport and the Regions (2000) *By Design – Urban Design in the Planning System: Towards a Better Place*. London: HMSO.

Dignan, J. (2005) *Understanding Victims and Restorative Justice*. Maidenhead: Open University Press.

Dixon, D. (1997) *Law in Policing: Legal Regulation and Policing Practices*. Oxford: Clarendon Press.

Dixon, M., Reed, H., Rogers, B. and Stone, L. (2006) *CrimeShare: The Unequal Impact of Crime*. London: IPPR.

Dobash, R. and Dobash, R. (1979) *Violence against Wives*. Shepton Mallet: Open Books.

Dobash, R. and Dobash, R. (1992) *Women, Violence and Social Change*. London: Routledge.

Dodsworth, F. (2007) 'Police and prevention of crime: commerce, temptation and the corruption of the body politic from Fielding to Colquhoun', *British Journal of Criminology*, 47: 439–54.

Dolowitz, D., Hulme, R., Nellis, M. and O'Neil, F. (eds) (2000) *Policy Transfer and British Social Policy: Learning from the USA*. Buckingham: Open University Press.

Dorling, D., Gordon, D., Hillyard, P., Pantazis, C., Pemberton, S. and Tombs, S. (2008) *Criminal Obsessions: Why Harm Matters Mone than Crime* (2nd edn). London: Center for Crime and Justice Studies.

Downes, D. and Morgan, R. (1994) 'Hostages to fortune?: the politics of law and order in post-war Britain', in M. Maguire, R. Morgan and R. Reiner (eds), *The Oxford Handbook of Criminology* (1st edn). Oxford: Oxford University Press.

Doyal, L. and Gough, I. (1984) 'A theory of human need', *Critical Social Policy*, 4(1): 96–135.

Doyal, L. and Gough, I. (1991) *A Theory of Human Need*. London: Macmillan.

Doyle, A. (2003) *Arresting Image: Crime and Policing in Front of the Television Camera*. Toronto: University of Toronto Press.

Doyle, A. and Ericson, R. (1996) 'Breaking into prison: news sources and correctional institutions', *Canadian Journal of Criminology*, 38(2): 155–90.

Dunhill, C. (ed.) (1989) *The Boys in Blue: Women's Challenge to the Police*. London: Virago.

Durham, M.G. and Kellner, D. (eds) (2006) *Media and Cultural Studies Keywords*. London: Blackwell.

Edwards, A. and Hughes, G. (2005) 'Comparing the governance of safety in Europe', *Theoretical Criminology*, 9(3): 345–63.

Edwards, S. (1989) *Policing 'Domestic' Violence*. London: Sage.

Ehrenreich, B. (2002) *Nickel and Dimed: Undercover in Low-wage USA*. London: Granta.

Eikemo, T., Bambra, C., Judge, K. and Ringdal, K. (2008) 'Welfare state regimes and differences in self-perceived health in Europe: a multi-level analysis', *Social Science and Medicine*, 66(11): 2281–95.

Eisner, M. (2001) 'Modernization, self-control and lethal violence: the long-term dynamics of European homicide rates in historical perspective', *British Journal of Criminology*, 41: 618–38.

Elias, N. (1987) *Involvement and Detachment*. Oxford: Blackwell.

Elias, N. (2000) *The Civilizing Process* (rev. edn) (trans. E. Jephcott). Oxford: Blackwell.

Emsley, C. (2007) 'Historical perspectives on crime', in M. Maguire, R. Morgan and R. Reiner (eds), *The Oxford Handbook of Criminology* (4th edn). Oxford: Oxford University Press.

Engels, F. (1968) 'Origins of the family, private property and the state', in K. Marx and F. Engels (eds), *Selected Works*. London: Lawrence and Wishart. pp. 449–583.

Epstein, L., Paluch, R., Gordy, C. and Dorn, J. (2000) 'Decreasing sedentary behaviors in treating pediatric obesity', *Archives of Pediatric and Adolescent Medicine*, 154(3): 220–6.

Ericson, R. (2007) *Crime in an Insecure World*. Cambridge: Polity Press.

Ericson, R., Baranek, P. and Chan, J. (1987) *Visualising Deviance: A Study of News Organisation*. Milton Keynes: Open University Press.

Ericson, R., Baranek, P. and Chan, J. (1989) *Negotiating Control: A Study of News Sources*. Milton Keynes: Open University Press.

Esping-Anderson, G. (1990) *The Three Worlds of Welfare Capitalism*. London: Polity Press.

Etzioni, A. (1993) *The Spirit of Community*. New York: Crown Publishing.

Etzioni, A. (1995) *The Spirit of Community: Rights, Responsibilities and the Communitarian Agenda*. London: Fontana Press.

Etzioni, A. (1997) *The New Golden Rule*. London: Profile Books.

Eurostat (2008) *Statistics in Focus, Crime and Criminal Justice*, 19, www.epp.eurostat.ec.europa. eu/portal/page?_pageid=1073,46587259&_dad=portal&_schema=PORTAL&p_product_code= KS-SF-08-019.

Evans, J. (2007) 'Intelligence, counter-terrorism and trust', Address to the Society of Editors, Manchester, 5 November, www.mi5.gov.uk/print/page562.html (accessed 05/11/07).

Fabian Society (2006) 'New British history in schools must be an honest "warts and all" story', *Fabian Society*, 16 January, www.fabiansociety.org.uk/press_office/display.asp?cat=43&id=526.

Fairclough, N. (1992) *Discourse and Social Change*. London: Polity Press.

Fairclough, N. (1995) *Critical Discourse Analysis: The Critical Study of Language*. London: Longman.

Fairclough, N. and Chouliaraki, L. (1995) *Discourse in Late Modernity: Rethinking Critical Discourse Analysis*. Edinburgh: Edinburgh University Press.

FCO/HO (2004) *Young Muslims and Extremism*. London: Foreign and Commonwealth Office/Home Office.

Feeley, M. (2003) 'Crime, social order and the rise of the neo-Conservative politics', *Theoretical Criminology*, 7(1): 111–30.

Feeley, M. and Simon, J. (1992) 'The new penology: notes on the emerging strategy of corrections and its implications', *Criminology*, 30(4): 449–74.

Fekete, L. (2008) *Integration, Islamophobia and Civil Rights in Europe*. London: Institute of Race Relations.

Fekete, L. and Webber, F. (1994) *Inside Racist Europe*. London: Institute of Race Relations.

Felson, M. (1998) *Crime and Everyday Life* (2nd edn). Thousand Oaks, CA: Pine Forge Press.

Ferrera, M. (1996) 'The southern model of welfare in social Europe', *Journal of European Social Policy*, 6(1): 17–37.

Findlay, M. (1999) *The Globalisation of Crime: Understanding Transitional Relationships in Context*. Cambridge: Cambridge University Press.

Fine, B. (1979) 'Law and class', in B. Fine et al. (eds), *Capitalism and the Rule of Law: From Deviancy Theory to Marxism*. London: Hutchinson.

Fine, B., Kinsey, R., Lea, J., Picciotto, S. and Young, J. (eds) (1979) *Capitalism and the Rule of Law: From Deviancy Theory to Marxism*. London: Hutchinson.

Finlayson, A. (2003) *Making Sense of New Labour*. London: Lawrence & Wishart.

Fiske, J. (1991) 'British cultural studies and television', in R.C. Allen (ed.), *Channels of Discourse, Reassembled: Television and Contemporary Criticism*. Chapel Hill, NC: University of North Carolina Press.

Fitzgerald, M. (1977) *Prisoners in Revolt*. Harmondsworth: Penguin.

Fitzgerald, M. (1993) *Ethnic Minorities and the Criminal Justice System*. Royal Commission on Criminal Justice, Research Study No. 20. London: HMSO.

Fitzgerald, M. and Hale, C. (1996) *Ethnic Minorities: Victimisation and Racial Harrassment: Findings from the 1988 and 1992 British Crime Surveys*. Home Office Research Study No. 154. London: Home Office.

Fitzgerald, M. and Sim, J. (1979) *British Prisons*. Oxford: Blackwell.

Foley, M. (1994) 'Professionalising the response to rape', in T. Gillespie and C. Lupton (eds), *Working with Violence*. Basingstoke: Macmillan.

Follett, M. (2006) 'The local politics of community safety: local policy for local people', in P. Squires (ed.), *Community Safety: Critical Perspectives on Policy and Practice*. Bristol: The Policy Press.

Fooks, G. (1999) 'The Serious Fraud Office: policing the city or policing for the city?', paper presented at the British Criminology Conference, Liverpool, 13–16 July.

Foot, P. (1990) 'Blair Peach', in *Words as Weapons: Selected Writings 1980–1990*. London: Verso.

Foster, V. (2005) *Success Stories? A Participatory Arts-based Project at Sure Start Parr*. Liverpool: School of Sociology, University of Liverpool.

Foucault, M. (1977) *Discipline and Punish*. London: Allen Lane.

Foucault, M. (1977) 'Truth and power', in A. Fontana and P. Pasquino (eds), *Microfisica del potere: interventi politici*. Turin: Einaudi. Reprinted in J. Faubion (ed.) (2002), *Power: Essential Works of Foucault 1954–1984*. London: Penguin.

Foucault, M. (1979) *The History of Sexuality, Vol. 1: An Introduction* (later *The Will to Knowledge*) (trans. R. Hurley). London: Allen Lane (1st edition published in Great Britain).

Frank, T. (2001) *One Nation under God: Extreme Capitalism, Market Populism and the End of Market Democracy*. London: Secker & Warburg.

Franklin, B. (2004) *Packaging Politics: Political Communication in Britain's Media Democracy*. London: Arnold.

Franklin, B. (2006) *Local Journalism and Local Media: Making the Local News*. London: Routledge.

Franzway, S., Court, D. and Connell, R.W. (1989) *Staking a Claim: Feminism, Bureaucracy and the State*. Cambridge: Polity Press.

Fraser, N. (1997) *Justice Interruptus: Critical Reflections on the 'Postsocialist' Condition*. London: Routledge.

Friend, A. and Metcalf, A. (1982) *Slump City: The Politics of Mass Unemployment*. London: Pluto Press.

Furedi, F. (1997/2002) *Culture of Fear: Risk Taking and the Morality of Low Expectation*. London: Continuum.

Gaines, S. (2008) 'Liverpool is England's most deprived district, government figures show', *The Guardian Society*, 30 April, www.guardian.co.uk/society/2008/apr/30/england.deprivation.

GALOP (Moran, L.J., Paterson, S. and Docherty, T.) (2004) *'Count me in!' A Report on the Bexley and Greenwich Homophobic Crime Survey*. London: GALOP.

GALOP (2005) *GALOP: A History*. London: GALOP.

Gamble, A. (1988) *The Free Economy and the Strong State*. Basingstoke: Macmillan.

Garland, D. (1996) 'The limits of the sovereign state', *British Journal of Criminology*, 36(4): 445–71.

Garland, D. (2001) *The Culture of Control: Crime and Social Order in Contemporary Society*. Oxford: Oxford University Press.

Garland, D. (2008) 'On the concept of moral panic', *Crime, Media Culture*, 4(1): 9–30.

Garnham, N. (1978) 'Contribution to a political economy of mass communication', *Media, Culture & Society*, 1(2): 130–4.

Gearty, C. (2008) *Human Rights, Civil Society and the Challenge of Terrorism*. London: Centre for Human Rights at the London School of Economics.

Gelsthorpe, L. and Morris, A. (2002) 'Restorative Justice: the vestiges of welfare?', in J. Muncie, G. Hughes and E. McLaughlin (eds), *Youth Justice: Critical Readings*. London: Sage/Open University Press.

Gelsthorpe, L. and Sharpe, J. (2006) 'Gender, youth crime and justice', in B. Goldson and J. Muncie (eds), *Youth Crime and Justice*. London: Sage.

Geraghty, T. (1998) *The Irish War: The Military History of a Domestic Conflict*. London: Harper Collins.

Getty, J.A. and Naumov, O.V. (2000) *The Road to Terror: Stalin and the Self-destruction of the Bolsheviks, 1932–1939*. New Haven, CT: Yale University Press.

Gibson, J.T. (1990) 'Factors contributing to the creation of a torturer', in P. Suedfeld (ed.), *Psychology and Torture*. New York: Hemisphere.

Giddens, A. (1998) *The Third Way: The Renewal of Social Democracy*. Cambridge: Polity Press.

Gifford, Lord (1986) *The Broadwater Farm Inquiry*. London: Karia Press.

Gill, P. (1994) *Policing Politics: Security Intelligence and the Liberal Democratic State*. London: Frank Cass.

Gill, P. (2004) 'Securing the globe: intelligence and the post-9/11 shift from "liddism" to "drainism"', *Intelligence and National Security*, 19(3): 467–89.

Gill, P. and Phythian, M. (2006) *Intelligence in an Insecure World*. Cambridge: Polity Press.

Gillespie, T. (1994) 'Under pressure: rape crisis centres, multi-agency work and strategies for survival', in C. Lupton and T. Gillespie (eds), *Working with Violence*. Basingstoke: Macmillan.

Gilling, D. (2007) *Crime Reduction and Community Safety*. Cullompton: Willan.

Gilling, D. and Barton, A. (1997) 'Crime prevention and community safety: a new home for social policy?', *Critical Social Policy*, 17: 63–83.

Gilroy, P. (1987) *There Ain't No Black in the Union Jack: The Cultural Politics of Race and Nation*. London: Routledge.

Glasbeek, H. (2002) *Wealth by Stealth: Corporate Crime, Corporate Law and the Perversion of Democracy*. Toronto: Between the Lines.

Golding, P. and Murdock, G. (1991) 'Culture, communications and political economy', in J. Curran and J. Gurevitch (eds), *Mass Media and Society*. London: Edward Arnold.

Goldson, B. (1997) 'Children, crime, policy and practice: neither welfare nor justice', *Children and Society*, 11: 77–88.

Goldson, B. (2001) 'The demonization of children: from the symbolic to the institutional', in P. Foley, J. Roche and S. Tucker (eds), *Children in Society: Contemporary Theory, Policy and Practice*. Basingstoke: Palgrave.

Goldson, B. (2002) 'New punitiveness: the politics of child incarceration', in J. Muncie, G. Hughes and E. McLaughlin (eds), *Youth Justice: Critical Readings*. London: Sage.

Goldson, B. (2005a) 'Taking liberties: policy and the punitive turn', in H. Hendrick (ed.), *Children and Social Policy: An Essential Reader*. Bristol: The Policy Press.

Goldson, B. (2005b) 'Child imprisonment: the case for abolition', *Youth Justice*, 5(2): 77–90.

Goldson, B. (2008) 'New Labour's youth justice: a critical assessment of the first two terms', in G. McIvor and P. Raynor (eds), *Developments in Social Work with Offenders*. London: Jessica Kingsley.

Goldson, B. and Coles, D. (2005) *In the Care of the State? Child Deaths in Penal Custody*. London: INQUEST.

Goldson, B. and Jamieson, J. (2002) 'Youth crime, the "parenting deficit" and state intervention: a contextual critique', *Youth Justice*, 2(2): 82–99.

Goldson, B. and Muncie, J. (eds) (2006) *Youth Crime and Justice*. London: Sage.

Goldson, B. and Yates, J. (2008) 'Youth justice policy and practice: reclaiming applied criminology as critical intervention', in B. Stout, J. Yates and B. Williams (eds), *Applied Criminology*. London: Sage.

Goodey, J. (2005) *Victims and Victimology*. London: Longman.

Gordon, D. and Pantazis, C. (1997) *Breadline Britain in the 1990s*. Aldershot: Ashgate.

Gough, I. and McGregor, A. (eds) (2007) *Wellbeing in Developing Countries: From Theory to Research*. Cambridge: Cambridge University Press.

Gramsci, A. (1971) *Selections from the Prison Notebooks*. London: Lawrence & Wishart.

Granada Television (2004) *Capital or Culture?*, 23 August.

Graziano, F. (1992) *Divine Violence: Spectacle, Psychosexuality and Radical Christianity in the Argentine 'Dirty War'*. Boulder, CO: Westview Press.

Green, D. (2006) *We're (Nearly) All Victims Now*. London: Civitas.

Green, P. (1990) *The Enemy Without: Policing and Class Consciousness in the Miners' Strike*. Milton Keynes: Open University Press.

Green, P. (2002) 'Researching the Turkish state', in S. Tombs and D. Whyte (eds), *Unmasking the Crimes of the Powerful*. New York: Peter Lang.

Green, P. and Ward, T. (2004) *State Crime: Governments, Violence and Corruption*. London: Pluto Press.

Green, P. and Ward, T. (2009) 'Torture and the paradox of state violence', in B. Clucas, G. Johnstone and T. Ward (eds), *Torture: Moral Absolutes and Ambiguites*. Baden-Baden: Nomos.

Greenberg, J. (2004) 'Tories, teachers and the media politics of education reform: news discourse and the 1997 Ontario teachers' strike', *Journalism Studies*, 5(3): 353–71.

Gregory, J. (1979) 'Sex discrimination, work and law', in B. Fine et al. (eds), *Capitalism and the Rule of Law: From Deviancy Theory to Marxism*. London: Hutchinson.

Griffith, P. and Leonard, M. (2002) *Reclaiming Britishness*. London: The Foreign Policy Centre.

Grossman, D. (1996) *On Killing*. Boston: Little, Brown & Co.

Guelke, A. (2006) *Terrorism and Global Disorder*. London: I.B. Tauris.

Haggerty, K.D. and Ericson, R.V. (2006) 'The new politics of surveillance and visibility', in K.D. Haggerty and R.V. Ericson (eds), *The New Politics of Surveillance and Visibility*. Toronto: University of Toronto Press.

Hall, S. (1979) 'The Great Moving Right Show', *Marxism Today*, January: 19–39.

Hall, S. (1980a) 'Popular-Democratic vs Authoritarian Populism: two ways of "taking democracy seriously"', in A. Hunt (ed.), *Marxism and Democracy*. London: Lawrence & Wishart.

Hall, S. (1980b) 'Nicos Poulantzas: state, power, socialism', *New Left Review*, 1(119): 60–9.

Hall, S. (1980c) *Drifting into a Law and Order Society*. London: Cobden Trust.

Hall, S. (1984) 'The Great Moving Right Show', *New Internationalist*, 133, www.newint.org/issue133/show.htm.

Hall, S. (1988) *The Hard Road to Renewal: Thatcherism and the Crisis of the Left*. London: Verso.

Hall, S. (2003) 'New Labour's double shuffle', *Soundings*, 24(Summer): 10–24.

Hall, S. (2005) 'New Labour's double-shuffle', *The Review of Education, Pedagogy, and Cultural Studies*, 27: 319–335.

Hall, S., Critcher, C., Jefferson, T., Clarke, J. and Roberts, B. (1978) *Policing the Crisis: Mugging, the State, and Law and Order*. Basingstoke: Macmillan.

Hall, S. and Jacques, M. (eds) (1983) *The Politics of Thatcherism*. London: Lawrence & Wishart.

Hall, S. and Jefferson, T. (eds) (1976) *Resistance through Rituals: Youth Subcultures in Post-war Britain*. London: Hutchinson.

Hall, T. and Hubbard, P. (1996) 'The entrepreneurial city: new urban politics, new urban geographies', *Progress in Human Geography*, 20(2): 153–74.

Hallin, D. (1994) *We Keep America on Top of the World*. New York: Routledge.

Halstead, M. (1988) *Education, Justice and Cultural Diversity: An Examination of the Honeyford Affair, 1984–85*. London: The Falmer Press.

Hamelink, C. (1994) *Trends in World Communication: On Disempowerment and Self-empowerment*. Penang: Southbound and Third World Network.

Hancock, L. (2001) *Community, Crime and Disorder: Safety and Regeneration in Urban Neighbourhoods*. Basingstoke: Palgrave.

Hancock, L. (2004) 'Criminal justice, public opinion, fear and popular politics', in J. Muncie and D. Wilson (eds), *Student Handbook of Criminal Justice and Criminology*. London: Cavendish.

Hancock, L. (2006) 'Community safety and social exclusion', in P. Squires (ed.), *Community Safety: Critical Perspectives on Policy and Practice*. Bristol: The Policy Press.

Hancock, L. (2007) 'Is urban regeneration criminogenic?', in R. Atkinson and G. Helms (eds), *Securing an Urban Renaissance: Crime, Community and British Urban Policy*. Bristol: The Policy Press.

Hancock, L. and Matthews, R. (2001) 'Crime, community safety and toleration', in R. Matthews and J. Pitts (eds), *Crime, Disorder and Community Safety*. London: Routledge.

Haney, C., Banks, C. and Zimbardo, P. (1973) 'Interpersonal dynamics in a simulated prison', *International Journal of Criminology and Penology*, 1: 69–97 www.prisonexp.org/pdf/ijcp1973.pdf

Hanmer, J. and Itzin, C. (eds) (2000) *Home Truths about Domestic Violence*. London: Routledge.

Harada, M. (1998) 'Changing relationship between work and leisure after the "bubble economy" in Japan', *Society and Leisure*, 21: 195–212.

Harcourt, B. (2001) *Illusion of Order: The False Promise of Broken Windows Policing*. Cambridge, MA: Harvard University Press.

Harding, R. (2007) 'Sir Mark Potter and the protection of the traditional family: why same-sex marriage is (still) a feminist issue', *Feminist Legal Studies*, 15(2): 223–34.

Harding, T., Oliver, T. and O'Neill, S. (2003) 'Murder fear after naming of IRA spy', *Daily Telegraph*, 12 May.

Hare, B. (2005) *Urban Grimshaw and the Shed Crew*. London: Hodder and Stoughton.

Haritos-Fatouros, M. (2003) *The Psychological Origins of Institutionalized Torture*. London: Routledge.

Harper, T. and Leapman, T. (2006) 'Reid accused of burying bad news by blocking research', *Daily Telegraph*, 2 July.

Hart, H.L.A. (1994) *The Concept of Law* (2nd edn). Oxford: Clarendon Press.

Harvey, D. (1973) *Social Justice and the City*. London: Edward Arnold.

Harwin, N. and Barron, J. (2000) 'Domestic violence and social policy: perspectives from Women's Aid', in J. Hanmer and C. Itzin (eds), *Home Truths about Domestic Violence*. London: Routledge.

Hatzfeld, J. (2005) *A Time for Machetes: The Rwandan Genocide – The Killers Speak* (trans. L. Coverdale). London: Serpent's Tale.

Havel, V. (1978) *The Power of the Powerless: Citizens against the State* (reprinted 1985). New York: M.E. Sharpe.

Havel, V. (1990) 'We live in a contaminated moral environment', in (ed.) (2005), *Speeches that Changed the World: The Stories and Transcripts of the Moments that Made History*. London: Smith-Davies Publishing.

Hay, C. (1995) 'Mobilization through interpellation: James Bulger, juvenile crime and the construction of a moral panic', *Social & Legal Studies*, 4: 197–223.

Hay, C. (1999) *The Political Economy of New Labour*. London: Unwin Hyman.

Hay, C. (2006) '(What's Marxist about) Marxist state theory?', in C. Hay, M. Lister and D. Marsh (eds), *The State: Theories and Issues*. Basingstoke: Palgrave Macmillan.

Hay, D., Linebaugh, P. and Thompson, E.P. and Winslow, C. (1975) *Albion's Fatal Tree*. London: Allen Lane.

Hayes, B. (2008) 'The development of the European Union', unpublished PhD, School of Social Policy, University of Ulster.

Hayes, B. (2009) 'Full Spectrum Dominance as European Union Security Policy: On the trail of the "Neoconopticon"', in K. Haggerty and M. Samatas (eds), *Surveillance and Democracy*. London: Routledge.

Haylett, C. (2001) 'Illegitimate subjects? Abject whites, neoliberal modernisation and middle-class multi-culturalism', *Environment and Planning D: Society and Space*, 19: 351–70.

Hayward, K. and Yar, M. (2006) 'The "chav" phenomenon: consumption, media and the construction of a new underclass', *Crime, Media Culture: An International Journal*, 2(1): 9–28.

Health and Safety Commission (2007) *Statistics of Fatal Injuries 2006/07, Health and Safety Commission/National Statistics*, www.hse.gov.uk/statistics/overall/fatl0607.pdf.

Heidensohn, F. and Gelsthorpe, L. (2007) 'Gender and crime', in M. Maguire, R. Morgan and R. Reiner (eds), *The Oxford Handbook of Criminology* (4th edn). Oxford: Oxford University Press.

Hendrick, H. (2006) 'Histories of youth crime and justice', in B. Goldson and J. Muncie (eds), *Youth Crime and Justice*. London: Sage.

Hennessy, P. (ed.) (2007) *The New Protective State: Government, Intelligence and Terrorism*. London: Continuum.

HMSO (2003) *Anti-Social Behaviour Act*. London: HMSO.

Her Majesty's Crown Prosecution Service Inspectorate/Her Majesty's Inspectorate of Constabulary (2007) *Without Consent: A Report on the Joint Inspection into the Investigation and Prosecution of Cases Involving Allegations of Rape*. London: Her Majesty's Inspectorate of Constabulary.

Herman, E. (2000) 'The propaganda model: a retrospective', *Journalism Studies*, 1(1): 101–12.

Herman, E. and Chomsky, N. (1988) *Manufacturing Consent: The Political Economy of the Mass Media*. New York: Pantheon Books.

Herring, E. and Robinson, P. (2003) 'Too polemical or too critical? Chomsky on the study of the news media and US foreign policy', *Review of International Studies*, 29: 553–68.

Hertz, N. (2001) *The Silent Takeover: Global Capitalism and the Death of Democracy*. London: Arrow.

Heseltine, M. (1987) *Where There's a Will*. London: Hutchinson.

Hewitt, S. (2008) *The British War on Terror*. London: Continuum.

Hills, J. (1988) *Income and Wealth, Vol. 2: A Summary of the Evidence*. York: Joseph Rowntree Foundation.

Hillyard, P. (1993) *Suspect Community*. London: Pluto Press.

Hillyard, P. (2007) 'Law's empire: socio-legal empirical research in the twenty-first century', *Journal of Law and Society*, 34(2): 266–79.

Hillyard, P. and Gordon, D. (1999) 'Arresting statistics', *Journal of Law and Society*, 26(4): 502–22.

Hillyard, P., Pantazis, C., Tombs, S. and Gordon, D. (eds) (2004) *Beyond Criminology: Taking Harm Seriously*. London: Pluto Press.

Hillyard, P., Pantazis, C., Tombs, S., Gordon, D. and Pemberton, S. (2008) *Criminal Obsessions: Why Harm Matters More Than Crime* (2nd edn). London: Centre for Crime and Justice Studies.

Hillyard, P. and Percy-Smith, J. (1988) *The Coercive State: The Decline of Democracy in Britain*. London: Fontana.

Hillyard, P., Sim, J., Tombs, S. and Whyte, D. (2004) 'Leaving a "stain upon the silence": contemporary criminology and the politics of dissent', *British Journal of Criminology*, 44(3): 369–90.

Hillyard, P. and Tombs, S. (2004) 'Beyond criminology?', in P. Hillyard, C. Pantazis, S. Tombs and D. Gordon (eds), *Beyond Criminology: Taking Harm Seriously*. London: Pluto Press.

Hintjens, H.M. (1999) 'Explaining the 1994 genocide in Rwanda', *Journal of Modern African Studies*, 37: 241–86.

Hinton, A.L. (ed.) (2002) *Genocide: An Anthropological Reader*. Oxford: Blackwell.

HMG (2006a) *Report of the Official Account of the Bombings in London on 7 July 2005*, HC 1087. London: HMSO.

HMG (2006b) *Countering International Terrorism: The United Kingdom's Strategy*, Cm 6888. London: HMSO.

Hoare, Q. and Nowell-Smith, G. (eds) (2005) *Antonio Gramsci: Selections from the Prison Notebooks*. London: Lawrence & Wishart.

Hobson, B. (2003) 'Recognition struggles in universalistic and gender distinctive frames: Sweden and Ireland', in B. Hobson (ed.), *Recognition Struggles and Social Movements: Contested Identities, Agency and Power*. Cambridge: Cambridge University Press.

Holdaway, S. (1983) *Inside the British Police*. Oxford: Blackwell.

Holden, C. (1999) 'Globalization: social exclusion and Labour's new work ethic', *Critical Social Policy*, 19(4): 529–38.

Home Office (1990) *Crime, Justice and Protecting the Public*, Cm 965. London: HMSO.

Home Office (1991) *Standing Conference on Crime Prevention: Safer Communities – The Local Delivery of Crime Prevention Through the Partnership Approach*. London: Home Office.

Home Office (1994) *CCTV: Looking Out for You*. London: Home Office.

Home Office (1997) *No More Excuses*, Cm 3809. London: Home Office. www.homeoffice.gov.uk/docs/nme.html.

Home Office (1998) *Guidance on Statutory Crime and Disorder Partnerships: Crime and Disorder Act 1998*. London: Home Office.

Home Office (2001) *Building Cohesive Communities: A Report of the Ministerial Group on Public Order and Community Cohesion*. London: Home Office.

Home Office (2003a) *Respect and Responsibility: Taking a Stand against Anti-Social Behaviour*, CM5778. London: Home Office.

Home Office (2003b) *Home Office Citizenship Survey: People, Families and Communities*. Home Office Research Study No. 289. London: Home Office.

Home Office (2004) *Prince of Wales to Attend First Citizenship Ceremony*, Home Office Press Release. London: Home Office.

Home Office (2006a) *A Coordinated Prostitution Strategy and a Summary of Responses to Paying the Price*. London: Home Office.

Home Office (2006b) *The New Asylum Model: Swifter Decisions – Faster Removals*, Home Office Press Release, 18 January. London: Home Office.

Hope, T. (2004) 'Pretend it works: evidence and governance in the evaluation of the reducing burglary initiative', *Criminal Justice*, 4: 287–308.

Hope, T. (2006) 'Things can only get better', *Criminal Justice Matters*, 62(Winter): 4–5.

Hope, T. (2008) 'A firing squad to shoot the messenger: Home Office peer review of research', in T. Hope and R. Walters, *Critical Thinking about the Uses of Research*. London: Centre for Crime and Justice Studies.

Hope, T. and Walters, R. (2008) *Critical Thinking about the Uses of Research*. London: Centre for Crime and Justice Studies.

House of Bishops (1991) *Issues in Human Sexuality: A Statement by the House of Bishops*. London: Church House Publishing.

House of Commons Home Affairs Committee (2007) *Black Young People and the Criminal Justice System*. London: HMSO, www.parliament.the-stationery-office.co.uk/pa/cm200607/cmselect/cmhaff/181/181i.pdf.

House of Commons Science and Technology Committee (2006) *Scientific Advice, Risk- and Evidence-based Policy Making*. Seventh Report of Session 2005–6 (Vol. 1). London: HMSO.

Howie, M. (2006) 'Executive "airbrushed" criticism from report on youth crime courts', *The Scotsman*, 5 December, p. 2.

Howie, M. (2007) 'Legal aid cash saving plan is a flop', *The Scotsman*, 11 January, www.cabinet-office.gov.uk/seu/2001/Action%20Plan/contents.htm.

Huber, E. and Stephens, J. (2001) *Development and Crisis of the Welfare State: Parties and Policies in Global Markets*. Chicago: Chicago University Press.

Hudson, B. (2003) *Justice in the Risk Society: Challenging and Re-affirming Justice in Late Modernity*. London: Sage.

Hudson, B. (2006) 'Beyond white man's justice: race, gender and justice in late modernity', *Theoretical Criminology*, 10(1): 29–47.

Hudson, B. (2007) 'Diversity, crime and criminal justice', in M. Maguire, R. Morgan and R. Reiner (eds), *The Oxford Handbook of Criminology* (4th edn). Oxford: Oxford University Press.

Huggins, M.K., Haritos-Fatouros, M. and Zimbardo, P.G. (2002) *Violence Workers: Police Torturers and Murderers Reconstruct Brazilian Atrocities*. Berkeley: University of California Press.

Hughes, G. (1998) *Understanding Crime Prevention: Social Control, Risk and Late Modernity*. Buckingham: Open University Press.

Hughes, G. (2002a) 'Crime and disorder reduction partnerships: the future of community safety', in G. Hughes, E. McLaughlin and J. Muncie (eds), *Crime Prevention and Community Safety: New Directions*. London: Sage.

Hughes, G. (2002b) 'Plotting the rise of community safety: critical reflections on research, theory and politics', in G. Hughes and A. Edwards (eds), *Crime Control and Community: The New Politics of Public Safety*. Cullompton: Willan.

Hughes, G. (2007) *The Politics of Crime and Community*. Basingstoke: Palgrave.

Hughes, G., McLaughlin, E. and Muncie, J. (2002) 'Teetering on the edge: the futures of crime control and community safety', in G. Hughes, E. McLaughlin and J. Muncie (eds), *Crime Prevention and Community Safety: New Directions*. London: Sage.

Hunt, J. (1985) 'Police accounts of normal force', *Urban Life*, 13: 315–42.

Hunt, T. (2004) *Building Jerusalem: The Rise and Fall of the Victorian City*. London: Phoenix.

Hunte, J. (1965) *Nigger Hunting in England*? London: West Indian Standing Conference.

Hutter, B. and Williams, G. (eds) (1981) *Controlling Women*. London: Croom Helm.

Igbokwe, U. (2004) 'Treating homosexuality as sickness', *British Medical Journal*, 328(7445): 955.

Ignatieff, M. (1978) *A Just Measure of Pain*. London: Macmillan.

Imrie, R. and Raco, M. (2003) 'New Labour and the turn to community regeneration', in R. Imrie and M. Raco (eds), *Urban Renaissance? New Labour, Community and Urban Policy*. Bristol: The Policy Press.

Innes, M. (1999) 'The media as an investigative resource in murder inquiries', *British Journal of Criminology*, 39(2): 268–85.

Innes, M. (2002) 'Police homicide investigations', *British Journal of Criminology*, 42(4): 669–88.

Institute of Race Relations (1987) *Policing against Black People*. London: Institute of Race Relations.

Institute of Race Relations (1991) *Deadly Silence: Black Deaths in Custody*. London: Institute of Race Relations.

Intelligence and Security Committee (2006) *Report into the London Terrorist Attacks on 7 July 2005*, Cm 6785. London: HMSO.

Itzin, C. (2000) 'Gendering domestic violence: the influence of feminism on policy and practice', in J. Hanmer and C. Itzin (eds), *Home Truths about Domestic Violence*. London: Routledge.

Iwasaki, K., Takahashi, M. and Nakata, Ai, (2006) 'Health problems due to long working hours in Japan: working hours, workers' compensation (*Karoshi*), and preventative measures', *Industrial Health*, 44(4): 537–40.

James, A.L. and James, A. (2001) 'Tightening the net: children, community and control', *British Journal of Sociology*, 52(2): 211–28.

Jamieson, J. (2006) 'New Labour, youth justice and the question of respect', *Youth Justice*, 5(3): 180–93.

Jamieson, J. (2008) 'Respect (government action plan)', in B. Goldson (ed.), *Dictionary of Youth Justice*. Cullompton: Willan.

Jamieson, R. and McEvoy, K. (2005) 'State crime by proxy and juridical othering', *British Journal of Criminology*, 45: 504–27.

Jefferson, T. (2008) 'Policing the crisis revisited: the state, masculinity, fear of crime and racism', *Crime, Media, Culture*, 4(1): 113–21.

Jefferson, T., Sim, J. and Walklate, S. (1992) 'Europe, the left and criminology in the 1990s: accountability, control and the construction of the consumer', in D. Farrington and S. Walklate (eds), *Victims and Offenders: Theory and Policy*. London: British Society of Criminology and the Institute for the Study and Treatment of Delinquency.

Jenkins, S. (2006) *Thatcher and Sons: A Revolution in Three Acts*. London: Allen Lane.

Jessop, B. (1990) *State Theory: Putting Capitalist States in their Place*. Cambridge: Polity Press.

Jessop, B. (1991) 'State theory', paper presented to the Deptartment of Politics, University of Manchester, May.

Jessop, B. (2002) *The Future of the Capitalist State*. Cambridge: Polity Press.

Jessop, B. (2004) 'Critical semiotic analysis and cultural political economy', *Critical Discourse Studies*, 1(2): 159–74.

Jessop, B., Bonnett, K., Bromley, S. and Ling, T. (1984) 'Authoritarian populism, two nations, and Thatcherism', *New Left Review*, 147(Sept.–Oct.): 33–60.

Johnson, P. (2007) 'Ordinary folk and cottaging: law, morality, and public sex', *Journal of Law and Society*, 34(4): 520–43.

Johnstone, G. and Bottomley, K. (1998) 'Labour's crime policy in context', *Policy Studies*, 19(3/4): 173–84.

Jones, C. (1983) *State Social Work and the Working Class*. Basingstoke: Macmillan.

Jones, C. (2001) 'Voices from the front line: social workers and New Labour', *British Journal of Social Work*, 31: 547–62.

Jones, C. and Novak, T. (1985) 'Welfare against the workers: benefits as a political weapon', in H. Beynon (ed.), *Digging Deeper*. London: Verso.

Jones, C. and Novak, T. (1999) *Poverty, Welfare and the Disciplinary State*. London: Routledge.

Jones, C. and Novak, T. (2000) 'Popular welfare', in M. Lavalette and G. Mooney (eds), *Class Struggle and Social Welfare*. London: Routledge.

Jones, D. (1996) 'Tough on crime and nasty to children', *Prison Report*, 36: 4–5.

Jones, D. (2001) 'Misjudged youth: a critique of the Audit Commission's reports on youth justice', *British Journal of Social Work*, 31(1): 57–79.

Jones, P., Hillier, D. and Comfort, D. (2003) 'Business improvement districts in town and city centres in the UK', *Management Research News*, 26(8): 50–9.

Jones, P. and Wilks-Heeg, S. (2004) 'Capitalising culture: Liverpool 2008', *Local Economy*, 19(4): 341–60.

Jones, T. and Newburn, T. (1997) *Policing after the Act: Police and Magistrates' Courts Act 1994*. London: Policy Studies Institute.

Jones, T. and Newburn, T. (2002) 'Learning from Uncle Sam? Exploring US influences on British crime control policy', *Governance: An International Journal of Policy, Administration, and Institutions*, 15(1): 97–119.

Joseph Rowntree Foundation (2007) *Poverty and Wealth across Britain – 1968 to 2005*. York: Joseph Rowntree Foundation.

Joshua, H. and Wallace, T. (1983) *To Ride the Storm: The 1980 Bristol 'Riot' and the State*. London: Heinemann.

Kaldor, M. (2006) *New and Old Wars: Organized Violence in a Global Era* (2nd edn). Cambridge: Polity Press.

Kantola, J. (2005) *Feminists Theorise the State*. Basingstoke: Palgrave.

Karmen, A. (1990) *An Introduction to Victimology*. Belmont, CA: Brooks-Cole.

Karn, J. (2007) *Narratives of Neglect: Community, Regeneration and the Governance of Security*. Cullompton: Willan.

Katz, J. (1988) *Seductions of Crime: Moral and Sensual Attractions in Doing Evil*. New York: Basic Books.

Kauzlarich, D. and Kramer, R.C. (1998) *Crimes of the American Nuclear State: At Home and Abroad*. Boston: Northeastern University Press.

Kegley Jr., C.W. (ed.) (2003) *The New Global Terrorism: Characteristics, Causes, Controls*. Upper Saddle River, NJ: Prentice-Hall.

Keith, M. (1993) *Race, Riots and Policing: Lore and Disorder in a Multi-racist Society*. London: UCL Press.

Kelman, H.C. and Hamilton, V.L. (1989) *Crimes of Obedience: Toward a Social Psychology of Authority and Responsibility*. New Haven, CT: Yale University Press.

Kelsen, H. (1967) *Pure Theory of Law*. Berkeley: University of California Press.

Kennedy, P. (2008) *Report of the Interception of Communications Commissioner for 2006*, HC 252. London: HMSO.

Kettle, M. and Hodges, M. (1982) *Uprising! The Police, the People and the Riots in Britain's Cities*. London: Pan Books.

Kidd-Hewitt, D. and Osborne, R. (eds) (1995) *Crime and the Media: The Post-Modern Spectacle*. London: Pluto Press.

King, N. (1999) *Heroes in Hard Times: Cop Action Movies in the US*. Philadelphia, PA: Temple University Press.

Kinsey, R. (1979) 'Despotism and legality', in B. Fine et al. (eds), *Capitalism and the Rule of Law: From Deviancy Theory to Marxism*. London: Hutchinson.

Kinsey, R., Lea, J. and Young, J. (1986) *Losing the Fight against Crime*. Oxford: Blackwell.

Klaehn, J. (2002) 'A critical review and assessment of Herman and Chomsky's "Propaganda Model"', *European Journal of Communication*, 17(2): 147–82.

Klaehn, J. (2003) 'Behind the invisible curtain of scholarly criticism: revisiting the Propaganda Model', 4(3): 359–69.

Klockars, K. (1996) 'A theory of excessive force and its control', in W.A. Gellner and H. Toch (eds), *Police Violence*. New Haven, CT: Yale University Press.

Knepper, P. (2007) *Criminology and Social Policy*. London: Sage.

Knightley, P. (1986) *The Second Oldest Profession: The Spy as Patriot, Bureaucrat, Fantasist and Whore*. London: Andre Deutsch.

Koo, J. and Cox, M. (2008) 'An economic interpretation of suicide: cycles in Japan', *Contemporary Economic Policy*, 26(1): 162–74.

Kramer, R.C. and Michalowski, R.J. (2005) 'War, aggression and state crime: a criminological analysis of the invasion and occupation of Iraq', *British Journal of Criminology*, 45: 446–64.

Kundnani, A. (2001) 'From Oldham to Bradford: the violence of the violated', *Race and Class*, 43(2): 105–10.

Kundnani, A. (2007a) *The End of Tolerance: Racism in 21st Century Britain*. London: Pluto Press.

Kundnani, A. (2007b) 'Integrationism: the politics of anti-Muslim racism', *Race and Class*, 48(4): 24–44.

Kundnani, A. (2007c) 'How liberals lost their anti-racism', *Institute of Race Relations News*, 3 October, www.irr.org.uk/2007/october/ha000008.html.

La'Porte, V. (1999) *An Attempt to Understand the Muslim Reaction to the Satanic Verses*. New York: The Edwin Mellen Press.

Lacey, N. (1994) 'Introduction: making sense of criminal justice', in N. Lacey (ed.), *A Reader on Criminal Justice*. Oxford: Oxford University Press.

LaFeber, W. (1988) 'Whose News?', *New York Times*, 6 November.

Lang, K. and Lang, G. (2004a) 'Noam Chomsky and the manufacture of consent for American foreign policy', *Political Communication*, 21(1): 93–101.

Lang, K. and Lang, G. (2004b) 'Response to Herman and Chomsky', *Political Communication*, 21(1): 109–11.

Lavalette, M. (2006) *George Lansbury and the Rebel Councillors of Poplar*. London: Bookmarks Publications.

Lavalette, M. and Money, G. (eds) (2000) *Class Struggle and Social Welfare*. London: Routledge.

Law, A. and Mooney, G. (2006) '"We've never had it so good": the "problem" of the working class in devolved Scotland', *Critical Social Policy*, 26: 523–42.

Law, I. (1981) *A History of Race and Racism in Liverpool, 1660–1950*. Liverpool: Merseyside Community Relations Council.

Lawrence, D. and Busby, M. (2006) *And Still I Rise: Seeking Justice for Stephen*. London: Faber & Faber.

Layard, R. (2003) 'Happiness: has social science a clue?', Lionel Robbins Memorial Lectures. London: London School of Economics.

Lea, J. and Young, J. (1984) *What is to be Done about Law and Order?* Harmondsworth: Penguin.

Lea, J. and Young, J. (1993) *What is to be Done about Law and Order?* (2nd edn). London: Pluto Press.

Lea, J., Jones, T. and Young, J. (1986) *Saving the Inner City – Broadwater Farm: A Strategy for Survival*. London: Middlesex Polytechnic.

Lee, J.A. (1981) 'Some structural aspects of police deviance in relations with minority groups', in C. Shearing (ed.), *Organisational Police Deviance*. Toronto: Butterworth.

Lee, Y.-S. and Yeoh, B. (2004) 'Introduction: globalisation and the politics of forgetting', *Urban Studies*, 41(12): 2295–301.

Lees, L. (2003) 'Visions of "Urban Renaissance": the Urban Task Force report and the Urban White Paper', in R. Imrie and M. Raco (eds), *Urban Renaissance? New Labour, Community and Urban Policy*. Bristol: The Policy Press.

Lees, S. (1996) *Carnal Knowledge*. London: Hamish Hamilton.

Lefebvre, H. (1996) *Writings on Cities*. London: Blackwell.

Leishman, F. and Mason, P. (2003) *Policing and the Media: Facts, Fictions and Factions*. Cullompton: Willan.

Levitas, R. (2000) 'Community, Utopia and New Labour', *Local Economy*, 15(3): 188–97.

Levitas, R. (2005) *The Inclusive Society: Social Exclusion and New Labour*. Basingstoke: Palgrave.

Lewis, J., Williams, A. and Franklin, B. (2008) 'A compromised Fourth Estate?: UK news journalism, public relations and news sources', *Journalism Studies*, 9(1): 1–20.

Liberty (2005) *Summary of the Prevention of Terrorism Act 2005*. London: Liberty.

Lifton, R.J. (1986) *The Nazi Doctors: Medical Killing and the Psychology of Genocide*. London: Macmillan.

Lilja, M., Mansson, I., Jahlenius, L. and Sacco-Peterson, M. (2003) 'Disability policy in Sweden: policies concerning assistive technology and home modification', *Journal of Disability Policy Studies*, 14(3): 130–5.

Liverpool City Council (2007) *Accelerating Delivery: Challenging Perceptions*. Liverpool: Liverpool First.

Loader, I. and Walker, N. (2001) 'Policing as a public good: reconstituting the connections between policing and the state', *Theoretical Criminology*, 5(1): 9–35.

Loader, I. and Walker, N. (2006) 'Necessary virtues: the legitimate place of the state in the production of security', in J. Wood and B. Dupont (eds), *Democracy, Society and the Governance of Security*. Cambridge: Cambridge University Press.

Loader, I. and Walker, N. (2007) *Civilising Security*. Cambridge: Cambridge University Press.

Lobban, P. (2005) 'Speech to the London Construction Awards', 11 October. London: Construction Industry Training Board.

Logan, J. and Molotch, H. 'The city as a growth machine', in J. Lin and C. Mele (eds) (2005), *The Urban Sociology Reader*. London: Routlege.

London Assembly Health and Public Services Committee (2005) *Building London, Saving Lives: Improving Health and Safety in Construction*. London: Greater London Authority.

Lowe, R. (1993) *The Welfare State in Britain since 1945*. Basingstoke: Macmillan.

Lupton, C. (1994) 'The British Refuge Movement: the survival of an ideal?', in C. Lupton and T. Gillespie (eds), *Working with Violence*. Basingstoke: Macmillan.

Lupton, C. and Gillespie, T. (eds) (1994) *Working with Violence*. Basingstoke: Macmillan.

Lustgarten, L. and Leigh, I. (1994) *In from the Cold: National Security and Parliamentary Democracy*. Oxford: Clarendon Press.

MacIntyre, D. (2003) 'Major on Crime: Condemn more, understand less', *Independent on Sunday*, 21 February 1993. http://www.independent.co.uk/news/major-on-crime-condemn-more-under-stand-less-1474470.html (accessed 2 March 2009).

Macnicol, J. (1987) 'In pursuit of the underclass', *Journal of Social Policy*, 16(3): 293–318.

MacPhee, C. (2007) 'Senior lecturer resigns over exec "corruption"', *Brig* (Stirling University student newspaper) Feb., p. 1.

Macpherson, W. (1999) *The Stephen Lawrence Inquiry*. Cm 4264-I. London: HMSO.

Maguire, M., Morgan, R. and Reiner, R. (eds) (2007) *The Oxford Handbook of Criminology* (4th edn). Oxford: Oxford University Press (1st edn, 1994).

Mahmood, C.K. (2000) 'Trials by fire: dynamics of terror in Punjab and Kashmir', in J.A. Sluka (ed.), *Death Squad*. Philadelphia, PA: University of Pennsylvania Press.

Mahon, R. (1979) 'Regulatory agencies: captive agents or hegemonic apparatuses?', *Studies in Political Economy*, 1(1): 162–200.

Maidment, B.E. (2000) '"Penny" wise, "penny" foolish? Popular periodicals and the "march of the intellect" in the 1820s and 1830s', in L. Brake, B. Bell and D. Finkelstein (eds), *Nineteenth Century Media and the Construction of Identities*. London: Palgrave.

Malik, K. (2006) 'Multiculturalism and the road to terror', KenanMalik.com, www.kenanmalik.com/essays/muslims_handelsblatt.html.

Mann, M. (1986) *The Sources of Social Power. Vol. I: A History of Power from the Beginning to 1760 AD*. Cambridge: Cambridge University Press.

Mann, M. (1993) *The Sources of Social Power. Vol. II: The Rise of Classes and Nation-States, 1760–1914*. Cambridge: Cambridge University Press.

Manning, P. (1998) *Spinning for Labour: Trade Unions and the New Media Environment*. Aldershot: Aldgate.

Manning, P. (2001) *News and News Sources: A Critical Introduction*. London: Sage.

Manningham-Buller, E. (2007) 'The international terrorist threat to the United Kingdom', in P. Hennessy (ed.), *The New Protective State: Government, Intelligence and Terrorism*. London: Continuum.

Marchak, P. (1999) *God's Assassins: State Terrorism in Argentina in the 1970s*. Montreal: McGill-Queen's University Press.

Marriott, J. (1999) 'In darkest England: the poor, the crowd and race in the nineteenth century metropolis', in P. Cohen (ed.), *New Ethnicities, Old Racisms*. London: Zed Books. pp. 82–100.

Marsh, D. and Rhodes, R. (eds) (1992) *Policy Networks in British Government*. Oxford: Clarendon Press.

Marshall, S.L.A. (1947) *Men against Fire*. New York: W. Morrow.

Marty, D. (2007) *Alleged Secret Detentions and Unlawful Inter-state Transfers of Detainees Involving Council of Europe Member States: Second Report*. Parliamentary Assembly, Council of Europe, 11 June.

Maruna, S. and King, A. (2004) 'Public opinion and community penalties', in A.E. Bottoms, S.A. Rex and G. Robinson (eds), *Alternatives to Prison: Options in an Insecure Society*. Cullompton: Willan.

Marx, K. and Engels, F. (1976) *Collected Works, Vol. 5* (trans. Richard Dixon). New York: International Publishers.

Maslow, A. (1954) *Motivation and Personality*. New York: Harper.

Mason, P. (2006) 'Lies, distortion and what doesn't work: monitoring prison stories in the British media', *Crime, Media, Culture*, 3(2): 251–67.

Mason, P. (2007) 'Misinformation, myth and distortion: how the press construct imprisonment in Britain', *Journalism Studies*, 8(3): 481–96.

Mason, P., Gross, B. and Mendes, K. (2006a) *Bulletin* No. 1 (Feb.). Cardiff: Prison Media Monitoring Unit, www.jc2m.co.uk/MarchBulletin.pdf.

Mason, P., Gross, B. and Mendes, K. (2006b) *Bulletin* No. 2 (March). Cardiff: Prison Media Monitoring Unit, www.jc2m.co.uk/MarchBulletin.pdf.

Mason, P., Gross, B. and Mendes, K. (2006c) *Bulletin* No. 3 (Apr.). Cardiff: Prison Media Monitoring Unit, www.jc2m.co.uk/MarchBulletin.pdf.

Mathiesen, T. (1974) *The Politics of Abolition*. London: Martin Robertson.

Mathiesen, T. (1997) 'The viewer society: Michel Foucault's panopticon revisited', *Theoretical Criminology*, 1(2): 215–34.

Mathiesen, T. (2001) 'Television, public space and prison population: a commentary on Mauer and Simon', *Punishment and Society*, 3(1): 35–42.

Mathiesen, T. (2003) 'Contemporary penal policy – a study in moral panics', European Committee on Crime Problems, 22nd Criminological Research Conference, Strasbourg.

Mathiesen, T. (2004) *Silently Silenced*. Winchester: Waterside Press.

Matthews, N. (1994) *Confronting Rape*. London: Routledge.

Matthews, R. (2003) 'Enforcing respect and reducing responsibility: a response to the White Paper on anti-social behaviour', *Community Safety Journal*, 2(4): 5–8.

Mauer, M. (2002) 'Mass imprisonment and the disappearing votes', in M. Mauer and M. Chesney-Lind (eds), *Invisible Punishment: The Collateral Consequences of Mass imprisonment*. New York: New Press.

Mawby, R. (2002) *Policing Images: Policing, Communication and Legitimacy*. Cullompton: Willan.

Mawby, R. (2003) 'Completing the half-formed picture? Media images of policing', in P. Mason (ed.), *Criminal Visions: Media Representatrions of Crime and Justice*. Cullompton: Willan.

Mawby, R. and Walklate, S. (1994) *Critical Victimology*. London: Sage.

Mayer, J. and Timms, N. (1970) *The Client Speaks*. London: Routledge and Kegan Paul.

McBarnet, D. (1981) *Conviction: Law, State and the Construction of Justice*. London: Macmillan.

McCann, E. (1981) 'The British press and Northern Ireland', in S. Cohen and J. Young (eds), *The Manufacture of News: Deviance, Social Problems and the Mass Media*. London: Constable.

McCartney, J. (2005) 'Foreword', in London Assembly Health and Public Services Committee, *Building London, Saving Lives: Improving Health and Safety in Construction*. London: Greater London Authority.

McChesney, R. and Nichols, J. (2002) *Our Media, Not Theirs: The Democratic Struggle against Corporate Media*. New York: Seven Stories Press.

McCulloch, J. (2001) *Blue Army: Paramilitary Policing in Australia*. Melbourne: Melbourne University Press.

McKelvey, T. (ed.) (2007) *One of the Guys: Women as Aggressors and Torturers*. Emeryville, CA: Seal Press.

McKie, L. (2005) *Families, Violence and Social Change*. Maidenhead: Open University Press.

McLaughlin, E. (1994) *Community, Policing and Accountability: The Policing of Manchester in the 1980s*. Aldershot: Avebury.

McLaughlin, E. (2002) '"Same bed, different dreams": postmodern reflections on crime prevention and community safety', in G. Hughes and A. Edwards (eds), *Crime Control and Community: The New Politics of Public Safety*. Cullompton: Willan.

McLaughlin, E. (2008) 'Hitting the panic button: policing/'mugging'/media/crisis', *Crime, Media, Culture*, 4(1): 145–54.

McMahon, B.M.E. (1974) 'The impaired asset: a legal commentary on the report of the Widgery Tribunal', *The Human Context*, VI: 681–99.

McNay, L. (2004) 'Situated intersubjectivity', in B. Marshall and A. Witz (eds), *Engendering the Social: Feminist Encounters with Sociological Theory*. Maidenhead: Open University Press.

McRobbie, A. (1994) 'Folk devils fight back', *New Left Review*, 202: 107–16.

McRobbie, A. and Thornton, S.L. (1995) 'Rethinking "moral panic" for multi-mediated social worlds', *British Journal of Sociology*, 46(4): 559–74.

Melossi, D. (1979) 'Institutions of social control and capitalist organization of work', in B. Fine et al. (eds), *Capitalism and the Rule of Law: From Deviancy Theory to Marxism*. London: Hutchinson.

Metropolitan Police Authority (2007) 'Counter-terrorism: The London Debate', February. London: Metropolitan Police Authority.

Michalowski, R. and Kramer, R. (2006) *State–Corporate Crime: Wrongdoing at the Intersection of Business and Government*. New Brunswick, NJ: Rutgers University Press.

Miers, D. (1978) *Responses to Victimization*. Abingdon: Professional Books.

Mies, M. (1991) *Patriarchy and Accumulation on a World Scale: Women in the International Division of Labour*. London: Zed Books.

Milgram, S. (1974) *Obedience to Authority*. New York: Harper & Row.

Miliband, R. (1969) *The State in Capitalist Society*. London: Quartet Books.

Miliband, R. (1977) *Marxism and Politics*. Oxford: Oxford University Press.

Miller, D. (1993) 'The Northern Ireland Information Service and the media: aims, strategy, tactics', in J. Eldridge (ed.), *Getting the Message: News, Truth and Power*. London: Routledge.

Miller, D. (1994) *Don't Mention the War: Northern Ireland, Propaganda and the Media*. London: Pluto Press.

Miller, D. and Reilly, J. (1994) *Food 'Scares' in the Media*. Glasgow: Glasgow Media Group.

Miller, D. and Williams, K. (1998) 'Sourcing AIDS news', in D. Miller, J. Kitzinger, K. Williams and P. Beharrell (eds), *The Circuit of Mass Communication*. Glasgow: Glasgow Media Group.

Miller, J. (2001) 'Bringing the individual back in: a commentary on Wacquant and Anderson', *Punishment and Society*, 3(1): 153–60.

Miller, P. and Rose, N. (1990) 'Governing economic life', *Economy and Society*, 19(1): 1–29.

Miller, S. and Markle, J. (2002) 'Social policy in the US: workfare and the American low wage labour market', in P. Townsend and D. Gordon (eds), *World Poverty: New Policies to Defeat an Old Enemy*. Bristol: The Policy Press.

Miller, S.L. (2005) *Victims as Offenders: The Paradox of Women's Violence in Relationships*. New Brunswick, NJ: Rutgers University Press.

Milne, K. (2005) *Manufacturing Dissent: Single-issue Protest, the Public and the Press*. London: Demos, www.demos.co.uk/files/manufacturingdissent.pdf.

Milne, S. (2004) *The Enemy Within*. London: Verso.

Milne, S. (2007) 'Pointless attack on liberty that fuels the terror threat', *The Guardian*, 8 November.

Mizen, P. (2004) *The Changing State of Youth*. Basingstoke: Palgrave Macmillan.

Monbiot, G. (2001) *Captive State: The Corporate Takeover of Britain*. London: Macmillan.

Mooney, G. (2004) 'Cultural policy and urban transformation? Critical reflections on Glasgow, European City of Culture 1990', *Local Economy*, 19(4): 327–40.

Mooney, J. (2000) 'Revealing the hidden figure of domestic violence', in J. Hanmer and C. Itzin (eds), *Home Truths about Domestic Violence: Feminist Influences on Policy and Practices*. London: Routledge.

Moore, R. (1975) *Racism and Black Resistance in Britain*. London: Pluto Press.

Morgan, R. (2000) 'The Politics of Criminological Research', in R. King and E. Wincup (eds), *Doing Research on Crime and Justice*. Oxford: Oxford University Press.

Morgan, R. and Newburn, T. (2007) 'Youth justice', in M. Maguire, R. Morgan and R. Reiner (eds), *The Oxford Handbook of Criminology* (4th edn). Oxford: Oxford University Press.

Morris, G. (2007) 'The real prison numbers scandal', *The Independent*, 6 December.

Morrison, Z. (2003) 'Cultural justice and addressing 'social exclusion': a case study of a Single Regeneration Budget project in Blackbird Leys, Oxford', in R. Imrie and M. Raco (eds), *Urban Renaissance? New Labour, Community and Urban Policy*. Bristol: The Policy Press.

Morrissey, B. (2003) *When Women Kill*. London: Routledge.

Mosco, V. (1995) *The Political Economy of Communication*. London: Sage.

Mosley, L. (2005) 'Globalisation and the state: still room to move?', *New Political Economy*, 10(3): 356–62.

Muir, Jr, W.K. (1977) *Police: Streetcorner Politicians*. Chicago, IL: University of Chicago Press.

Muncie, J. (1998) 'Reassessing competing paradigms in criminological theory', in P. Walton and J. Young (eds), *The New Criminology Revisited*. London: Macmillan.

Muncie, J. (2000a) 'Decriminalising criminology', in G. Lewis, S. Gerwitz and J. Clarke (eds), *Rethinking Social Policy*. London: Sage.

Muncie, J. (2000b) 'Pragmatic realism? Searching for criminology in the new youth justice', in B. Goldson (ed.), *The New Youth Justice*. London: Russell House Publishing.

Muncie, J. (2002c) 'Failure never matters: detention centres and the politics of deterrence', in J. Muncie, G. Hughes and E. McLaughlin (eds), *Youth Justice: Critical Readings*. London: Sage.

Muncie, J. (2004) *Youth and Crime: A Critical Introduction* (2nd edn). London: Sage.

Muncie, J. (2006) 'Governing young people: coherence and contradiction in contemporary youth justice', *Critical Social Policy*, 26(4): 770–93.

Muncie, J. and Goldson, B. (2005) 'England and Wales: the new correctionalism', in J. Muncie and B. Goldson (eds), *International Developments in Juvenile Justice*. London: Sage.

Muncie J. and Hughes, G. (2002) 'Modes of youth governance: political rationalities, criminalization and resistance', in J. Muncie, G. Hughes and E. McLaughlin (eds), *Youth Justice: Critical Readings*. London: Sage.

Murdock, G. and Golding, P. (1973) 'For a political economy of mass communications', in R. Miliband and J. Saville (eds), *Socialist Register*. London: Merlin Press.

Murray, C. (1990) *The Emerging British Underclass*. London: Institute of Economic Affairs, Health and Welfare Unit.

Murray, C. (1994) 'The new Victorians ... and the new rabble', *The Sunday Times*, 29 May. Reproduced in R. Lister (ed.) (1996) *Charles Murray and the Underclass: The Developing Debate*. Choice in Welfare No. 33. London: The Health and Welfare Unit.

Murray, C. (2005) 'The advantages of social apartheid', *The Sunday Times*, 3 April.

Mydans, S. (2007) 'What makes a monk mad', *The New York Times*, 30 September.

Navarro, V. and Shi, L. (2001) 'The political context of social inequalities and health', *Social Science and Medicine*, 52(3): 481–91.

Nazir-Ali, M. (2006) 'Multiculturalism is to blame for perverting young Muslims', *Telegraph Online*, 15 August, www.telegraph.co.uk/opinion/main.jhtml?xml=/opinion/2006/08/15/do1501.xml.

Nellis, M. (2001) 'Community penalities in historical perspective', in A.E. Bottoms, L. Gelsthorpe and S. Rex (eds), *Community Penalities: Change and Challenges*. Cullompton: Willan.

Nelson, J. (1989) *Sultans of Sleaze: Public Relations and the Media*. Toronto: Between the Lines.

Neocleous, M. (2000) 'The social police and mechanisms of prevention: Patrick Colquhoun and the condition of poverty', *British Journal of Criminology*, 40: 710–26.

Neocleous, M. (2003) *Imagining the State*. Maidenhead: Open University Press.

Nessein, T. (2003) 'Markets versus planning: an assessment of the Swedish housing model in the post-war period', *Urban Studies*, 40(7): 1259–82.

Newburn, T. (2002) 'Young people, crime and youth justice', in M. Maguire, R. Morgan and R. Reiner (eds), *The Oxford Handbook of Criminology* (3rd edn). Oxford: Oxford University Press.

Newburn, T. (2007) *Criminology*. Cullompton: Willan.

Ní Aolain, F. (2000) *The Politics of Force: Conflict Management and State Violence in Northern Ireland*. Belfast: Blackstaff Press.

Nicholas, S., Kershaw, C. and Walker, A. (2007) *Crime in England and Wales*. London: HMSO.

Norrie, A. (1993) *Crime, Reason and History: A Critical Introduction to Criminal Law*. London: Butterworths.

Novak, T. (1988) *Poverty and the State*. Milton Keynes: Open University Press.

Nyman, C. (1999) 'Gender equality in "the most equal country in the world"? Money and marriage in Sweden', *The Sociological Review*, 47(4): 766–93.

Nzongola-Ntalaja, G. (2002) *The Congo from Leopold to Kabila: A People's History*. London: Zed Books.

O'Donnell, I. (2003) 'A new paradigm for understanding violence? Testing the limits of Lonnie Athens' theory', *British Journal of Criminology*, 43: 750–71.

O'Kane, R.T. (1996) *Terror, Force and States*. Cheltenham: Edward Elgar.

O'Malley, J. (1977) *The Politics of Community Action: A Decade of Struggle in Notting Hill*. Nottingham: Bertrand Russell Peace Foundation.

O'Neill, B. (2006) 'Watching you, watching me', *New Statesman*, 2 October.

OECD (2003) *Transforming Disability into Ability: Policies to Promote Work and Income Security for Disabled People*. Paris: OECD.

OECD (2006a) *Measures of Material Deprivation in OECD Countries*. OECD Social, Employment and Migration Working Paper No. 37. Paris: OECD

OECD (2006b) *Society at a Glance: OECD Social Indicators* (2006 edn). Paris: OECD.

OECD (2007a) *Babies and Bosses – Reconciling Work and Family Life: A Synthesis of Findings for OECD Countries*. (Vol 5). Paris: OECD.

OECD (2007b) *Factbook 2007: Economic, Environmental and Social Statistics*. Paris: OECD.

Office for National Statistics (2007) 'News release: more than 18,000 civil partnerships formed', London: Office for National Statistics.

Oliver, J. (2005) 'Colditz camps for families from hell', *The Mail on Sunday*, 9 October.

Osawa, M. (2000) 'Government approaches to gender equality in the mid-1990s', *Social Science Japan Journal*, 3(1): 3–19.

Osborne, D. and Gaebler, T. (1992) *Reinventing Government: How the Entrepreneurial Spirit is Transforming the Public Sector*. Reading, MA: Addison-Wesley.

Osiel, M. (2001) *Mass Atrocity, Ordinary Evil and Hannah Arendt*. New Haven, CT: Yale University Press.

Panitch, L. (2000) 'The new imperial state', *New Left Review*, 2(Mar./Apr.): 5–20.

Pantazis, C. (2004) 'Gendering harm from a life course perspective', in P. Hillyard, C. Pantazis, S. Tombs and D. Gordon (eds), *Beyond Criminology: Taking Harm Seriously*. London: Pluto Press.

Pantazis, C. and Pemberton, S. (2006) 'The new suspect communities: an examination of the impacts of recent UK counter-terrorist measures', The Social Impacts of the War on Terror, British Academy Seminar, Melbourne Trades Hall, 12–13 July.

Pantazis, C. and Pemberton, S. (2008) 'Globalization, governance and the UK's domestic "war on terror"', in P. Kennett (ed.), *Governance, Globalization and Public Policy*. Cheltenham: Edward Elgar.

Pantazis, C., Gordon, D. and Levitas, R. (eds) (2006) *Poverty and Social Exclusion in Britain: The Millennium Survey*. Bristol: The Policy Press.

Parry, C. (2007) 'Lecturer quits in research row', *The Stirling Observer*, 5 January.

Passas, N. (1990) 'Anomie and corporate deviance', *Contemporary Crises*, 14: 157–78.

Patten, Lord (1999) *A New Beginning: Policing in Northern Ireland. The Report of the Independent Commission on Policing in Northern Ireland* (Patten Report). Belfast: Northern Ireland Office.

Pavlich, G. (1999) 'Criticism and criminology: in search of legitimacy', *Theoretical Criminology*, (3): 29–50.

Peakin, W. (2006) 'Censored: the Executive stands accused of manipulating the work of independent researchers and misleading the public on success of its policies', *Holyrood, The Official Magazine of the Scottish Parliament*, December: 24–6.

Pearce, F. (1973) 'Crime, corporations and the American social order', in I. Taylor and L. Taylor (eds), *Politics and Deviance*. Harmondsworth: Penguin.

Pearce, F. (1976) *Crimes of the Powerful: Marxism, Crime and Deviance*. London: Pluto Press.

Pearce, F. and Tombs, S. (1990) 'Ideology, hegemony and empiricism: compliance theories of regulation', *British Journal of Criminology*, Autumn: 423–43.

Pearce, F. and Tombs, S. (1991) 'Policing corporate "Skid Rows": safety, compliance, and hegemony', *British Journal of Criminology*, Autumn: 415–26.

Pearce, F. and Tombs, S. (1998) *Toxic Capitalism: Corporate Crime and the Chemical Industry*. Aldershot: Ashgate.

Pearce, F. and Tombs, S. (2001) 'Crime, corporations and the "new" social order', in G. Potter (ed.), *Controversies in White-collar Crime*. Cincinnati, OH: Anderson.

Pearson, G. (1983) *Hooligan: A History of Respectable Fears*. London: Macmillan.

Pemberton, S. (2004) 'The production of harm in the United Kingdom: a social harm perspective', PhD dissertation, University of Bristol, Bristol.

Pemberton, S. (2005) 'Deaths in police custody: the acceptable consequences of a law and order society?', *Outlines: Critical Social Studies*, 7(2): 23–42.

Pemberton, S. (2007) 'Social harm future(s): exploring the potential of the social harm approach', *Crime, Law and Social Change*, 48(1–2): 27–41.

Pemberton, S. (2008) 'Demystifying deaths in police custody: challenging state talk', *Social and Legal Studies*, 17(2): 237–62.

Penna, S. (2005) 'The Children Act 2004: child protection and social surveillance', *Journal of Social Welfare and Family Law*, 27(2): 143–57.

Petras, J. (1997) 'Imperialism and NGOs in Latin America', *Monthly Review*, 49(7) www. monthlyreview. org/1297petr.htm.

Phillips, C. and Bowling, B. (2007) 'Ethnicities, racism, crime and criminal justice', in M. Maguire, R. Morgan and R. Reiner (eds), *The Oxford Handbook of Criminology* (4th edn). Oxford: Oxford University Press.

Phoenix, J. and Oerton, S. (2005) *Illicit and Illegal: Sex, Regulation and Social Control*. Cullompton: Willan.

Piachaud, D. (1987) 'Problems in the definition and measurement of poverty', *Journal of Social Policy*, 16(2): 146–64.

Pickering, S. (2002) *Women, Policing and Resistance in Northern Ireland*. Belfast: Beyond the Pale.

Pilger, J. (1998) *Hidden Agendas*. London: Vintage.

Pilger, J. (2006) *Freedom Next Time*. London: Bantam Press.

Pilkington, E. (1988) *Beyond the Mother Country: West Indians and the Notting Hill White Riots*. London: I.B. Tauris.

Píon-Berlin, D. (1989) *The Ideology of State Terror: Economic Doctrine and Political Repression in Argentina and Peru*. London: Rienner.

Pitts, J. (1988) *The Politics of Juvenile Crime*. London: Sage.

Pitts, J. (1990) *Working with Young Offenders*. London: Macmillan.

Pitts, J. (2000) 'The new youth justice and the politics of electoral anxiety', in B. Goldson (ed.), *The New Youth Justice*. Lyme Regis: Russell House Publishing.

Pitts, J. (2001) *The New Politics of Youth Crime: Discipline or Solidarity?* Lyme Regis: Russell House Publishing.

Pitts, J. (2008) *Reluctant Gangsters: The Changing Face of Youth Crime*. Cullompton: Willan.

Police Ombudsman for Northern Ireland (2007) 'Statement of the Police Ombudsman for Northern Ireland on her investigation into the circumstances of the death of Raymond McCord Junior and related matters'. Belfast: Police Ombudsman for Northern Ireland.

Poulantzas, N. (1975) *Classes in Contemporary Capitalism*. London: New Left Books.

Poulantzas, N. (1978a) *Political Power and Social Classes*. London: Verso.

Poulantzas, N. (1978b) *State, Power, Socialism*. London: New Left Books.

Poulantzas, N. (2000) *State, Power, Socialism* (new edition with an introduction by Stuart Hall). London: Verso.

Powell, M. (2007) *Understanding the Mixed Economy*. Bristol: The Policy Press.

Poynter, J.R. (1969) *Society and Pauperism: English Ideas on Poor Relief 1795–1834*. London: Routledge and Kegan Paul.

Poynting, S., Noble, G., Tabar, P. and Collins, J. (2004) *Bin Laden in the Suburbs: Criminalising the Arab Other*. Sydney: Sydney Institute of Criminology.

Pratt, J. (1989) 'Corporatism: the third model of juvenile justice', *British Journal of Criminology*, 29(3): 226–54.

Presdee, M. and Walters, R. (1999) 'Governing criminological knowledge – "state", power and the politics of criminological research', in M. Corsianos and J. Train (eds), *Interrogating Social Justice: Culture, Politics and Identity*. Toronto: Canadian Scholars Press.

Prison Reform Trust (2007) *Bromley Briefings: Prison Factfile, May 2007*. London: Prison Reform Trust.

Prosser, T. (1997) *Law and the Regulators*. Oxford: Clarendon Press.

Quinney, R. (1975) 'Crime control in capitalist society: a critical philosophy of legal order', in I. Taylor, P. Walton and J. Young (eds), *Critical Criminology*. London: Routledge.

Radford, J. and Stanko, E. (1991) 'Violence against women and children: the contradictions of crime control under patriarchy', in K. Stenson and D. Cowell (eds), *The Politics of Crime Control*. London: Sage.

Ramamurthy, A. (2006) 'The politics of Britain's Asian youth movements', *Race and Class*, 48(2): 38–60.

Ray, L. and Smith, D. (2001) 'Racist offenders and the politics of "hate crime"', *Law and Critique*, 12: 203–21.

Reid, J. (2007) John Reid interview transcript on *The Politics Show*, Sunday 11 February, www.news.bbc.co.uk/1/hi/programmes/politics_show/6337799.stm.

Reid, M. (2007) 'Nearly all cameras are illegal', *The Times*, 31 May.

Reiman, J. (1979) *The Rich Get Richer and the Poor Get Prison: Ideology, Class and Criminal Justice*. New York: John Wiley.

Reiner, R. (2000) 'Romantic realism: policing and the media', in F. Leishman, B. Loveday and S. Savage (eds), *Core Issues in Policing*. Cullompton: Willan.

Reiner, R. (2007) 'Media-made criminality: the representation of crime in the mass media', in R. Reiner, M. Maguire and R. Morgan (eds), *The Oxford Handbook of Criminology* (4th edn). Oxford: Oxford University Press.

Reiner, R., Livingstone, S. and Allen, J. (2003) 'From law and order to lynch mobs: crime news since the Second World War', in P. Mason and Paul (eds), *Criminal Visions: Media Representations of Crime and Justice*. Cullompton: Willan.

REMHI (Recovery of Historical Memory Project) (1999) *Guatemala: Never Again!* Maryknoll, NY: Orbis.

Renderson, J. (2006) 'DNA of 37% of black men held by the police', *The Guardian*, 5 January .

Research Development and Statistics Directorate (2004) *Ethnicity, Victimisation and Worry about Crime: Findings from the 2001/02 and 2002/03 British Crime Surveys*. London: Research Development and Statistics Directorate.

Rhodes, R.W. (1996) 'The new governance: governing without government', *Political Studies*, 44: 652–67.

Rhodes, R.W. (1997) *Understanding Governance: Policy Networks, Governance, Reflexivity and Accountability*. Milton Keynes: Open University Press.

Rice, J., Bather, H., Slack, A., McHarron, S. and Slack, C. (2005) 'Section 30 scandal exposed', *Nerve*, 6, www.catalystmedia.org.uk/issues/nerve6/section30.htm.

Richan, W.C. and Mendelsohn, A.R. (1973) *Social Work: The Unloved Profession*. New York: New Viewpoints.

Richardson, J. (2007) *Analysing Newspapers: An Approach from Critical Discourse Analysis*. New York: Palgrave Macmillan.

Riddle, P. (1989) *The Thatcher Effect*. Oxford: Blackwell.

Risse, T., Ropp, S.C. and Sikkink, K. (eds) (1999) *The Power of Human Rights: International Norms and Domestic Change*. Cambridge: Cambridge University Press.

Risse, T. and Sikkink, K. (1999) 'The socialization of international human rights norms into domestic practice: introduction', in T. Risse, S.C. Ropp and K. Sikkink (eds), *The Power of Human Rights: International Norms and Domestic Change*. Cambridge: Cambridge University Press.

Roberts, J. and Hough, M. (2005) 'Sentencing young offender: public opinion in England and Wales', *Criminal Justice*, 5(3): 211–32.

Robinson, P. (2001) 'Theorizing the influence of media on world politics: models of media influence on foreign policy', *European Journal of Communication*, 16(4): 523–44.

Rodger, J.J. (2008) *Criminalising Social Policy: Anti-social Behaviour and Welfare in a De-civilised Society*. Cullompton: Willan.

Rolston, B. (1991) 'Containment and its failure: the British state and the control of conflict in Northern Ireland', in A. George (ed.), *Western State Terrorism*. New York: Routledge.

Rolston, B. and Scraton, P. (2005) 'In the full glare of English politics: Ireland, inquiries and the British state', *British Journal of Criminology*, 45(4): 547–64.

Rose, N. (1996) 'The death of the social? Re-figuring the territory of government', *Economy and Society*, 25(3): 327–56.

Rose, N. and Miller, P. (1992) 'Political power beyond the state: problematics of government', *British Journal of Sociology*, 43(2): 173–205.

Rosenbaum, M. (1997) *From Soapbox to Soundbite: Party Political Campaigning in Britain since 1945*. Basingstoke: Macmillan.

Rowe, M. (1998) *The Racialisation of Disorder in Twentieth-century Britain*. Aldershot: Ashgate.

Rowe, M. (2004) *Policing, Race and Racism*. Cullompton: Willan.

Rummel, R.J. (1994) *Death by Government*. New Brunswick, NJ: Transaction Books.

Runnymede Trust (1997) *Islamophobia: A Challenge for Us All*. London: Runneymede Trust.

Russell, B. (2006) 'Police stop and search 100 people a day under new anti-terror laws', *The Independent*, 25 January, www.independent.co.uk/news/uk/crime/police-stop-and-search-100-people-a-day-under-new-antiterror-laws-524447.html?service=Print.

Russell, J. (2007) *Charge or Release: Terrorism Pre-charge Detention Comparative Law Study*. London: Liberty.

Rutherford, A. (1992) *Growing Out of Crime: The New Era*. Winchester: Waterside Press.

Rutherford, A. (1995) 'Signposting the future of juvenile justice policy in England and Wales', in Howard League for Penal Reform (ed.), *Child Offenders: UK and International Practice*. London: Howard League for Penal Reform.

Ryan, M. (1978) *The Acceptable Pressure Group*. Farnborough: Teakfield.

Ryan, M. (1999) 'Penal policy making towards the millennium: elites and populists; New Labour and the new criminology', *International Journal of the Sociology of Law*, 27: 1–22.

Ryan, M. (2003) *Penal Policy and Political Culture in England and Wales*. Winchester: Waterside Press.

Ryan, M. and Ward, T. (1989) *Privatisation and the Penal System*. Milton Keynes: Open University Press.

Ryggvik, H. (2000) 'Offshore safety regulations in Norway: from model to systems in erosion', *New Solutions*, 10(1–2): 67–116.

Sainsbury, D. (2006) 'Immigrants' social rights in comparative perspective: welfare regimes, forms of immigration and immigration policy regimes', *Journal of European Social Policy*, 16(3): 229–44.

Salmi, J. (2004) 'Violence in democratic societies: toward an analytic framework', in P. Hillyard, C. Pantazis, S. Tombs and D. Gordon (eds), *Beyond Criminology: Taking Harm Seriously*. London: Pluto Press.

Sampson, A., Stubbs, P., Smith, D., Pearson, G. and Blagg, H. (1988) 'Crime, localities and the multi-agency approach', *British Journal of Criminology*, 28: 478–93.

Sanders, A. and Young, R. (2007) *Criminal Justice* (3rd edn). Oxford: Oxford University Press.

Sandland, R. (2005) 'Feminism and the Gender Recognition Act 2004', *Feminist Legal Studies*, 13(1): 43–66.

Saunders, P. (1983) *Urban Politics: A Sociological Interpretation*. London: Hutchinson.

Savage, M., Warde, A. and Ward, K. (2003) *Urban Sociology, Capitalism and Modernity* (2nd edn). Basingstoke: Palgrave.

Scammell, M. (1995) *Designer Politics: How Elections Are Won*. Basingstoke: Macmillan.

Scarman, Lord (1981) *The Scarman Report: The Brixton Disorders, 10–12 April 1981*. London: HMSO.

Scheff, T.J. (1994) *Bloody Revenge: Emotions, Nationalism and War*. Boulder, CO: Westview Press.

Schiller, H. (1989) *Culture, Inc.: The Corporate Takeover of Public Expression*. Oxford: Oxford University Press.

Schiller, H. (1991) 'Not yet the post-imperialist era', *Critical Studies in Mass Communication*, 8: 13–28.

Schirmer, J. (1998) *The Guatemalan Military Project*. Philadelphia, PA: University of Pennsylvania Press.

Schlesinger, P. (1989) 'From production to propaganda?', *Media, Culture Society*, 11(3): 283–306.

Schlesinger, P. (1990) 'Rethinking the sociology of journalism: source strategies and the limits of media-centrism', in M. Ferguson (ed.), *Public Communication. The New Imperatives: Future Directions for Media Research*. London: Sage.

Schlesinger, P. and Tumber, H. (1994) *Reporting Crime: The Media Politics of Criminal Justice*. Oxford: Clarendon Press.

Schult, B. (2002) 'A European definition of poverty: the fight against poverty and social exclusion in the member states of the European Union', in P. Townsend and D. Gordon (eds), *World Poverty: New Policies to Defeat an Old Enemy*. Bristol: The Policy Press.

Schur, E. (1974) *Radical Non-Intervention*. New York: Prentice-Hall.

Schwendinger, H. and Schwendinger, J. (1975) 'Defenders of order or guardians of human rights?', in I. Taylor, P. Walton and J. Young (eds), *Critical Criminology*. London: Routledge.

Scott-Samuel, A. (ed.) (1990) *Total Participation, Total Health: Reinventing the Peckham Health Centre for the 1990s*. Edinburgh: Scottish Academic Press.

Scoular, J. and O'Neill, M. (2007) 'Regulating prostitution: social inclusion, responsibilization and the politics of prostitution reform', *British Journal of Criminology*, 47(5): 764–78.

Scraton, P. (1985a) *The State of the Police: Is Law and Order Out of Control?* London: Pluto Press.

Scraton, P. (1985b) 'The State v. The People: an introduction blood on the coal', *Journal of Law and Society*, 12(3): 251–66.

Scraton, P. (ed.) (1987) *Law, Order and the Authoritarian State: Readings in Critical Criminology*. Milton Keynes: Open University Press.

Scraton, P. (1997) 'Whose "childhood"? What "crisis"?', in P. Scraton (ed.), *Childhood in Crisis?* London: UCL Press.

Scraton, P. (1999) *Hillsborough: The Truth*. Edinburgh: Mainstream.

Scraton, P. (2001) 'A response to Lynch and Schwendingers', *The Critical Criminologist: Newsletter of the ASC's Division on Critical Criminology*, 11(2): 1–3.

Scraton, P. (2003) 'Streets of terror: marginalisation, criminalisation and authoritarian renewal', paper presented at a conference in Chester, England, 22–24 April, hosted by the Centre for Studies in Crime and Social Justice (Edge Hill) in collaboration with the European Group for the Study of Deviance and Social Control, www.statewatch.org/news/2003/aug/13scraton.htm.

Scraton, P. (2007a) 'The neglect of power and rights: a response to "problem solving"', in Z. Davies and W. McMahon (eds), *Debating Youth Justice: From Punishment to Problem Solving*. London: Centre for Crime and Justice Studies.

Scraton, P. (2007b) *Power, Conflict and Criminalisation*. London: Routledge.

Scraton, P. and Chadwick, K. (1991) 'The theoretical and political priorities of critical criminology', in K. Stenson and D. Cowell (eds), *The Politics of Crime Control*. London: Sage.

Scraton, P., Jemphrey, A. and Coleman, S. (1995) *No Last Rights: The Denial of Justice and the Promotion of Myth in the Aftermath of the Hillsborough Disaster*. Oxford: Alden Press.

Sebba, L. (2001) 'On the relationship between criminological research and policy: the case of crime victims', *Criminal Justice*, 1(1): 27–58.

Secretary of State for the Home Department, Secretary of State for Children, Schools and Families and Lord Chancellor and Secretary of State for Justice (2008) *Youth Crime Action Plan*. London: HMSO.

Sedgwick, E.K. (1990) *Epistemology of the Closet*. Berkeley: University of California Press.

Sharpe, A.N. (2007) 'Endless sex: the Gender Recognition Act 2004 and the persistence of a legal category', *Feminist Legal Studies*, 15(1): 57–84.

Shaw, H. and Coles, D. (2007) *Unlocking the Truth: Families' Experience of the Investigation of Deaths in Custody*. London: INQUEST.

Shaw, M., Dorling, D., Gordon, D. and Davey Smith, G. (1999) *The Widening Gap: Health Inequalities and Policy in Britain*. Bristol: The Policy Press.

Shearing, C.D. and Stenning, P.C. (2003) 'From the panopticon to Disney World: the development of discipline', in E. McLaughlin, J. Muncie and G. Hughes (eds), *Criminological Perspectives: Essential Readings*. Milton Keynes: Open University Press.

Sheptycki, J. (2000) 'Introduction', in J. Sheptycki (ed.), *Issues in Transnational Policing*. London: Routledge.

Shimazu, T., Kuriyama, S., Hozawa, A., Ohmori, K., Sato, S., Nakaya, N., Nishino, Y., Tsubono, Y. and Tsuji, I. (2007) 'Dietary patterns and cardiovascular disease mortality in Japan: a prospective cohort study', *Journal of Epidemiology*, 36(3): 600–9.

Sim, J. (1994) 'The abolitionist approach: a British perspective', in A. Duff, S. Marshall, R.E. Dobash and R.P. Dobash (eds), *Penal Theory and Practice: Tradition and Innovation in Criminal Justice*. Manchester: Manchester University Press.

Sim, J. (2000) 'Against the punitive wind: Stuart Hall, the state and the lessons of the Great Moving Right Show', in P. Gilroy, L. Grossberg and A. McRobbie (eds), *Without Guarantees: In Honour of Stuart Hall*. London: Verso.

Sim, J. (2009) *The Carceral State: Power and Punishment in a Hard Land*. London: Sage.

Sim, J., Scraton, P. and Gordon, P. (1987) 'Introduction: crime, the state and critical analysis', in P. Scraton (ed.), *Law, Order and the Authoritarian State*. Milton Keynes: Open University Press.

Simon, B. (1974) *The Two Nations and the Educational Structure 1780–1870*. London: Lawrence & Wishart.

Simon, R. (1982) *Gramsci's Political Thought*. London: Lawrence & Wishart.

Simpson, J. (2004) 'Statistics of racial segregation: measures, evidence and policy', *Urban Studies*, 41(3): 661–81.

Singh, R. (2002) *The Struggle for Racial Justice from Community Relations to Community Cohesion: The Story of Bradford 1950–2002*. Bradford: Ramindar Singh.

Sion, A.A. (1977) *Prostitution and the Law*. London: Faber & Faber.

Sivanandan, A. (1976/1982) 'Race, class and the state: the black experience in Britain', in *A Different Hunger: Writings on Black Resistance*. London: Pluto Press.

Sivanandan, A. (1986) *From Resistance to Rebellion: Asian and Afro-Caribbean Struggles in Britain*, Race and Class Pamphlet No. 10 (2nd impression). London: Institute of Race Relations.

Sivanandan, A. (2000) 'Macpherson and after', *Institute of Race Relations News*, 19 February, www.irr.org.uk/2000/february/ak000001.html.

Sivanandan, A. (2006) 'Attacks of multicultural Britain pave the way for enforced assimilation', *Guardian Unlimited*, 13 September, www.commentisfree.guardian.co.uk/a_sivanandan/.

Sivard, R.L. (1996) *World Military and Social Expenditures 1996*. Washington, DC: World Priorities.

Skeggs, B. (2004) *Class, Self, Culture*. London: Routledge.

Skolnick, J. and Fyfe, J. (1993) *Above the Law*. New York: Free Press.

Slack, J. (2007) 'Police put 100,000 innocent children on DNA database', *The Daily Mail*, 23 May.

Sluka, J.A. (ed.) (2000) *Death Squad*. Philadelphia, PA: University of Pennsylvania Press.

Small, N. (1987) 'AIDS and social policy', *Critical Social Policy*, 7(21): 9–29.

Smart, C. (1978) *Women, Crime and Criminology*. London: Routledge and Kegan Paul.

Smart, C. (1989) *Feminism and the Power of Law*. London: Routledge.

Smart, C. (1990) 'Feminist approaches to criminology, or postmodern woman meets atavistic man', in L. Gelsthorpe and A. Morris (eds), *Feminist Perspectives in Criminology*. Milton Keynes: Open University Press.

Smart, C. (1995) *Law, Crime and Sexuality*. London: Sage.

Smart, C. and Smart, B. (eds) (1978) *Women, Sexuality and Social Control*. London: Routlege and Kegan Paul.

Smith, A.M. (1992) 'Resisting the erasure of lesbian sexuality: a challenge for queer activism', in K. Plummer (ed.), *Modern Homosexualities: Fragments of Lesbian and Gay Experience*. London: Routledge.

Smith, G., Bartlett, A. and King, M. (2004) 'Treatments of homosexuality in Britain since the 1950s – an oral history: the experience of patients', *British Medical Journal*, 328(7437): 427–9.

Smith, N. (1996) *The New Urban Frontier: Gentrification and the Revanchist City*. London: Routledge.

Smith, N. (2005) 'Neo-critical geography, or, the flat pluralistic world of business class', *Antipode*, 37: 887–9.

Smith, R. (2007) *Youth Justice: Ideas, Policy and Practice* (2nd edn). Cullompton: Willan.

Snider, L. (1991) 'The regulatory dance: understanding reform processes in corporate crime', *International Journal of Sociology of Law*, 19(2): 209–37.

Snider, L. (2000) 'The sociology of corporate crime: an obituary (or: Whose knowledge claims have legs?)', *Theoretical Criminology*, 4(2): 169–206.

Snider, L. (2009) 'Accommodating power: the "common sense" of regulators', *Social & Legal Studies*, 18(2): 179–97.

Social Exclusion Unit (SEU) (2001) *A New Commitment to Neighbourhood Renewal: A National Strategy Action Plan*. London: SEU.

Sofsky, W. (1997) *The Order of Terror: The Concentration Camps*. Princeton, NJ: Princeton University Press.

Solomon, E. (2006) 'Crime soundbites: a view from both sides of the microphone', in P. Mason (ed.), *Captured by the Media: Prison Discourse in Popular Culture*. Cullompton: Willan.

Solomon, E., Eades, C., Garside, R. and Rutherford, M. (2007) *Ten Years of Criminal Justice under Labour: An Independent Audit*. London: Centre for Crime and Justice Studies.

Solomon, E. and Garside, R. (2008) *Ten Years of Labour's Youth Justice Reforms: An Independent Audit*. London: Centre for Crime and Justice Studies.

Somerville, P. (2004) 'State rescaling and democratic transformation', *Space and Polity*, 8(2): 137–56.

Southern and Eastern Regional Trades Union Congress (2005) *Evidence from Southern and Eastern Regional Trades Union Congress to the Greater London Assembly Scrutiny Inquiry: Health and Safety of Construction Workers in London*, www.tuc.org.uk/h_and_s/tuc-9752-f0.cfm?regional=7.

Spalek, B. (2006) *Crime Victims: Theory, Policy and Practice*. London: Palgrave.

Sparks, C. (2007) 'Extending and refining the propaganda model', *Westminster Papers in Communication and Culture*, 4(2): 68–84.

Sparrow, A. (2008) 'Smith's speech aims to reclaim crime issue for Labour', *The Guardian*, 8 May.

Spurgeon, A., Harrington, J. and Cooper, C. (1997) 'Health and safety problems associated with long working hours: a review of the current position', *Occupational and Environmental Medicine*, 54(3): 367–75.

Squires, P. (2006) 'Conclusion. Contradictions and dilemmas: the rise and fall of community safety', in P. Squires (ed.), *Community Safety: Critical Perspectives on Policy and Practice*. Bristol: The Policy Press.

Squires, P. and Stephen, D. (2005) *Rougher Justice: Anti-Social Behaviour and Young People*. Cullompton: Willan.

Stålenheim, P., Perdomo, C. and Sköns, E. (2007) 'Military expenditure', in *Stockholm International Peace Research Institute, SIPRI Yearbook 2007*. Oxford: Oxford University Press.

Stalker, J. (1988) *Stalker*. London: Harrap.

Statewatch (2003a) 'Anti-terrorist stop and searches target Muslim communities, but few arrests', *Statewatch Bulletin*, 13(6), Nov.–Dec., www.statewatch.org/news/2004/jan/13uk-stop-and-search-targets-Muslim-communites.htm.

Statewatch (2003b) 'UK: data retention and access consultation farce', *Statewatch Bulletin*, 13(2).

Statewatch (2007) 'Observatory on the exchange of data on passengers (PNR) with USA', www.statewatch.org/pnrobservatory.htm.

Staub, E. (1989) *The Roots of Evil: The Origins of Genocide and Other Group Violence*. Cambridge: Cambridge University Press.

Steinert, H. (2003) 'The indispensable metaphor of war: on populist politics and the contradictions of the state's monopoly of force', *Theoretical Criminology*, 7: 265–91.

Stenson, K. (2002) 'Community safety in middle England – the local politics of crime control', in G. Hughes and A. Edwards (eds), *Crime Control and Community: The New Politics of Public Safety*. Cullompton: Willan.

Stenson, K. and Edwards, A. (2001) 'Rethinking crime control in advanced liberal government: the "third way" and the return to the local', in K. Stenson and R.R. Sullivan (eds), *Crime, Risk and Justice: The Politics of Crime Control in Liberal Democracies*. Cullompton: Willan.

Stenson, K. and Edwards, A. (2003) 'Crime control and local governance: the struggle for sovereignty in advanced liberal polities', *Contemporary Politics*, 9(2): 203–17.

Stevens, A. (2006) *Confronting the 'Malestream': The Contribution of Feminist Criminologies*. Issues in Community and Criminal Justice Monograph No. 7. London: NAPO.

Stevens, J. (2003) *Stevens Enquiry: Overview and Recommendations*. London: HMSO.

Stockholm International Peace Research Institute (2006) *SIPRI Yearbook 2006: Armaments, Disarmament and International Security*. Stockholm: Stockholm International Peace Research Institute.

Stonewall (2007a) *The School Report: The Experience of Young Gay People in Britain's Schools*. London: Stonewall.

Stonewall (2007b) *Living Together: British Attitudes to Lesbian and Gay People*. London: Stonewall.

Stonewall (2008) *Serves You Right: Lesbian and Gay People's Expectations of Discrimination*. London: Stonewall.

Stychin, C.F. (2006) 'Not (quite) a horse and carriage: the Civil Partnership Act 2004', *Feminist Legal Studies*, 14(1): 79–86.

Sumner, C. (1997) 'The decline of social control and the rise of vocabularies of struggle', in R. Bergalli and C. Sumner (eds), *Social Control and Political Order: European Perspectives at the End of the Century*. London: Sage.

Swinton, T. (2007) *Report of the Interception of Communications Commissioner for 2005–2006*, HC 315. London: HMSO.

Swyngedouw, E. (1996) 'Reconstructing citizenship, the re-scaling of the state and the new authoritarianism: closing the Belgian mines', *Urban Studies*, 33(8): 1499–521.

Takei, N., Kawai, M. and Mori, N. (2000) 'Sluggish economics affect health of Japanese "business warriors"', *The British Journal of Psychiatry*, 176(5): 494–5.

Tata, C. and Stephen, F. (2007) 'When paying the piper gets the "wrong": the impact of fixed payments in case management', in P. Pleasance, (ed.), *Transforming Lives, Law and Social Processes*. Glasgow: Legal Aid Commission.

Tatchell, P. (1991) 'Criminal injustice: the homophobic bias of the criminal justice system', *The Pink Paper*, 26 October.

Taylor, I., Walton, P. and Young, J. (1973) *The New Criminology: For a Social Theory of Deviance*. London: Routledge and Kegan Paul.

Taylor, I., Walton, P. and Young, J. (eds) (1975) *Critical Criminology*. London: Routledge.

Temkin, J. (2000a) 'Rape and criminal justice at the millennium', in D. Nicolson and L. Bibbings (eds), *Feminist Perspectives on Criminal Law*. London: Cavendish. pp. 183–204.

Temkin, J. (2000b) 'Prosecuting and defending rape: perspectives from the bar', *Journal of Law and Society*, 27(2): 219–48.

Temkin, J. and Ashworth, A. (2004) 'Rape, sexual assaults and the problems of consent', *Criminal Law Review*, May: 328–46.

Thomas, P.A. (1993) 'The nuclear family, ideology and AIDS in the Thatcher years', *Feminist Legal Studies*, 1(1): 23–44.

Thompson, E.P. (1975) *Whigs and Hunters: the Origin of the Black Act*. Harmondsworth: Penguin.

Thorpe, D.H., Smith, D., Green, C.J. and Paley, J.H. (1980) *Out of Care: The Community Support of Juvenile Offenders*. London: Allen and Unwin.

Tift, L. and Sullivan, D. (2001) 'A needs-based, social harm definition of crime', in S. Henry and M. Lanier (eds), *What is Crime? Controversies over the Nature of Crime and What To Do about It*. Lanham, MD: Rowman & Littlefield.

Tilley, N. (1993) 'Crime prevention and the safer cities story', *The Howard Journal of Criminal Justice*, 32(1): 40–57.

Tilley, N. (2002) 'Crime prevention in Britain, 1975–2010: breaking out, breaking in and breaking down', in G. Hughes, E. McLaughlin and J. Muncie (eds), *Crime Prevention and Community Safety: New Directions*. London: Sage.

Tilly, C. (1985) 'War making and state making as organised crime', in P. Evans, D. Rueschmeyer and T. Skocpol (eds), *Bringing the State Back In*. Cambridge: Cambridge University Press.

Tilly, C. (1992) *Coercion, Capital, and European States, AD 1990–1992*. Oxford: Blackwell.

Tinic, S. (2007) '(En)Visioning the televisual audience: revisiting questions of power in the age of interactive television', in K. Haggerty and R. Ericson (eds), *The New Politics of Surveillance and Visibility*. Toronto: University of Toronto Press.

Tombs, S. (1996) 'Injury, death and the deregulation fetish: the politics of occupational safety regulation in UK manufacturing', *International Journal of Health Services*, 26(2): 327–47.

Tombs, S. (2001) 'Thinking about "white-collar" crime', in S.-Å. Lindgren (ed.), *White-collar Crime Research: Old Views and Future Potentials*. Lectures and Papers from a Scandinavian Seminar (BRÅ-Rapport 2001:1). Stockholm: Brottsförebyggande råde/Fritzes.

Tombs, S. (2007) 'Violence, "safety" crimes and criminology', *British Journal of Criminology*, 47(4): 531–50.

Tombs, S. and Whyte, D. (1998) 'Capital fights back: risk, regulation and profit in the UK offshore oil industry', *Studies in Political Economy*, 57(Sept.): 73–101.

Tombs, S. and Whyte, D. (eds) (2003a) *Unmasking Crimes of the Powerful: Scrutinizing States and Corporations*. New York: Peter Lang.

Tombs, S. and Whyte, D. (2003b) 'Corporations beyond the law? Regulation, risk and corporate crime in a globalised era', *Risk Management*, 5(2): 9–16.

Tombs, S. and Whyte, D. (2007) *Safety Crimes*. Cullompton: Willan.

Tombs, S. and Whyte, D. (2008) *A Crisis of Enforcement: The Decriminalisation of Death and Injury at Work*. London: Centre for Crime and Justice Studies.

Tosh, J. (2004) 'Hegemonic masculinity and the history of gender', in S. Dudink, K. Hagermann and J. Tosh (eds), *Masculinities in Politics and War*. Manchester: Manchester University Press.

Toynbee, P. (2003) *Hard Work: Life in Low-pay Britain*. London: Bloomsbury.

Travis, A. (1994) 'Ministers suppress research: findings contradict Howard crackdown', *The Guardian*, 4 July.

Travis, A. (2003) 'New Britons to pledge loyalty to country', *The Guardian*, 26 July.

Travis, A. (2008) 'Planned changes to youth justice system aimed at keeping more children out of jail', *The Guardian*, July 17, www.guardian.co.uk/society/2008/jun/17/youthjustice.justice1.

Traynor, I. (2008) 'Government wants personal details of every traveller', *The Guardian*, 23 February.

Turner, B. (1996) 'Sweden', in P. Balchin (ed.), *Housing Policy in Europe*. London: Routledge.

Turrow, J. (2007) 'Cracking the consumer code: advertisers, anxiety and surveillance', in K. Haggerty and R. Ericson (eds), *The New Politics of Surveillance and Visibility*. Toronto: University of Toronto Press.

Uglow, S. (1988) *Policing Liberal Society*. Oxford: Oxford University Press.

Uildriks, N. and van Mastrigt, H. (1991) *Policing Police Violence*. Dordrecht: Kluwer.

UK Children's Commissioners (2008) *UK Children's Commissioners' Report to the UN Committee on the Rights of the Child*. London/Belfast/Edinburgh/Swansea: 11Million/NICCY/SCCYP/Children's Commissioner for Wales, www.11million.org.uk/resource/31f7xsa2gjgfc3l9t808qfsi.pdf.

Unison/Centre for Corporate Accountability (2002) *Safety Last? The Under-enforcement of Health and Safety Law: Full Report*. London: Unison/Centre for Corporate Accountability.

Urban Task Force (1999) *Towards an Urban Renaissance: Report of the Urban Task Force – Executive Summary*. London: HMSO.

US Census Bureau (2007) *Income, Poverty and Health Insurance: Coverage in the United States: 2006*. Washington, DC: US Department of Commerce, Economics and Statistics Administration.

van Dijk, J., van Kestern, J. and Smit, P. (2007) *Criminal Victimisation in International Perspective: Key Findings from the 2004–2005 International Crime Victim Survey and The European Crime and Safety Survey*. The Hague: Ministry of Justice Research and Documentation Centre.

van Dijk, T. (1988) *New Analysis: Case Studies of International and National News in the Press*. Hillsdale, NJ: Erlbaum.

van Dijk, T. (1991) *Racism and the Press*. London: Routledge.

van Dijk, T. (1993) *Elite Discourse and Racism*. Newbury Park, CA: Sage.

van Swaaningen, R. (2002) 'Towards a replacement discourse on community safety: lessons from the Netherlands', in G. Hughes, E. McLaughlin and J. Muncie (eds), *Crime Prevention and Community Safety: New Directions*. London: Sage.

Wacquant, L. (2001) 'The penalisation of poverty and the rise of neo-liberalism', *European Journal on Criminal Policy and Research*, 9(4): 401–12.

Wacquant, L. (2002) 'Scrutinizing the street: poverty, morality and the pitfalls of urban ethnography', *American Journal of Sociology*, 107(6): 1468–532.

Wacquant, L. (2008) *Urban Outcasts*. Cambridge: Polity Press.

Waldron, J. (1993) *Liberal Rights: Collected Papers, 1981–91*. Cambridge: Cambridge University Press.

Walker, C. (2002) *Blackstone's Guide to the Anti-Terrorism Legislation*. Oxford: Oxford University Press.

Walker, C. (2007) 'The legal definition of "terrorism" in UK law and beyond', *Public Law*, Summer: 331–52.

Walklate, S. (2005) 'Victimhood as a source of oppression', *Social Justice: Emerging Imaginaries of Repression and Control*, Special edn, edited by T. Kearon and R. Lippens, 32(1) May: 89–99.

Walklate, S. (2007) *Imagining the Victim of Crime*. Maidenhead: McGraw-Hill/Open University Press.

Waller, I. (1988) 'International standards, national trail blazing and the nest steps', in M. Maguire and J. Pointing (eds), *Victims of Crime: A New Deal?* Milton Keynes: Open University Press.

Walmsey, R. (2002) *The World Prison Population List* (4th edn). Findings No. 188. London: Home Office.

Walsh, C. (2002) 'Curfews: no more hanging around', *Youth Justice*, 2(2): 70–81.

Walters, R. (2003) *Deviant Knowledge: Criminology, Politics and Policy*. Cullompton: Willan.

Walters, R. (2006a) 'Boycott, resistance and the role of the deviant voice', *Criminal Justice Matters*, 62: 6–7.

Walters, R. (2006b) 'Critical criminology and the "new" authoritarian state: reflection and horizons', in A. Barton, D. Scott and D. Whyte (eds), *The Criminological Imagination*. Cullompton: Willan.

Walters, R. (2007) 'Embedded criminology', in G. Brannigan and G. Pavlich (eds), *Critical Studies in Social Control: The Carson Paradigm and Governmentality*. London: Routledge Cavendish. pp. 309–28.

Walters, R. (2008) 'Government manipulation of criminological knowledge and policies of deceit', in T. Hope and R. Walters (eds), *Critical Thinking about the Uses of Research*. London: Centre for Crime and Justice Studies.

Ward, C. (2000) *Social Policy: An Anarchist Response*. London: Freedom Press.

Ward, T. and Young, P. (2007) 'Elias, organised violence and terrorism', in M. Mullard and B. Cole (eds), *Globalisation, Citizenship and the War on Terror*. Cheltenham: Edward Elgar.

Watney, S. (1997) *Policing Desire: Pornography, AIDS and the Media* (3rd edn). London: Cassell.

Webber, F. (2004) 'The war on migration', in P. Hillyard, C. Pantazis, S. Tombs and D. Gordon (eds), *Beyond Criminology: Taking Harm Seriously*. London: Pluto Press.

Weber, L. and Bowling, B. (2002) 'The policing of immigration in the new world disorder', in P. Scraton (ed.), *Beyond September 11: An Anthology of Dissent*. London: Pluto Press.

Weber, M. (1968) *Economy and Society* (vol. 3). New York: Bedminster Press.

Weeks, J. (1990) *Coming Out* (2nd edn). London: Quartet Books (1st edn, 1977).

Weiss, L. (1997) 'Globalisation and the myth of the powerless state', *New Left Review*, 225: 3–27.

Weiss, L. (2005) 'The state-augmenting effects of globalisation', *New Political Economy*, 10(3): 345–53.

West, P. (2005) *The Poverty of Multiculturalism*. London: Civitas.

Westmarland, L. (2002) *Gender and Policing*. Cullompton: Willan.

Wetherell, M. (2003) 'Themes in discourse research: the case of Diana', in M. Wetherell, S. Taylor and S. Yates (eds), *Discourse Theory and Practice: A Reader*. London: Sage.

Wheeler, C. (2006) Freedom of Information Request Reference Number T10229/6, www.homeoffice. gov.uk/about-us/freedom-of-information/released-information/foi-archive-rese.

White, J. (1986) *The Worst Street in North London*. London: Routledge and Kegan Paul.

Whittle, S., Turner, L. and Al-Alami, M. (2007) *Engendered Penalties: Transgender and Transsexual People's Experiences of Inequality and Discrimination*. London: Press for Change.

WHO (2002) *World Report on Violence and Health*. Geneva: World Health Organization.

WHO (2005) *Mental Health Atlas*. Geneva: World Health Organization.

Whyte, D. (2003) 'Lethal regulation: state–corporate crime and the UK government's new mercenaries', *Journal of Law and Society*, 30(4): 575–600.

Whyte, D. (2004) 'Corporate crime and regulation', in J. Muncie and D. Wilson (eds), *The Student Handbook of Criminology and Criminal Justice*. London: Cavendish.

Whyte, D. (2006) 'Regulating safety, regulating profit: cost-cutting, injury and death in the North Sea after Piper Alpha', in E. Tucker (ed.), *Working Disasters: The Politics of Recognition and Response*. New York: Baywood.

Whyte, D. (2007) 'Market patriotism and the war on terror', *Social Justice*, 35(2–3): 111–31.

Whyte, D. (2007/2008) 'Gordon Brown's charter for corporate criminals', *Criminal Justice Matters*, 70(Winter): 31–2.

Wiles, P. (2002) 'Criminology in the 21st century: public good or private interest?', The Sir John Barry Memorial Lecture, *The Australian and New Society of Criminology Journal*, 35: 238–52.

Wilkinson, R. (1996) *Unhealthy Societies*. London: Routledge.

Williams, B. (1999) *Working with Victims of Crime: Policies, Politics and Practice*. London: Jessica Kingsley.

Williams, B. (2003) 'Community justice, victims and social justice', Professorial Inaugural Lecture, De Montfort University, Leicester.

Wilson, D. (2006) 'Seduced by the politics of penal populism', *The Independent*, 16 August.

Wilson, D. and Fowles, T. (2005) 'Attrition in reported rape cases', *The Howard Journal of Criminal Justice*, 44(3): 326–8.

Wilson, J.Q. and Kelling, G.L. (2003) 'Broken windows: the police and neighborhood safety', in E. McLaughlin, J. Muncie and G. Hughes (eds), *Criminological Perspectives: Essential Readings* (2nd edn). London: Sage.

Wilson, R.A. (ed.) (2005) *Human Rights in the 'War on Terror'*. New York: Cambridge University Press.

Wodak, R. and Meyer, M. (2001) *Methods of Critical Discourse Analysis*. London: Sage.

Wootton, B. (1959) *Social Science and Social Pathology*. London: Allen and Unwin.

Worden, R.E. (1996) 'The causes of police brutality: theory and evidence on police use of force', in W.A. Geller and H. Toch (eds), *Police Violence*. New Haven, CT: Yale University Press.

Worrall, A. (1997) *Punishment in the Community: The Future of Criminal Justice*. London: Longman.

Worrall, A. (1999) 'Troubled or troublesome? Justice for girls and young women', in B. Goldson (ed.), *Youth Justice: Contemporary Policy and Practice*. Aldershot: Ashgate.

Worrall, A. (2002) 'Rendering women punishable: the making of a penal crisis', in P. Carlen (ed.), *Women and Punishment*. Cullompton: Willan.

Worrall, A. (2004) 'Twisted sisters, ladettes, and the new penology', in C. Alder and A. Worrall (eds), *Girls' Violence: Myths and Realities*. New York: State University of New York Press.

Wright Mills, C. (1970) *The Sociological Imagination*. Harmondsworth: Penguin.

Yates, J. (2008) 'Informal action', in B. Goldson (ed.), *Dictionary of Youth Justice*. Cullompton: Willan.

Yates, J. 'Youth justice: Moving in an anti-social direction', in J. Wood and J. Hine (eds) *Work with Young People*. London: Sage.

Young, A. (1996) *Imagining Crime*. London: Sage.

Young, J. (1971) *The Drug Takers*. London: Paladin.

Young, J. (1999) *The Exclusive Society: Social Exclusion, Crime and Difference in Late Modernity*. London: Sage.

Young, J. (2002) 'Morals, suicide and pyschiatry: a view from Japan', *Bioethics*, 16(5): 412–24.

Young, J. (2003) 'Searching for a new criminology of everyday life: a review of the *Culture of Control* by D. Garland', *British Journal of Criminology*, 43(1): 228–43.

Young, L. and Nestle, M. (2002) 'The contribution of expanding portion sizes to the US obesity epidemic', *American Journal of Public Health*, 92(2): 246–9.

Zedner, L. (2002) 'Victims', in M. Maguire, R. Morgan and R. Reiner (eds), *The Oxford Handbook of Criminology* (3rd edn). Oxford: Oxford University Press.

Zimbardo, P. (2007) *The Lucifer Effect: Understanding How Good People Turn Evil*. New York: Random House.

Cases

Brown [1994] 1 AC 212; [1993] 2 WLR 556.

Corbett v. Corbett [1971] P 83; [1970] 2 All ER 33.

Re G (children) (FC) [2006] UKHL 43

Wilkinson v. Kitzinger [2006] EWHC 2022 (Fam); [2006] HRLR 36.

INDEX